THE EVICTION BOOK FOR CALIFORNIA

Judicial Council forms used in evictions (unlawful detainers) change periodically. The forms in this book were current as of February, 2006. Go to the Judicial Council website (courtinfo.ca.gov/forms/) to check for more recent form changes.

Dedication

This book is dedicated to Muriel, who evicted me at an early age and made me scrupulous about evicting others.

Acknowledgements

Kudos to Brad Albom, Jean Barnhardt, Jackie Bassis, Peter Berger, Virgil Bolin, Kathryn Brunner, Nelly Bunn, C.E. Cauffman, Denzil Clements, Betty Cole, Chris Collins, Sonja Darling, Theo Evans, Fred Felder, Joe Fletcher, Ruth Furey, Vernon Graves, Paul Jensen, James Kerr, Donald Kirby, Jeanette Loureiro, Ted Luebkeman, Charles Marshall, Paula Martinez, Ben McClinton, Margaret Miglia, Rita Moore, Terry Moore, Joy Nelson, David Patton, Carol Pladsen, Jeff Pollack, Phil Pridham, Dario Robinson, Ivy Robinson, Robert Saunders, Ira Serkes, John Sporleder, Gerald Studier, Monica Tutson, and Paul Warren, scrupulous people, all of them, for their help in putting this book together.

The Usual Caveat

THE EVICTION BOOK FOR CALIFORNIA

A HANDYMANUAL FOR SCRUPULOUS LANDLORDS AND LANDLADIES WHO DO THEIR OWN EVICTIONS!

NINTH EDITION

written by
LEIGH ROBINSON

illustrated by
DAVID PATTON

published by

P.O. BOX 1639
EL CERRITO, CA 94530-4639
landlording.com

FIRST EDITION   August, 1980
    Revised   January, 1981
SECOND EDITION   October, 1982
    Revised   September, 1983
THIRD EDITION   November, 1984
    Reprinted   July, 1985
FOURTH EDITION   August, 1986
    Revised   July, 1987
FIFTH EDITION   July, 1988
    Revised   June, 1989
    Revised   August, 1990
SIXTH EDITION   November, 1991
    Revised   March, 1993
    Revised   May, 1994
SEVENTH EDITION   March, 1995
    Revised   February, 1996
EIGHTH EDITION   February, 1998
    Revised   February, 1999
NINTH EDITION   October, 2004
    Revised   December, 2004
    Revised   February, 2006

COVER AND BOOK DESIGN by David Patton

COMPOSED ON A MACINTOSH® USING ADOBE PAGEMAKER®

INTERNATIONAL STANDARD BOOK NUMBER: 0-932956-29-7

PRINTED IN THE U.S.A.

ExPress Publishing has a Web site (landlording.com) where, among other items of interest to landlords, you will find "what's news" about evictions.

The LANDLORDING SERIES™, of which this is Book Two, and the "Landlording Character," who first appears here on the preface page, are trademarks of ExPress and Leigh Robinson.

Preface

Originally, the nucleus of *The Eviction Book for California* was but a single chapter in *Landlording*, a book which I wrote in 1975 for scrupulous landlords and landladies doing business in California. Eventually that book began selling so well outside the Golden State that I felt obligated to prepare a completely new edition which might be useful to landlords and landladies no matter where they happened to be in the United States. So, early in 1980, I completed the third edition of *Landlording*, which was intended for distribution nationwide.

In preparing that third edition, I had to eliminate all the information in the earlier editions which was specific to California; consequently, all the legal information about evicting tenants in California courts had to go. After all, why should a landlady in Kansas care how her counterpart in California evicts a tenant through the courts for nonpayment of rent when the laws in her state dictate that she must use a very different procedure?

Because the eviction information in the earlier editions of *Landlording* had proven to be useful to many landlords and landladies in California over the years, however, I decided to expand it and publish it separately rather than toss it into my circular file.

You hold in your hands this descendant of *Landlording*. It is a rather specialized manual, a kind of companion volume to the national version of *Landlording*. I hope that you find it useful when you need it, but I also hope that you won't need it very often, for evictions are unpalatable and costly medicine.

Because they are so unpalatable and costly, I hope that you will take the time to learn how to prevent them. To help you learn how, I have included one short chapter here on the rudiments of preventing evictions, chapter 1, some of which

also appears in *Landlording*. This is material which always bears repeating. Although it may not be pertinent to the legal eviction that you want to pursue right now, it certainly will be pertinent to your situation when you regain possession of your rental dwelling once more and begin dealing with another tenant. Heed this advice, and you won't have to bother reading anything more about evictions ever again.

Chapter 2 also includes some material which appears in *Landlording*. These suggestions for getting problem tenants out without going to court will work as well in California as they will in Kansas or in the Land of Oz, and I should hope that you would consider trying the legal alternatives mentioned in this chapter before you ever go rushing headlong into the very uncertain and very imperfect world of the courts.

Courts are the provinces of attorneys and of judges, most of whom have been attorneys, and you may have wondered when you first picked up this book, why the letters "LL.B." or "J.D." did not appear after my name as an indication that I had paid my dues at law school and was fully qualified to write a manual explaining the intricacies of the legal procedure used in California to evict tenants. I don't use those letters after my name because I am not an attorney. In truth, I have never attended a single day of classes at even a storefront law school. I am a former high school English teacher who has toiled at landlording for years, and in doing so I have acquired certain knowledge about evictions which I have always believed would be useful to any other landlord or landlady struggling to survive, knowledge which attorneys may know but which they do not generally stress in a way most helpful to the distraught landlord or landlady who needs to get a tenant out today, right now, or go stark mad.

I became aware that my own approach to evictions was indeed different from those of attorneys when I appeared as a panelist at a public gathering hosted by the Berkeley Community Affairs Committee. The panel was comprised of four attorneys, all of whom had some unique perspective on housing problems, plus myself. One of the authors of the *California Tenants' Handbook* was there, along with two other attorneys sympathetic to tenants, and there was one attorney who specialized in representing property management companies. He and I were supposed to balance the panel. At one point in the discussion, the question arose concerning the shortest possible time an eviction for nonpayment of rent might possibly take, and there was only one person on the panel who knew the answer. You're right. I was the one. I knew the answer because it was in my interest to know. I'd already done the calculations. Besides, I had actually performed evictions myself in the shortest period of time allowed by law. They hadn't.

Attorneys don't particularly care how long evictions take, so long as the period of time is reasonable enough to keep their clients paying their bills. Only the landlord and landlady care enough about such things to find out, and then to turn that knowledge to their advantage.

My perspective on the subject of evictions, then, is not that of the attorney. It is the perspective of the landlord who has to deal on a daily basis, perhaps even on an emergency basis, with a tenant who is either a robber, a cheat, a devastator, or a nuisance. I want that tenant out as quickly as possible. For the sake of my business and my sanity, I have to get that tenant out. So my perspective is one similar to yours.

Because I have this perspective, I made it my business to develop certain eviction techniques which were as swift and as sure as possible, whether or not they involved going to court. I found out, for example, how best to offer bribes to tenants for moving and which days of the week are best for serving a 3-Day Notice to Pay Rent or Quit. The chances are good that you won't find an attorney who can give you such information because he won't have learned it in law school and he won't have taken the time to figure it out. It isn't in an attorney's best interest to know.

I do not mean to put down attorneys. Some of my closest relatives, some of my best friends, ahem, are attorneys. I am merely concerned that you understand my perspective as you read this book. I have walked in your moccasins, and I have trembled in them.

🍃 🍃 🍃

Changes in California's eviction procedures, laws, and forms occur all the time. Go to the landlording.com website to see whether anything referred to in this book has changed since it was published.

Table of Contents

Introduction

You, dear reader, are most likely involved in very painful circumstances, or else you wouldn't be reading this book. Somehow or other, you have become stuck with tenants who are constantly on your mind, tenants who are making your life miserable. You are plagued with self-doubts, and you are wondering whether you ought to be in this business at all, whether it's worth the trouble.

You have a substantial investment in your property, so naturally you have a lot to lose. Your tenants, on the other hand, very likely have nothing to lose by attempting to thwart your every effort to evict them, and they are doing just that.

You are wondering now what your options are, whether you can possibly get rid of the tenants without having to use an attorney, without having to wait very long, and without having to spend very much. You are wondering whether there is any good way for you to minimize your losses under the circumstances, whether there is any way you might handle the situation with a minimum of aggravation for all concerned so you might please almost everyone involved.

I can sympathize with you, for I have been in just such a mess more times than I care to remember. I have lost many hours of sleep while being involved with tenants who absolutely had to be evicted. I have the gray hairs to show for the experiences, but I have survived, too, in spite of the threats on my life and the unmentionable damage which some tenants have done to my rental dwellings. Somehow I survived eviction after eviction with my life and my self-respect intact, and in the process I learned a few things about dealing with people under trying circumstances.

Rough as these experiences are to live through, you can, and you will, live through them just as I have. At least, I trust that you will, and even though you will undoubtedly ask yourself at times just why such revolting developments should happen to you of all people, don't expect any solid answers to questions like that, certainly not here. Do expect to find solid answers here to those nitty-gritty questions you have about evictions, answers which will enable you to get an eviction over with quickly and inexpensively so you can get on with more important business.

You will profit most from this book if you skim through it quickly first, reading only the section headings in each chapter and the key points worth remembering which appear at the end of each chapter. They will give you a clue about what to expect so you can go directly to the section which answers the questions plaguing you now. If you are preparing to evict a tenant for breach of contract or failure to vacate, be sure you become familiar with chapter 5 first because it explains thoroughly the entire legal eviction procedure for nonpayment of rent, and parts of that procedure apply to the other two. If you wonder what "breach of contract" or any of the other terms used in this book mean, look them up in the glossary before you forge ahead. If you happen to be unlucky enough to own property in a rent-controlled area, read chapter 4, by all means.

Incidentally, I believe that the laws governing evictions in California are outmoded. They are crying for reform. There are fairer, faster, less complicated ways to handle evictions (landlord-tenant courts modeled after small-claims courts are one possibility), and we should be clamoring for them to be adopted. You have only to be initiated into the eviction procedure yourself to realize how elusive, and hence frustrating, the pursuit of justice through legal channels can be. When merely the presence or absence of a single mark on a single piece of paper will give your tenant an extra fifteen days of free rent, you begin to wonder about our legal machinery for handling what should be a relatively simple matter. When your tenants are handed an opportunity at the eleventh hour to delay their impending eviction if only they will claim that one of their number wasn't named in the court papers and therefore they should all get to stay longer free of charge, you begin to wonder about fairness. Afterwards, you won't wonder any more why some landlords get so exasperated over the legal technicalities which prevent them from evicting a nonpayer promptly that they take matters into their own hands.

In theory, the eviction procedure is supposed to keep us and our tenants from taking advantage of one another. In practice, it has become a convoluted legal exercise which has undone more than one landlord I know and has given savvy tenants the opportunity to live rent free legally for many a month.

Little by little, some improvements are occurring (the Judicial Council's website is one (courtinfo.ca.gov); the extensive set of unlawful detainer forms approved by the Judicial Council of California for use throughout the state and available over the council's website as Adobe Acrobat documents is another; the law enabling court clerks to enter default judgments is still another), but the whole machinery really needs to be overhauled, not patched piecemeal.

I hope that once you become familiar with the eviction procedure we have now, you will make some effort to change it. Write a letter or two to your state legislators. Tell them you think that the current procedure probably worked satisfactorily back in the good ol' days when people felt moral obligations to pay their bills on time and care for other people's property, when tenants would move out voluntarily if ever they were served with a notice to vacate, and when the attorneys who had to handle the few evictions which did actually reach the courthouse were charging a flat $25 per case and enjoying the challenge. Those days are long gone. Times have changed; eviction proceedings haven't. They need to be changed.

There is a better way.

Every county ought to have at least one landlord-tenant court holding sessions every day of the week or whenever there is a need for a session, and it ought to be run informally like a small claims court.

Scream loudly enough for change, for simplification. Your tenants are out there screaming, and look at what they have accomplished.

You should know that the information given here has been thoroughly researched and is believed to be accurate at the time of publication, but because certain practices vary from place to place and because the laws and the interpretation of those laws change all the time, whereas the words in this book are fixed on paper, you would be wise to consider double-checking what you read here and to check the landlording.com website for any eviction updates.

To help you avoid the most common pitfalls in doing an eviction yourself, I have tried wherever possible to be conservative about the various decisions involved. There's always the chance that I might have been too conservative or not conservative enough or that I might have overlooked something. Should you encounter any errors in this book or any problems with your eviction which you think might fall within the scope of this book, please write me in care of ExPress. I will share this knowledge with other landlords so they might avoid having to suffer as you did.

1
Preventing Evictions

Those people who are concerned enough about their health to exercise regularly and eat their apple a day, practicing preventive medicine all their lives, seldom wind up on an operating table undergoing the big fix, and they seldom suffer the many ailments common to those who ignore their health.

Preventive landlording is similar. Practice it religiously, and you should be able to avoid the numerous ailments common to the landlord-tenant relationship. You should also be able to avoid landlording's big fix, an eviction. Preventive landlording is well worth the effort. It will keep your blood pressure and your pulse rate as near normal as possible, and it will contribute significantly to your overall success in this business.

So, how does one go about practicing preventive landlording as it relates to evictions? Are the methods some kind of magic or voodoo? Hardly! They are nothing more than well-developed, workable procedures for selecting tenants, insuring compliance, enforcing agreements, and collecting rents, all applied with as much diligence and consistency as possible.

Each of these methods in itself is a fascinating subject of particular importance to one's success in landlording. My intention here is not to expand on these subjects to any great degree. It is simply to underscore the relationship of these procedures to evictions and to suggest a few ideas worth remembering and using. Read the *Landlording* book for a detailed treatment of the subjects.

Selecting Tenants

To understand how evictions relate to tenant selection, think of each landlord-tenant relationship as a continuum with a short beginning, a lengthy middle, and a short end. Each relationship begins normally when you choose someone to be your tenant and that someone chooses you to be his landlord. It continues in a somewhat balanced fashion until the tenant chooses to leave and move on. You normally do not choose for the tenant to leave. You exercise only the one choice in the matter, at the very beginning of the relationship. If you fail to exercise that choice wisely or at all, you run the risk of having to end the relationship abruptly and abnormally, that is, with an eviction.

Since you surely don't want to evict tenants any more than you absolutely have to, you must choose your tenants wisely.

Even in this age of tenants' rights and landlords' responsibilities, you still do have some leeway in choosing your tenants. You don't have to rent to the first person who comes along and waves all the move-in money in your face. You do have to rent to the first person who comes along and meets all of your legal and consistently applied standards, standards which you yourself determine to a great degree.

When you set your tenant standards, you should set them according to what's legal and nondiscriminatory for the rental dwelling you have available. These standards should include factors such as amount of income, stability of income, credit rating, amount of assets, rental history, pets, number of vehicles, number of people in the household, smoking habits, drinking habits, permanence, and cleanliness. They should not include factors such as whether there are any children in the household, whether the applicants are married, whether the applicants are Mexican-American, African-American, Chinese-American, or Italian-American, whether the applicants are 21 or 65 years of age, whether the applicants are atheists or holy rollers, or whether they are HIV-positive.

Once you set your reasonable standards and

put them in writing, you need to gather all the relevant information you can on the applicants. Give a rental application to everyone who is interested in renting from you. Then check the applications thoroughly to see whether the information is truthful.

Next, you must satisfy yourself as to whether the applicants measure up to your standards. All in all, you're mainly interested in determining whether they have the ability and the inclination to pay the rent, whether they will take care of your property, and whether they will likely get along with the other tenants.

Making these determinations requires some science and some sorcery. It's a judgment call, albeit an informed judgment call.

When you're making one of these judgment calls, remember that a wayward suitor makes a wayward spouse, and a poor applicant makes a poor tenant. If you doubt whether an applicant will make a good tenant, don't rent to him. You're not going to change him. Remember, also, that a vacant rental is better than one rented to someone who is going to have to be evicted later. A vacant rental isn't going to drive your good tenants away, nor is it going to develop holes in the walls, burns in the carpets, clogs in the toilet, tears in the linoleum, cracks in the windows, or chips in the tile. It isn't going to generate any rent, that's true, but, on the other hand, neither will a dwelling which you have rented to a deadbeat tenant.

Refuse to rent to someone you believe would become one of your eviction statistics if you did rent to him. That is the cheapest, least agonizing "eviction" you can possibly perform.

Insuring Compliance

We Americans buy more insurance to cover ourselves for more calamities than any other people on this earth. We are insurance junkies. We can't seem to get enough of the stuff. Yet, we landlords seldom consider insuring ourselves in case an untested tenant turns sour. Believe it or not, nobody sells this kind of insurance. Nobody sells it because it's absolutely free. Because it's free, there's nobody promoting it, and we, therefore, tend to forget that it's available to us at all.

This insurance which I am referring to is *co-signer involvement*. When you're selecting tenants and you're somewhat dubious about

whether a particular applicant would make a good tenant, request that he secure a co-signer, someone of means to insure that he will comply with the terms of the rental agreement. Get the co-signer to sign a co-signer agreement (the *Landlording* book has one) as an addendum to the rental agreement. Then, if the tenant does turn sour, you may proceed to collect on your free insurance policy from the co-signer.

Enforcing Agreements

When you and your tenant began your relationship, you should have agreed on any number of terms besides just the rent and how long the agreement was to last. Your terms might have covered the tenant's obligations regarding noise, cleanliness, pets, redecorating, damage, number of occupants, subletting, and the like.

If either of you manages to violate these terms you have agreed upon, the other naturally has grounds for a lawsuit.

Many times you may have grounds for a lawsuit, all right, and you may wish to hustle into court. Don't! Don't be hasty about going to court when you see a St. Bernard puppy sitting on the tenant's doorstep, when your new tenant begins practicing his trombone at 6 a.m., when an extra roommate appears, when the tenant paints all his walls flat black, or when the tenant drains his motor oil onto the driveway and into the gutter. But don't neglect those matters either. Instead of being hasty about settling them in court, be hasty about dealing with them on a person-to-person, face-to-face basis.

No problem you will ever encounter in this business will become any easier to deal with if you neglect it for a while. It will not disappear. It *will* become tougher to deal with because it will have assumed greater proportions over time. Left alone long enough, the problem will result in neighbors' complaints, the departure of your best tenants (if the building is a multiple-family dwelling), the transgressing tenant's eviction, your property's deterioration, your impoverishment, your capitulation, or all six of these mournful eventualities.

Consider the St. Bernard puppy which has appeared mysteriously on the doorstep. It's a cute, cuddly animal when it's young, but it grows–fast. Confront the tenant when you first see the puppy, and the tenant will likely get rid of it or move. Wait some time before confronting the tenant, and you will likely have a battle on your hands that will lead you straight into court. Why? The tenant has become attached to his growing pet and has assumed that since you haven't approached him on the matter, you are permitting him to keep it in spite of what the agreement says. You are doing precisely that, too, if you don't enforce the agreement as soon as you recognize that it has been broken.

To its chagrin, the San Francisco Housing Authority, which operates San Francisco's public housing projects, had to learn the hard way about the problems of failing to enforce its own rental agreement some time ago. The agreement specifically prohibited "cats, dogs, snakes, etc.," but many tenants traditionally had ignored this ban, and the housing authority itself had overlooked the matter completely until certain tenants who were without pets began to grow weary of having to play hopscotch on the sidewalks and having to wear plugs in their ears in order to adapt to the habits of their fellow tenants' pets. These inconvenienced tenants finally complained so loudly that they couldn't be ignored. The problem had festered so long, and the controversy had escalated so dramatically that only the intervention of the mayor could quell it.

Actually, the tenants' landlord, the housing authority, had wronged them all, pets included, for when any landlord fails to enforce an agreement which has been broken by a single tenant, he is failing all the tenants, especially the ones who are conscientious about observing the agreement's terms in the first place.

Rental agreement terms are for the benefit of all concerned, yours as landlord, your tenants in general, and your tenants individually. You, in the role of agreement maker and enforcer, must try to be fair to all, and that means setting understandable, enforceable rules for your relationship in advance (if you can't understand a rule, don't include it in your agreement; if you can't envision yourself enforcing a rule, don't include it in your agreement). Make sure your tenants know what to expect of you from the very first (if you can, avoid changing the rules in the middle of your relationship), and then deliver. Rules and regulations serve no useful purpose otherwise. They become only a source of endless friction.

Notwithstanding the rental agreement, your tenants will test you constantly to determine what your limits are, (kids test their parents; students test their teachers; workers test their bosses; and spouses test each other). Testing for limits is human nature. Show your tenants at the outset, in your role as agreement enforcer, that you mean business, that you simply will not allow them to break the agreement you have made with them. Be tough in the beginning, and you won't have to resort to the courts to settle your disputes later. Going to court is a big waste of money and an even bigger waste of time, and you can never know for sure just how you'll be treated there. Stay out of court if you possibly can. I repeat. Stay out of court if you possibly can.

Collecting Rents

The last eviction prevention method is none other than a reasonable, lucid, and strict rent collection policy.

Remember that everyone hates to pay rent. Few would pay it at all if they didn't believe they would be thrown out otherwise. Establish yourself, therefore, as a landlord who expects the rent to be paid promptly. When it isn't, you should become menacing, a force to contend with.

Make it more troublesome for your tenants not to pay you than not to pay anyone else they owe money to. Explain precisely what your policy is regarding rent collection. Tell them before you ever rent to them just when their rent is due, when it is late, and what's going to happen to them if they don't pay on time. I tell mine that their rent is due on the first, it is late on the fifth, and if it's not paid by the fifth, I'll give them three days to pack up and leave. Talk tough. Be tough when you collect rents. You won't be understood any other way.

In practice, this four-day grace period works well. You no longer have to listen to those hackneyed excuses tenants make for not having paid you on or before the first. You know and, what's more, they know that if the rent hasn't been paid by the fourth, either they do have a serious excuse or they're making a conscious attempt to avoid paying altogether. You save innumerable calls and trips on the second or third or fourth of the month to inquire after the rent, and you can feel entirely justified in collecting a late fee from a tenant who has missed the due date by at least four days.

If your tenant hasn't paid you the rent or bothered to advise you that it'll be delayed for some good reason or another, visit him yourself on the

PAYMENT PLEDGE

Dear Landlord/Landlady:

On or before ___July 28, XXXX___, I promise to pay you $__750⁰⁰__ for rent and other charges now owing on the dwelling which I rent from you located at the following address:

45 Wellington Way, Apt. 367
(Street Address)

Bonkers   California   95556
(City)   (State)   (Zip)

I expect to be receiving sufficient funds to pay you from the following sources:

Name	Address	Phone	Amount Expected
Ellen Dore	Route 4, Box 221, Littleton, CA	123-0707	$250
One Arm Credit Union, 111 Main St., Littleton, CA		123-5000	$500

Should you wish to, you have my authorization to verify these sources.

If I fail to honor this pledge, I understand that I will be evicted and that this pledge will be used against me as evidence of my bad faith in paying what I owe.

_ET_ I acknowledge receipt of a 3-Day Notice to Pay Rent or Quit as required by law to begin eviction proceedings. I understand that the 3-Day Notice may show a balance owed which is different from that given above because a 3-Day Notice by law can demand only delinquent rent. I also understand that the three-day period mentioned in this Notice is being extended to the date given above, at which time I promise to pay you what I owe. If I fail to pay on or before that date, you have the right to continue the legal eviction (unlawful detainer) procedure against me without having to serve me another 3-Day Notice to Pay Rent or Quit. I have already been served. I am being given the extra time to pay only as a courtesy and only this once.

Signed _Extra Terrestrial_
Extra Terrestrial

Dated _July 10, XXXX_

You will find a blank copy of this form in the FORMS section of this book and in Eviction Forms Creator.

fifth to learn what's the matter. Listen to his explanation sympathetically, and then decide whether you ought to give him a little bit of leniency or none at all.

Whether he is to get leniency or not, he ought to get a 3-Day Notice to Pay Rent or Quit then and there (see chapter 5). Have the notice already filled out so you can hand it to him before you leave. Tell him, "We give everybody one of these notices if the rent isn't paid by the fifth, regardless of who he is. We treat everybody the same way."

only does it help each of you remember the details of the agreement, it helps both of you understand the situation more fully.

"Whoa, now," you might say, "there could be a problem here! If you're giving the tenant a 3-day notice at the same time you're getting him to sign a payment pledge stating that you'll still take the rent at some time after the 3-day notice expires, the tenant could argue in court that you're sending him confusing signals. On the one hand, you're saying, 'Pay up in three days,' and on the other, you're saying, 'It's okay to take more

If he doesn't deserve any leniency, tell him that unless he comes up with the rent money in the next three days, he'd better get a move on and move out.

If you're inclined to show him some leniency, have him make a definite commitment to pay on or before a certain date, not over two weeks hence for the best of tenants and within just a few days for those doubtful ones. Put that commitment in writing using a payment pledge form like the one shown here. It specifies exactly when the delinquent rent and other charges will be paid, how much will be paid at that time, what sources will provide the funds, and what will happen if the rent isn't paid by then. It formalizes whatever verbal agreement you make with the tenant. Not

than three days to pay up.' Which is it?"

So as not to be accused of giving the tenant confusing signals about when the rent really has to be paid in order to avoid court action, get the tenant to acknowledge that the 3-Day Notice to Pay Rent or Quit is being served at this time for legal reasons and that the tenant has until the date agreed upon in the payment pledge to pay. After that date, having already served him with the legal notice which initiates eviction proceedings, you may go right ahead and file the summons and complaint. Have him initial the acknowledgment to that effect on the pledge form.

Because you want to circumvent problems with 3-Day Notice to Pay Rent or Quit provisions which require that the final day for payment must be a normal banking day, make the pledge's final day a banking day as well. In other words, don't make the final day a Saturday, Sunday, or holiday; it should be any other day. And because you want to circumvent problems involving dollar amounts, make sure that your 3-day notice demands only rent, no late fees, no bad check charges, or the like. The payment pledge, however, may include whatever sums the tenant owes you, including late fees.

Incidentally, besides those already mentioned, there is another significant advantage in serving a payment pledge along with a 3-day notice. You get the tenant to acknowledge in writing that he has received the notice. You cannot understand how important this advantage is until you have to stand toe-to-toe with a tenant in court sometime and listen to him lie through his incisors, denying under oath that he ever received your notice. How are you going to prove otherwise? With a pledge form in hand, you have his initials and signature to prove that he received it. He can hardly deny that.

Also, going to the trouble of giving your tenant more time than the law requires will make you look good if you have to go to court later. You would not appear hasty. You would appear entirely reasonable. Giving the tenant the 3-day notice at the same time you come to terms using the pledge form is prudent, too. It's your fallback position in case he doesn't come through. You absolutely must give your tenant some form of proper notice before you can proceed with his eviction. You might as well do it now.

If you fail to give the tenant notice along with the pledge, and he doesn't pay on the appointed day, you'll have to deliver it later anyway, and then you'll have to wait the required number of days following service of the notice before you can file your court papers. That wastes precious days. Whereas, if you deliver the notice on the fifth day after the rent due date, and the tenant doesn't pay up on the date agreed upon in the pledge, you may go right ahead, if you wish, and file your court papers the very next day because you have already served the notice and you should already have waited the required number of days specified in the notice. That's prudent indeed!

Taking the Consequences

Collecting your rents swiftly and doggedly on a scheduled basis will prevent evictions for non-payment of rent more than anything else you might do. Your tenants will know full well what to expect of you. They may test you once, but they won't test you a second time. It's too costly. If they have to, they will borrow the money from someone else to pay you their rent rather than risk your wrath and risk being evicted.

Not collecting your rents systematically can only result in losses and frequent trips to the courthouse. I know. How I know! I estimate that I lost at least $6,000 in rents, which were owed to me but never paid, before I finally decided that collections were sufficiently important to warrant more careful treatment. How do you think I learned how to evict? That's right; I wore a path to the courthouse door.

If you stick with reasonable policies for selecting tenants, securing co-signers, enforcing agreements, and collecting rents, you will forestall at least 90% of all your potential evictions. You will be running a healthy business, and your own health will flourish as well.

- Select your tenants with care. "Evict" those *applicants* whom you'd likely have to evict later if they were to become your tenants.
- Get a co-signer to insure the compliance of an untested tenant.
- Be an "enforcer" of your rental agreement. Do not delay; enforce promptly. There's no time like the present, right now, this very minute!
- Be a "heavy" whenever you're collecting rent. Collecting rent is what landlording is all about. That rent money is your paycheck. There's nothing more important in this business than your paycheck, absolutely nothing!
- When you're inclined toward leniency, use the winning combination of a 3-Day Notice to Pay Rent or Quit and a written payment pledge.

2
Getting Problem Tenants Out Without Going To Court

There are legal and there are illegal self-help eviction methods which landlords and landladies may use to get obstreperous, obnoxious, deadbeat tenants to move. I recommend that you try whatever legal methods seem appropriate in your situation before you ever resort to the courts, and I recommend that you learn about the illegal methods so that you will know what to avoid doing to stay out of trouble.

We Americans have become positively obsessed with litigation, running to court optimistically expecting to resolve every kind of problem imaginable, from determining what constitutes reasonable language for high school student assemblies to challenging our deceased Aunt Agatha's last will and testament, in which she left all her money to Rufus, her pet cockatoo. We have come to believe that we will be treated fairly only if we have our day in court, so we blithely file suit after suit after suit at a rate of more than 18,000,000 civil suits a year, and we pay our attorney's fees unquestioningly. We have been clogging our courts with patently frivolous suits; we have been spending more and more unproductive time on jury duty; we have been awarding damage claims so astronomical that they force old and established companies into bankruptcy; we have developed such a fascination for watching court-related programs on television that there are any number of shows like "People's Court" and "Judge Judy," and there's even an entire cable channel called Court TV for people who can't get enough of such programming; we have been devouring convoluted legal thrillers written by attorneys; we have elevated certain attorneys to celebrity status; and we have been educating far too many attorneys.

Japan has only one attorney for every 10,000 people; Germany has one for every 2,000; California has one for every 400; and San Francisco has one for every 50. Which geographical area is going to be the first to have one attorney for every single inhabitant? Which area will have nobody but attorneys? You can be sure that it will be someplace here in the United States, which has a whopping 70% of the world's supply. Will it be Boston, Chicago, Los Angeles, Miami, New York City, San Francisco, or Washington, D.C.? Stay tuned.

If you can stay out of the bailiwick of attorneys, that is, if you can stay out of court, and still accomplish your primary objectives, do so. When faced with an eviction possibility, whatever the reason, you obviously don't have to go to court to evict your tenant if you can come to some resolution of your differences between yourselves. At the very least, you should try something or other before dragging your tenant into a court of law and subjecting yourself to a host of arcane procedures, confusing forms, new frustrations, and constant worries.

What might landlords try other than going to court? Let's examine some of the legal alternatives available first. Then we'll take a look at some of the illegal alternatives. You ought to know the difference.

Legal Alternatives

• TALKING—How do you convince tenants to vacate simply by talking with them? Go to their dwelling. Do not summon them to yours and do not talk with them by telephone. Show them how important this matter is to you by making a personal appearance yourself on their turf. Make sure when you arrive that the decision-maker of the group is there. If not, arrange another meeting at a definite time later that day.

When you meet with them, ask them to explain, first of all, what unusual circumstances have occurred which might have forced them to break their agreement with you. Tell them you have had confidence in them in the past, and you have always felt that it was well placed. Then outline the situation matter-of-factly as you understand it, and suggest alternatives. After that, ask them what they would do if they were in your shoes. If they offer up some unacceptable solution, tell them quite frankly why it wouldn't work and pose your own.

Can you get someone to do something he absolutely doesn't want to do? No, you can't. Yet you can get people to do things which they never thought they would do. You convince them with diplomacy.

One of the many stories told about the redoubtable Winston Churchill occurred at the estate of a friend who was giving a lavish dinner party. The hostess became upset and frustrated when she happened to notice one of her wealthiest guests pocketing a sterling silver salt shaker. She didn't know how to go about retrieving her expensive heirloom without creating a scene and embarrassing the fellow, so she asked her good friend Winston for help. He told her to leave the task to him. Nonchalantly, Winston sidled up to man later in the evening and engaged him in conversation, at the end of which he pulled a salt shaker from his own pocket and said to the fellow, "I think we've been seen. We'd better put them back." Both of them did.

What kind of a stir would Churchill have created had he approached the man like a policeman and told him he had been seen stealing a salt shaker and that if he didn't return it, he'd be arrested? It would have caused great embarrassment and lasting damage. The salt shaker would have been retrieved all right, but the man would have become a social pariah, and no one would have been pleased with the outcome. There is an immense difference between approaching someone as a companion in crime and approaching him as a strong arm of the law. The diplomat knows those two approaches and others and knows when to use each. He knows that one approach won't work in every situation with everyone. Had the saltshaker thief been a streetwise Cockney beggar, the strong-arm approach would have worked well enough. The companion-in-crime approach, as a matter of fact, might have backfired, generating a very different response. The beggar would probably have told his supposed companion in crime that he was a fool for returning his shaker. "Go ahead and return yours if you want to. I'll keep mine. That's

why I pinched it!" he might have said.

Using diplomacy, you as landlord approaching a tenant who has failed to pay his rent when due could play the role of the strong-arm or the companion-in-crime. You know the strong-arm approach. That involves looking the tenant straight in the eye and telling him, "I want my money or else." Someone trying the companion-in-crime approach would say, "I have to pay my rent, too. I pay it to the bank. It's "rent" on the money I borrowed in order to buy this place, and I need your rent money to keep them from repossessing it."

Talk with your tenants using just the diplomatic approach which is right for the situation. Try to be understanding and try to reach an agreement that allows them to save face. You might want to put your agreement in written form, something like the payment pledge introduced in chapter 1. Then again, you might not. Be flexible up to a point. Give a little, take a little. Be reasonable. Be businesslike.

If you simply cannot reach an agreement you consider fair, tell them you are left with no alternative but to evict them in a court of law. Tell them you are loathe to go to that extreme because they will be identified in public records as having been evicted.

This bad news will haunt them for a long time to come because eviction registries will pick it up and make it readily accessible to rental property owners nationwide. Renting another dwelling will be all the more difficult for them in the future. Some landlords will simply not rent to them at all. Others may rent to them only if they will put up a larger deposit and find a co-signer.

Credit bureaus will pick up the information, too, and include it on their personal credit reports. Their credit rating will suffer, and bill collectors will begin hounding them.

In addition, they will never again be able to answer honestly on rental applications that they have not been evicted (to some this may sound hilarious because they seldom tell the truth anyway; to others, unaccustomed to lying in matters such as this, it may be a serious prospect; you will have to decide whether to mention it at all).

After stating these consequences candidly, see if the tenants still persist in being unreasonable. If so, depart and say, "I'm disappointed that you have left me no choice. I had very much hoped we could work something out." Don't get into an argument. Don't leave in a huff. Just go.

Your success or failure in using this maneuver will depend upon the kind of relationship you have already developed with your tenants, as well as upon your skills of persuasion and diplomacy. Tailor the appeal to the people you are dealing with. Above all, be firm and be polite. Don't antagonize them. Don't call them names or impugn their ancestry. You may believe very strongly that they are doing you wrong, but keep your head. Swallow your pride. Keep the dialogue open-ended. If you cut off the dialogue, your impending eviction suit will be all the more difficult to pursue. You want the tenants to be available to be served with court papers as the case progresses. You don't want to alienate them so much that they will avoid service and thereby delay your case ten days here and ten days there. That can be expensive.

For some good ideas on the subject of negotiating, read *Getting to Yes*, which appears among the listings in the References section of this book.

Perhaps you have already tried talking your tenants into leaving, or you feel that talk just wouldn't work. Well, how about mediation?

• MEDIATION—Mediation has become more and more popular because it works. It works so well that some courts require that every small claims case be mediated before it ever comes before a judge, and they have mediators available at the courthouse to assist the litigants in finding a solution to their dispute.

Compared to litigation, mediation is quicker, more convenient, less costly, and more informal.

In case you aren't familiar with mediation, you should know that it introduces a third party, a mediator, into the mix. The mediator, who may or may not be an attorney, is experienced in resolving conflicts and gives each disputant enough time to speak his mind and say how he prefers to resolve the dispute. The mediator listens and suggests possible ways to settle the dispute, ways which might benefit both parties. The mediator does not pass judgment or make decisions. He suggests, and the disputants are free to take the suggestions or continue their dispute.

If you are inclined to use a mediator, arrange a mediation session before you file your unlawful detainer papers with the court because a successful outcome resulting from mediation will save you a heap of fees. You won't have to bother going to court.

To arrange mediation, ask the tenants whether they would agree to attend a meeting where you would try to work out your differences with the help of an impartial third party. If they agree, ask them for some convenient times when they could meet with you and the mediator.

Next, select a mediator. To find one, ask at the courthouse for the names of mediators, use an internet search engine, call your county bar association, or look in the Yellow Pages under "Mediation Services."

When making the first contact, ask whether they feel qualified to mediate a landlord-tenant dispute, ask about the times when they are available, ask about places where they will meet with you, and ask about their charges. You, of course, will be paying the bill, but it should be similar to the cost of filing your unlawful detainer papers.

If successful, mediation will benefit you and your tenants. You'll put the matter behind you quickly, and the tenants won't have a court judgment on their record for all to see.

If unsuccessful, mediation will still benefit you. It will prove to the court that you have made every effort to resolve the dispute before resorting to the courts. Judges tend to sympathize with anyone who exhausts all the legal alternatives, especially mediation, before appearing in their courtrooms.

If you are not inclined to use a mediator, consider bribery. Yes, I know that some people won't even say the "B" word. They consider it a despicable act used by dishonest politicians and business people. It isn't.

• BRIBERY—Bribery has several real advantages. It is quick and, comparatively speaking, it is inexpensive. If you required enough in deposits from your tenants before they moved in, you should, if you act fast, have enough money available from their deposits to pay them for leaving. This was one of the reasons for requiring a deposit in the first place, wasn't it?

Obviously, should you succeed in suing to evict them, the money judgment, including court costs, would be subtracted from their deposits, and they could expect to receive little or no money back. In fact, they'd probably owe you something. An offer to return what's left of their deposits after you deduct for the rent they owe you might be enough to get them moving. It's worth a try.

Calculate about how much an eviction and lost rent would cost you (especially if an attorney is handling the case) before making your offer, and you'll likely find that a bribe will cost you far less. Even if you do have to sweeten the offer somewhat out of your own pocket because you have delayed so long that there's only a paltry deposit balance remaining of, say, less than $100 (few tenants would move for less), you will come out ahead by bribing them to leave, and so will they.

There are some good variations on the bribery gambit, too. You might offer to store the tenant's goods in one of your garages or pay the rent at a self-storage facility for a few months. You might offer to arrange and pay for a U-Haul

grown ventriloquist dummies courting extraterrestrials, acting like escaped loonies, and chattering like blithering simpletons. Sure, they're exhibitionists, but they're also greedy when the price is right. Tenants, too, suddenly feel a great urge to make their move when the price is right.

•INTIMIDATION (SHOW YOUR MUSCLE)—Another maneuver which is perfectly legal and ofttimes prompts tenants to vacate without your ever having to resort to the courts is "show your muscle" intimidation. I don't mean hiring goons or gorillas to intimidate. They're anything but official. I mean hiring a peace of-

van and a small crew to move the tenant's possessions. You might cut a $100 bill in half right before the tenant's eyes, give him half, and keep half yourself until he has moved out completely. Or you might offer to buy his TV, stereo, appliances, furniture, aquarium, or pet parakeet.

Unless the tenant is unable to comprehend what an eviction will mean to him, you will likely be successful with one of these bribes. Don't be ashamed or afraid to try. Money, especially when offered in the right way, will get people to do things they wouldn't begin to consider doing without it. You have probably seen full-grown people making fools of themselves on those old television game shows, dressing up like half-

ficer to scare your tenants out. How? Go to the sheriff's or marshal's office and pay the fee to have one of them serve your notices. Sure, you can serve the notices yourself, but you're too familiar a face to your tenants. You're simply not intimidating enough. You cannot possibly impress upon them the gravity of the matter as much as can an armed and uniformed peace officer who's handing out a notice signed by you and stipulating that the tenants have a fixed number of days to clear out. That is quite intimidating to most people. They simply do not want to get mixed up with the law if they can help it, and they frequently will mistake your notice for one which actually announces their impending eviction. It all looks so official and imperative.

NOTA BENE: Some peace officers don't serve notices at all when on duty. They're too busy serving official court documents, and your notice does not qualify as an official court document. Some are terribly slow. They may have such a backlog of work that they may take more than a week to get around to yours. Before you hire one of them to serve your notice, ask them to estimate how long they'll take to serve it, and then weigh the intimidation factor of their serving the notice versus the time factor of your or someone else's serving it more quickly.

you might want to consider posting your official paperwork on their door for twenty-four hours before you file it with the court clerk. They may get the message and move without a word, or they may get the message and call you to arrange the best terms they can get for moving out. If they don't move and they don't call, call them yourself and tell them they have one last chance to move before you file the court papers.

This form of intimidation has worked many times before. It could work for you, and it could save you time and money. In order for it to work, you must be firm and assertive.

A variation of this method involves the direct hiring of an off-duty law-enforcement officer or a security patrolman to serve your notices. In most areas, they may wear their uniforms while off duty and may hire themselves out as process servers. They look quite intimidating when they appear on a doorstep in full-dress attire complete with a firearm strapped to their waist and they hand your tenant his notice. They seem to carry *clout*, and they frequently get the desired response.

• INTIMIDATION (SHOW YOUR PAPERWORK)—Because some tenants believe you're a dolt and a tightwad and a pushover who will never get around to evicting them in court,

Illegal Alternatives

In some respects we ought to consider ourselves fortunate that there are laws to keep us landlords from acting rashly when we're trying to force problem tenants to move out. After being frustrated repeatedly, some of us might be driven to near distraction and feel compelled to take the law into our own hands, only to wind up doing something we regret later.

Unscrupulous, bullheaded, devil-may-care landlords use illegal self-help eviction methods anyway, laws or no laws. These methods generally work as effectively as a gangster chieftain's dictum, but sometimes they don't. Sometimes the results are disastrous, and you read about them on the front page of your daily newspaper. No matter what the risks are, some people are willing to take them. So be it.

Just in case you don't know what these illegal self-help eviction methods are, I'll identify a few. Perhaps you weren't aware that they are illegal.

• CONSTRUCTIVE EVICTION—Unscrupulous landlords and landladies might disturb what the law calls "the tenant's right to quiet enjoyment of his domicile" by arranging for 130-decibel punk rock to play at all hours in an adjoining apartment or encouraging the elephants living upstairs to keep up their tap dancing. Like

This monster man stops by at dinnertime and bangs threateningly on the tenant's door, perhaps loosening a hinge or two. When the tenant opens the door, he is staring directly into a hairy navel, and he hears a husky voice from on high echoing down to him, "Your landlord wants you out of here by 6 o'clock tonight or we'll come by to move you out." Now that's an appeal that's mighty hard to resist. Few tenants do. They're cowed into submission. But it's as illegal as drug peddling, and the consequences can be just as disastrous.

Don't use any of these methods unless you're

some of the other methods described here, this is what is known as a "constructive eviction," and the tenant's responsibility to pay rent ceases whenever a constructive eviction occurs.

They might cut off the water and lights, unhinge the outside doors, chop down the stairway to a second floor apartment, or collect the neighborhood population of rodents and keep them around by feeding them daily on the premises.

They might change the locks on the doors, rummage through the tenant's belongings, keep the good stuff, and throw the rest out on the sidewalk.

They might hire a burly bear of a man to scare the tenant out.

willing to risk a very angry tenant and legal action in which you are the defendant not the plaintiff, an action that may actually delay the tenant's departure and then cost you big bucks in a settlement.

You might wonder why laws keep us from using these methods. They seem so perfectly reasonable to use in certain cases. After all, it's our property, and we don't want the tenants to stay there anymore. If we want to remove the front door or chop down the stairway, that's our business. We own the place, including the door and the stairway. Why can't we do with it what we want to do with it? Why should such an act be against the law? The simple reason is that these eviction methods disturb the peace. They enrage tenants and endanger the lives and limbs of everyone concerned, yours too, to say nothing of the possible property damage they might cause. People get hurt when they're being tossed out. They break bones when they go to descend a flight of stairs and discover belatedly that the stairs have disappeared. People become infuriated when their belongings are peremptorily confiscated. People become incensed when someone "locks" them inside their home by removing the front door so they can't leave or when someone locks them out of their home by changing the locks.

and landladies who resort to such methods when they believe the circumstances are right for these methods to work, that is, when they anticipate no complications. The secret to using self-help methods successfully, they say, is to keep a low profile, be unobtrusive and very canny.

• LOCKOUT—One landlady told me how she locked out a tenant some time ago, seemingly a dangerous act, certainly an illegal one. Maybe it would have been dangerous in other circumstances, but she thought otherwise. You be the judge.

It so happened that one of her tenants was

They strike back. Tempers flare. Problems grow out of all proportion, and the police have to be called in to quell the disturbances. Sometimes the coroner even has to be called in to cart off the dead. The object of these laws is to keep people from resorting to street remedies and to bring their potentially destructive disputes into court instead, where they can be judged impartially in a neutral atmosphere.

Avoid illegal self-help eviction methods if you want to keep your property, your fortune, your health, and your life pretty much intact. Use them only if you don't mind taking the risk of losing everything you've worked for.

Still, I must admit that I know some landlords

two weeks in arrears, and at great inconvenience to herself, she had been trying several times a day for the previous ten days to find him. Upon making inquiries, she learned that none of the neighbors had seen him during that period, and she was unable to reach any of the contacts listed on his rental application. To determine whether he had indeed flown the coop or whether he was just being evasive, she peered through the windows, and seeing what appeared to be little but trash inside, she decided to enter with her passkey. When she did so, she committed her first illegal act, forcible entry, believe it or not, but she rationalized her action by saying to herself that she thought the tenant might be dead and she'd better find out for sure.

Strange to say, from what she saw in this house which she had rented out unfurnished, she couldn't tell whether he was still living there or not. There was a mattress on the floor in the bedroom and a table and chair in the kitchen. That's all there was for furniture. On the back porch was a fair-sized heap of trash, and the usual junk one finds in a recently vacated rental was scattered throughout the rooms. The place looked abandoned.

Under these circumstances, she should really have used the abandonment procedure outlined

to move out within two days, and so he did. In fact, the very next day he moved out everything, including the trash.

She believed he had been eluding her all that time, coming in late and leaving early, and that he would have continued playing cat and mouse with her, occupying the premises rent-free much longer, if she had not forced him to meet with her. Her stratagem had worked. She had outsmarted her tenant. She had recovered possession of her house, and she had done it quickly, much more quickly than if she had followed the legal means available to her. Of course, her ac-

in chapter 14 to regain possession, but she decided instead to change the locks, using old replacements exactly like the originals so that her locking out the tenant would not appear obvious to him if he did return. His key would fit into the keyway, but it wouldn't turn.

That night at 2 a.m. the tenant called to let her know that he couldn't get his key to work. Apologizing for the "defective" lock, she let him in after pretending to have trouble opening the lock herself. She gave him another key. They talked cordially. He apologized for not contacting her earlier about the rent. He said that all kinds of unfortunate things had happened to him lately and he had just forgotten, but he promised

tion might have resulted in her tenant's breaking a door or a window to get in. It might also have resulted in a lawsuit, but fortunately for her, it resulted only in the tenant's departure, and that was her prime objective.

Do the ends justify the means? It's an age-old question. This landlady believed that they did in her case. Otherwise she would never have gambled and she never would have won.

The point of this narrative and the next is that there are certain pragmatic methods which might accomplish one's objectives in a given situation quickly, cheaply, and painlessly should one choose to use them. I do not advocate their use because they must be carefully chosen and carefully executed, they require extra-careful judgment, they don't always work, they may actually backfire, and they are, after all, illegal, but I think you should be familiar with them and their drawbacks nonetheless, just as you should be familiar with the applicable legal eviction procedures.

• PHONY EVICTION—The next illegal method is rather an inventive one, staging a phony eviction. It capitalizes on the tenant's ignorance of the legal eviction process and his unwillingness to become a respondent in the case. When you examine the eviction procedures outlined in chapters 5-9, you will notice that none of them

tenants, he prepares forms for the phony eviction just as carefully as if he were going through court. He covers the original names, dates, and other particulars with correction fluid, photocopies the papers, types in the tenant's name and the other information relevant to this case, photocopies the doctored copies, and then serves those copies himself by posting them on the door. Each time another form is "due," it too is dummied up and served. The tenant doesn't know the difference but believes that when the final date is set, he'd better clear out. The success of this method, to be sure, depends on the tenant's

actually forces the stalwart but submissive tenant to appear in court. If he chooses not to answer the summons, he never goes near the courthouse. The legal machinery just keeps grinding away behind his back. He knows it is because he keeps getting papers from the court. The only thing he can hope to do is delay matters by making himself unavailable, and that insures the phony eviction's success. He never sees the landlord who's posting the notices on his door.

To stage an eviction, the landlord follows all the steps of an ordinary legal eviction through the courts, but he dummies up the papers. Using originals of all the appropriate forms which he obtained from authentic cases against former

lack of sophistication in legal matters.

The landlord I know who uses this method claims that it saves him inconvenience and money and that it works especially well in cases where he has already delayed matters too long and the tenant regards eviction as inevitable anyway.

These illegal, self-help eviction methods are quite different one from the other, but they have one thing in common. They create some pretty apprehensive landlords and landladies. Don't even try using them yourself. You may be creating more problems for yourself than you ever thought possible.

Evict legally. You want the law to be on your side, not on the side of the tenant who is making your life miserable.

- Avoid litigation if you possibly can.
- Try some friendly persuasion first.
- Try mediation.
- Consider how much litigation is going to cost you and then try offering your tenant some cash money as an enticement to leave.
- Eschew methods used by the unscrupulous.

3
Preparing for Your Court Case

When you have tried and failed to rid yourself of problem tenants by hook or by crook, you have no alternative but to try an eviction by the book. You need legal clout to get them out.

Before you begin, however, you should know a thing or two about legal terminology, eviction statistics, courts, ownership entity, attorneys, eviction services, local practices, court clerks, time demands, fictitious name statements, equipment and supplies, computer programs, and costs, and if your property is located in an area under rent control, you should definitely know something about how rent control will affect your eviction. You'll find information about rent control in the next chapter. First, let's take a look at the various things which might have some bearing upon your eviction, no matter where in California you happen to be.

Legal Terminology

In almost every pursuit there's a jargon understood only by its initiates. Perhaps because those who practice law, work so much with words and try so hard to be precise, they have developed more special terminology than have people in most other pursuits. To help you understand certain special meanings of the terms you are likely to encounter when you handle an eviction through the courts, there is a glossary at the back of this book.

One term you will see so frequently that it should be introduced here is "unlawful detainer." Generally speaking, it means wrongfully possessing real property which belongs to someone else, but in the strict legal sense it refers to the legal proceeding which culminates in the sheriff (or) marshal's removing tenants from the landlord's property. Most frequently, it is used interchangeably with the term "eviction," but it will almost always be the term used in legal proceedings to refer to an eviction action.

Actually, the term "eviction" has a broader definition. You may say that you evicted a tenant when you merely asked him to leave and he went, when you served him with a notice and he left, when you made his dwelling uninhabitable and he moved, or when you filed a complaint against him in court and had the sheriff preside over his departure. Those are all evictions, but only the last one is an unlawful detainer.

Eviction Statistics

The news media love horror stories. They thrive on horror stories, so much so that you'd think Stephen King were every reporter's patron saint. If you pay any attention to the news media, you have encountered horror stories about evictions which took some poor landlord months to consummate and practically sent him to the poor house, and you may be wondering whether you might be embarking upon a horror story of your own as you prepare to evict some tenants. Well, just in case you're becoming apprehensive about your chances of successfully evicting your tenants in court, consider some statistics gathered by the California Apartment Law Information Foundation (CALIF) on unlawful detainers filed during 1990 (the last year anybody studied unlawful detainers so exhaustively).

In that year, there were 236,817 unlawful detainers filed throughout the state of California, and the plaintiff/landlord prevailed in 99.4% of them. Imagine that! Landlords won 99.4 out of every 100 unlawful detainers they filed! The Procter & Gamble people claim that Ivory soap is 99.99% pure, and we tend to think of that as being pretty pure. It is. Prevailing in 99.4% of all unlawful detainer cases is almost as sure as Ivory is pure. Think about that as you begin your own unlawful detainer action. You are going to prevail. You are not going to lose. The statistics are

Unlawful Detainer: Filed a complaint w/ the Court & the sheriff force the move out

Landlords must jump thru the legal antiquated loops

with you. They are with you overwhelmingly!

Don't let that 99.4% figure go to your head, though. Whereas your eventual triumph is about as close to a sure thing as you'll ever find in this world, you still must jump through all the hoops which our antiquated legal system insists you jump through. Some of the hoops are flaming and may singe you slightly. Some are small and may be a tight squeeze. Some are moving and may require special concentration. Jump through them anyway. Jump through every one of them, or the bureaucrats, the badge wearers, and the black-robed potentates operating the system will not let you prevail.

Then there's the matter of time. Time is not on your side in an unlawful detainer action. Time is your enemy. The longer your unlawful detainer takes, the more your tenants gain. Time is on their side. It's their ally, not yours.

Time is on the tenant side not the Landlord

Let's look at some more eviction statistics gathered by CALIF, and we'll see just how tenants use time to their advantage in unlawful detainers. Statewide, the average unlawful detainer takes 48 days, that is, from the date when the landlord files his first document with the court until he gets his judgment. Mind you, this is not the elapsed time for the entire eviction cycle because it does not include the notice period before the first court papers are filed, nor does it include the lag time between the filing of the Writ of Execution and the actual departure of the tenants. The shortest amount of time the notice period might take is three days, and the final lag time is going to be at least five days, so we have to add at least eight days to the 48 days. The average unlawful detainer in California, then, takes at least 56 days. That's close to two months! That's a long time. That's a very long time when every one of those days is costing you money.

Avg Time for an unlawful Detainer 40 days (60)

Hold on, it gets worse. On average, landlords in Los Angeles take a week longer than the statewide average to evict their tenants. Landlords in Berkeley take over two weeks longer than the statewide average. Landlords in Compton, of all places, require more than twice as much time to evict their tenants as landlords elsewhere. Sounds pretty bad, eh? Read on.

There are two primary eviction delaying tactics used by unscrupulous tenants. You'll be learning more about them later in this book. The one is a tenant claim that an adult actually living in the rental dwelling failed to receive proper no-tice of the landlord's unlawful detainer action. This is called an "Arrieta claim" because it's the result of a California Supreme Court decision in the Arrieta case [*Arrieta v. Mahon* (1982) 31 CA3d 381]. The other delaying tactic is bankruptcy, generally filed at the eleventh hour, right before the sheriff comes to turn the tenants out. If tenants make an Arrieta claim, statistics show that they require an extra month to be evicted. If they file bankruptcy, they require an extra five weeks to be evicted. If they go for broke, making both an Arrieta claim *and* filing bankruptcy, they require an extra six weeks more than the average to be evicted, or three-and-a-half months in all!

Clearly, time is the tenants' ally. Initially, the statistics about unlawful detainers look good for the landlord. The landlord is going to win. It's a sure thing. Press the statistics further for information, however, and things change. Sure, the landlord is going to win in the end, but the tenant is going to be dragging his feet all the way out the door and living rent-free as long as possible.

"Time" is the watchword in unlawful detainers. You have to be concerned as much about time in an unlawful detainer as anything else. It's important to you, very important. Ignoring time is not going to result in your losing your case completely, but it is going to result in your losing money, lots of it, and that after all is what most civil lawsuits are all about.

You *can* beat the time averages when doing an eviction yourself. I always do. I have never once needed as much time as the statewide average to consummate an eviction. My average is about half the statewide average. You should be able to beat the averages, too, even if you have never evicted a tenant through the courts before. All you have to do is pay close attention to the ticking clock while you're pursuing your unlawful detainer, and you will beat the averages.

Don't worry much about whether you will win or lose. Worry only about how long your winning will take. Stay tuned to your case. Follow it closely. Check out the various timetables in this book, and play "Beat the Clock."

Courts

Small claims courts can no longer hear eviction cases in California. Nowadays you have no choice. You must use superior court to evict a tenant.

Common delay Tactic used by a tenant #1 An Adult living-n property was not served notices Properly aka "Arrieta claim" # Filing of a B.K

Utilize Small Claim Court for other disputes?- beside Rent @ of 2008
Limit $7,500 Rowever
LLC, corp, partnership
Chapter 3: Preparing for Your Court Case   29
mid X 75k

In some ways, being denied access to small claims courts for evictions is no great loss for landlords because small claims courts were always notoriously slow in carrying an eviction through to its conclusion, no matter how justified it was. Landlords who chose to evict their tenants through small claims courts could wind up winning their judgments (but) losing lots of rent money because the entire procedure was so slow and so weighted in favor of tenants. Any tenant bent on delaying his ouster as long as legally possible could stay on for months by taking advantage of the perfectly legal stratagems available to him and following a timetable far slower than

simple, straightforward procedures and forms.

You may, of course, still use small claims court for other money disputes involving tenants. Let's say that a tenant won't reimburse you for a window his son broke, or he drove his uninsured Ford into the side of your storage shed and refuses to pay to repair the damage, or he won't pay you the balance of the security deposit he promised to pay during the second month of his tenancy. Go after him in small claims court.

Just make sure that the compensation you seek falls within the monetary limits of the court.

Those monetary limits have increased quite substantially over the years. You may have heard

the one which applies to evictions pursued in superior court, where evictions are entitled to speedy processing.

Nonetheless, small claims courts did have certain advantages as eviction battlegrounds—neither landlord nor tenant could be represented by counsel; the landlord as plaintiff could expect special help with the paperwork from small claims court clerks skilled in advising neophytes about their cases; the landlord could expect to pay a cheaper filing fee; and the whole procedure was simpler. Perhaps these advantages will return one of these days if the legislature ever gets around to establishing landlord-tenant courts using

that you as an individual can now sue somebody for $7,500 in a California small claims court. You heard right. As of January 1, 2006, it is $7,500, but there is one important condition. You may sue for a maximum of $7,500 *no more than twice in any given year*, whereas you may sue for anything up to $2,500 as often as you like.

The $7,500 limit applies to all small claims courts throughout the state, not to each of them separately. You can't sue twice for the maximum in San Diego, for example, and then twice in Los Angeles in the same year. You can sue once for the maximum in San Diego and then once in Los Angeles or any other place in the state in a single year, and that's all. After that, you have to limit your suits to $2,500 each until the following year.

There are two other small claims court limitations you should know something about because they could affect you as a landlord.

First, if you own your property in the name of a corporation or a general partnership or a limited liability company or any other entity which files its own income tax return, then you cannot sue for more than $5,000. The top limit of $7,500 is available only to individuals.

Second, if you are suing a co-signer, AKA a "guarantor," you cannot sue for more than $4,000, but if that person charged nothing for co-signing, then the limit is $2,500.

Keeping those limitations in mind, whenever you are pursuing a tenant who owes you money and you're not also trying to evict him, take him to small claims court. Before you go, though, read a copy of the Department of Consumer Affairs' booklet called "The Dos and Don'ts of Using the Small Claims Court," which is available on the internet at dca.ca.gov/legal/small_claims/small_claims.pdf or by mail. Then proceed. You must know something about preparing your case for small claims court if you expect to convince a judge that you're telling the truth and deserve a favorable judgment.

Now that you no longer have the option of taking evictions to small claims court, which is the one court most people know something about from having seen "People's Court" and "Judge Judy" on television, you should know a little about the one court you can use for evictions, superior.

First of all, you should know that superior courts are under county jurisdiction, not city, not state, and not federal. Counties are responsible for administering them and maintaining their operations. Hence, you must know the county where your rental property is located, for you must use a court in that county to evict. You cannot use the court which is nearest to your rental property unless it happens to be in the same county as the property.

Secondly, you should know that the name "superior court" is misleading. Whereas juvenile courts and probate courts have names which indicate what kinds of cases they handle, who would know what happens in superior courts? They have a "poker-face" name. Their name offers no clues as to what happens there. Superior courts are not

inherently "superior" to other courts, and they are definitely not one step below the Supreme Court. In fact, they are many steps below that esteemed court. Don't suppose that you could ever take a case decided against you in superior court directly to the Supreme Court. You couldn't, nor would you want to. You'd have to spend piles of money and calendars of time to take a case to the Supreme Court from superior court. Forget about it, and forget what you might imagine is happening in superior courts if you know no more about them than the name. The name is not descriptive. They're simply the courts for evictions in California.

By the way, municipal courts, which used to hear most evictions in California, no longer exist. They were legislated out of existence. They became superior courts, and when they became superior courts, their judges became superior court judges.

Ownership Entities and Their Representation Requirements

The ownership entity holding title to your rental property determines who may handle your unlawful detainer, you or an attorney.

Let's say that you formed a corporation to protect your personal assets from lawsuits, and your corporation holds title to your rental property. Can you represent your corporation in court in an unlawful detainer? No, you cannot. No matter what kind of corporation you formed, you cannot represent it in superior court. You may represent it in small claims court when litigating security deposit disputes and such, but you cannot represent it in superior court when litigating unlawful detainers. An attorney must represent the corporation there.

The same holds true for limited liability companies, commonly known as L.L.C.'s. Like corporations, they are not "natural persons," and they must have attorney representation in superior court. At least such is the case in the state of California. Other states allow members of a limited liability company to represent the company. If you do business as an L.L.C. in other states besides California, check the statutes in those states for a determination.

Partnerships, both general and limited, are not natural persons either, and according to Corporations Code 24000, neither are churches, labor unions, political parties, professional or trade associations, social clubs, or homeowners associations. All of them fall under the same restrictions as corporations and L.L.C.'s (see *Clean Air Trans. Sys. v San Mateo County Transit District* (1988) 198 CA 3d 576). They must have an attorney represent them in superior court.

A good way to determine whether the owner of a property requires representation is to consider whether the owner reports the property's income and expenses on a tax return other than a personal return. If so, the owner is not a natural person and requires representation.

Individuals over the age of 18 years who hold title may represent themselves. Couples, married or not, as well as unrelated persons who have formed a joint venture and hold title together, qualify as individuals and may represent themselves, too. Of course, individuals may have an attorney represent them if they so desire.

Unlawful detainer paperwork requires identification of the plaintiff's particulars, including the ownership entity. The choices are as follows: an individual over the age of 18 years, a public agency, a partnership, a corporation, or "other."

Because the public records related to your rental property identify its ownership entity, you must be certain that your paperwork conforms with the public records, or you could face trouble later if the defendants or their attorney discovers that you are representing yourself even though public records show that your corporation or L.L.C. owns the property and you ought not to be representing yourself.

Attorneys

Regardless of whether you do your own evictions or have an attorney do them for you, you should know an attorney to consult when there are legal entanglements. You'll feel more confident about handling your whole landlording business if you do. Besides, attorneys are absolutely indispensable in our society, regardless of how we feel about them and the whole business of litigation in America today.

They are not absolutely indispensable for doing evictions, however. In most evictions, ones which might be called routine, you can do the same thing yourself more quickly and more inexpensively. Attorneys, after all, delegate the paperwork to a legal secretary and become involved only when a court appearance is necessary.

Unless they have an "eviction mill" set up,

most attorneys don't even want to do evictions for landlords (ah, but from reading the *California Eviction Defense Manual*, methinks there are those attorneys who get a perverse thrill out of championing the rights of "downtrodden" tenants) because they're penny-ante stuff compared to other types of legal cases. Many attorneys handle them for the same reason that some real estate agents handle rental property management operations, to promote themselves so you'll think of them first when you need their other more lucrative services.

Now you might think that an attorney, a professional in the field of law, would take less time to evict a tenant than you, a rank amateur, would. You might think that, but you'd be wrong.

Here are three reasons why an eviction handled by an attorney will take longer than one you do yourself. First, because you know that an attorney will charge you $200 to $1,500 in fees (depending on whether court appearances are necessary) plus attendant costs amounting to upwards of $300, you will tend to delay longer than you should before turning to him to begin eviction proceedings, accepting the tenant's excuses more credulously and hoping he will move out without your having to spend all that money. Second, an attorney will handle from 50 to 150 cases at one time, and yours may be delayed because another case needs attention at the same time yours does. Third, an attorney has no incentive to push your eviction through to completion as rapidly as is legally possible. You do. Every extra day the tenant stays without paying rent is money out of your pocket. On the other hand, the attorney is going to be compensated for his time regardless of how long the eviction takes.

You can do an eviction yourself in superior court for between $260 and $290 in out-of-pocket costs and a total of two to five hours of your own time. If your time is more important than your money, hire an attorney to handle your evictions. It's an attorney's business. Otherwise, do it yourself.

Some have said that acting as your own attorney is akin to doing your own brain surgery. That may be true if you're trying to defend yourself on murder charges. Evictions are not murder charges. They're more like the common cold.

Do be shrewd enough to recognize when you need to engage the services of an attorney, however. Generally you need one when your tenants have hired an attorney themselves, when your tenants in an apartment house have organized against you (hell hath no fury like all the tenants in a building who are being evicted at one time), or when there are any complications you don't understand. That's when you should hire yourself an attorney, and remember that even though you have begun an action on your own, you may always hire an attorney to assist you whenever you feel you need one as your case progresses.

I should mention here that there are several special advantages in using an attorney for evictions if you're so inclined. Both relate to bungling. First, because attorneys are independent contractors, you can't be sued by your tenant if your attorney makes an error which gives the tenant a cause of action. Second, if the attorney bungles the paperwork so badly that you lose your suit to your tenant, you may sue your attorney for malpractice.

If you, on the other hand, bungle an eviction, you'll have to go back to square one and start all over again. You'll have nobody to blame for the bungling but yourself. Considering the advantages in handling routine evictions on your own, though, I'd say that the advantages in using an attorney really aren't substantial enough to warrant using one for every garden-variety eviction you have.

Eviction Services

In the Yellow Pages and on the internet you will find eviction services, companies which specialize in doing evictions for the landlord or in helping the landlord do them himself. These services may be run by attorneys or by independent paralegals who may or may not be affiliated with attorneys.

You already know that attorneys have had to demonstrate their knowledge of the law in order to practice any legal specialty, including landlord-tenant law. You may not know that independent paralegals who handle evictions have had to satisfy certain state-mandated requirements before they could open for business. They must be licensed by the state; they must register in every county where they do business; and they must post a $25,000 bond covering only their eviction work. In other words, they are professionals, too, and they know the practical aspects of evictions as well as anybody.

The big differences between eviction services

are in their cost and in their latitude to provide you with advice and representation in court. Attorneys charge more for their eviction services than do paralegals, but attorneys can give you legal advice and can represent you in court, whereas paralegals cannot.

Paralegals can still analyze your case, orient you to the whole mechanical process, steer you in the right direction without giving you legal advice, prepare the paperwork, do the legwork, help you avoid an unsympathetic judge should you have to go to court (whereas you cannot specify a particular judge, you may be able to specify a time for your court appearance, and paralegals may know what times are better than others for avoiding a particular judge who tends to be unsympathetic to landlords), and hold your hand. They can also refer you to an attorney if they see any red flags when they first analyze your case or later as it progresses. They can even help you with mediation, especially when legal aid is involved. They can prepare stipulated judgments which sometimes work to keep the tenant in possession with or without an exit date, so long as the tenant continues to make payments to you on an agreed-upon schedule.

If you cannot make sense out of this book, if you feel too timid to handle an eviction yourself, if you live too far away from the court of jurisdiction, if you encounter difficulties doing an eviction yourself, or if you cannot call upon anybody when you need help, look for a local eviction service in the Yellow Pages or search for one on the internet. You will find attorneys and independent paralegals operating as eviction services. Just remember that the two are different in their training, their approaches, their costs, and their services.

If you live in an area which has no eviction services as such available and you want to use an attorney, check under "attorneys" in the Yellow Pages (I guarantee you'll find some of them listed) and call several who advertise that they are a general practice law firm specializing in, among other things, landlord-tenant law.

To find the attorney or independent paralegal in your area who ought to know more about evictions than anybody, ask the court clerk for the name of the person who files the most evictions in her court. The clerk will know right away who that person is and will probably even have the telephone number memorized. In my local court, one person files more than half of all the evictions filed there. You can bet that he knows what he's doing.

Local Practices

Within California there are some variations in forms, practices, costs, and schedules. Some courts, for example, hear unlawful detainers on only one day every week; some allow a declaration in lieu of actual appearance in court to get a default judgment; some require that two-sided forms be copied always on one sheet of paper, never on two; and some have special forms all their own which they require litigants to use (forms approved by the Judicial Council of California are used throughout the state). Acquaint yourself with the forms and procedures given here first and then ask your court clerk certain questions about local practices when you first call her or when you actually file the summons and complaint. Then you won't be surprised later.

In chapter 5, you will find cautionary information related to local practices discovered the hard way by readers of this book. Read it carefully. Don't let unusual local practices trip you up and delay you.

Court Clerks

Your primary contact with your court will be the court clerk. She can make your job easier and speedier in many ways, by giving you helpful hints when you need them, by supplying you with the correct forms for her court, by squeezing you onto an already full calendar, and by holding your hand as you traverse strange legal territory. She knows it all. Be patient around her (she's often harried), trust her (she's experienced), be nice to her even if she does sometimes appear gruff and uncivil (it's a stressful job), and she will be of great help to you. It wouldn't hurt for you to bring her a flower or two to cheer her up when appropriate. Courthouses aren't the most cheerful places in which to work, you know.

Lest you think that your court clerk is being especially curt or aloof to you because you don't belong to the "attorney guild," consider this. One eviction expert, an attorney who has handled over 3,000 evictions himself, told me that three years elapsed before any of the court clerks in one of the courts he uses frequently, ever treated him civilly.

Don't despair if your court clerk is unfriendly

to you at first. She's not discriminating against you because you're an outsider. She likely treats attorneys that way as well.

Time Demands

The eviction process will take some of your personal time. You will have to type up the papers, visit the clerk's and sheriff or marshal's offices, make telephone calls, possibly appear in court, and finally, supervise the actual eviction if necessary. Be certain you have the time necessary for the whole process. Either you or your spouse may do the work, but, for the sake of convenience, the one not tied to a daytime job should be the one to do it. Court offices are generally open from 8-12 a.m. and from 1-5 p.m., and your court hearing is usually set for 9 a.m. Be certain you can make your hearing.

As an added precaution, you should list both yourself and your spouse or partner as plaintiffs in the complaint, and then any one of you could appear in court. Some courts will allow your manager to appear in court as well, even though he is not mentioned in the complaint. If you live at a distance from your property or you would be greatly inconvenienced by appearing in court yourself, include your manager's name on the complaint as a plaintiff as well, and then he could appear, but he must be considered one of the owners if he appears in court on an unlawful detainer since the only one who may legally represent an owner in court is an attorney licensed to practice before the bar.

[handwritten margin note: who can appear in court on your behalf?]

Fictitious Name Statements

If you have adopted a fictitious name for your landlording business or for a particular building you own *and* if your rental agreements are written in that name rather than your own (if rent checks are made out in the name of the building or in your business name, that doesn't matter; this requirement refers only to the name used on the agreement), you will have to file a fictitious name statement before you may evict a tenant through the courts. It's a simple procedure really, costing around $60 all told, but since it involves publishing a legal notice, it cannot be done overnight; it takes about four weeks. If you are using a fictitious name on your agreements, you must include a statement in your complaint verifying that you have filed the fictitious name statement. If you haven't filed one yet and you have been using a fictitious name, file immediately and then proceed with the first steps of your unlawful detainer. Only the court action itself need wait upon final publication of the name.

Where you file your fictitious name is important, for a devious attorney may attack your eviction action by claiming that you filed in the wrong county, and this claim may delay the eviction considerably. Remember to file it in the county where you conduct most of your business under a particular name. If you live in one county, own buildings in several other counties, and operate all of them under one fictitious name, then the location where you have your central office would be

If you don't have a computer around the house or have access to one, you'll need to get a ballpoint pen with black ink, a typewriter (preferably one with a correction key), typewriter correction tape (necessary only if your typewriter lacks a correction key), correction fluid, carbon paper, copies of appropriate preprinted forms, and pleading paper (paper with numbers down the left margin; necessary only if you don't or can't use preprinted forms; you'll find a blank in the FORMS section of this book). With all that, this book, and, of course, your checkbook, you're ready to do battle with your tenant through the courts.

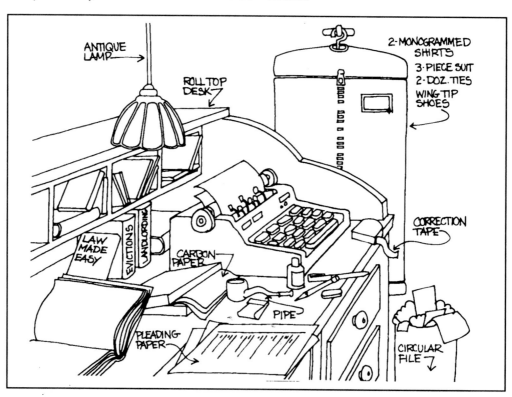

the county to file in. If you live in one county and have several properties in other counties, operating them under various fictitious names, file separate fictitious name statements, and file them in the counties where the properties are located.

Equipment and Supplies

To handle an eviction yourself, you won't have to invest in a three-piece suit, monogrammed shirts, and wingtip shoes, trappings of the newly initiated attorney, but you will have to gather together some equipment and a few supplies, most of which you probably already have around the house or at your office.

If you do have a computer around the house or have access to one, you may use it to fill out the forms. Following are three different ways you may use a computer to fill out the forms. Each of them shows you exactly what the forms look like right on your computer screen. You select the forms you need, enter the data appropriate to your case, review it, and print out as many copies of the forms on your printer as you need.

Judicial Council Forms in Adobe Portable Document Format

The Judicial Council now makes its forms available free of charge in the Adobe Portable

Document Format (pdf) on its website (courtinfo.ca.gov). From the home page on that site, go to the Self-Help Center and select "Landlord/Tenant" under "More Topics." There you'll find "Eviction (Unlawful Detainer) Forms." Go to the list of forms, and you'll find the ones available for downloading.

Download all you think you'll ever use, and you may use them offline whenever you wish.

You'll need a recent copy of Adobe® Reader® to open the forms and use them, of course. It's a freebie. Go to adobe.com and download it if you don't already have a copy.

Once you open the forms, you may print them just the way they appear and use a typewriter to fill in the blanks and checkboxes with data specific to your case, but that wouldn't be taking advantage of the forms' primary feature. They are "fillable." You don't need to use a typewriter to fill them out. You may use your computer.

Click on the checkboxes to put a check in them, and click wherever else you think the form calls for data, and a box will appear to accept your data. When you finish entering your data, print the form and smile at how good it looks.

Not to be outdone by a state agency, counties are beginning to offer their local forms as pdf's, too. Check your county's court website to see what's available. Go to courtinfo.ca.gov/courts/trial/courtlist.htm for a list of courts.

EZ Legal File

EZ Legal File is something new, and it shows great promise. It's a web-based interactive program found at ezlegalfile.org. Users select the type of case they're pursuing and the jurisdiction where they're filing the case. Then they answer a set of questions, and the program completes the forms.

The program is usable now, but it is under development and will have more features as it develops. When fully developed, it will enable users to complete the forms online and submit them directly to the court online. The court will accept them, open the case, and notify the plaintiff of the timeframe for the case. It has potential for being a real time saver.

Eviction Forms Creator™

Eviction Forms Creator, a computer program I wrote myself to fill out eviction forms, goes beyond both the Judicial Council's and EZ Legal File's forms. It also is not web-based.

It does require a computer, either a Windows machine or a Mac, but it does not require an internet connection. It comes on a CD-ROM, so you can load it onto your computer and use it whenever and wherever you wish and as many times as you wish.

It includes all the applicable Judicial Council forms plus a large number of the local forms which courts use. It's designed strictly to save you the drudgery of having to re-enter data. You enter data once, and then the program uses that same data to populate all the forms.

You'll find some information about Eviction Forms Creator in the back of this book, and you will see what the main menu looks like as well.

All of the sample forms shown in this book were created using Eviction Forms Creator. In all, it can create over fifty forms.

Costs

Your out-of-pocket expenses for doing an eviction yourself will vary somewhat, depending upon your court's filing fees (filing fees average around $180); the process server's fees (if you can con a friend into serving the papers for you, you may not have to pay anything; otherwise you'll pay approximately $75 per person served), and the number of tenants you serve (each one costs extra because each one must be served a separate set of papers).

There are other fees which you will have to pay for certain services as well, but they will hardly break you—issuing the writ by the court ($15) and evicting the tenant by the sheriff or marshal ($75).

All together, your out-of-pocket expenses will be somewhere between $345 and $425 if you elect to do an unlawful detainer yourself.

Next

The particular reason you have for evicting your tenant will dictate the kind of notice you serve, as well as how you complete the complaint. In chapters 5-9, we will cover the steps used for evicting tenants legally for any of these reasons: 1) nonpayment of rent; 2) breach of contract; 3) waste, nuisance, or unlawful acts; 4) failure to vacate after receiving proper notice; and 5) failure to vacate after losing or relinquishing ownership. But before we cover these steps, let's consider how rent control affects evictions. That's the subject of the next chapter.

- Learn the legal lingo and use it.
- Start your eviction case expecting to win; stay with it in order to win promptly.
- Use an attorney only if you must.
- Be nice to court clerks.
- Adapt quickly to local practices.
- Know the time demands.
- Use a computer to fill out the forms.
- Keep between $345 and $425 handy to pay your eviction costs.

4
Considering Rent Control's Effects on Evictions

Although many states, Massachusetts and Texas included, prohibit their local governments from enacting any form of rent control, California is not among these enlightened states. Some form of rent control extends to approximately one-quarter of all the rental dwellings in the Golden State. In addition, many communities and counties have adopted rent control specifically for mobilehome parks.

Whereas the rent control bandwagon was rolling merrily along from the late '70s through the early '80s here in California, it hasn't been going anywhere lately. Having been lulled into a dream world with sweet songs about rent control's benefits, many people have come to their senses, for rent control's drawbacks are plain to see. We can only hope that something will happen at the ballot box or in a courtroom to eliminate this scourge from our state forever.

Fortunately, good things are happening because good people, such as the Pacific Legal Foundation, are challenging rent control's actual effectiveness in real life. We know that communism doesn't work in real life, and we know that rent control doesn't work in real life either. The world has rejected communism because it doesn't work, and California courts may one day reject rent control because it doesn't work.

Along these lines, the best thing to happen in many a year has been the appellate court decision in *152 Valparaiso Associates v. City of Cotati*. In that decision, the court held that "it is the result produced, not merely the result intended, which must be examined in determining whether a rent control ordinance has unconstitutionally taken private property without just compensation." The court challenged the city of Cotati to come up with evidence proving that its rent control law is benefitting the poor as intended. It is supposed to produce evidence that "poor people have in fact more recently flocked to Cotati to live in an increasing inventory of rental apartments [and] that respondents' rent control laws are applied so as to lure private investors and builders." If the city cannot come up with such evidence, then its rent control law must go. Imagine that, a court decision which makes perfect sense! The court is telling Cotati to prove that the good intentions in its rent control ordinances are actually coming true, or else the city must eliminate the ordinances.

The city of Berkeley saw the handwriting on the wall in this decision and tried to get it delisted, so that it could not be used elsewhere in supporting other decisions, but that naked attempt to thwart justice for all was denied.

While we are waiting for further developments to occur to restore the free market to all of California's rental properties, owners of rentals in rent-control areas must cope with the laws as they are, not as they will be in the future, and unfortunately those laws affect both rents and evictions.

Double Trouble

What many people do not realize is that the high-minded Robin Hoods who enacted rent control in certain California cities not only gave themselves a license to steal from landlords' pockets every month, they gave themselves a license to meddle with evictions. That's right! Where there are rent controls, expect to find eviction controls as well. Berkeley proudly and euphemistically calls its rent control ordinance the "Rent Stabilization and Eviction for Good Cause Ordinance." Controls on rents are only half the sad story of the "landlord bashing" going on there and elsewhere. Controls on evictions are the other half.

Why do the two occur together? You might say that once the rent control crusaders tasted power, they lusted after more, and you'd be at least partly right. They included eviction controls in their rent control ordinances for four primary reasons. Let's look at them one by one.

The first reason why rent control crusaders decided to meddle with evictions was to make vacancy decontrol provisions work. The vacancy decontrol provisions in some rent control ordinances permit landlords to increase their rents to market levels whenever there's a vacancy. So long as a tenant occupies a dwelling, the landlord must keep the rent as artificially low as rent control laws dictate, but as soon as the tenant vacates, the landlord is no longer bound by rent controls. He may charge whatever he likes, or so the rent control crusaders think.

(Actually, no landlord may ever charge whatever he likes; he may charge only whatever he can get, whatever someone will pay. The market sets rents. Landlords don't. You know that, and so does anyone else who's ever been in any kind of business.)

Okay now, if a vacancy were to release a landlord from rent control, even for a time, he'd be stupid not to create a vacancy periodically to take advantage of vacancy decontrol and increase his rents to market levels. Wouldn't he? Absolutely!

The rent control crusaders in their finite wisdom knew that such would be the case, so they added extra conditions to the steps normally required for landlord-initiated vacancies. They set up eviction controls. They felt they had to, to protect good tenants from being arbitrarily evicted by greedy landlords bent on getting rid of old tenants expressly so they could raise the rent on new ones.

They were right. Vacancy decontrol, to work at all, does require eviction controls. But not all rent control laws include vacancy decontrol provisions. Some control rents so strictly that if you decide to evict a tenant in order to move into your own building, what you are allowed to charge for rent whenever you finally move out must be based on whatever the rent was before you first moved in. Wow! In that case, there are no vacancy decontrol problems to worry about, are there?

The second reason why rent control crusaders decided to meddle with evictions was to protect tenants from landlord retaliation.

You can imagine how pleased you would be if a tenant of yours informed the rent control board that you were not complying with the rent con-

trol laws. You'd be eternally grateful, I'm sure. You want to be told when you're breaking the law, both good laws and bad, don't you? Other landlords wouldn't be so pleased. They would try to evict the informer at the first opportunity. That's why local eviction control laws prohibit evictions in retaliation against tenants who exercise their rent control rights.

The third reason why rent control crusaders decided to meddle with evictions was to "discipline" those landlords who refuse to register their rental property.

In most rent control areas, the rent control board raises revenue to pay for offices, paper shufflers, paper, and paper clips by charging landlords annual registration fees. Landlords who refuse to register are denying the board the revenue it needs to survive. That makes the board most unhappy, but there's not much it can do to collect because it doesn't have enough staff to force every landlord in town to pay his dues. So it requires that every landlord be registered in order to use the court system for an eviction. Evictions through the system have thus become the means for the board to exact its tribute, to demand its pounds of flesh. You must comply with the rent control ordinances in order to avail yourself of a court's authority to evict your tenant, and you must state in your complaint, even when the eviction is for a simple nonpayment of rent matter, that you have complied with all the applicable requirements of the ordinances. Presumably, if you are required to register your rental dwelling with the rent control board, and you neglect or refuse to do so, you would not be able to evict your tenants through the courts no matter what. You'd have to try some other way to get them out. What they're saying in effect is this, "Either you play our game or we won't allow you to play yours."

The fourth reason why rent control crusaders decided to meddle with evictions was to eliminate what they perceived to be "one of the great disasters of California law." What's that? You've never heard of a greater law disaster in California than rent control? You're right, of course. But rent controls are not a disaster from the crusaders' point of view. They're your disaster, not theirs. As far as they are concerned, rent-gouging landlords need controlling, so rent controls are fair and just.

The so-called "disaster" they're concerned

about is the state law which permits landlords to terminate a tenancy for no reason at all by giving a tenant a thirty-day Notice to Terminate. Rent control crusaders do not like this law one bit. They're certain that landlords abuse it.

Now, as any landlord knows, nobody is going to evict a tenant for no reason at all, just as no tenant is going to vacate voluntarily for no reason at all. There's always some reason, stated or not. Getting good tenants is too expensive a proposition for a landlord to evict a tenant for no reason, and moving is too expensive and traumatic for tenants to vacate for no reason.

Rent control crusaders don't know the economics or the agonies of the landlording business, so they don't know why it's utterly foolish for any landlord to evict a tenant unless there really is a good reason. They also don't seem to know why it's wise for a landlord to evict an uncooperative tenant without giving a reason (see chapter 8). Yet, when they as tenants can't get along with a fellow tenant, they want their landlord to "do something right away." Try getting rid of a tenant who's creating friction among other tenants or who's letting his dog loose to wander the neighborhood when you have to show a "just cause" for doing so. It's difficult, if not impossible. Judges won't let you evict a tenant from his home merely because he's being nasty to his neighbors or his landlord or because his dog is indiscriminate about elimination, not when there's a just-cause restriction on the books.

Believe it or not, there are some unscrupulous tenants in our world who make life miserable for all of us, scrupulous tenants and landlords alike, and those tenants are mighty hard to get rid of without 30-day notices. Rent control crusaders don't believe that. They believe that landlords would throw good tenants out on the streets if there were no just-cause eviction controls. It happens all the time in that three-quarters of California without eviction controls, doesn't it? You have to wonder how they would react if landlords tried to pass a law requiring that tenants must have a just cause to vacate. Then they would howl about a law disaster!

So much for why rent controls and eviction controls appear together. You might be wondering whether there are any local areas which have adopted eviction controls alone? No, there aren't. Crusaders can't get the people in a community quite so stirred up about controlling evictions as they can about controlling rents. Controlling rents appeals to people's greed; controlling evictions appeals to their principles. You know which one motivates them more. Once the rent control crusaders have organized and forced local authorities to adopt rent control measures, they say sweetly, "By the way, we can't just have rent controls unless we have eviction controls as well." You already know their reasons. After the struggle for rent control is won, there's no struggle for eviction controls. It's no contest, no contest at all, and so the landlord bashing goes on.

Local Eviction Controls

You should know that although courts have ruled that rent and eviction controls imposed by local ordinance are a legitimate use of "police power" (does that sound Orwellian or doesn't it?), local ordinances cannot ban evictions altogether, nor can they interfere with the summary nature of the proceedings as spelled out in state law. You see, evictions are entitled to summary treatment; it's the fastest treatment allowed in any civil case. It may not seem fast to you sometimes, but it's faster than anything else available. Local ordinances may not require longer time periods for the various steps in an eviction than are required by state law. They cannot, for example, require you to serve a 10-day notice to pay rent or quit since state law allows a 3-day notice, nor can they extend the time period provided for answering an unlawful-detainer summons beyond the five days state law provides.

Local eviction controls can, however, impose additional conditions on the eviction process, conditions which serve to make evictions more difficult and more expensive to pursue. Every attorney who handles evictions in both rent control and non-rent control jurisdictions knows this and charges extra for handling evictions in rent control jurisdictions. He knows they will take more of his time. He has to do more research to get everything right because there are more laws and legal precedents to review. He also knows that each eviction will be scrutinized all the more by the opposition.

The additional conditions in local eviction controls go beyond state laws. Here are the most common ones.

As a general rule, you cannot evict anyone from a rent controlled dwelling unless you have registered your rental property with the rent control board. That's pretty much a given wherever registration is required. Refuse to register and you can bet that your tenant will beat your eviction action, no matter how merited. All he has to do is reveal to the court that you haven't registered, and you'll lose.

You cannot evict a tenant from a rent controlled dwelling unless you are charging a legal rent. Should you and your tenant have mutually agreed in happier times on a higher-than-legal rent, you will not be able to evict him now that he's stopped paying you his rent altogether, at least not without complications.

You cannot evict a tenant from a rent controlled dwelling unless you follow whatever special notice requirements there are. You may have to submit to the rent board within ten days of service a copy of your 3-Day Notice to Pay Rent or Quit or any other notice you serve. You may have to state on the notice that there are tenant counseling services available from the rent control board at a certain address. Fail to do so, and you invalidate the notice.

Then there are the "just cause" requirements. You cannot evict a tenant from a rent controlled dwelling unless you have a just cause. They affect evictions more than anything else in rent control areas.

Just causes fall into two categories—those which are tenant-initiated and those which are landlord-initiated. Always the question is the same, "Is this matter substantial enough as a reason for the court to order an eviction?"

Here are the usual tenant-initiated just causes: failure to pay rent (state law applies in all areas), breaking the rental agreement, using the premises for unlawful acts, refusing to allow the landlord access, refusing to execute a new lease, creating a nuisance, and subletting.

Here are the usual landlord-initiated just causes: rehabilitating the unit, demolishing or converting the unit, going out of business, and moving himself or a relative into the unit.

Naturally, there are varying conditions and restrictions on these just causes, lots of them. San Francisco's ordinance, for example, specifically permits evictions when the tenant "habitually pays the rent late" or "gives checks which are frequently returned because there are insufficient funds in the checking account." Berkeley's ordinance, on the other hand, would not consider those as "just causes" for eviction. Tenants have

RENT CONTROL CITIES AND THEIR OFFICIAL WEBSITES

BERKELEY
www.ci.berkeley.ca.us/

BEVERLY HILLS
www.ci.beverly-hills.ca.us/

CAMPBELL
www.ci.campbell.ca.us/

EAST PALO ALTO
www.ci.east-palo-alto.ca.us/

FREMONT
www.ci.fremont.ca.us/

HAYWARD
www.ci.hayward.ca.us/

LOS ANGELES
www.ci.la.ca.us/

LOS GATOS
www.ci.los-gatos.ca.us/

OAKLAND
www.ci.oakland.ca.us/

PALM SPRINGS
www.ci.palm-springs.ca.us/

SAN FRANCISCO
www.ci.sf.ca.us/

SAN JOSE
www.ci.san-jose.ca.us/

SANTA MONICA
www.ci.santa-monica.ca.us/

THOUSAND OAKS
www.ci.thousand-oaks.ca.us/

WEST HOLLYWOOD
www.ci.west-hollywood.ca.us/

If you have trouble locating your rent control board's information through the city's website, try www.tenant.net and you may find a link to the site you're looking for.

to be more than check kiters to get evicted in Berkeley.

The just-cause requirement for evictions sounds good. It sounds as if it's righting a wrong, but it doesn't work that way in real life. It's a nuisance, as are all eviction controls imposed on a local level.

What to Do, What to Do?

Local eviction controls make your job as a scrupulous landlord all the more burdensome, all the more exacting, all the more trying, all the more impossible. Of that there's no doubt. Landlording under local eviction controls is like playing tackle football without pads or helmet against a team suited up for gridiron combat. You get hurt a lot in such a contest. The other team doesn't feel a thing. You feel badly beaten sometimes when you try so hard to play fair and do the right thing and an unscrupulous tenant without hardly trying makes you suffer by taking advantage of the laws and legal interpretations so favorable to tenants today.

Short of throwing up your hands, mortgaging your property to the hilt and surrendering it entirely to the rent control board or to your tenants (may not be such a bad idea; it would be a "just" reward, don't you think?), you are stuck with few alternatives when you want to evict a tenant. Until things change, heed these suggestions.

• GO TO THE SOURCE AND GET THE LATEST AUTHORITY—For specific information about local rent and eviction control ordinances, secure a copy of the full text of the latest ordinances from the same source your tenants use, the rent control board's office. Go there and ask for a copy, or look for the rent control board's website, and you'll likely find a copy of the ordinances there.

Do not expect the ordinances to speak for themselves. They won't, at least not at first. They're written in legalese. The rent control board knows that tenants don't understand legalese any more than you do, so they'll have a fifth-grade-vocabulary version available, too. Ask for one. At the same time, ask whether any recent ordinance has changed the information in either publication.

Remember, only the ordinances are the authority. A judge won't refer to the simplified version when he's deciding your case. Use the simplified version to help you understand the ordinances, and refer to the ordinances themselves for clarification of fine points.

• FIND OUT WHETHER YOUR RENTAL PROPERTY FALLS UNDER EVICTION CONTROLS AT ALL—Read through the rent and eviction control ordinances carefully to learn whether they apply to your kind of rental dwelling. Whereas the rent control ordinances may exempt houses, condos, smaller owner-occupied buildings, new construction, and higher-priced units, the eviction controls may not exempt any kind of rental housing at all. You may be surprised to learn that although local rent controls do not apply to your little duplex because you occupy half of it yourself, local eviction controls do apply to it when you're trying to evict that tenant from the other half. Find out what the law says.

If you don't want to read through the ordinances or can't understand them, ask someone at the rent control board whether your kind of rental property must comply with local eviction controls. Or if you'd rather not push the rent control board's buttons, call your rental property owners association. Someone there will know.

• BECOME FAMILIAR WITH THE REQUIREMENTS—Learn the specific requirements you must meet in order to pursue the particular type of eviction you intend to conduct.

You already know that local eviction controls may impose special requirements about notices, legal rent, your registration status, and just causes.

Get the details. Find out what are the special requirements for conducting an eviction in your rent controlled area.

• COMPLY, COMPLY, COMPLY—You might as well save the money and time required to seek a legal eviction in any eviction-control area unless you intend to comply with the ordinances. Distasteful and difficult as it may be, you have to be prepared to jump through the rent control board's hoops, or you simply will not get the tenant evicted. It's their show. You're just a bit player to them, a bit player who must play his part perfectly or else. The court doesn't care whether you have a legitimate reason to evict a tenant for something so easy to prove as nonpayment of rent. You must comply with the local ordinances, or you will lose your case. Count on it.

What choice do you have?

- Expect rent control areas to have some kind of eviction controls.
- Familiarize yourself with the very latest rent and eviction control ordinances in your area.
- Comply with the ordinances or despair of ever evicting anyone legally.

5 Handling an Eviction for Nonpayment of Rent

You have tried everything possible short of going to court to get your deadbeat tenants either to pay you their delinquent rent or to leave the place, but they are as unyielding as they can be. Nothing moves them. You have despaired of ever getting them to pay you another cent, and quite frankly you have had enough of their excuses, their promises, their rubber checks, and their shenanigans. You want to get them out as quickly as possible before you lose much more rent than what you have lost already.

Your best alternative now is to use the full strength of the laws written to protect you from such deadbeats. Get the full force of the law behind you, and get them out.

To save yourself both time and money, you have decided to handle the eviction yourself, and you are now ready to proceed. Here are the steps you should follow, from preparing the proper notice to having them removed bodily, if necessary.

Step 1. Prepare a 3-Day Notice to Pay Rent or Quit.

If you have accepted any rent monies since you last served a notice or if you haven't already served a notice, you should now prepare a 3-Day Notice to Pay Rent or Quit. If you have already served a notice and it is still valid, proceed to Step 3.

Every unlawful detainer for nonpayment of rent must begin with a written notice served properly on the tenant. Because you hope that the very appearance of your notice will stimulate your tenant to react as you want him to, use a form which is noticeable. The ones I use have bold headings which cannot be ignored. Anybody who sees one of them can tell at a glance from a distance of twenty paces what it is. They catch the eye. They look impressive. They look legal. They command attention.

The notice itself ought to contain the following:
1) Name(s) of the known tenant(s);
2) Reference to unknown persons in possession;
3) Address of the dwelling in question;
4) Amount of rent due;
5) Period for which the rent is due;
6) Number of days allowed for payment;
7) Consequences of nonpayment;
8) Payment particulars;
9) Date of the notice; and
10) Your signature.

Be careful that all of this information is complete and correct, and make it thoroughly consistent throughout your paperwork. Any deviation could give your tenant grounds for responding to your complaint on just this one technicality alone, and after you glance at chapter 10, you will understand a little better why you want to avoid giving the tenants the slightest opportunity to respond.

• TWO NOTICE FORMS—You may use any 3-Day Notice to Pay Rent or Quit form which includes the necessary elements. This book gives you two to choose from. Choose the one which most closely matches the form you would draw up yourself if you were starting from scratch. The first is more matter-of-fact than the second. The second contains several "asides" to help the landlord, tenant, and server understand what they ought to be doing.

• NAMES ON THE NOTICE—One sad reality of landlording in California these days is this–unless you give notice specifically to all the adults who claim to be living in a rental dwelling, regardless of whether they're mentioned in the rental agreement or are responsible for paying the rent, you may encounter difficulties in evicting anybody at all. So, make a conscientious effort to discover whether there are any adults liv-

3-DAY NOTICE TO PAY RENT OR QUIT

TO: Richard Renter, Rose Renter

and all other occupants, tenants, and subtenants in possession of the premises described as:

456 Sweet Street
(Street Address)

Littletown   California   91111
(City)   (State)   (Zip)

PLEASE TAKE NOTICE that the rent is now due and payable on the above-described premises which you currently hold and occupy.

Your rental account is delinquent in the amount itemized as follows:

Rental period ___9/1/XXXX___ through ___9/30/XXXX___ RENT DUE $___780.00___

less partial payment of $___50.00___

equals TOTAL RENT DUE of $___730.00___

YOU ARE HEREBY REQUIRED to pay said rent in full within three (3) days or to remove from and deliver up possession of the above-described premises, or legal proceedings will be instituted against you to recover possession of said premises, to declare the forfeiture of the Lease or Rental Agreement under which you occupy said premises and to recover rents and damages, together with court costs and attorney's fees, according to the terms of your Lease or Rental Agreement.

RENT MUST BE PAID IN FULL AND IN PERSON TO THE FOLLOWING PERSON OR ENTITY:
Name Lester Landlord   Phone 555-123-4567
Address where rent is to be paid 123 Neat Street Littletown
Usual days and times for payment of rent Mon.-Fri., 1P-6P; Sat., 10A-5P; Sun., 1P-3P
Please phone in advance to make sure that someone will be available to accept payment.

Dated: 9/10/XXXX   *Lester Landlord*
                                          Owner/Manager

PROOF OF SERVICE (Server should complete this proof of service only AFTER serving tenants.)

I, the undersigned, being at least 18 years of age, declare under penalty of perjury that I served the above notice, of which this is a true copy, on the following tenant(s) in possession in the manner(s) indicated below: *Richard Renter*

☒ On _9/12/XXXX_, I handed the notice to the tenant(s) personally.

☐ On _____, after attempting personal service, I handed the notice to a person of suitable age and discretion at the residence/business of the tenant(s), AND I deposited a true copy in the U.S. Mail, in a sealed envelope with postage fully prepaid, addressed to the tenant(s) at his/her/their place of residence (date mailed, if different _____).

☐ On _____, after attempting service in both manners indicated above, I posted the notice in a conspicuous place at the residence of the tenant(s), AND I deposited a true copy in the U.S. Mail, in a sealed envelope with postage fully prepaid, addressed to the tenant(s) at his/her/their place of residence (date mailed, if different _____).

Executed on _9/12/XXXX_, at _Littletown_, California.

Served by *Lester Landlord*

efc

You will find a blank copy of this form in the FORMS section of this book and in Eviction Forms Creator.

ing in your rental besides the original tenants, and mention them all by first and last names on the notice. Include everybody's middle initials if you know what they are.

Don't identify a married couple as "Mr. & Mrs. Richard Renter." Identify them as "Richard H. Renter and Rose Renter." Include the co-signer, too, if there is one. He should be made aware of what's happening so that he has a chance to come forward and pay what's owed and so that you can get a judgment against him if he doesn't.

Don't bother to include on the notice the names of children who are eighteen years old or thereabouts unless they work and help pay the rent. Including the older children who don't work generally upsets the parents and needlessly complicates service of court papers later. Should their absence on the notice become an issue, you can always add their names if you have to. You are making provisions for such problems by having the notice read either "and all other tenants in possession of the premises" or "and all other occupants, tenants, and subtenants in possession of the premises."

A single notice may have everyone's name on it. You don't have to prepare a bunch of notices, each with a different person's name on it, so long as all of the people mentioned are living in the same dwelling or are responsible for paying the rent on it. A single notice will suffice for a single eviction.

• AMOUNT TO ASK FOR—In listing the amount of rent due, be sure you include only rent. You may not demand late charges or bad check charges or cleaning fees (if you use a discounted rent method, you may get away with asking for the entire non-discounted or gross rent, but don't count on it; to be safe, use the net rent when you calculate rent due). To recover whatever late charges or bad check charges or cleaning fees are owed to you, you may include them in the complaint filed later. Just don't include them here on the notice.

Rent is all you may ask for on the notice, and the rent stated there must be *delinquent* for the current rental period. For example, if you serve the notice on the seventh of June because the tenant hasn't paid any rent for May or June, and the rent is due on the first of the month, include June's rent, too, because his rent is also delinquent for June. Remember, though, that it must be delinquent, not merely due, to be included. If

you serve the notice on the 29th or 30th of May, obviously it should include only May's rent and not June's because the tenant is not yet delinquent for the June rental period. But what do you do if you plan to serve the notice on the first of June and he hasn't paid for either May or June? Is June's rent delinquent on the first of June and should it be included in the notice? No, it isn't delinquent yet, and it should not be included in the notice. Don't hesitate to serve the notice on the first of June if he hasn't yet paid May's rent; just don't include June's rent on the notice. You'll have the opportunity later to add June's rent to the amount owed.

Actually, his rent may or may not even be delinquent on the second or third of the month either. Whether his rent is delinquent around the beginning of a rental period depends upon the availability of a banking day on which to pay and upon the grace period, if any, allowed by the rental agreement. If, for instance, his rent is due on the first, and the first falls on a Saturday, then legally he wouldn't have to pay his rent until Monday, which would be the first banking day after the due date, and if Monday were a holiday, then the first day he'd have to pay would be Tuesday. Unless otherwise stated in the rental agreement, you shouldn't count his rent delinquent until the day after the first banking day following the rental due date, and if the rental agreement specifically allows, say, a four-day grace period, then the rent is not delinquent until the day after that grace period.

Serving a 3-Day Notice to Pay Rent or Quit which includes any rent not yet delinquent might be regarded as premature and might precipitate a legal challenge.

Treat the second month involved in the same way you treat the first month. Include the second month's rent on the notice only if it, too, is delinquent.

Whenever you're unsure exactly how much the tenant owes, estimate the amount with a figure which is certain to be below the actual amount owed. If you indicate on your three-day notice that the tenant owes you more than he actually does, you may lose your whole case on this one technicality alone and have to begin again from the beginning, all of which may affect you deleteriously by forcing you to drink too much, smoke too much, eat too much, worry too much, or become promiscuous. Don't let yourself go

3-DAY NOTICE TO PAY RENT OR QUIT

This notice supersedes any previously served 3-day notice to pay rent or quit.

TO: Richard Renter, Rose Renter

and all other occupants, tenants, and subtenants in possession of the premises described as:

456 Sweet Street
(Street Address)

Littletown   California   91111
(City)   (State)   (Zip)

Penal Code Section 594 states, "Every person who maliciously injures or destroys any real or personal property not his own... is guilty of a misdemeanor."

(LANDLORD: Include the names of all known adult occupants. Include only rent which is due and delinquent. Do not include rent due and delinquent for longer than twelve months. Do not include items such as unpaid late fees, damages, utilities, deposits, etc. Put them in a separate 3-day notice to perform covenant. Serve a 30- or 60-day notice to terminate tenancy concurrently with this notice to those month-to-month tenants you wish to evict even if they comply with this notice.)

PLEASE TAKE NOTICE that the rent is now due and payable on the above-described premises which you currently hold and occupy.

Your rental account is delinquent in the amount itemized as follows:

Rental period ___9/1/XXXX___ through ___9/30/XXXX___ RENT DUE $___780.00___

less partial payment of $___50.00___

equals TOTAL RENT DUE of $___730.00___

YOU ARE HEREBY REQUIRED to pay said rent in full within three (3) days or to remove from and deliver up possession of the above-described premises, or legal proceedings will be instituted against you to recover possession of said premises, to declare the forfeiture of the Lease or Rental Agreement under which you occupy said premises and to recover rents and damages, together with court costs and attorney's fees, according to the terms of your Lease or Rental Agreement.

RENT MUST BE PAID IN FULL AND IN PERSON TO THE FOLLOWING PERSON OR ENTITY:
Name Lester Landlord   Phone 555-123-4567
Address where rent is to be paid   123 Neat Street Littletown
Usual days and times for payment of rent Mon.-Fri., 1P-6P; Sat., 10A-5P; Sun., 1P-3P
Please phone in advance to make sure that someone will be available to accept payment.

Dated: __9/10/XXXX__   *Lester Landlord*
                              Owner/Manager

(OCCUPANTS: If you receive other notices along with this notice, you must comply with all of them. Compliance with this notice alone does not entitle you to remain in possession. Be advised that your landlord has the right to make a negative credit report to a credit reporting agency if you fail to meet your payment obligations.)

PROOF OF SERVICE

(SERVER: Complete this proof of service only AFTER serving tenants. Serve every adult occupant, whether named in the rental agreement or not. Try the first method, personal delivery, first; if unsuccessful, try the second, substituted service. Only if both methods are unsuccessful should you try the third, posting and mailing.)

I, the undersigned, being at least 18 years of age, declare under penalty of perjury that I served the above notice, of which this is a true copy, on the following tenant(s) in possession in the manner(s) indicated below: _Richard Renter_

☒ On __9/12/XXXX__, I handed the notice to the tenant(s) personally.
☐ On _____, after attempting personal service, I handed the notice to a person of suitable age and discretion at the residence/business of the tenant(s), AND I deposited a true copy in the U.S. Mail, in a sealed envelope with postage fully prepaid, addressed to the tenant(s) at his/her/their place of residence (date mailed, if different _____).
☐ On _____, after attempting service in both manners indicated above, I posted the notice in a conspicuous place at the residence of the tenant(s), AND I deposited a true copy in the U.S. Mail, in a sealed envelope with postage fully prepaid, addressed to the tenant(s) at his/her/their place of residence (date mailed, if different _____).
Executed on __9/12/XXXX__, at __Littletown__, California.
Served by __Lester Landlord__

efc

You will find a blank copy of this form in the FORMS section of this book and in Eviction Forms Creator.

to ruin just because you lost an unlawful detainer on a technicality. Do the thing right the first time.

• "CORRECTING" THE NOTICE—After you have served your tenant a notice showing what you believe is the correct amount of rent owed and you discover that he owes you *more* because you just learned that his last check bounced or you somehow neglected to calculate properly, do not bother serving him another notice. You'll have the opportunity to prove he owed you more once you get into court.

Ah, but should you discover that he owes you *less* than what you indicated as of the date on the notice, you will have to prepare a new notice with the correct figures and serve it. You cannot amend a notice once it has been served. An incorrect notice will cause you to lose your case if the tenant catches the error and answers you in court. It may even cause you to lose your case if the tenant doesn't answer you in court, that is, if the judge happens to spot the error during the prove-up trial.

The notice you serve may be incorrect, and its erroneousness won't matter one bit until you file your papers with the court. Then it must be absolutely correct, for it can no longer be changed. Your case lives or dies on the correctness of that notice. Until you file, you may "correct" your notice all you want by serving new notices.

If you discover that you must serve another notice, you will want to avoid any confusion regarding earlier incorrect notices. Indicate clearly on your "final" notice that it is the notice which counts, the "notice of notices." Some notices, including the second one shown here, include a statement saying, "This notice supersedes any previously served 3-day notice to pay rent or quit." On the top of any notice lacking such verbiage, write or type something like this: "IGNORE PREVIOUS NOTICE. THIS IS THE CONTROLLING NOTICE."

If you served more than one incorrect notice, put this on top: "IGNORE PREVIOUS NOTICES SERVED ON [date] AND [date]. THIS IS THE CONTROLLING NOTICE."

You do not want to confuse your tenant, nor do you want to confuse the judge with a bunch of different notices, different figures, and different dates.

• RENTAL PERIOD MENTIONED IN THE NOTICE—Although no law absolutely requires that you mention in the notice the rental period for which the rent is due, I recommend that you do mention it. Almost all preprinted notices to pay rent or quit, including the ones given here and the one drafted by the California Apartment Association, contain space for the rental period. Judges, therefore, are accustomed to seeing the rental period on notices, and rightly or wrongly, they might question the legality, the completeness, or the clarity of your notice if you choose to omit it. You don't need the extra hassle of being called upon to cite a code or a precedent to prove your notice's legitimacy in court.

Mentioning the rental period in the notice also helps to clarify for your tenants just how you arrived at the total balance due.

If you use either 3-Day Notice to Pay Rent or Quit form which appears in this book, you should have no trouble indicating the period for which rent is owed and the amount of rent owed. That's in the notice's itemization section. Put down the rental period(s) for which there is any rent delinquent at all. Total the rent normally due for each of those periods, subtract any partial payments which apply to the periods listed, and *voila*, there you have it, the TOTAL BALANCE DUE. You don't have to make any complex calculations.

If you are using a 3-Day Notice to Pay Rent or Quit form which calls only for the amount of rent due and the period for which it is due, you'll have no problem determining the period for which the rent is due or the amount, so long as the tenant owes rent for full months, but if the tenant owes you partial rent because you have accepted half a month's rent or some other sum less than usual, calculating the rental period for your notice can be confusing.

Do your calculating this way—divide the full month's rent by 30 (whether the month you're dealing with really has 28, 29, 30, or 31 days doesn't matter to the court; calculations based on a 30-day month are considered "fair"), and then divide that per-diem rental figure into the amount of partial rent already paid. Your answer will be in days paid, but it may include a fraction as well. The rental period for which rent is owed should start on the day after those days have been added to the previous full rental period for which rent was paid.

As an example, let's say that your tenant's rent is $975; the rental period is August 1 through 31; the amount paid by the tenant toward his

August rent was $485; and you're serving the 3-Day Notice to Pay Rent or Quit on September 5th. We would divide $975 by 30 and get the rent per diem, $32.50; then we would divide the amount which the tenant paid toward his August rent, $485, by $32.50. Our answer would be 14.92. We would round this number off upwards to 15 and consider that 15 days' rent had been paid. The rental period which should be mentioned in the notice, then, would be August 16 through September 30, and the total amount of rent owed would be $1,465 (remember that we must now add September's rent because we are serving the notice after the delinquent date for September's rent).

Whatever you do, be certain that the rent you are asking for covers *consecutive* periods and none of them more than twelve months in the past. Your case will be thrown out of court if you are asking for rent more than one year past due. As for consecutive periods, if your tenant failed to pay you any rent in January but did pay in February and again in March, you should give him a rent receipt for January when he pays in February and for February when he pays in March. Courts will not allow you to seek delinquent rents for periods with gaps in them, such as January and April. They assume that tenants who have a rent receipt to show for a recent period have paid rent for all prior months. If you somehow make the mistake of creating a gap in a tenant's receipts, forget about trying to collect for the gap. Go after rent for the most recent consecutive periods only.

• THE ALTERNATIVE—Note that the 3-Day Notice to Pay Rent or Quit forms shown here contain an either/or alternative. The alternative is this—either pay up or get out. If the tenant complies with the alternative, then the notice is of no further consequence.

If you want to eliminate the alternative so that the tenant must move out even though he complies with your notice to pay, serve him a Notice to Terminate Tenancy when you serve him the notice to pay.

The Notice to Terminate Tenancy gives the tenant no alternative. He must vacate within thirty days.

Before you serve your tenants a Notice to Terminate Tenancy, though, determine whether it's valid in your case. You cannot use such a notice in certain California jurisdictions which have their own eviction controls except under special circumstances (see chapter 4). You cannot serve Section 8 tenants a Notice to Terminate Tenancy unless you follow HUD guidelines. And you cannot use a Notice to Terminate Tenancy at all if your tenant has an unexpired lease which continues beyond the expiration of the notice.

• COLLECTING FROM MOVE-OUTS—If a tenant moves out before the three days are up and he still owes you rent money, don't go to superior court. It's a waste of money under the circumstances. Instead, proceed in small claims court to get a money judgment and then set out to collect your judgment using the suggestions in chapter 13. If he moves before the three days are up and you think there's little chance you might collect anything from him at all, do what you can to smirch his credit rating using the suggestions in chapter 13. Whatever you decide to do following the deadbeat's hasty departure, be grateful that he's no longer your headache, and chalk the whole affair up to experience, part of your schooling at Landlording's Hard Knocks School.

• THE PROOF OF SERVICE—At the bottom of each notice is a declaration to prove to the court that the notice was, in fact, served on a qualifying date, in a prescribed manner, and by an eligible server. Some people use a separate sheet of paper for their declarations, but there's nothing wrong with saving paper and including it right on the notice itself. Don't fill out the declaration on the notice which is handed to the tenant. Fill it out only on the copies which you keep for your own and for the court's use.

• COPIES—At the beginning of the FORMS section in the back of this book you will find suggestions you might want to follow for determining how many copies you need to make of the various forms. Always make sure that you keep at least one copy of every form for yourself.

Step 2. Serve the 3-Day Notice to Pay Rent or Quit.

• WHO MAY SERVE—You, your manager, a process server, or anyone else at least 18 years of age may legally serve the notice. In some areas, you may even use the sheriff or marshal to serve the notice for you (see discussion in chapter 2 about using a uniformed officer or security patrolman to intimidate).

If you believe that your tenant is enough of a

scoundrel to perjure himself and claim in court that your unlawful detainer against him should be thrown out because he never received a notice, consider any of the following so you'll be able to prove otherwise: serve a copy in person yourself and mail one, too, using the certificate-of-mailing method described shortly; serve it along with a payment pledge as outlined in chapter 1 and get the tenant himself to acknowledge service; serve it yourself in the presence of a witness; hire a professional to serve it; or get a friend or another tenant to do it for you.

recommend that you make the effort to serve each tenant individually just to be on the safe side. I don't myself because I believe that serving notices should be a part of the rent collection process (see chapter 1), and I serve lots of them. If I had to serve each adult tenant individually every time I served a notice, I'd be wasting a lot of time trying to find everybody. Consequently, I serve only one notice to a household. I have yet to encounter a problem in an unlawful detainer which resulted from my serving tenants in this way.

If your tenant swears that he did not receive any notice and you swear that he did, the burden of proof rests upon you to show that he did. If you can't prove that he received it beyond your swearing that he did, you will lose in a standoff.

Oddly enough, if you do elect to pay a professional to serve the notice, you may not count this as one of your reimbursable costs. Courts apparently consider this more a matter of convenience than a matter of necessity.

• WHO SHOULD BE SERVED—You don't have to bother serving everyone named in the notice individually, for service of the notice on one of your tenants is considered to be service on all of them [*USC v. Weiss* (1962) 208 CA3d 759, 769, 25 CR 475]. Even so, some experts

If you feel convinced that your notice is going to be the first step in evicting certain tenants through the courts and that you are going to have to fight them every step of the way, consider serving them individually. Otherwise, I don't think it's worth the trouble.

By all means, do prepare and serve a second copy of your notice if you are aware that the premises have been sublet, with or without your approval, for both the primary tenant and the subtenant should be notified of the nonpayment of rent and should have an opportunity to pay up.

See that any co-signer involved gets a separate copy, too. Although you don't have to serve the co-signer in order to evict whoever's living on the premises, you should certainly make the co-signer aware of what's happening. Once he knows, he may pay you what the tenant owes or he may put pressure on the tenant in ways you cannot. After all, what's a co-signer for?

• THE SERVICE—To serve a 3-Day Notice to Pay Rent or Quit properly per CCP §1162, you must serve it (keep the original to show the court or attach to the original complaint; serve a copy) in one of these three ways:

1) Hand it to the tenant personally;

2) Hand it to someone else on the property or at the tenant's place of business who is at an age of suitable discretion; make note somewhere of the person's name and/or of his description because you'll need this information later when you fill out the complaint; and also send a copy by first-class mail. To prove that you mailed it, take the stamped envelope to the post office; ask for a "Certificate of Mailing," USPS Form 3817 (you may download the form from the USPS website at usps.com/forms/miscforms.htm); complete the form and hand it, the envelope, and 95¢ to the clerk; and wait for the clerk to stamp the form and return it to you. Courts have held that someone sixteen years old is "at an age of suitable discretion." Someone younger may or may not qualify. You'd be risking a challenge by serving the notice to a 13-year-old, a challenge which you might win, and then again you might not.

3) Do what attorneys call "nail and mail," that is, post the notice by the main entrance where it is unavoidable, *and* send a copy by first-class mail. Don't bother with registered or certified mail. That's overkill. Get a Certificate of Mailing as proof that you mailed it.

Try the first method first, personal service. It's the best because it's simple and forthright. Try to serve the tenant at his residence first and then try the place where he works if you know where he works. According to an appellate court decision [*Hozz v. Lewis* 215 CA3d 314, 263 CR 577], though, you do not have to try repeatedly to serve the tenant at home and at work. Once is enough.

Having tried to serve the tenant in person, you may resort straightaway to either of the other two methods, both of which are called "constructive-service" or "substituted-service" methods.

By the way, if the tenant refuses the notice when you hand it to him, that's his problem; you need only let him know he's being served and

put the notice where he can get it. You may drop it at his feet, or if you're talking to him through a closed door, you may tell him that you're leaving it under the mat. You aren't expected to do the impossible. After all, it's for his benefit that you are serving him in the first place. You are taking the trouble to inform him that you are going to initiate some legal action which will affect him directly in some way or another.

If you can't find the tenant anywhere and you have good reason to suspect that he may have abandoned the premises, you may want to consider following the abandonment procedure as outlined in chapter 14. It has some very definite advantages over an unlawful detainer for nonpayment of rent, especially if you've already delayed serving a 3-Day Notice to Pay Rent or Quit for a couple of weeks. If fourteen or more days have passed since the rent became delinquent and you have seen neither skin nor limb of the tenant during that time, all you have to do is send him a Notice of Belief of Abandonment and wait eighteen days for a response. If you get no response, you take possession. It's that simple.

Although you may use the abandonment procedure in conjunction with an eviction for nonpayment of rent and take advantage of whichever is successful sooner, you should not even think of using it as an underhanded legal maneuver just to benefit from its advantages. That could get you into terrible trouble. Use it only as it was intended to be used, only if you honestly believe that the tenant has given up possession without notifying you. Don't use it if you think the tenant is merely trying to avoid being served. Use constructive service in that case.

• TIME TO SERVE—You may serve a 3-Day Notice to Pay Rent or Quit on the first day a tenant's rent becomes delinquent and not before. As mentioned already, a tenant's rent becomes delinquent the day after it is due unless the due date falls on a day when the banks are closed (Saturday, Sunday, or holiday), in which case it is delinquent the day after the first banking day following the due date, or it is delinquent the day after whatever grace period was specified in the rental agreement. Serving the notice before the rent is delinquent will cause your case to be thrown out of court as premature and will require you to begin the entire procedure again from the beginning.

• LEASES, LAST MONTH'S RENT, AND

TIME TO SERVE—Some landlords puzzle over when they ought to serve a 3-Day Notice to Pay Rent or Quit to a tenant who's on a lease or to a tenant who's paid the last month's rent in advance. Should they delay serving the notice until the last month's rent is used up? No, no, no! Treat anyone on a lease and anyone who's paid the last month's rent in exactly the same way as you'd treat someone who's on a month-to-month agreement and hasn't paid any last month's rent. Serve them all a 3-Day Notice to Pay Rent or Quit as soon as their *current* rent becomes delinquent. Do not allow any tenant to apply his "last month's rent" to any month other than the "last month."

What happens to a tenant's last month's rent when he's evicted? Like his deposits, it's applied to the judgment.

• BEST TIME TO SERVE—You are more likely to serve a 3-Day Notice to Pay Rent or Quit belatedly rather than prematurely. Try to do neither. Keep on top of your rent collections and serve a 3-day notice to every tenant on a regular schedule the day after his rent becomes delinquent.

If you have procrastinated longer than that, you will be all the more anxious to evict your tenants as swiftly as possible, and you will want to take advantage of every opportunity to save time. One way to speed the process is to serve the notice when you may take advantage of every intervening day, including weekends. To get a decided advantage, serve the notice anytime Sunday or Monday (see calendars at the end of this chapter). Because of the way weekends affect the various time limits in an eviction, they're the two best days for serving a 3-day notice.

Even though the persistent landlord or landlady can hope to pursue an eviction within the shortest possible time by serving the notice on a

Sunday or Monday, don't you wait for a Sunday or Monday to come along before serving your notice. The best time to serve it is *now, right now, today.*

• COUNTING THE DAYS—Begin your three-day countdown on the day *after* you serve your notice to everyone who's supposed to get a notice. If you serve the primary tenant on Friday and the subtenant on Sunday, start your counting with Monday. Count Monday, Tuesday, and Wednesday as the three days you are giving them to pay up. The earliest you may then file the summons and complaint is Thursday. You may wait longer if you want to, believing that they will either vacate or pay, but legally you don't have to.

Be aware that the third day after service must

Serve Notice on...	Notice Expires at Midnight on...	File Summons & Complaint on...
Sunday	Wednesday	Thursday
Monday	Thursday	Friday
Tuesday	Friday	Monday
Wednesday	Monday	Tuesday
Thursday	Monday	Tuesday
Friday	Monday	Tuesday
Saturday	Tuesday	Wednesday

be a "business day." It must not be a weekend day or a holiday. If the third day falls on a Sunday and there's a Monday holiday the following day, you must give the tenant until Tuesday to pay, and you must not file your summons and complaint until Wednesday. If the third day falls on a Friday, though, you may file on the following Monday.

If you couldn't serve the tenants personally and you had to resort to either method two or method three, you might think that you should wait some extra days before filing your summons and complaint because that's what people have been doing for years and years now, waiting an extra five days. Forget that.

According to a court decision [*Losornio v. Motta* (1998) 67 CA4th 110, 115, 78 CR2d 799, 801], you don't have to wait any extra days following service of a 3-day notice when mailing is used in conjunction with substituted service or "nail and mail" service, as it must be under CCP §1162, which is the code defining how eviction notices must be served. A 3-day notice means three days and no more, regardless of which legal method of service you use. The court held that the extra five-day wait provisions of CCP §1013(a) do not apply to eviction cases because the mailing of the notice is only *one component* of service under CCP §1162. It isn't the sole means of service. Mailing alone, in fact, is not sufficient for service of 3-day notices. It has to accompany another means of service.

Always try to serve your 3-day notices personally. Go through hot coals and high water to serve them if you have to, but don't despair if you cannot locate the tenants because you can still proceed with the eviction in a timely manner when you have no choice other than to resort to substituted service.

• BEWARE ESTOPPEL—Did you know that by law your rents are not due in advance unless you stipulate in your rental contract that they are? It's true! Did you know also that if you continually accept a tenant's rent late, say fifteen days after it's due, and you decide one month to give him a 3-Day Notice to Pay Rent or Quit five days after the rent is due, that your case may be thrown out of court because you gave the notice prematurely? Well, it's true!

In this latter situation, your tenant could argue the "estoppel defense." He could say that because you have shown by your past conduct that you have agreed to accept the rent late, you may not, therefore, give a 3-Day Notice to Pay Rent or Quit before the 16th day after the due date, or whenever in the month the tenant could establish was the day after which you have accepted his rent in the past without regarding it late. You set a precedent by accepting rent late on a regular basis, a precedent which becomes a danger to you when you're involved in an unlawful detainer.

To preclude the estoppel defense from being used against you in an unlawful detainer, set a definite grace period before you pass out pay-rent-or-quit notices every month, and then consistently give notices to everyone who hasn't paid you the rent by that day. In those cases where you have been accepting rent later than that in the past, give the tenants each a Notice to Change Terms of Tenancy outlining your new rent collection policy. In any case where you have been accepting a certain tenant's rent late in the past and "late" is becoming "later" month by month, until it has finally reached the point where you are now pretty apprehensive about collecting any

rent at all, give the tenant a notice one month and a day following the date when you last accepted rent and then proceed without fear that estoppel will be used as a defense against you.

• PAYMENT IN FULL—Your 3-Day Notice to Pay Rent or Quit requires that the tenant pay the rent owing in full within three days. If the tenant offers you payment in full within three days, take it. He has complied with your notice, and you have nothing to gain by refusing it. In fact, the law requires you to take it.

If you have already waited the three days and you haven't yet filed the summons and complaint and the tenant offers you payment in full, you may refuse the payment if you want or you may take it. You decide. I wouldn't refuse it myself because I much prefer getting paid than evicting, and I know that I can always evict the tenant sometime later if the need arises again.

If you have waited the three days *and* you have filed the summons and complaint and the tenant offers to pay you everything he owes in full, you may take it or reject it. You decide. Should you be inclined to take it, tell the tenant that he owes you for your out-of-pocket expenses, too, but that they are much less than the court costs and attorney fees which he probably agreed to pay in his lease or rental agreement. Sometimes I split the expenses with the tenant if I want him to stay and I believe that his reasons for paying so late are legitimate and unlikely to recur.

• PARTIAL PAYMENT—You never have to accept partial payment for the rent that a tenant owes you. No law requires you to accept part of the rent owed when a tenant claims to be unable to pay it all at one time. You get to decide for yourself whether you should accept the fistful of dollars your tenant is waving in your face when you're there on his doorstep ready to serve him with a 3-Day Notice to Pay Rent or Quit.

At this time, before you have served the notice, you have nothing to lose by accepting the money, no matter how much or how little it is. It's "found" money, money you're probably never going to see if you refuse it now. Take it, and tell the tenant that you will have to adjust the notice to reflect the amount of his partial payment.

Make the adjustment then and there. Initial it, and give him the revised notice. It's still a *three-* day notice, mind you. It still gives the tenant only three days to come up with the balance of the money or else.

So what have you lost by accepting the money? Not a thing!

You haven't lost any time because you aren't extending the notice by even one day. You may if you want to, but you don't have to. You haven't lost any money because you haven't yet paid any court costs or attorney fees, and you get to pocket whatever money the tenant pays you. You haven't lost any of your reputation as a business person because you still served the notice. You may even gain a better reputation as a reasonable business person sensitive to your tenants' problems. That's a triple win for you—a time win, a money win, and a reputation win.

Would that the answers to all your landlording problems were so simple and had such winning results!

Should the tenant offer you partial payment one day, two days, three days, or more after you serve the notice, the situation is different. Again you may or may not accept it. If you do accept it, you send the tenant a message that you don't mean what you say in your notices. You say that you require payment in full in the notice and then you accept less. That's not good landlording, and you may come to regret showing your tenants how weak you can be in such matters.

Even at this early stage of the eviction, you ought to accept partial payment only if it's big enough because accepting partial payment at this stage is going to cost you some time. You'll have to serve a new notice and restart the three-day clock. The very minimum you should accept would be half the amount owed. Immediately after you accept it, serve another notice covering the balance, for your accepting even one dollar invalidates the old notice (actually the law is vague about this matter, but courts have held that landlords accepting partial payments after serving a notice are "interrupting their own proceedings" and must serve a new notice following acceptance of any rent monies).

• BAD CHECK—If you give your tenant a 3-Day Notice to Pay Rent or Quit and he gives you a bad check as payment, you needn't serve him another notice before you file the summons and complaint. The original notice still applies because he never paid you what he owes you. He gave you a worthless piece of paper and nothing more. Just in case the tenant made an inadvertent accounting error, you might want to contact him and tell him that his check was worthless and that if he wants to keep from being evicted, he'd better pay you in full with a money order *today*. You aren't obligated to contact him, of course, just as you aren't obligated to serve him with another notice, but you ought to try.

Step 3. Prepare the Summons, Complaint, and Cover Sheet.

After you have served your notice, and as far as you are concerned, the tenant has made an inadequate response or no response at all in the time allowed, you should prepare to file a Summons (Unlawful Detainer) and Complaint (Unlawful Detainer), along with a Civil Case Cover Sheet, all of which are state-mandated Judicial Council forms.

• THE SUMMONS—The summons is a notice to the tenant that he is being summoned to court as a defendant in a lawsuit and that he must answer the complaint accompanying the summons within five days or risk certain eviction. Blank summons forms are available from a number of different sources. You may get them at your court clerk's office, or you may copy the blank one found in the FORMS section of this book, or you may download the one available on the Judicial Council's website (see REFERENCES), or you may use the one in Eviction Forms Creator™ (see REFERENCES).

Like many other Judicial Council of California forms, the summons form has two sides to it. The back side is upside down so that when the clerk mounts it in a two-hole, top-grip binder, anybody browsing through the binder won't have to keep turning it around every time they flip a page. The print will always be right side up.

If you opt to make copies of multi-page forms with their pages printed on both sides of a sheet of paper, preserve this page orientation. If you opt to print multi-page forms on separate sheets of paper, don't bother trying to paste two sheets together so they resemble a double-sided copy. Merely put them right side up in numerical order. That way, when mounted in a two-hole, top-grip binder, they will still be readable from a single perspective.

If this is your first case as a lay attorney, at this point you should call the clerk of the court which has jurisdiction over the area where your property is located. You will find the telephone number under "Government Offices" in the Yellow Pages. You will also find the number on the

SUMMONS
(CITACION JUDICIAL)
UNLAWFUL DETAINER—EVICTION
(RETENCIÓN ILÍCITA DE UN INMUEBLE—DESALOJO)

SUM-130

FOR COURT USE ONLY
(SOLO PARA USO DE LA CORTE)

NOTICE TO DEFENDANT: Richard Renter
(AVISO AL DEMANDADO): Rose Renter
       AND DOES 1 TO 10 INCLUSIVE

YOU ARE BEING SUED BY PLAINTIFF:
(LO ESTÁ DEMANDANDO EL DEMANDANTE):
      Lester Landlord, Leslie Landlord

You have 5 CALENDAR DAYS after this summons and legal papers are served on you to file a written response at this court and have a copy served on the plaintiff. (To calculate the five days, count Saturday and Sunday, but do not count other court holidays. If the last day falls on a Saturday, Sunday, or a court holiday then you have the next court day to file a written response.) A letter or phone call will not protect you. Your written response must be in proper legal form if you want the court to hear your case. There may be a court form that you can use for your response. You can find these court forms and more information at the California Courts Online Self-Help Center (www.courtinfo.ca.gov/selfhelp), your county law library, or the courthouse nearest you. If you cannot pay the filing fee, ask the court clerk for a fee waiver form. If you do not file your response on time, you may lose the case by default, and your wages, money, and property may be taken without further warning from the court.

There are other legal requirements. You may want to call an attorney right away. If you do not know an attorney, you may want to call an attorney referral service. If you cannot afford an attorney, you may be eligible for free legal services from a nonprofit legal services program. You can locate these nonprofit groups at the California Legal Services Web site (www.lawhelpcalifornia.org), the California Courts Online Self-Help Center (www.courtinfo.ca.gov/selfhelp), or by contacting your local court or county bar association.

Tiene 5 DÍAS DE CALENDARIO después de que le entreguen esta citación y papeles legales para presentar una respuesta por escrito en esta corte y hacer que se entregue una copia al demandante. (Para calcular los cinco días, cuente los sábados y los domingos pero no los otros días feriados de la corte. Si el último día cae en sábado o domingo, o en un día en que la corte esté cerrada, tiene hasta el próximo día de corte para presentar una respuesta por escrito).*Una carta o una llamada telefónica no lo protegen. Su respuesta por escrito tiene que estar en formato legal correcto si desea que procesen su caso en la corte. Es posible que haya un formulario que usted pueda usar para su respuesta. Puede encontrar estos formularios de la corte y más información en el Centro de Ayuda de las Cortes de California (www.courtinfo.ca.gov/selfhelp/espanol/), en la biblioteca de leyes de su condado o en la corte que le quede más cerca. Si no puede pagar la cuota de presentación, pida al secretario de la corte que le dé un formulario de exención de pago de cuotas. Si no presenta su respuesta a tiempo, puede perder el caso por incumplimiento y la corte le podrá quitar su sueldo, dinero y bienes sin más advertencia.*

Hay otros requisitos legales. Es recomendable que llame a un abogado inmediatamente. Si no conoce a un abogado, puede llamar a un servicio de remisión a abogados. Si no puede pagar a un abogado, es posible que cumpla con los requisitos para obtener servicios legales gratuitos de un programa de servicios legales sin fines de lucro. Puede encontrar estos grupos sin fines de lucro en el sitio web de California Legal Services, (www.lawhelpcalifornia.org), en el Centro de Ayuda de las Cortes de California, (www.courtinfo.ca.gov/selfhelp/espanol/) o poniéndose en contacto con la corte o el colegio de abogados locales.

1. The name and address of the court is:
   (El nombre y dirección de la corte es):
   Saddleback Superior Court
   100 State Street
   Littletown, California 91111

CASE NUMBER:
Número del caso):
   1234567890

2. The name, address, and telephone number of plaintiff's attorney, or plaintiff without an attorney, is:
   (El nombre, la dirección y el número de teléfono del abogado del demandante, o del demandante que no tiene abogado, es):

   Lester Landlord & Leslie Landlord   Phone: 555-123-4567
   123 Neat Street
   Littletown, CA 91111

3. *(Must be answered in all cases)* An unlawful detainer assistant (Bus. & Prof. Code, §§ 6400-6415) [X] did not [ ] did for compensation give advice or assistance with this form. *(If plaintiff has received any help or advice for pay from an unlawful detainer assistant, complete item 6 on the next page.)*

Date: Clerk, by _____ , Deputy
(Fecha)   *(Secretario)*   *(Adjunto)*

(For proof of service of this summons, use Proof of Service of Summons (form POS-010).)
(Para prueba de entrega de esta citatión use el formulario Proof of Service of Summons(POS-010)).

[SEAL]

4. **NOTICE TO THE PERSON SERVED:** You are served
   a. [ ] as an individual defendant.
   b. [ ] as the person sued under the fictitious name of *(specify):*
   c. [ ] as an occupant
   d. [ ] on behalf of *(specify):*
       under: [ ] CCP 416.10 (corporation)   [ ] CCP 416.60 (minor)
              [ ] CCP 416.20 (defunct corporation)   [ ] CCP 416.70 (conservatee)
              [ ] CCP 416.40 (association or partnership) [ ] CCP 416.90 (authorized person)
              [ ] CCP 415.46 (occupant)   [ ] other *(specify):*
5. [ ] by personal delivery on *(date):*

Page 1 of 2

Form Adopted for Mandatory Use
Judicial Council of California
SUM-130 [Rev. January 1, 2004]

SUMMONS—UNLAWFUL DETAINER—EVICTION

Code of Civil Procedure, §§ 412.20, 415.456, 1167

You will find a blank copy of this form in the FORMS section of this book and in Eviction Forms Creator.

court's own website, a link to which appears on www.courtinfo.ca.gov/otherwebsites, the California Courts' website.

Tell the clerk that you are planning to file an unlawful detainer and that you need to know whether your particular rental property is within this court's judicial district. You also need to know what the filing fee is, whether the court will accept a personal check or credit card for the filing fee, what the names of the court and judicial district are, and where exactly the courthouse is located.

With this information and what you already know about the tenants, you should be able to fill out the summons and complaint.

By the way, whenever you are filling out official court papers, you generally capitalize every letter in names and words of special importance. You don't have to follow this convention, however, if you prefer to follow standard capitalization usage. Either one is perfectly acceptable. By all means, do make sure that everything's legible. That's much more important than capitalization concerns.

Just below the words, "NOTICE TO DEFENDANT" on the summons, put the names of all known adult tenants you want to evict.

In addition to naming the known tenants, put down a reference to all the *unknown* adult tenants you want to evict. Unknown tenants are known as "Does" in the legal world. They're phantom people who may turn out to be real people later. Maybe they've been living on the premises all along or maybe they'll move in while your unlawful detainer is wending its way through legal channels.

If a mother-in-law, her boyfriend, and his teenage son have all moved in with your tenant and his wife, and you don't know any of their names, you'll have to use "Does" for them here. This is a common legal maneuver to keep people who might be defendants in a lawsuit from being excluded. Mentioning "Does" will allow you to amend your complaint later if you make a "discovery" of people and names. Putting, say, "AND DOES 1-10 INCLUSIVE" on the summons can't hurt your case; it can only help. To learn what to do in case you do make a discovery, see Appendix A under the "Does" section.

Below the words, "YOU ARE BEING SUED BY PLAINTIFF," put your name and the name of anyone else who owns the property. You don't have to include the names of all the owners, just those who might be of some help in handling the case. When there are several people listed as plaintiffs, any one of them may handle the paperwork or appear in court. They don't all have to appear.

In item 1, put the name and address of the court you are using, so the tenant will know which court he is being summoned to.

Put your name, address, and telephone number in item 2, and check one of the boxes in item 3 to indicate whether you did or did not receive any assistance from an unlawful detainer assistant.

If you did receive assistance, provide information about the assistant in item 6 on the second page of the form. There is no sample shown here of page two because it is self-explanatory.

Don't supply the date; leave that for the clerk.

Do check an appropriate box under item 4. In most circumstances, this would be box 4a.

Do not check box 5 or supply a date there. Leave them for the process server.

Make an original and one copy of your prepared summons, and make one additional copy for each additional defendant whom you want to have served.

• THE COMPLAINT—The complaint which you must prepare for filing along with the summons form should do the following—review your tenancy arrangement with the tenant; declare that you have performed all the conditions according to your arrangement; state your case against him; indicate that you have complied with the laws about giving the tenant proper notice; ask the court to return the premises to you; and ask for a money judgment to cover the amount owed, your costs, and any damages.

To do all that in times past, you would have had to draft at least a three-page typewritten document following a certain legal format and using just enough legal jargon to sound impressive, or you might have used the three-page form which appeared in the first edition of this book back in 1980 (see the similar one in chapter 9 especially drafted for holdover owners). But in 1982 the Judicial Council of California finally came up with a straightforward two-page form, now a three-page form, which you may use to do the very same thing today. It's a time-saver, and it helps you remember to include the essentials.

Ah, but don't be misled by the form's simplicity. Those choice boxes can be deceptive. You

---

	UD-100
ATTORNEY OR PARTY WITHOUT ATTORNEY *(Name, State Bar number, and address):* Lester Landlord & Leslie Landlord 123 Neat Street Littletown, CA 91111	FOR COURT USE ONLY

TELEPHONE NO.: 555-123-4567   FAX NO. *(Optional):* 555-123-4568
E-MAIL ADDRESS *(Optional):* lesterlandlord@yahoo.com
ATTORNEY FOR *(Name):* Plaintiff in Propria Persona

SUPERIOR COURT OF CALIFORNIA, COUNTY OF SADDLEBACK
STREET ADDRESS: 100 State Street
MAILING ADDRESS:
CITY AND ZIP CODE: Littletown 91111
BRANCH NAME: Creekside

PLAINTIFF: Lester Landlord
                    Leslie Landlord
DEFENDANT: Richard Renter, Rose Renter

[X] DOES 1 TO ___10___ INCLUSIVE   DEMAND AMOUNT $730

COMPLAINT — UNLAWFUL DETAINER*	CASE NUMBER:
[X] **COMPLAINT** [ ] **AMENDED COMPLAINT** *(Amendment Number):* _____	

Jurisdiction *(check all that apply):*

[X] **ACTION IS A LIMITED CIVIL CASE**
Amount demanded   [X]   **does not exceed $10,000**
              [ ]   **exceeds $10,000, but does not exceed $25,000**
[ ] **ACTION IS AN UNLIMITED CIVIL CASE** (amount demanded exceeds $25,000)
[ ] **ACTION IS RECLASSIFIED** by this amended complaint or cross-complaint *(check all that apply):*
     [ ]   **from unlawful detainer to general unlimited civil** (possession not in issue)   [ ]   **from limited to unlimited**
     [ ]   **from unlawful detainer to general limited civil** (possession not in issue)   [ ]   **from unlimited to limited**

1. PLAINTIFF *(name each):*
   Lester Landlord, Leslie Landlord
   alleges causes of action against DEFENDANT *(name each):*
   Richard Renter, Rose Renter

2. a. Plaintiff is (1) [X] an individual over the age of 18 years.   (4) [ ] a partnership.
               (2) [ ] a public agency.   (5) [ ] a corporation.
               (3) [ ] other *(specify):*
      b. [ ] Plaintiff has complied with the fictitious business name laws and is doing business under the fictitious name of *(specify):*

3. Defendant named above is in possession of the premises located at *(street address, apt. no., city, zip code, and county):*
   123 Neat Street, Littletown 91111, Saddleback County

4. Plaintiff's interest in the premises is [X] as owner [ ] other *(specify):*
5. The true names and capacities of defendants sued as Does are unknown to plaintiff.
6. a. On or about *(date):* 12/14/XXXX   defendant *(name each):*
        Richard Renter   Rose Renter

        (1) agreed to rent the premises as a [X] month-to-month tenancy [ ] other tenancy *(specify):*
        (2) agreed to pay rent of $ 700.00   payable [X] monthly [ ] other *(specify frequency):*
        (3) agreed to pay rent on the [X] first of the month [ ] other day *(specify):*
      b. This [X] written [ ] oral   agreement was made with
        (1) [X] plaintiff.   (3) [ ] plaintiff's predecessor in interest.
        (2) [ ] plaintiff's agent.   (4) [ ] other *(specify):*

* NOTE: Do not use this form for evictions after sale (Code Civ. Proc., § 1161a).   Page 1 of 3

Form Approved for Optional Use Judicial Council of California UD-100 [Rev. July 1, 2005]	**COMPLAINT—UNLAWFUL DETAINER**	Civil Code, § 1940 et seq. Code of Civil Procedure §§ 425.12, 1166 *www.courtinfo.ca.gov*

You will find a blank copy of this form in the FORMS section of this book and in Eviction Forms Creator.

Checking the right box is Key

must be careful when making your selections, very careful. While getting used to your new trifocals, you might easily check a wrong box and find to your chagrin that your case was thrown out of court by a sharp-eyed judge. You will have to be hawk-eyed yourself to use this form correctly and stay out of trouble. Get accustomed to your trifocals while reading your newspaper's comics, not here. Use your most reliable reading glasses here.

When you complete the form, read it aloud to yourself or have someone else read it to you, reading only the portions you have checked. Think carefully about whether those statements reflect your own case accurately, and if they don't, change them so they do.

Here's an explanation of the entire form, line by line and box by box, and here's also a sample complaint form filled out as it should be if you were Lester and Leslie Landlord evicting Richard and Rose Renter for nonpayment of rent.

Complete the top portion of the complaint with the information called for. You'll notice that it has the same elements as the summons except that they're in a different sequence. In the section "ATTORNEY OR PARTY WITHOUT ATTORNEY," enter "Plaintiff in Pro Per" or "Plaintiff in Propria Persona" where the form says "Attorney for (Name)." "Plaintiff" is the legal term for the person who's doing the suing. "In pro per" is an abbreviation of the Latin expression, "in propria persona," meaning simply that you are acting as your own attorney.

When entering the court's address and branch name, remember to enter the county on the first line after "SUPERIOR COURT OF CALIFORNIA, COUNTY OF."

Make certain that the names and addresses of the plaintiffs and defendants are exactly the same on every document you prepare, right down to the middle initials if any. Again, do not use "Mr. & Mrs." Use first and last names. Do not use "Richard and Rose Renter" either. Use each person's full name like this: "Richard H. Renter" and "Rose Renter."

Check the box in front of "DOES 1 TO ___," and put "10" in the blank. Beside the blank, put the word "INCLUSIVE," and to the right of that put "DEMAND AMOUNT $XX." The "$XX" dollar figure you enter should be the same one you put in 17c. It's the past-due rent.

Check the "COMPLAINT" box. Check the "AMENDED COMPLAINT" box only if you already filed a complaint and needed to amend it to include more defendants or to correct a defect in the original.

In the "Jurisdiction" section, check two boxes, "ACTION IS A LIMITED CIVIL CASE" and "does not exceed $10,000," that is, unless your case fits into one of the other two monetary categories. If it does, shame on you! Next time begin eviction proceedings sooner! Stop believing those tenant excuses!

1. Item 1 repeats the names of the plaintiffs and defendants as already entered. Enter them again here.

2. Item 2a presents a problem for some rental property owners because, strictly speaking, people cannot represent themselves in court unless they are an "individual." If you as plaintiff are a public agency, a partnership, a corporation, or any ownership entity other than an individual, you must hire an attorney to represent you in court.

Lest you think that "individual" in 2a means only one person, though, think again. Here it means any single person or group of people who own property in their own names and report their ownership activity on their own tax returns. In other words, they do not file a separate tax return strictly for the property ownership entity and then reflect their portion of ownership on their individual returns. Clearly then, a husband and wife or several unrelated people who have a "handshake" or "joint venture" ownership arrangement do qualify as an "individual" plaintiff, whereas corporations and partnerships of any kind, be they family or limited liability, do not qualify here as an "individual" plaintiff and cannot represent themselves in an unlawful detainer action.

If you are filing "in pro per," you must check box 2a(1). Checking any other box will leave you open to questioning should your case come before a judge, although a judge who does determine that you are not an ownership entity entitled to represent yourself will most likely let you continue with your unlawful detainer action so long as you get an attorney to represent you from then on.

If you have adopted a fictitious business name such as Greenbrier Apartments or Overlook Terrace, and you have been using that name on your rental agreements and rent receipts (just having a sign out in front of the property doesn't count), then you must comply with the laws about filing

PLAINTIFF *(Name)*: Lester Landlord	CASE NUMBER:
DEFENDANT *(Name)*: Richard Renter	

6. c. ☐ The defendants not named in item 6a are
    (1) ☐ subtenants.
    (2) ☐ assignees.
    (3) ☐ other *(specify)*:

  d. ☒ The agreement was later changed as follows *(specify)*:
    Rent raised to $780 as of 7/1/XXXX

  e. ☒ A copy of the written agreement, including any addenda or attachments that form the basis of this complaint, is attached and labeled Exhibit 1. *(Required for residential property, unless item 6f is checked. See Code Civ. Proc., § 1166.)*

  f. ☐ *(For residential property)* A copy of the written agreement is **not** attached because *(specify reason)*:
    (1) ☐ the written agreement is not in the possession of the landlord or the landlord's employees or agents.
    (2) ☐ this action is solely for nonpayment of rent (Code Civ. Proc., §1161(2)).

7. ☒ a. Defendant *(name each)*:
    Richard Renter, Rose Renter

    was served the following notice on the same date and in the same manner:
    (1) ☒ 3-day notice to pay rent or quit   (4) ☐ 3-day notice to perform covenants or quit
    (2) ☐ 30-day notice to quit   (5) ☐ 3-day notice to quit
    (3) ☐ 60-day notice to quit   (6) ☐ Other *(specify)*:

  b. (1) On *(date)*:   9/15/XXXX   the period stated in the notice expired at the end of the day.
    (2) Defendants failed to comply with the requirements of the notice by that date.
  c. All facts stated in the notice are true.
  d. ☒ The notice included an election of forfeiture.
  e. ☒ A copy of the notice is attached and labeled Exhibit 2. *(Required for residential property. See Code Civ. Proc. § 1166.)*

  f. ☐ One or more defendants were served (1) with a different notice, or (2) on a different date, or (3) in a different manner, as stated in Attachment 8c. *(Check item 8c and attach a statement providing the information required by items 7a-e and 8 for each defendant.)*

8. a. ☒ The notice in item 7a was served on the defendant named in item 7a as follows:
    (1) ☒ by personally handing a copy to defendant on *(date)*:   9/12/XXXX
    (2) ☐ by leaving a copy with *(name or description)*:
        a person of suitable age and discretion, on *(date)*:   at defendant's
        ☐ residence ☐ business AND mailing a copy to defendant at defendant's place of residence on *(date)*:   because defendant cannot be found at defendant's residence or usual place of business.
    (3) ☐ by posting a copy on the premises on *(date)*:   ☐ AND giving a copy to a person found residing at the premises AND mailing a copy to defendant at the premises on *(date)*:
        (a) ☐ because defendant's residence and usual place of business cannot be ascertained OR
        (b) ☐ because no person of suitable age or discretion can be found there.
    (4) ☐ *(Not for 3-day notice; see Civil Code, § 1946 before using)* by sending a copy by certified or registered mail addressed to defendant on *(date)*:
    (5) ☐ *(Not for residential tenancies; see Civil Code, § 1953 before using)* in the manner specified in a written commercial lease between the parties.
  b. ☒ *(Name)*: Richard Renter
    was served on behalf of all defendants who signed a joint written rental agreement.
  c. ☐ Information about service of notice on the defendants alleged in item 7f is stated in Attachment 8c.
  d. ☒ Proof of service of the notice in item 7a is attached and labeled Exhibit 3.

You will find a blank copy of this form in the FORMS section of this book and in Eviction Forms Creator.

that name with the county and advertising it in a publicly circulated newspaper before you may file an unlawful detainer. Use of a fictitious name which includes your surname, such as Lester Landlord's Sun Garden Apartments, won't require filing and won't require you to check this box unless you use Sun Garden Apartments in place of Lester Landlord on your rental agreement and elsewhere in your rental property dealings. If you are using a true fictitious name, as I do for certain of my property holdings, then be sure to check box 2b and give the name there (see the discussion of fictitious name statements in chapter 3).

3. Item 3 asks for the location of your property which your tenants, now the defendants in this case, are occupying—their street address, apartment number, city, zip code, and county. In addition to that, be certain you include whatever suite, space, building, or room number further identifies the exact premises. This information should match what is shown on the notice and on the rental agreement.

4. Whether you own a minuscule percentage or one hundred percent of the property in question, check the owner box. If you are anything else, such as an original tenant trying to evict a subtenant, check the second box and state enough facts to show that you have the right to possession of the premises. Some courts will allow managers and agents to act as plaintiffs and handle unlawful detainers for absentee owners, and some won't. Check with your court about its requirements before you file. Even if your court does require the owner to be the plaintiff in an unlawful detainer, the physical presence of the owner would be required only for a court appearance, and even that may not be necessary. Everything else could be handled by someone other than the plaintiff once the signatures have been obtained.

5. To take advantage of item 5 in the complaint, be sure you put a number in the "DEFENDANT" section of the complaint up above, where you see "DOES 1 TO ____." This number should match the one you put on the summons.

6. In section 6, you have an opportunity to establish for the court the precise terms of the agreement made with the tenant. Indicate the date of the agreement and the names of those mentioned in the agreement. They should be the defendants named in the complaint. If the people

you originally rented to have sublet to someone else, name here the original renters whose names appear in the agreement, even though they no longer live on the premises and indicate in 6c whether there are any additional defendants and if so, what category they fit under. The term "other" in 6c might refer to guests, licensees, trespassers, or co-signers, all of whom must be mentioned in the original notice to be included here.

Next, indicate in 6a(1) with an "X" whether the tenancy is month-to-month or another arrangement, in which case you should specify what kind of an arrangement it is, week-to-week, year-to-year, one-year lease, three-year lease, lease-option, or some such.

In the blank 6a(2) following "rent of $____," put down the net rent *as given in the rental agreement or as agreed upon verbally.* This may or may not be the current rent. Don't worry about that right now. Then indicate whether the rent is payable monthly or at some other interval and also when it is due, on the first or on some other day.

Remember that these names, intervals, figures, and days should reflect what you agreed upon when you *first* rented the place to the tenant, and that they are not necessarily current. In 6d, you have an opportunity to specify how the agreement has been changed.

Indicating in 6b whether the agreement is written or oral is extremely important, and that's what you do next. A crafty attorney taught me that lesson the hard way once by filing a demurrer (see GLOSSARY) because my complaint failed to specify that the rental agreement was written. In the context of life, specifying whether an agreement is written or oral is about as important as the hair growing between your toes, but in the context of pursuing an unlawful detainer, it's as important as the hair on your head. Naturally this attorney's challenge was a frivolous one, made on a legal technicality, and designed only to delay the case, thereby winning the tenant a few more days of free rent. It was easily answered, but it was frustrating to be thwarted over something which appeared to be so insignificant.

If you were the one who made this agreement with your tenant, check the "plaintiff" box 6b(1); if it was your manager or agent, check the agent box; if it was someone you bought the property from, a "predecessor in interest," check that box; if someone else did it, check the "other" box and specify who it was.

PLAINTIFF *(Name)*: Lester Landlord	CASE NUMBER:
DEFENDANT *(Name)*: Richard Renter	

9. ☐ Plaintiff demands possession from each defendant because of expiration of a fixed-term lease.

10. ☒ At the time the 3-day notice to pay rent or quit was served, the amount of **rent due** was $ 730.00

11. ☒ The fair rental value of the premises is $26.00   per day.

12. ☐ Defendant's continued possession is malicious, and plaintiff is entitled to statutory damages under Code of Civil Procedure section 1174(b). *(State specific facts supporting a claim up to $600 in Attachment 12.)*

13. ☒ A written agreement between the parties provides for attorney fees.

14. ☐ Defendant's tenancy is subject to the local rent control or eviction control ordinance of *(city or county, title of ordinance, and date of passage):*

    Plaintiff has met all applicable requirements of the ordinances.

15. ☐ Other allegations are stated in Attachment 15.

16. Plaintiff accepts the jurisdictional limit, if any, of the court.

17. **PLAINTIFF REQUESTS**
    a. possession of the premises.
    b. costs incurred in this proceeding: $265.00
    c. ☒ past-due rent of $ 730.00
    d. ☐ reasonable attorney fees.
    e. ☒ forfeiture of the agreement.
    f. ☒ damages at the rate stated in item 11 from *(date):* 10/1/XXXX   for each day that defendants remain in possession through entry of judgment.
    g. ☐ statutory damages up to $600 for the conduct alleged in item 12.
    h. ☐ other *(specify):*

18. ☒ Number of pages attached *(specify):* __5__ Rental Agreement, Notice to Pay or Quit, Proof of Service of Notice

UNLAWFUL DETAINER ASSISTANT (Bus. & Prof. Code §§ 6400-6415)

19. *(Complete in all cases.)* An unlawful detainer assistant ☒ did **not** ☐ did for compensation give advice or assistance with this form. *(If plaintiff has received any help or advice for pay from an unlawful detainer assistant, state:)*
    a. Assistant's name:
    b. Street address, city, and zip code:
    c. Telephone No.:
    d. County of registration:
    e. Registration No.:
    f. Expires on *(date):*

Date: September 16, XXXX

_____Lester Landlord & Leslie Landlord_____   ▶ *Lester Landlord   Leslie Landlord*
(TYPE OR PRINT NAME)   (SIGNATURE OF PLAINTIFF OR ATTORNEY)

VERIFICATION

(Use a different verification form if the verification is by an attorney or for a corporation or partnership.)

I am the plaintiff in this proceeding and have read this complaint. I declare under penalty of perjury under the laws of the State of California that the foregoing is true and correct.

Date: September 16, XXXX

_____Lester Landlord & Leslie Landlord_____   ▶ *Lester Landlord   Leslie Landlord*
(TYPE OR PRINT NAME)   (SIGNATURE OF PLAINTIFF)

UD-100 [Rev. July 1, 2005]   **COMPLAINT—UNLAWFUL DETAINER**   Page 3 of 3

You will find a blank copy of this form in the FORMS section of this book and in Eviction Forms Creator.

In the box at the top of page two, put the first and last name of the lead plaintiff and the first and last name of the lead defendant. Leave the "CASE NUMBER" box blank for the court clerk to fill in.

Should there be any other defendants listed in your complaint whose names did not appear in 6a, check the box after "c" and indicate whether they are subtenants (renting from the original tenants and responsible to them), assignees (tenants who have assumed the original tenants' agreement and are responsible to you directly), or other (co-signers would fit into this category).

Unless the tenants being evicted are relatively new, you will probably have something to include in 6d. Check the box first and then list any relevant changes which have been made to the tenants' original rental agreement—rent increases, tenant additions or deletions, and the like.

6e and 6f are related and concern attaching the rental agreement to the complaint. Look at them closely before you check any of their boxes.

Unless he must, the virtuoso eviction attorney whom I consult for good ideas does not attach the rental agreement to the complaint because he believes that omitting it "reduces the demurrability" of the complaint. In other words, he believes that attaching the rental agreement increases the chances that the tenant or the tenant's attorney will find something to object to. If you elect to follow this practice whenever possible and omit attaching the agreement to the complaint, you will have to make a copy available for the judge to see later, but not now.

Note that attaching the agreement to the complaint is mandatory for residential tenancies unless there never was a written agreement, unless it cannot be found, or unless you are pursuing the tenant solely for nonpayment of rent.

If the agreement was verbal or was lost, check box 6f(1). If you are pursuing the tenants solely for nonpayment and you don't want to attach the agreement, check box 6f(2). Otherwise, check box 6e.

7. This section refers to the type of notice you served, the people who received it, and the date when it expired. Check box 7 and list to the right the names of all those defendants who were served. Then check the box next to the type of notice you served. For nonpayment of rent, check the first one.

In 7b, give the date when the notice period ended. Be careful in making your calculations for this date. It should be exactly correct. Take the date given on the notice and add the number of days granted for compliance. If, for example, a 3-Day Notice to Pay Rent or Quit were given on July 12th, the notice expiration day would be July 15th. If it were given on July 31st, the notice expiration day would be August 3d.

Ah, but remember that a 3-Day Notice to Pay Rent or Quit does not always expire after three days. It must expire on a day when the banks are open. Notices served on a Wednesday or Thursday do not expire in three days. Notices served on a Wednesday expire in five days, and notices served on a Thursday expire in four days. Notices served on either of these days of the week expire on the following Monday (review the chart shown earlier in this chapter) unless that Monday is a holiday. Then they expire on the following Tuesday. Be mindful of this quirk when you identify in 7b the date the notice period ended for your 3-Day Notice to Pay Rent or Quit.

The waiting periods for other notices are not subject to this same quirk because there's no money involved. There's no need for the tenant to have access to his bank account in order to comply with a 30-Day Notice to Terminate Tenancy, for example. A 30-day notice given on July 3d would expire August 2d. "Thirty days" means thirty days. More would be all right, of course, but fewer would not be.

Electronic calculators aren't always helpful in calendar calculations. Fingers and toes are better, especially when they count off the days on an actual calendar.

Check box 7d if your notice included a statement requesting the tenant to forfeit his rental agreement. The 3-Day Notice to Pay Rent or Quit, 3-Day Notice to Quit, and Notice to Terminate Tenancy given in this book all do include such a statement, but the 3-Day Notice to Perform Covenant does not. Look carefully at the particular notice you used. Whether the rental agreement is forfeited or not involves some legal complexities for underemployed attorneys to argue about. Suffice it to say here that when you do *not* elect to forfeit a rental agreement in a nonpayment-of-rent case, the court *may* allow the tenant to pay up and still continue to occupy the premises. When you serve any of the three notices above which request the tenant to forfeit his agreement, you want him to leave, not linger.

MC-025

SHORT TITLE:		CASE NUMBER:
LANDLORD VS. LEWNO		1234567890

ATTACHMENT *(Number):*   7 f   Page __4__ of __4__
(This Attachment may be used with any Judicial Council form.)   *(Add pages as required)*

1

2   On July 12, XXXX, at 6:12 a.m., Plaintiff Lester Landlord did serve Defendant

3   Muretta Lewno by personal service a copy of the 3-Day Notice to Pay Rent or Quit

4   referred to in this Complaint and showing a balance owed of $1,215 as of July 5,

5   XXXX.

6   Service occurred at the residence of the Defendants, 999 Sweet Street,

7   Littletown, California.

8

9

10

11

12

13

14

15

16

17

18

19

20

21

22

23

24

25

26

27   *(If the item that this Attachment concerns is made under penalty of perjury, all statements in this Attachment are made under penalty of perjury.)*

Form Approved for Optional Use
Judicial Council of California
MC-025 [New July 1, 2002]

ATTACHMENT
to Judicial Council Form

Cal. Rules of Court, rule 982

You will find a blank copy of this form in the FORMS section of this book and in Eviction Forms Creator.

When you serve him the 3-Day Notice to Perform Covenant, you may want him to leave, but you definitely want his tenancy responsibilities to continue, especially if there's a lease involved, so you do not request forfeiture.

Box 7e should be checked and a copy of the notice you served or had served on the defendant should be attached to the complaint whenever you're proceeding against residential tenants. Attaching it is mandatory.

Identify the attached notice as "Exhibit 2." Don't fret over whether you ought to call it "Exhibit 1" because you decided not to attach a copy of the written agreement and thus would have no Exhibit 1 otherwise. Identify it as "Exhibit 2" whether you have an Exhibit 1 or not.

Check box 7f if you served other defendants with a different notice or you served them on a different date or in a different manner, and attach a statement to that effect as Attachment 8c.

Use Judicial Council attachment form MC-025 for your statement.

8. Check the box directly after 8a and also check the appropriate one of the other five numbered boxes describing the service of the notice. If the defendant was served personally, the first method, check that box and give the date of service. If the notice was left with someone "of suitable age and discretion," check that box, give the name or description of the person whom the notice was left with and the date when it was left, indicate whether it was served this way at the defendant's residence or place of business, and give the date when it was mailed. If the notice was posted and mailed, check that box, give the date when it was posted and when a copy was mailed, check whether a copy was also given to someone on the premises (it doesn't have to be), and then check one of the two boxes to indicate why you chose this method. If you used the fourth method, sending a copy by certified or registered mail, check that box and tell when it was sent (please note that this method by itself may not be used for three-day notices). Check the fifth box if you served a commercial tenant in a manner specified in your lease.

Check box 8b if you served one tenant on behalf of every tenant who signed the rental agreement, and name the person who was served.

Check box 8c if you checked box 7f and have already prepared a statement identified as Attachment 8c explaining how you served the additional defendants referred to in 7f. Incidentally, you need not use a totally separate page for each attached statement. You may use one page for all the attachments. Use an additional page only if you need more space.

Check box 8d to indicate that you attached the proof of service of the notice as Exhibit 3. Notices in this book which include the proof of service at the bottom of the notice may bear identification as both Exhibit 2 and Exhibit 3.

9. Check box 9 only if the tenants failed to leave when their fixed lease term expired.

10. Check box 10 if you are evicting for nonpayment of rent, and include the precise amount of rent due when you served the notice. This amount should be exactly what you put on the notice, regardless of whether more rent is now owed and delinquent.

By the way, whereas attaching the agreement to the complaint may increase its demurrability, attaching the notice to the complaint decreases its demurrability. The defendant cannot claim that the form complaint is "ambiguous" and "uncertain" as to the statement of the amount of rent due in the notice. The notice speaks for itself.

11. Check box 11 no matter what kind of eviction you are pursuing and indicate the current rent per day. Regardless of how many days there are in the actual months involved, use a 30-day month for this calculation. Courts have held that a 30-day month is proper and consistent to use for rent calculations and that it represents a fair rental value. To calculate your rental's monthly value, merely divide the monthly rent by 30. If the rent were $975 per month, for example, the per-diem rent would be $32.50.

12. You are no longer entitled to treble damages awarded by the court for proving that the tenant was extra ornery in harassing or cheating you. Instead, you are entitled to a maximum of $600. I caution you against asking for this sum unless you believe you can prove beyond any doubt in an attachment that the tenant has been malicious. "Malicious" here would mean that he has threatened you, damaged the rental dwelling intentionally, or tried numerous and obvious delaying tactics. Calling you names wouldn't suffice. Brandishing a weapon at you would. These damages are seldom awarded, except in extreme cases, so I no longer include them in my complaints because they tend to complicate what I want to be kept simple. Some tenants' attorneys

CM-010

ATTORNEY OR PARTY WITHOUT ATTORNEY *(Name, State Bar number, and address)*:	FOR COURT USE ONLY
Lester Landlord & Leslie Landlord 123 Neat Street Littletown, CA 91111 TELEPHONE NO.: 555-123-4567 FAX NO.: 555-123-4568 ATTORNEY FOR *(Name)*: Plaintiff in Propria Persona	

SUPERIOR COURT OF CALIFORNIA, COUNTY OF Saddleback
STREET ADDRESS: 100 State Street
MAILING ADDRESS:
CITY AND ZIP CODE: Littletown   91111
BRANCH NAME: Creekside

CASE NAME:
LANDLORD VS. RENTER

CIVIL CASE COVER SHEET	Complex Case Designation	CASE NUMBER:
☐ Unlimited ☒ Limited (Amount (Amount demanded demanded is exceeds $25,000) $25,000 or less)	☐ Counter ☐ Joinder Filed with first appearance by defendant (Cal. Rules of Court, rule 1811)	1234567890
		JUDGE: DEPT:

Items 1-5 below must be completed (see instructions on page 2).

1. Check **one** box below for the case type that best describes this case:

Auto Tort	Contract	Provisionally Complex Civil Litigation (Cal. Rules of Court, rules 1800-1812)
☐ Auto (22)	☐ Breach of contract/warranty (06)	☐ Antitrust/Trade regulation (03)
☐ Uninsured motorist (46)	☐ Collections (09)	☐ Construction defect (10)
Other PI/PD/WD (Personal Injury/Property Damage/Wrongful Death) Tort	☐ Insurance coverage (18)	☐ Mass tort (40)
☐ Asbestos (04)	☐ Other contract (37)	☐ Securities litigation (28)
☐ Product Liability (24)	**Real Property**	☐ Environmental/Toxic tort (30)
☐ Medical malpractice (45)	☐ Eminent domain/Inverse condemnation (14)	☐ Insurance coverage claims arising from the above listed provisionally complex case types (41)
☐ Other PI/PD/WD (23)	☐ Wrongful eviction (33)	**Enforcement of Judgment**
Non-PI/PD/WD (Other) Tort	☐ Other real property (26)	☐ Enforcement of judgment (20)
☐ Business tort/unfair business practice (07)	**Unlawful Detainer**	**Miscellaneous Civil Complaint**
☐ Civil rights (08)	☐ Commercial (31)	☐ RICO (27)
☐ Defamation (13)	☒ Residential (32)	☐ Other complaint *(not specified above)* (42)
☐ Fraud (16)	☐ Drugs (38)	**Miscellaneous Civil Petition**
☐ Intellectual property (19)	**Judicial Review**	☐ Partnership and corporate governance (21)
☐ Professional negligence (25)	☐ Asset forfeiture (05)	☐ Other petition *(not specified above)* (43)
☐ Other non-PI/PD/WD tort (35)	☐ Petition re: arbitration award (11)	
Employment	☐ Writ of mandate (02)	
☐ Wrongful termination (36)	☐ Other judicial review (39)	
☐ Other employment (15)		

2. This case ☐ is ☒ is not complex under rule 1800 of the California Rules of Court. If the case is complex, mark the factors requiring exceptional judicial management:
   a. ☐ Large number of separately represented parties d. ☐ Large number of witnesses
   b. ☐ Extensive motion practice raising difficult or e. ☐ Coordination with related actions pending in one or more courts
   novel issues that will be time-consuming to resolve   in other counties, states or countries, or in a federal court
   c. ☐ Substantial amount of documentary evidence f. ☐ Substantial postjudgment judicial supervision
3. Type of remedies sought *(check all that apply)*:
   a. ☒ monetary b. ☒ nonmonetary; declaratory or injunctive relief c. ☐ punitive
4. Number of causes of action *(specify)*: 1
5. This case ☐ is ☒ is not a class action suit.
6. If there are any known related cases, file and serve a notice of related case. *(You may use form CM-015.)*

Date: September 16, XXXX

Lester Landlord   ▶ *Lester Landlord*
_____   _____
(TYPE OR PRINT NAME)   (SIGNATURE OF PARTY OR ATTORNEY FOR PARTY)

NOTICE
- Plaintiff must file this cover sheet with the first paper filed in the action or proceeding (except small claims cases or cases filed under the Probate Code, Family Code, or Welfare and Institutions Code). (Cal. Rules of Court, rule 201.8.) Failure to file may result in sanctions.
- File this cover sheet in addition to any cover sheet required by local court rule.
- If this case is complex under rule 1800 et seq. of the California Rules of Court, you must serve a copy of this cover sheet on **all** other parties to the action or proceeding.
- Unless this is a complex case, this cover sheet will be used for statistical purposes only.

Page 1 of 2

Form Adopted for Mandatory Use
Judicial Council of California
CM-010 [Rev. January 1, 2006]   **CIVIL CASE COVER SHEET**   Cal. Rules of Court, rules 201.8, 1800-1812;
Standards of Judicial Administration, § 19
www.courtinfo.ca.gov

You will find a blank copy of this form in the FORMS section of this book and in Eviction Forms Creator.

will file a motion to strike unless the request for such damages includes what might be considered an allegation of willfulness, in other words, behavior which is deliberate, intentional, or obstinate. If you are bent upon attempting to secure these damages from your tenant, include your allegations as Attachment 12. As for myself, I wouldn't bother. Why ask for them and leave yourself open to an attorney's response when you have so little chance of being awarded them anyway and even less of a chance of collecting?

13. Check box 13 only if your rental agreement entitles you to ask for attorney fees. Checking the box does not mean you are asking for attorney fees. It means only that your agreement includes a clause which entitles you to ask for them.

Some agreements no longer ask that attorney or legal services fees go to the prevailing party. Some landlords have been stung badly. After losing lengthy eviction suits, they have had to pay their own legal costs plus those of their tenants. Check your rental agreement to see what it says.

14. Check box 14 only if there is a rent or eviction control ordinance covering the premises. State whether it's a city or a county ordinance and give the title and date. If you don't know what to enter here, call your local rent control board and ask them for the information or look for it on the rent control board's website.

Note that item 14 also includes a statement saying that you as plaintiff have met all the applicable requirements of the ordinance. You have, haven't you?

15. Check box 15 only if you need to add some more allegations to your complaint, something which just hasn't been covered by any of the choices in the complaint form thus far. Add your allegations in an attachment.

16. In item 16, you agree to excuse the tenant for any monetary claims you may have against him which exceed the court's limits.

17. The eight requests under item 17 sum up the entire complaint. You have no choice about the first two. They're at the heart of every eviction. Request "a" states the first item of importance, that is, you want possession of the premises. Request "b" states the second item of importance, that is, you want your tenant to reimburse you for your out-of-pocket costs to pursue the eviction. These costs include filing fees, process serving fees, court reporter's fees for hearings and for depositions if there are any, and witness fees. Request "c" echoes item 10 above; check box "c" if you checked box 10 above and put the same rental figure there, too. Request "d" asks for reasonable attorney fees. Don't check box "d" even if you did check box 13 above, that is, if you are acting "in pro per." Anybody representing himself in court, even an attorney representing himself in court, is not entitled to attorney fees. If you decide to hire an attorney later, you may ask for them then.

Incidentally, if your rental agreement includes a clause which provides for "legal services fees" rather than or in addition to "attorney fees," you may ask for self-representation fees when filing "in pro per" [*Jacobson v. Simmons Real Estate* (1994) 23 CA4th 1285, 28 CR2d 699, 702-703]. Calculate them based upon an hourly rate equal to that paid an office worker in your area, and put them in item 17h.

Request "e" asks for forfeiture of the agreement. Check box "e" only if you checked box 7d and you want the agreement forfeited. Request "f" refers to damages. Here the word "damages" does not mean physical damages. In nonpayment cases, it means rent which would have been charged from one day following the last rental period given in the notice to pay. In evictions for other than nonpayment, damages begin on the day following the date their rent is paid through. Put in the blank here the date when damages begin. Request "g" echoes item 12 above. Check box "g" if you checked box 12. Finally, check box "h" if you have any further request which you want to specify, such as late fees, bad check charges, damages, legal services fees, and so on.

18. Add up the pages you are attaching to the complaint, give the number, name the attachments, and check box 18.

19. As you do on the summons, you must indicate on the complaint whether you received any help from an unlawful detainer assistant. If you did, provide information about the assistant where indicated.

After completing item 19, type or print your name legibly on the two lines below and to the left, sign your name on the two lines to the right, and date both the complaint itself and the verification. Don't overlook the dates. They're easy to overlook because they're in the same space where the plaintiff's typed or printed name goes both above and beneath the verification.

The verification on the complaint is for a plaintiff only. Wording for an attorney's verification appears in Appendix A.

Now that you have completed your complaint, go back to the first item and begin reading it out loud, reading only those sections which you checked and the others which apply. See if it makes any sense to you and if it's consistent. When it does make sense and is consistent, you are ready to file your complaint with the court clerk and arrange to have it served.

• THE COVER SHEET—The cover sheet is a Judicial Council form which you must include with the summons and complaint when you first file your case. Your tenant won't be getting a copy when he's served because courts use cover sheets for statistical purposes only.

General instructions for completing the cover sheet appear as page 2 of the form itself (see FORMS section of this book). Here are more specific instructions for unlawful detainers. Enter the same information in the upper-left-hand section of the form that you entered on the complaint. The case name is simply the plaintiff's (your) last name "vs." the defendant's (your tenant's) last name.

Below the case name, check the box next to "Limited" to indicate that you are asking for less than $25,000. Check neither box under "Complex Case Designation." Your unlawful detainer is neither.

In item 1, enter an "X" in the box for a residential unlawful detainer (32) or an "X" in the box for a commercial unlawful detainer (31). In item 2, enter an "X" in the box indicating that yours is not a complex case. In item 3, enter an "X" in boxes "a" and "b" because you are seeking both monetary and nonmonetary remedies in an eviction for nonpayment of rent. If you are seeking a nonmonetary remedy only, enter an "X" in box "b" only. In item 4, enter a "1" because you have only one cause of action. In item 5, enter an "X" in the "is not" box because you are not bringing a class action suit. Then date the form, type or print your name, and sign it.

• COVER SHEET ADDENDUM, LOS ANGELES—Los Angeles Superior Court now requires an additional cover sheet. It's their Civil Case Cover Sheet Addendum and Statement of Location. It's a four-page form you may pick up from the office of the court or download from the court's website (lasuperiorcourt.org/forms).

Follow the step-by-step instructions on the first page of the form. They're simple enough.

Step 4. File the Summons, Complaint, and Cover Sheet.

• INTIMIDATION (SHOW YOUR PAPERWORK)—In case you missed the remarks in chapter 2 about the intimidating tactic of showing your legal paperwork to the tenant before you file it with the court clerk, I am repeating the gist of those remarks here because you now have the opportunity to try this tactic if you think it has any chance of succeeding.

Simply put, the tactic consists of posting the completed summons and complaint on the tenant's door for twenty-four hours to let him know that you are deadly serious about dragging him into court. Some tenants will respond by crying "uncle" and will pay up or move. Some tenants will respond by thumbing their noses at you and saying, "So, take me to court!"

Even a modest success rate warrants trying the tactic because you have much to gain if it succeeds and little or nothing to lose if it fails. The perfect time to post the paperwork is one day before you can legally file it with the court clerk. That way you don't lose a single hour in pressing your case if the tactic fails, and you might save the fees and costs of the suit and regain possession much sooner if it succeeds.

• THE FILING—With your paperwork completed and checked, at last you're ready to file it with the court clerk. Take the correct number of copies (see the first page of the FORMS section for guidance) to the court clerk's office which you located earlier. If possible, go in the morning so the process server will have a chance to serve the papers that same day.

Give the clerk the summons, complaint, and cover sheet originals, the copies, and the filing fee. She will assign your case a number and open a corresponding file, stamping your papers and hers with an array of rubber stamps so numerous and so varied that you'd swear she could write a book with them. Don't swear to that, though, not in this office. You don't want to perjure yourself.

After the necessary stamping and signing, she will hand you a receipt for the filing fee and return all the papers except the originals of your complaint and cover sheet. She keeps them for the court's records.

If she appears friendly, ask her for advice about serving the defendant, your tenant, with the papers. Practices and preferences regarding service vary, and you should listen carefully to the clerk's recommendations.

Since some courts hear unlawful detainers on certain days of the week, ask also about specific scheduling so you can be prepared. There's no feeling worse than getting everything ready for court on the Friday before a three-day holiday, only to learn that unlawful detainers aren't heard on Fridays in your local court, and you'll have to wait until Tuesday before you can get in, thereby losing four days in the process. You might as well learn now what to expect in the way of court scheduling.

In addition, while you're still there, ask the clerk whether there have been any updates to the forms you're most likely to use next, all of which are Judicial Council forms and all of which appear in the back of this book—the Request for Entry of Default (982(a)(6)), the Declaration for Default Judgment by Court (UD-116), the Judgment (UD-110), and the Writ of Execution (EJ-130). The court may use a local form or two as well. Ask. If it does, ask for a copy of each.

• DELAYED ACCESS—California courts now delay public access to court papers in limited civil cases for sixty days from the date of filing (see CCP §1161.2 for specifics).

This delay is a real boon to landlords because it has virtually stopped the unscrupulous eviction defense services. They would send somebody down to the courthouse every day to sift through recently filed unlawful detainer complaints looking for potential business. They would identify who's being sued, and then they would contact the defendants directly with offers to obstruct the eviction as long as legally possible.

Believe me, almost any attorney can obstruct almost any eviction for some time if he wants to. Whether the case has merit or not doesn't matter in the least. The unscrupulous attorney knows all the gimmicks for exploiting the legal system. He can create a snowstorm of paperwork which will stop your eviction efforts cold, at least for a while. Any obstruction of the eviction is a "win" for your tenant, and when he's being evicted, he'd rather pay an attorney than pay you. These "eviction chasers" would also identify complaints which might have special value to them, complaints which might generate some damages as-

sessed against you, you "rent-gouging, feelthy-reech landlord with them deep pockets and that bulging purse."

Now that public access to unlawful detainer filings is delayed, nobody can just go down to the courthouse and examine the paperwork. They have to wait sixty days, and by then, you should have already evicted the tenants.

• SAVING TRIPS AND TIME—By knowing just what to do, which includes calling the court clerk at the right time of day, having certain papers already prepared, and taking advantage of weekends, you may save precious days in the eviction process, and you may also keep your trips to the courthouse to a minimum. I have had to make as many as three trips there in a single day because I wasn't completely prepared the first time. If you follow the advice given here and if your case is uncontested, you may be able to do everything in only two or three visits to the courthouse all told, and you may be able to do everything in a total of sixteen days from start (delivery of the 3-Day Notice to Pay Rent or Quit) to finish (removal of the tenants by an officer of the court).

Step 5. Arrange Service of the Summons and Complaint.

Although you may legally serve the notice which initiates eviction proceedings yourself, you may not legally serve the summons and complaint yourself. That's absolutely *verboten*. You have to arrange for someone else to do it.

Any person in the following three categories may serve the summons and complaint for you:
1) A uniformed law enforcement officer;
2) A professional process server; or
3) Someone else who is at least eighteen years old and not a party to the suit.

Personally, I prefer to have a uniformed law enforcement officer serve the papers if I think it will be intimidating to the tenant or if the tenant is potentially dangerous *and* if I know service will be fast. It appears legally sanctioned, as if you're "making a federal case out of the matter," one which has a foregone conclusion, and it stifles the tenant's will to respond. Since you want the tenant out as soon as possible, you don't want him wasting any of your time with a response to the complaint.

To have an on-duty law enforcement officer serve your papers, find out from the court clerk

POS-010

ATTORNEY OR PARTY WITHOUT ATTORNEY *(Name, State Bar number, and address):*	FOR COURT USE ONLY
Lester Landlord & Leslie Landlord 123 Neat Street Littletown, CA 91111 TELEPHONE NO.: 555-123-4567 FAX NO. *(Optional)*: 555-123-4568 E-MAIL ADDRESS *(Optional)*: ATTORNEY FOR *(Name)*: Plaintiff in Propria Persona	

SUPERIOR COURT OF CALIFORNIA, COUNTY OF Saddleback
STREET ADDRESS: 100 State Street
MAILING ADDRESS:
CITY AND ZIP CODE: Littletown 91111
BRANCH NAME:

PLAINTIFF/PETITIONER: Lester Landlord Leslie Landlord DEFENDANT/RESPONDENT: Richard Renter, Rose Renter	CASE NUMBER: 1234567890

PROOF OF SERVICE OF SUMMONS	Ref. No. or File No.

(Separate proof of service is required for each party served.)

1. At the time of service I was at least 18 years of age and not a party to this action.

2. I served copies of the summons and
   a. [X] complaint
   b. [ ] Alternative Dispute Resolution (ADR) package
   c. [ ] Civil Case Cover Sheet *(served in complex cases only)*
   d. [ ] cross-complaint
   e. [ ] other *(specify documents):*

3. a. Party served *(specify name of party as shown on documents served):*
      Rose Renter

   b. Person served: [X] party in item 3a   [ ] other *(specify name and relationship to the party named in item 3a):*

4. Address where the party was served:
      123 Neat St., Littletown, CA 91111

5. I served the party *(check proper box)*
   a. [X] **by personal service.** I personally delivered the documents listed in item 2 to the party or person authorized to
      receive service of process for the party (1) on *(date):*   9/16/XXXX   (2) at *(time):* 3:12 p.m.

   b. [ ] **by substituted service.** On*(date):*   at *(time):*   I left the documents listed in item 2 with or
      in the presence of *(name and title of relationship to person indicated in item 3b):*

      (1) [ ] **(business)** a person at least 18 years of age apparently in charge at the office or usual place of business
              of the person to be served. I informed him or her of the general nature of the papers.

      (2) [ ] **(home)** a competent member of the household (at least 18 years of age) at the dwelling house or usual
              place of abode of the party. I informed him or her of the general nature of the papers.

      (3) [ ] **(physical address unknown)** a person at least 18 years of age apparently in charge at the usual mailing
              address of the person to be served, other than a United States Postal Service post office box. I informed
              him or her of the general nature of the papers.

      (4) [ ] I thereafter mailed (by first-class, postage prepaid) copies of the documents to the person to be served
              at the place where the copies were left (Code Civ. Proc., § 415.20). I mailed the documents on
              (date):   from *(city):*   **or** [ ] a declaration of mailing is attached.

      (5) [ ] I attach a **declaration of diligence** stating actions taken first to attempt personal service.

Page 1 of 2

Form Adopted for Mandatory Use Judicial Council of California POS-010 [Rev. January 1, 2004]	**PROOF OF SERVICE OF SUMMONS**	Code of Civil Procedure § 417.10

You will find a blank copy of this form in the FORMS section of this book and in Eviction Forms Creator.

whether one can serve the papers (certain areas no longer have the manpower, so you may have to use somebody else) and where they have offices. Usually the office is close by. Ask them when they will make the first effort to serve your papers and when they might expect to complete the service. Some officers are extremely diligent. They'll attempt to serve the papers the very next morning between 5 and 7:30. That's 5 a.m. in the morning! In addition, they'll keep trying day after day until they succeed. Others act as if they have a monopoly on process serving in their bailiwick. They won't even try to serve the papers for two weeks.

You're going to be paying for the sheriff or marshal's service. You have a right to know how long they will take. Don't assume that your papers will be served quickly. Find out for sure. Time is extremely important here. Get the papers served as soon as possible so the eviction clock can continue ticking. Until they are served, nothing is happening to get the eviction moving. Its clock has stopped dead.

In most cases, a professional process server will do just as well as a sheriff or marshal, if not better, because he is bound to be more prompt and more diligent. For instance, if you file Friday afternoon, a sheriff or marshal probably won't make his first effort to serve until Monday morning because he doesn't work Friday nights or weekends, and that means you have just added two days to the eviction process. Professional process servers, on the other hand, will serve any time, any day. Those who are diligent and passionate about their work have been known to impersonate an Avon lady, climb up a ship's swaying mainmast, crash cocktail parties, and fend off killer pit bulls to get their papers served. That's free enterprise in action!

You will find them listed under "Process Serving" in the Yellow Pages and on the internet as well. Contact several. Ordinarily they're quite competitive in price, but do compare their charges with the sheriff or marshal's before committing yourself. Ask whether they charge by the address or by the person served. If they charge by the address, and you have three people to serve at one address, you will pay a third of what you would pay if they were to charge by the person served instead. Also check to see that they are licensed by the state and registered with the county so their acknowledgment of service will

be accepted readily by the court.

Remember that professional process servers dress like ordinary people. They have no uniforms, no badges, no smart hats, and no guns. They don't look so imposing as does an officer of the law, but then this is sometimes an advantage, too, because tenants tend to be less wary about being served when someone ordinary-looking knocks on the door. You needn't worry whether ordinary-looking process servers will get the job done quickly and correctly. They will. After all, they're professionals.

If you want to save some money, if you can't find a good professional process server, or if the tenant is successfully avoiding service, you can always have someone else, an amateur, serve the papers, and you can even accompany him to identify the defendant. It's just as legal a service as any, mind you, but it isn't quite so overwhelming as being served by a sheriff or marshal, and because an amateur's doing it rather than a professional, the service might get bungled.

If you do elect to use a friend or acquaintance as your process server, make sure that he serves one copy of the summons and one copy of the complaint on each defendant and that he completes item 5 on the summons and fills out the Proof of Service of Summons correctly.

Take a good look at the two-page Proof of Service of Summons sample shown here. Notice that it's a general form used for evictions and other causes of action as well. Parts of it do not apply to evictions. The sample shows how an unregistered amateur would fill out the form after having served Richard Renter personally on behalf of Lester Landlord.

As you can see, it's reasonably straightforward. Page 1's whole upper section is already familiar to you. It's typical of the Judicial Council forms you have seen.

In ordinary cases, the server would complete the upper section, put an "X" in 2a, identify the party served in 3a, put an "X" in 3b (party in item 3a), provide the address where the party was served in item 4, and put an "X" in 5a along with the date and time when the party was served.

Section 7 of the Proof of Service asks for information on the server, and there's a place (7d) where the server may put down a fee. $45, or whatever the law enforcement officers in your area charge, would be a reasonable figure. Your amateur server should check boxes 7e.1, 7e.2, and 8.

PLAINTIFF/PETITIONER: Lester Landlord	CASE NUMBER:
DEFENDANT/RESPONDENT: Richard Renter	1234567890

c. ☐ **by mail and acknowledgment of receipt of service.** I mailed the documents listed in item 2 to the party, to the address shown in item 4, by first-class mail, postage prepaid.

    (1) on *(date)*:   (2) from *(city)*:

    (3) ☐ with two copies of the *Notice and Acknowledgment of Receipt* (form 982(a)(4)) and a postage-paid return envelope addressed to me. *(Attach completed* Notice and Acknowledgement of Receipt *(form 982(a)(4).)* (Code Civ. Proc., § 415.30.)

    (4) ☐ to an address outside California with return receipt requested. (Code Civ. Proc., § 415.40.)

d. ☐ **by other means** *(specify means of service and authorizing code section):*

    ☐ Additional page describing service is attached.

6. The "Notice to the Person Served" (on the summons) was completed as follows:
    ☒ as an individual defendant.
    ☐ as the person sued under the fictitious name of *(specify):*
    ☐ On behalf of *(specify):*
    under the following Code of Civil Procedure section:

☐ 416.10 (corporation)	☐ 415.95 (business organization, form unknown)
☐ 416.20 (defunct corporation)	☐ 416.60 (minor)
☐ 416.30 (joint stock company/association)	☐ 416.70 (ward or conservatee)
☐ 416.40 (association or partnership)	☐ 416.90 (authorized person)
☐ 416.50 (public entity)	☐ 415.46 (occupant)
	☐ other:

7. **Person who served papers**
  a. Name: Jane Granzow
  b. Address: 2222 Oak Street, Littletown, CA
  c. Telephone number: 555.123.4444
  d. **The fee** for service was: $ 45.00
  e. I am:
    (1) ☒ not a registered California process server
    (2) ☒ exempt from registration under Business and Professions Code section 22350(b).
    (3) ☐ registered California process server:
      (i) ☐ Employee or independent contractor.
      (ii) Registration No.:
      (iii) County:

8. ☒ I **declare** under penalty of perjury under the laws of the State of California that the foregoing is true and correct.
    or
9. ☐ I am a California sheriff or marshal and I certify that the foregoing is true and correct.

Date: 5/16/XXXX

Jane Granzow   *Jane Granzow*
(NAME OF PERSON WHO SERVED PAPERS/SHERIFF OR MARSHAL)   (SIGNATURE)

You will find a blank copy of this form in the FORMS section of this book and in Eviction Forms Creator.

You might like to know that "B&P §22350(b)," referred to in 7e.2, gives those who serve no more than ten summonses in any one calendar year an exemption from registering with the county.

Don't forget that there must be a separate Proof of Service form submitted for each person served, even if they were all served at once.

Which one of the three types of process servers you select to serve your summons and complaint will depend upon four factors: speed, cost, intimidation potential, and likelihood of completing the service correctly.

Check the chart here to see how the three possible process servers differ on the four factors,

Step 6. Serve the Summons and Complaint.

• WHO SHOULD BE SERVED WITH THE SUMMONS AND COMPLAINT?—To evict all the adult tenants from a dwelling and make them all responsible for paying the judgment, you must mention each of them by name in the complaint and serve each of them separately with a summons and complaint. You could chance serving only the dominant adult or the breadwinner alone and hope that the eviction of that one person would precipitate a mass exodus, but you couldn't be absolutely certain of it,

	SHERIFF or MARSHAL	PROFESSIONAL	OTHER (AMATEUR)
SPEED	varies (check locally)	excellent	good
COST	good (check locally)	varies	excellent
INTIMIDATION POTENTIAL	excellent	poor	poor
SERVICE CORRECTNESS	good	good	fair

and select the one who ought to do the best job for you in a given situation.

Make the process server's job as easy as possible. Give whomever you select to serve the papers as much information as you can about the tenant, especially his appearance, his possible whereabouts at different times, and his occupation (process servers know that they're likely to catch a bartender at one time of the day and a carpenter at another). A picture would help if you have one (if you copied his driver's license when he moved in, make a copy of your copy and give it to the process server for better identification). Make certain that the address correctly identifies the tenant's dwelling. If you tell the process server to look for the tenant at 140 Marina Way, and there are six apartments at that address, don't expect the process server to find which apartment this particular tenant lives in. Give him the apartment number.

not nowadays anyway.

Some freeloaders know the legal loopholes in the eviction procedure well enough so that they can frustrate your best efforts to evict them, and the California Supreme Court (the old "Bird Court") gave them still another loophole to use in the Arrieta case. In it, the court held that a sheriff or marshal can evict only those adults whose names appear on the complaint. He cannot remove an adult unnamed in the resulting writ who is physically present during the actual eviction, resists eviction, and claims a right of possession commencing before the unlawful detainer was filed. As you might imagine, this decision popped the lid off a bucket of worms, for it made evictions even costlier, more troublesome, and more time-consuming than they already were. If you want to get all the tenants out, you now have to prepare an additional set of papers for each defendant, pay added process servers' fees to serve each defendant, and wait until every one of them is served.

Consequently, you simply must name and serve all the adults who are currently living in your rental, regardless of whether they're mentioned in the rental agreement or are responsible for paying the rent. And if you want to forestall the possibility that some strangers might appear at the very last minute and claim that they, too, have tenants' rights and that nobody can be evicted as a consequence, you might want to take advantage of the "prejudgment claim" procedure, which I will explain shortly.

To get a judgment against a co-signer, you have to name and serve him as well, though most landlords prefer to ignore the co-signer during the unlawful detainer. They want to avoid any potential complications in getting the tenants out, and involving another person in the action tends to cause unforeseen delays. Once the tenants are out, the landlord proceeds against the co-signer in small claims court.

Please note that some courts won't even allow you to proceed against both the tenant and the co-signer in an unlawful detainer. Ask your court clerk.

As mentioned before regarding whose names should be on the notice, don't bother serving children who are upwards of eighteen years old unless they are mature enough to be helping support the family. Serving them antagonizes the parents. Serving them also tends to be difficult because they're hard to find at home.

• DECIDING WHETHER TO USE THE PREJUDGMENT CLAIM PROCEDURE— Eight years following the lamebrained Arrieta decision, after thousands upon thousands of fraudulent claims of right to possession had been filed against hapless landlords (only 3% of such claims were found to be legitimate), the state legislature finally came up with something to help the situation (CCP §415.46). It combines different methods of service and uses a special form called a Prejudgment Claim of Right to Possession (see FORMS section) to insure that nobody, known or unknown, who claims to have a right to live in the dwelling could later plead ignorance about the unlawful detainer and put a halt to the eviction at the very last minute.

Here's how it works. You tell the court clerk that you intend to use the prejudgment claim procedure. You make up three additional copies of the summons and complaint. You attach a blank copy of the Prejudgment Claim of Right to Possession to each of these three sets of papers. One set is for whoever comes to the door; one is for posting on or near the primary entrance; and one is for mailing to the address of the premises. You tell the process server (must be a sheriff or marshal or a professional process server, not an amateur server) that you want to serve any unknown occupants with a Prejudgment Claim of Right to Possession when you drop off all the papers you want served.

You then wait ten days following service. If nobody responds with a claim during that period, you go right ahead and complete your normal unlawful detainer paperwork, except that you indicate on both the Request for Entry of Default and the Writ of Execution that you have complied with CCP §415.46 and that your judgment includes "all tenants, subtenants, named claimants and other occupants of the premises." That wording authorizes the sheriff or marshal to evict everybody he finds.

If one or more people do make a claim, they are added as defendants to the unlawful detainer, and they then have five days in which to respond to the summons and complaint. If they make no response within five days, you may go ahead and file a Request for Entry of Default on them and proceed normally with your unlawful detainer. If they do make a response within five days, you treat the matter like any other contested case (see chapter 10).

Although some attorneys use this procedure as a matter of course now, you should be aware that it does have several disadvantages. It adds at least five extra days to the whole eviction process and it increases both the copying costs and the fees for service.

Should you use it anyway? Maybe yes and maybe no. If you believe that the tenants you want to evict are neither savvy nor devious enough to get somebody to file a post-judgment third-party claim, don't bother to use the procedure. If, on the other hand, you have reason to believe that they might file a claim because they know all the angles and aren't afraid to take advantage of them, or because they have proven to be devious people, or because they might really have somebody else living with them who is unbeknownst to you, or because you don't have a clue who is actually living there and you need to "smoke 'em all out," go ahead and use the procedure and save yourself any uncertainty about whether someone will show up out of nowhere to halt the eviction when the sheriff or marshal is there to put the tenants out on the street.

VERY IMPORTANT!! Please note that you do not have to wait ten days to request an entry of default on the *named* defendants. You can, and you should, request an entry of default on them five days after they have been served, so they cannot file a response later.

• SUBSTITUTED SERVICE—If, after three tries, your process server cannot find the tenant, then the process server must use "substituted service," a procedure which the officer or professional will resort to automatically. It will delay things a bit, but it will definitely advance them. The problems with substituted service, though, are that you need an additional copy of the complaint for each defendant served under substituted service, that somebody must be found on the premises to take the papers, and that the tenant has fifteen days to respond to the complaint rather than the usual five.

• POSTING—Consider resorting to the posting procedure according to CCP §415.45 to serve those tenants who are difficult to find. Like substituted service, posting gives the tenant fifteen days to respond and requires additional copies of the papers. Unlike substituted service, it does not require anyone to be found on the premises. You may use this procedure after the process server has made three attempts to serve the tenant on different days and at different times. Instruct the process server to return your papers with enough information so you can get an order for posting if you want to use this procedure. Then go to the courthouse and get your order signed by the judge. You'll find forms and instructions for posting in Appendix A.

In exceptional circumstances, you may seek a Writ of Immediate Possession (see chapter 14), but you may find that proving what is necessary to get this writ is more difficult than the other alternatives.

• WAITING—When counting the five days, count every day including Saturdays and Sundays, but *do not count court holidays*, those thirteen days a year when the courts are closed (currently, they are New Year's Day, M.L. King Jr. Day Observance, Lincoln's Birthday, Presidents' Birthday Observance, Cesar Chavez Day, Memorial Day, Independence Day, Labor Day, Columbus Day Observance, Veteran's Day, Thanksgiving Day, Day after Thanksgiving, and Christmas Day). The final day on which the tenant may respond to your complaint must be a court day, a day when court offices are open and he at least has the opportunity to file. If his final day falls on a Saturday, Sunday, or holiday, he has the following court day in which to respond (CCP §1167). You cannot claim the tenant has defaulted until the day following the last day given him to respond to the complaint. If you have any doubts about waiting the prescribed number of days, consult Calendar 2 at the end of this chapter or ask your court clerk.

Whoever serves your summons and complaint will prepare the Proof of Service and return it to you. If you haven't received this evidence of successful service by the fourth day after you arranged service of the summons and complaint, by all means, take the initiative and call the server. Find out what's happening. Remember that you may begin counting the days allowed for the tenant's response only after service of the summons and complaint has been completed, so serving it promptly is extremely important.

Step 7. Inquire About a Response.

You are hoping that your tenant won't bother to file a response to your complaint because doing so will only delay and complicate matters for you.

If he does file a response with the court, you will receive a copy by mail, but you may have to wait a while for the U.S. Postal Service to deliver it, and you cannot afford to waste precious time doing so, especially if it wasn't filed until the last possible moment. So you should wait until the last day, and virtually the last hour, for the tenant to file before calling the court clerk's office to inquire whether he has filed a response. If the tenant has made a response to your summons and complaint, whether the response is substantial or frivolous in nature, go to chapter 10 to learn what to do next. If the tenant has not made a response, ask the clerk when is the earliest possible date she can schedule you on the court calendar, and then decide which of the alternatives in Step 8 to follow.

• LIKELIHOOD OF A RESPONSE BEING FILED—Fortunately the odds are in your favor that the tenant won't file a response (between 75 and 80% of all unlawful detainer complaints filed in my local court are never responded to). There are three reasons why responses are made infrequently to unlawful detainers for nonpayment of rent. Responses require 1) that the defendant either prepare a written paper himself or get an attorney to do it for him, 2) that he file the response with the court, and 3) that he either pay a filing fee or file a form stating that he's too poor to pay the fee.

Most defendants are simply unwilling to take the time and spend the money to make a response when they know full well that they are most likely going to lose anyway. They'd rather spend their time and money finding new accommodations someplace else where they can begin the cycle of free living and troublemaking all over again.

Certain tenants may go so far as to contact a legal-aid attorney, and because you are representing yourself, you may get some phone calls about the matter, but if you have a good case and you explain it frankly and fully, the legal-aid attorney will seldom bother to file a response. He has plenty of other cases with real merit to work on. He doesn't have the time to defend a tenant who's up to no good.

Step 8. Consider Your Alternatives and Select One.

Let's say you happen to be lucky. Your tenant hasn't filed a response to your complaint, and now you face the pleasant prospect of evicting him legally within days. Don't start feeling too smug yet. There are still some pitfalls which could delay everything, and there are still more hoops you have to jump through before the sheriff or marshal puts him out.

Right now it's decision time. You have to select one of at least three, and in some cases four, alternative paths to follow, each with certain advantages. Consider the four carefully.

1) The first alternative used to be the only one available; not any more. It involves setting up a court date, doing the paperwork necessary to appear in court, actually appearing in court for what is sometimes called a "prove-up trial," and getting a judgment for the restitution of your rental dwelling and for the money owed to you. Consider using this option when you don't have to wait more than a day or two to get into court, and you have reason to believe that the tenant

has attachable assets or garnishable wages.

2) The second alternative involves doing the paperwork necessary for the clerk to enter the tenant's default and to give you a default judgment for restitution. It's a timesaving procedure which is explained in CCP §1169 (see Appendix B). *You don't have to appear in court, but then neither do you get a money judgment.* Only a judge can grant a money judgment. Consider using this alternative when you're in a hurry to get your tenant evicted and you despair of ever getting any money out of him. It definitely saves you time because you do not have to wait for a court date *or* appear in court.

3) The third alternative combines the best features of the first two alternatives. Just as in the second alternative, it involves doing the paperwork necessary for the clerk to enter the tenant's default and to give you a default judgment for restitution, so you do get the tenants evicted quickly. At the same time, you arrange to get a money judgment, too, either by making a routine appearance in court or by filing a declaration. Consider using this alternative when you're in a hurry to have the tenant evicted and you think you might collect some money from him by attaching his assets or wages after he's long gone.

4) The fourth alternative adds some paperwork and some time to the procedure, but it's convenient, for you don't have to appear in court, and you do get judgments for both restitution and money. It involves preparing and filing all the other paperwork, plus something called a Declaration for Default Judgment by Court (sometimes known as a Declaration for Default Judgment in Lieu of Personal Testimony). You should know, though, that this procedure is discretionary, that is, it depends entirely upon the practice decided upon by your local judicial district. Some courts allow a declaration, and some courts don't, and the only way you can find out whether yours does is to ask. Consider using this alternative when you don't want to, or can't, appear in court, but you still want a money judgment and you're willing to endure some delay in the eviction.

Attorneys tend to favor the first alternative, the old-fashioned way, because they're used to it and it takes care of everything at once, restitution and money, but, as you know, attorneys aren't particularly interested in evicting their clients' tenants as quickly as possible. You have a different timetable. You want the bums out sooner rather than later, today rather than tomorrow. Consequently, I recommend that you try the second or the third alternative because either one of them should enable you to evict your tenants sooner. Getting into court generally means delays of one sort or another, and CCP §1169 recognizes this fact. Using it to expedite your tenants' eviction is in your best interest.

If you have any doubts about which alternative you ought to follow, read through Steps 9-14 for each alternative, and then decide. Note that the third alternative follows an "A" path first to get the judgment for restitution and then a "B" path to get the money judgment.

By the way, the fees for each alternative are identical.

Regardless of which alternative you select, plan to make a trip to the courthouse anyway on the sixth day following service of the summons and complaint. This is an extremely important trip, which is necessitated by your having to beat the tenant to the court clerk's office to file your request before the tenant gets around to filing his response. You see, after the tenant has had his five days to respond to your summons and complaint, he still has additional time to respond, up until you file the request.

Once you file the Request for Entry of Default, you no longer need to worry about whether your tenant will respond to the complaint. He can't. He has already had five days in which to respond and he has chosen not to. After you file the request, he gets no further opportunity to respond, even though you may not be able to get your default judgment immediately. You don't want to give him any more time than the law requires, so go ahead and beat him to the courthouse. Get there early, before the clerk has even had enough time to put on her lipstick.

CAUTION! In most California courts, the clerk takes the papers of the first person to get through the door on the sixth day following service of the summons and complaint. If you beat your tenant by one second, that's good enough. You'll get your default judgment. This practice follows the letter and the spirit of the law which gives the tenant five days to respond, not five and a quarter or six.

Alas, there are some courts which give the tenant more time to respond than they should. If you file your Request for Entry of Default at 8:15

a.m. in one of these courts, and the tenant files his answer at 4:46 p.m. on the same day, they give the tenant's answer precedence. As far as I am concerned, this practice is contrary to law and obviously weighted in favor of tenants.

Still other courts will refuse to enter your default request for several days, allowing the extra time for the tenant's paperwork to be forwarded from any court in the county. That, too, is just plain wrong. It's a double standard. You don't get that privilege. You can't file your papers with any court in the county. You must go to one certain court and keep going to that same court.

If you are treated in either of these ways, get mad about it. Scream "bloody murder" to all the powers that be, for you as a landlord are being taken advantage of! You are being treated unfairly.

Even if your court does give tenants extra time in which to answer and won't change its ways, you still should get to the court on the sixth day. That's the only way you can keep advancing your cause as quickly as possible.

Steps 9-14

These steps vary according to which of the four alternatives you selected in Step 8. To understand how they all work, you should note what they are once more:

1) Normal procedure requiring court appearance;
2) Clerk entering default judgment for restitution only;
3) Clerk entering default judgment for restitution, then judge awarding money judgment;
4) Declaration for default by court in lieu of personal testimony involving no court appearance, while providing judgment for both restitution and money.

VERY IMPORTANT! No matter which of the four alternatives you choose, you should be aware that your earlier decision to use or not to use the Prejudgment Claim of Right to Possession procedure *must be indicated* on the Request and the Writ. Both forms have check boxes for this purpose. On the Request, if you followed the prejudgment claim procedure, you should check the box [under 1e(1)] next to the words "Include in the judgment all tenants, subtenants, named claimants...." If you did not follow the procedure, do not check this box. On the Writ, if you followed the procedure, check box 24a(1). If you

982(a)(6)

ATTORNEY OR PARTY WITHOUT ATTORNEY *(Name, State Bar number, and address):*	FOR COURT USE ONLY
Lester Landlord & Leslie Landlord 123 Neat Street Littletown, CA 91111 TELEPHONE NO: 555-123-4567　　FAX NO. *(Optional):* 555-123-4568 E-MAIL ADDRESS *(Optional):* lesterlandlord@yahoo.com ATTORNEY FOR *(Name):* Plaintiff in Propria Persona	

SUPERIOR COURT OF CALIFORNIA, COUNTY OF SADDLEBACK
STREET ADDRESS: 100 State Street
MAILING ADDRESS:
CITY AND ZIP CODE: Littletown 91111
BRANCH NAME: Creekside

PLAINTIFF/PETITIONER: Lester Landlord
　　　　　　　　　　　　Leslie Landlord
DEFENDANT/RESPONDENT: Richard Renter, Rose Renter

REQUEST FOR (Application)	[X] **Entry of Default** [X] **Court Judgment**	[ ] **Clerk's Judgment**	CASE NUMBER: 1234567890

1. **TO THE CLERK:** On the complaint or cross-complaint filed

　a. on *(date):* 9/16/XXXX

　b. by *(name):* Lester Landlord

　c. [X] Enter default of defendant *(names):*

　　　Richard Renter, Rose Renter

　d. [X] I request a court judgment under Code of Civil Procedure sections 585(b), 585(c), 989, etc., against defendant *(names):*

　　　Richard Renter, Rose Renter

　　　(Testimony required. Apply to the clerk for a hearing date, unless the court will enter a judgment on an affidavit under Code Civ. Proc., § 585(d).)

　e. [ ] Enter clerk's judgment
　　　(1) [ ] for restitution of the premises only and issue a writ of execution on the judgment. Code of Civil Procedure section 1174(c) does not apply. (Code Civ. Proc., § 1169.)
　　　　　[ ] Include in the judgment all tenants, subtenants, named claimants, and other occupants of the premises. The *Prejudgment Claim of Right to Possession* was served in compliance with Code of Civil Procedure section 415.46.
　　　(2) [ ] under Code of Civil Procedure section 585(a). *(Complete the declaration under Code Civ. Proc., § 585.5 on the reverse (item 5).)*
　　　(3) [ ] for default previously entered on *(date):*

2. **Judgment to be entered.**

		Amount	Credits acknowledged	Balance
a. Demand of complaint	$	730.00	$	$ 730.00
b. Statement of damages *				
(1) Special	$		$	$
(2) General	$		$	$
c. Interest	$		$	$
d. Costs *(see reverse)*	$	250.00	$	$ 250.00
e. Attorney fees	$		$	$
f. **TOTALS**	$	980.00	$	$ 980.00

　g. **Daily damages** were demanded in complaint at the rate of: $ 26.00　per day beginning *(date):* 10/1/XXXX
　(Personal injury or wrongful death actions; Code Civ. Proc., § 425.11.)*

3. [X] *(Check if filed in an unlawful detainer case)* **Legal document assistant or unlawful detainer assistant** information is on the reverse *(complete item 4).*

Date: 9/23/XXXX

　　　Lester Landlord　　　　　　　　　　　　　▶ *Lester Landlord*
　　(TYPE OR PRINT NAME)　　　　　　　　　　　　(SIGNATURE OF PLAINTIFF OR ATTORNEY FOR PLAINTIFF)

	(1) [ ] Default entered as requested on *(date):*	
FOR COURT USE ONLY	(2) [ ] Default NOT entered as requested *(state reason):*	
	Clerk, by _____, Deputy	

Page 1 of 2

Form Adopted for Mandatory Use Judicial Council of California 982(a)(6) [Rev. February 18, 2005]	**REQUEST FOR ENTRY OF DEFAULT** **(Application to Enter Default)**	Code of Civil Procedure, §§ 585-587, 1169 www.courtinfo.ca.gov

You will find a blank copy of this form in the FORMS section of this book and in Eviction Forms Creator.

did not follow the procedure, check box 24a(2). Checking the boxes to show that you have followed the procedure alerts everyone that you are entitled to its benefits.

NOTA BENE—As shown here, the sample Request for Entry of Default and the sample Writ of Execution assume that Lester Landlord has *not* followed the prejudgment claim procedure.

Now follow the various steps for each alternative to its conclusion.

Step 9. (Alternative 1). Prepare Request, Judgment, and Writ.

Prepare the three forms: Request for Entry of Default, Judgment (Default), and the Writ of Execution as shown on the following pages (they must be typed).

Besides the usual information called for in the upper third of the Request for Entry of Default, check the "Entry of Default" and "Court Judgment" boxes.

Enter the date when you filed the complaint in item 1a.

Enter your name in 1b.

Check box 1c and enter the name(s) of the defendant(s) in item 1c whose default you are seeking. If you are proceeding against two tenants and neither tenant has answered, put both names here. If one tenant has answered and one hasn't, put here the name of the tenant who did *not* answer (use alternative 2 to eliminate one of several tenants; you gain little by taking the time to follow this alternative, that is, alternative 1).

Check box 1d and enter the name(s) of the defendant(s) whose default you are seeking through a court judgment.

Leave section 1e and all of its subsections blank. It's for clerk's judgments only, and you're pursuing a court judgment, not a clerk's judgment.

In section 2a under "Amount," enter the exact amount of your demand as given in the complaint.

Check box 3. You always check this box for an unlawful detainer because you must complete a statement on the backside about whether you used a legal document assistant or an unlawful detainer assistant.

Now turn the form over. In the box at the top, put the same names next to "PLAINTIFF/ PETITIONER" and "DEFENDANT/RE-SPONDENT" as those which appear on the first page of the form. Enter the case number in the CASE NUMBER box.

In section 4, indicate whether you did or did not use and pay an assistant for help. If you did use and pay one, include the particulars requested about the assistant.

Check box 5, and then check the three "is not" boxes in that section. They are not relevant to an unlawful detainer.

Check box 6a only if you were unable to mail a copy of the Request for Entry of Default to certain defendants because you lacked their addresses. Give their names.

Check box 6b to indicate that you mailed a copy of the request to each of the defendants whose last-known addresses you have, and complete the information called for: names, addresses, and dates. List each defendant separately.

In section 7, "Memorandum of Costs," you may list the various costs you have already paid to bring the unlawful detainer against your tenant, as well as certain other costs which you will incur, but you may not include your costs for such things as mileage, postage, and copying.

In 7a, enter what you paid for clerk's filing fees.

In 7b, enter what you paid for process server's fees. If you used an officer or a registered process server, enter the exact amount paid. If you used an amateur, you may pay him an amount no greater than a professional's fee and request reimbursement here.

In 7c, enter the cost of the fee for filing the writ. The clerk will tell you how much it is, or you may look for it on the court's website.

In 7d, enter the cost you'll incur for having the sheriff or marshal come out to post the Notice to Vacate and to come out again to evict the tenants bodily. Ask at the sheriff or marshal's office for the amount of this fee.

Total the costs at 7e.

Enter today's date and your name under sections 6, 7, and 8.

Check box 8 to indicate that no defendant is in the active military. Reserves don't count.

You should know that the Soldiers' and Sailors' Civil Relief Act of 1940 protects those on active duty from default judgments specifically and requires courts to appoint an attorney to represent the military defendant who fails to respond to a complaint. The assumption is that the military defendant may be unable to respond to the com-

PLAINTIFF/PETITIONER: Lester Landlord	CASE NUMBER:
DEFENDANT/RESPONDENT: Richard Renter	1234567890

4. **Legal document assistant or unlawful detainer assistant (Bus. & Prof. Code, § 6400 et seq.).** A legal document assistant or unlawful detainer assistant ☐ did ☒ did **not** for compensation give advice or assistance with this form. *(If declarant has received **any** help or advice for pay from a legal document assistant or unlawful detainer assistant, state):*

    a. Assistant's name: c. Telephone no.:
    b. Street address, city, and zip code: d. County of registration:
                                                  e. Registration no.:
                                                  f. Expires on *(date):*

5. ☒ **Declaration under Code of Civil Procedure Section 585.5** *(required for entry of default under Code Civ. Proc., § 585(a)).* This action

    a. ☐ is ☒ is not on a contract or installment sale for goods or services subject to Civ. Code, § 1801 et seq. (Unruh Act).
    b. ☐ is ☒ is not on a conditional sales contract subject to Civ. Code, § 2981 et seq. (Rees-Levering Motor Vehicle Sales and Finance Act).
    c. ☐ is ☒ is not on an obligation for goods, services, loans, or extensions of credit subject to Code Civ. Proc., § 395(b).

6. **Declaration of Mailing (Code Civ. Proc., § 587) .** A copy of this *Request for Entry of Default* was

    a. ☐ **not mailed** to the following defendants, whose addresses are **unknown** to plaintiff or plaintiff's attorney *(names):*

    b. ☒ **mailed** first-class, postage prepaid, in a sealed envelope addressed to each defendant's attorney of record or, if none, to each defendant's last known address as follows:

    (1) Mailed on *(date):*   (2) To *(specify names and addresses shown on the envelopes):*
        9/23/XXXX   Richard Renter
                                               458 Sweet Street
                                               Littletown, California 91111

I declare under penalty of perjury under the laws of the State of California that the foregoing items 4, 5, and 6 are true and correct.
Date: 9/23/XXXX

Lester Landlord   ▶ *Lester Landlord*
_____   _____
(TYPE OR PRINT NAME)   (SIGNATURE OF DECLARANT)

7. **Memorandum of costs** *(required if money judgment requested).* Costs and disbursements are as follows (Code Civ. Proc., § 1033.5):

    a. Clerk's filing fees. . . . . $ 180.00
    b. Process server's fees. . . . . $ 70.00
    c. Other *(specify):* . . . . $
    d. . . . . $
    e. **TOTAL** . . . . $ 250.00
    f. ☐ Costs and disbursements are waived.
    g. I am the attorney, agent, or party who claims these costs. To the best of my knowledge and belief this memorandum of costs is correct and these costs were necessarily incurred in this case.

I declare under penalty of perjury under the laws of the State of California that the foregoing is true and correct.
Date: 9/23/XXXX

Lester Landlord   ▶ *Lester Landlord*
_____   _____
(TYPE OR PRINT NAME)   (SIGNATURE OF DECLARANT)

8. ☒ **Declaration of nonmilitary status** *(required for a judgment).* No defendant named in item 1c of the application is in the military service so as to be entitled to the benefits of the Servicemembers Civil Relief Act (50 U.S.C. App. §501 et seq.)

I declare under penalty of perjury under the laws of the State of California that the foregoing is true and correct.
Date: 9/23/XXXX

Lester Landlord   ▶ *Lester Landlord*
_____   _____
(TYPE OR PRINT NAME)   (SIGNATURE OF DECLARANT)

982(a)(6) [Rev. February 18, 2005]   **REQUEST FOR ENTRY OF DEFAULT**   Page 2 of 2
                                          (Application to Enter Default)

You will find a blank copy of this form in the FORMS section of this book and in Eviction Forms Creator.

plaint because of military commitments beyond his control.

If your tenant is in the active military, follow the suggestions in the last chapter of this book rather than try to comply with the burden the act puts on the plaintiff who is seeking a default judgment against a military defendant. You'll get more immediate results.

Now, note the total in 7e, turn the form over, and enter that same 7e figure in the "Amount" column at 2d, "Costs." Total all of the amounts at 2f.

Whatever appears in the "Amount" column should also appear in the "Balance" column, that is, unless the tenant has any credits coming. Do not credit the tenant here for any security deposit he has paid. That's still yours to use for its intended purpose after the tenants move out.

At 2g, enter the figure given in the complaint as daily damages, and indicate in the space immediately following the words "per day beginning (date):" when these damages are supposed to begin. In nonpayment-of-rent cases, they begin the day following the rental period for which you have demanded rent in the complaint.

Let's say, for example, that you demanded rent through September 30th in your complaint. Damages, being equal to rent not demanded in the complaint, would then begin on October 1st. In termination-of-tenancy cases, they begin the day following the expiration of the notice.

Below box 3, next to "Date:" enter today's date, and type your name below that.

Sign your name four times to the right of the triangular black pointers, once on the front side and three times on the back side. Try to avoid getting writer's cramp when you're signing your name these four times. You won't qualify to receive workers' compensation if you do.

Take a cappuccino break now if you need one, but don't relax too much. You're not through yet. There's still more to do.

The next form you need to deal with is the judgment. There is now a Judicial Council version approved for optional use throughout the state. Because it is optional, you may find that your court still uses a local form. Ask the clerk whether you may use the Judicial Council version. If so, follow the instructions here. If not, look for common elements in the two. You'll find that every element in a local form will match one in the multipurpose Judicial Council version, and

you'll be able to complete the local form from knowing how to fill out the Judicial Council version.

Let's go.

Except for the identifiers, the upper part of the form is only too familiar to you. Enter your particulars where indicated and identify yourself as the "Judgment Creditor."

Enter the court's particulars where indicated.

Name yourself as the plaintiff and your tenant as the defendant.

Next, check the box beside "By Court" and also the box beside "By Default." Leave the other four boxes empty.

In section 1, check the box following the "1" to indicate that you are seeking a default judgment.

Check box 1e to indicate that you are expecting a court judgment.

Check box 1e(1) to indicate that you are appearing in court to give testimony and present other evidence.

Turn the form over.

Enter the names of the lead plaintiff and the lead defendant plus the case number.

Check box beside "THE COURT" because you are getting a court judgment.

Check box 3a, and give the name of every plaintiff where indicated and every defendant where indicated.

In section 4, check the first box, and identify the property by address.

Section 5 refers to the procedure which uses the Prejudgment Claim of Right to Possession form to eliminate everybody who might claim an interest in the property. Since you did not use this procedure and you did not wait the ten days before filing for default, skip this section.

Section 6 covers the amount and terms of the judgment. Do not fill in any of the amounts. The clerk will do that for you. Check box 6a, and check an appropriate box beside 6c.

That's the extent of what you can do to complete the judgment in advance of your court appearance.

Next, you'll need to complete either an Application for Writ of Possession (Orange and Los Angeles counties require applications and make them available on their websites) and the Writ of Execution/Possession or just the Writ of Execution/Possession itself. Ask the clerk whether you need to complete the application and the writ or

UD-110

ATTORNEY OR PARTY WITHOUT ATTORNEY *(Name, state bar number, and address)*: Lester Landlord & Leslie Landlord 123 Neat Street Littletown, CA 91111	FOR COURT USE ONLY

TELEPHONE NO.: 555-123-4567   FAX NO. *(Optional)*: 555-123-4568
E-MAIL ADDRESS *(Optional)*:
ATTORNEY FOR *(Name)*: Plaintiff in Propria Persona

[ ] ATTORNEY FOR   [X] JUDGMENT CREDITOR   [ ] ASSIGNEE OF RECORD

SUPERIOR COURT OF CALIFORNIA, COUNTY OF Saddleback
STREET ADDRESS: 100 State Street
MAILING ADDRESS:
CITY AND ZIP CODE: Littletown 91111
BRANCH NAME:

PLAINTIFF: Lester Landlord
      Leslie Landlord

DEFENDANT: Richard Renter, Rose Renter

JUDGMENT—UNLAWFUL DETAINER	CASE NUMBER:
[ ] By Clerk [X] By Default [ ] After Court Trial [X] By Court [ ] Possession Only [ ] Defendant Did Not Appear at Trial	1234567890

JUDGMENT

1. [X] **BY DEFAULT**
   a. Defendant was properly served with a copy of the summons and complaint.
   b. Defendant failed to answer the complaint or appear and defend the action within the time allowed by law.
   c. Defendant's default was entered by the clerk upon plaintiff's application.
   d. [ ] **Clerk's Judgment** (Code Civ. Proc., § 1169). For possession only of the premises described on page 2 (item 4).
   e. [X] **Court Judgment** (Code Civ. Proc., § 585(b)). The court considered
      (1) [X] plaintiff's testimony and other evidence.
      (2) [ ] plaintiff's or others' written declaration and evidence (Code Civ. Proc., § 585(d)).

2. [ ] **AFTER COURT TRIAL.** The jury was waived. The court considered the evidence.
   a. The case was tried on *(date and time)*:
      before *(name of judicial officer)*:
   b. Appearances by:
      [ ] Plaintiff *(name each)*:   [ ] Plaintiff's attorney *(name each)*:
                                                             (1)
                                                             (2)
      [ ] Continued on *Attachment 2b* (form MC-025).
      [ ] Defendant *(name each)*:   [ ] Defendant's attorney *(name each)*:
                                                             (1)
                                                             (2)
      [ ] Continued on *Attachment 2b* (form MC-025).
   c. [ ] Defendant did not appear at trial. Defendant was properly served with notice of trial.
   d. [ ] A statement of decision (Code Civ. Proc., § 632)   [ ] was not   [ ] was   requested.

Form Approved for Optional Use
Judicial Council of California
UD-110 [New January 1, 2003]

JUDGMENT—UNLAWFUL DETAINER

Code of Civil Procedure, §§ 415.46,
585(d), 664.6, 1169

You will find a blank copy of this form in the FORMS section of this book and in Eviction Forms Creator.

PLAINTIFF: Lester Landlord	CASE NUMBER:
DEFENDANT: Richard Renter	1234567890

JUDGMENT IS ENTERED AS FOLLOWS BY: [X] THE COURT ☐ THE CLERK

3. **Parties.** Judgment is

   a. [X] for plaintiff *(name each):* Lester Landlord, Leslie Landlord

      and against defendant *(name each):* Richard Renter, Rose Renter

      ☐ Continued on *Attachment 3a* (form MC-025).

   b. ☐ for defendant *(name each):*

4. [X] Plaintiff ☐ Defendant is entitled to possession of the premises located at *(street address, apartment, city, and county):*
      456 Sweet Street, Littletown 91111, Saddleback County

5. ☐ Judgment applies to all occupants of the premises including tenants, subtenants if any, and named claimants if any (Code Civ. Proc., §§ 715.010, 1169, and 1174.3).

6. **Amount and terms of judgment**

   a. [X] Defendant named in item 3a above must pay plaintiff on the complaint:
      b. ☐ Plaintiff is to receive nothing from defendant named in item 3b.

      ☐ Defendant named in item 3b is to recover costs: $

      ☐ and attorney fees: $

(1) [X] Past-due rent	$	730.00
(2) ☐ Holdover damages	$	
(3) ☐ Attorney fees	$	
(4) [X] Costs	$	205.00
(5) ☐ Other *(specify):* Int. Special Damages	$	
(6) **TOTAL JUDGMENT**	$	935.00

   c. [X] The rental agreement is canceled.   ☐ The lease is forfeited.

7. ☐ **Conditional judgment.** Plaintiff has breached the agreement to provide habitable premises to defendant as stated in *Judgment—Unlawful Detainer Attachment* (form UD-110S), which is attached.

8. ☐ **Other** *(specify):*

   ☐ Continued on *Attachment 8* (form MC-025).

Date: ☐ _____
                    JUDICIAL OFFICER

Date: ☐ Clerk, by _____ , Deputy

[SEAL]

CLERK'S CERTIFICATE *(Optional)*

I certify that this is a true copy of the original judgment on file in the court.

Date:

Clerk, by _____ , Deputy

UD-110 [New January 1, 2003]	**JUDGMENT—UNLAWFUL DETAINER**	Page 2 of 2

You will find a blank copy of this form in the FORMS section of this book and in Eviction Forms Creator.

EJ-130

ATTORNEY OR PARTY WITHOUT ATTORNEY *(Name, State Bar number, and address):*	FOR COURT USE ONLY
Lester Landlord & Leslie Landlord 123 Neat Street Littletown, CA 91111	

TELEPHONE NO.: 555-123-4567   FAX NO. *(Optional):* 555-123-4568
E-MAIL ADDRESS *(Optional):* lesterlandlord@yahoo.com
ATTORNEY FOR *(Name):* Plaintiff in Propria Persona

☐ ATTORNEY FOR   ☒ JUDGMENT CREDITOR   ☐ ASSIGNEE OF RECORD

SUPERIOR COURT OF CALIFORNIA, COUNTY OF Saddleback
STREET ADDRESS: 100 State Street
MAILING ADDRESS:
CITY AND ZIP CODE: Littletown 91111
BRANCH NAME: Creekside

PLAINTIFF: Lester Landlord
           Leslie Landlord
DEFENDANT: Richard Renter, Rose Renter

WRIT OF	☒ EXECUTION (Money Judgment) ☒ POSSESSION OF ☐ Personal Property ☒ Real Property ☐ SALE	CASE NUMBER: 1234567890

1. **To the Sheriff or Marshal of the County of:**   Saddleback
   You are directed to enforce the judgment described below with daily interest and your costs as provided by law.

2. **To any registered process server:** You are authorized to serve this writ only in accord with CCP 699.080 or CCP 715.040.

3. *(Name):* Lester Landlord & Leslie Landlord
   is the ☒ judgment creditor ☐ assignee of record   whose address is shown on this form above the court's name.

4. **Judgment debtor** *(name and last known address):*

   Richard Renter
   458 Sweet Street
   Littletown, California 91111

   Rose Renter
   458 Sweet Street
   Littletown, California 91111

   ☐ Additional judgment debtors on next page

5. **Judgment entered on** *(date):*   9/23/XXXX
6. ☐ **Judgment renewed on** *(dates):*

7. **Notice of sale** under this writ
   a. ☒ has not been requested.
   b. ☐ has been requested *(see next page).*
8. ☐ Joint debtor information on next page.
   [SEAL]

9. ☒ See next page for information on real or personal property to be delivered under a writ of possession or sold under a writ of sale.
10. ☐ This writ is issued on a sister-state judgment.
11. Total judgment . . . . $ 980.00
12. Costs after judgment (per filed order or memo CCP 685.090) . . . . $
13. Subtotal *(add 11 and 12).* . . . . $ 980.00
14. Credits. . . . . $
15. Subtotal *(subtract 14 from 13).* . . . . . $ 980.00
16. Interest after judgment (per filed affidavit CCP 685.050) (not on GC 6103.5 fees) . . . $
17. Fee for issuance of writ . . . . $ 15.00
18. **Total** *(add 15, 16, and 17).* . . . . $ 995.00
19. Levying officer:
    (a) Add daily interest from date of writ *(at the legal rate on 15)* (not on GC 6103.5 fees) of . . . . $ 0.27
    (b) Pay directly to court costs included in 11 and 17 (GC 6103.5, 68511.3, CCP 699.520(i)). . . . . $
20. ☐ The amounts called for in items 11-19 are different for each debtor. These amounts are stated for each debtor on Attachment 20.

Issued on *(date):* 9/23/XXXX   Clerk, by _____ , Deputy

NOTICE TO PERSON SERVED: SEE NEXT PAGE FOR IMPORTANT INFORMATION.

Page 1 of 2

Form Approved for Optional Use
Judicial Council of California
EJ-130 [Rev. January 1, 2006]

WRIT OF EXECUTION

Code of Civil Procedure, §§ 699.520, 712.010, 715.010
Government Code, § 6103.5
www.courtinfo.ca.gov

You will find a blank copy of this form in the FORMS section of this book and in Eviction Forms Creator.

just the writ. The two have such closely corresponding elements that we will cover only the writ here because it is used throughout the state. The application is used selectively. If you know how to complete a writ, you know how to complete an application.

The writ should look pretty familiar to you by now. It's a Judicial Council form.

You already know how to fill in most of the upper third of the form. Go to it.

Notice that an email address is optional. You might want to ask your court clerk why you ought to include it. Will she use it to communicate with you? If she says she will and if you have an email address, include it. It might speed up communications between the court and you. Otherwise, don't bother to include it.

Check the "JUDGMENT CREDITOR" box under your name.

Check the "EXECUTION" box, the "POSSESSION" box, and the "REAL PROPERTY" box just above item 1 to indicate what specific type of writ this is. It's a "Writ of Execution (Money Judgment), as well as a Writ of Possession of Real Property."

In section 1, enter your county's name.

In section 3, enter your own name and check the "judgment creditor" box there.

In section 4, enter each judgment debtor's name and address separately, one per box (there's space enough for two more on the back of the form).

Skip section 5 for right now unless you know already when the judgment was entered.

Skip section 6. Yours is not a renewed judgment.

Check box 7a to show that you're not requesting any sale at this time.

Skip section 8.

Check box 9 to indicate that you have described your property on the back of the writ in item 24e.

Skip section 10.

That's all you can do on the front of the writ at this time. The rest has to wait until you get the actual judgment.

Now turn the writ over.

Enter the names of the lead plaintiff and the lead defendant plus the case number.

Notice that section 21 corresponds to section 4. Section 22 corresponds to section 7b. Section 23 corresponds to section 8. Section 24 corresponds to section 9.

Check box 24 and enter the date when you filed the complaint.

Check box 24a and check *either* 24a(1) *or* 24a(2), whichever one applies.

No matter which one you checked, 24a(1) or 24a(2), you must indicate in 24a(2)(a) the daily rental value, a figure you have probably committed to memory by now.

Make sure you complete 24e, too. "Description" here is merely the address of the property.

Step 9. (Alternative 2). Prepare Request, Judgment, and Writ.

When following alternative 2, make these *changes* in the request, judgment, and writ forms from the way they're shown here in the samples (see "very important" note on page 75).

On the request, check the "CLERK'S JUDGMENT" box near the top rather than the "COURT JUDGMENT" box, check boxes 1e and 1e(1) rather than 1d, enter either nothing or the words "possession only" in section 2 and nothing in 7a through 7f.

Ask the court clerk whether you should use the Judicial Council's Judgment–Unlawful Detainer form or a Judgment (Default) by Clerk form prepared by the local judicial district.

You have already seen the Judicial Council's two-page judgment form. Alternative 1 used it.

Let's assume that you can use it for alternative 2. Of the six boxes in the upper third of the form, the sample shows two checked. You should check three: "By Clerk," "By Default," and "Possession Only." Check box 1 and 1d; check no boxes under 1e.

On the back side, change only one thing near the top of the form. Check the "THE CLERK" box rather than "THE COURT" box.

On the writ, check the "POSSESSION" and "REAL PROPERTY" boxes just above item 1, and omit the amounts on lines 11-18.

Remember now, everything else on the forms should be the same as on the samples.

In addition, you may have to make up a simple application to use CCP §1169 or use a form prepared by your court for this purpose (ask the clerk). If you have to make one up, type the following on a piece of typing paper:

```
Court Clerk, [name & address of
the court]
```

EJ-130

PLAINTIFF: Lester Landlord	CASE NUMBER:
DEFENDANT: Richard Renter	1234567890

—Items continued from page 1—

21. ☐ **Additional judgment debtor** *(name and last known address):*

22. ☐ **Notice of sale** has been requested by *(name and address):*

23. ☐ **Joint debtor** was declared bound by the judgment (CCP 989-994)
    a. on *(date):*   a. on *(date):*
    b. name and address of joint debtor: b. name and address of joint debtor:

    c. ☐ additional costs against certain joint debtors *(itemize):*

24. ☒ *(Writ of Possession or Writ of Sale)* **Judgment** was entered for the following:
    a. ☒ Possession of real property: The complaint was filed on *(date):*   9/16/XXXX
         (Check (1) or (2)):
         (1) ☐ The Prejudgment Claim of Right to Possession was served in compliance with CCP 415.46.
                  The judgment includes all tenants, subtenants, named claimants, and other occupants of the premises
         (2) ☒ The Prejudgment Claim of Right to Possession was NOT served in compliance with CCP 415.46.
             (a) $26.00   was the daily rental value on the date the complaint was filed.
             (b) The court will hear objections to enforcement of the judgment under CCP 1174.3 on the following
                 dates *(specify)*:
    b. ☐ Possession of personal property.
        ☐ If delivery cannot be had, then for the value *(itemize in 9e)* specified in the judgment or supplemental order
    c. ☐ Sale of personal property.
    d. ☐ Sale of real property.
    e. Description of property: 458 Sweet Street
                        Littletown, California 91111

— NOTICE TO PERSON SERVED —

WRIT OF EXECUTION OR SALE. Your rights and duties are indicated on the accompanying Notice of Levy (Form EJ-150).
WRIT OF POSSESSION OF PERSONAL PROPERTY. If the levying officer is not able to take custody of the property, the levying officer will make a demand upon you for the property. If custody is not obtained following demand, the judgment may be enforced as a money judgment for the value of the property specified in the judgment or in a supplemental order.
WRIT OF POSSESSION OF REAL PROPERTY. If the premises are not vacated within five days after the date of service on the occupant or, if service is by posting, within five days after service on you, the levying officer will remove the occupants from the real property and place the judgment creditor in possession of the property. Except for a mobile home, personal property remaining on the premises will be sold or otherwise disposed of in accordance with CCP 1174 unless you or the owner of the property pays the judgment creditor the reasonable cost of storage and takes possession of the personal property not later than 15 days after the time the judgment creditor takes possession of the premises.

▶ *A Claim of Right to Possession form accompanies this writ (unless the Summons was served in compliance with CCP 415.46).*

EJ-130 [Rev. January 1, 2006]   **WRIT OF EXECUTION**   Page 2 of 2

You will find a blank copy of this form in the FORMS section of this book and in Eviction Forms Creator.

```
Due to continued occupancy of
resident defendant, I herewith
make application for you to enter
the default of [defendant's name]
and immediately enter judgment
for restitution of the premises
located at [address] and issue a
writ of execution.
     [Plaintiff's Signature]
```

Step 9. (Alternative 3). Prepare Request, Judgment, and Writ.

To follow the third alternative, prepare one set of these same forms as outlined in step 9 (alternative 2) and prepare a second set to use for getting your money judgment *after* the tenants have been evicted (with the tenants gone, you can complete an accurate reckoning and account for their security deposit correctly). When preparing the second set, make them exactly like the samples shown for alternative 1. You needn't change a thing.

Step 9. (Alternative 4). Prepare Request, Judgment, and Declaration.

You are proceeding under CCP §585.4, also known as §585(d). Without ever appearing in court, you are seeking both restitution of your property and a judgment for the money your tenant owes you.

Prepare the Request for Entry of Default and the judgment forms as shown in the samples (see "very important" note on page 75).

You must also prepare a declaration for default judgment. In the declaration, you restate your case much as you first stated it in the complaint, testifying in writing to what you would have testified in court had you made a personal appearance, and you sign your name to this statement under penalty of perjury.

The Judicial Council has an optional three-page declaration form for this purpose. It's entitled Declaration for Default Judgment by Court. Since it's an optional form and more complex than it needs to be, ask the court clerk whether you must use it or whether you may use a simpler two-page alternative, a Declaration for Default Judgment in Lieu of Personal Testimony, submitted on pleading paper.

Use the simpler declaration if possible. You'll find one in the FORMS section of this book. It's on pleading paper with blanks for you to fill in. It's simple enough for you to complete without even following a sample.

The Judicial Council declaration is not quite so simple. It appears here as a sample.

If you use it, pay close attention to what it says in items 4b and 4c about attaching the rental agreement and what it says in items 5e and 5f about attaching an agreement for change in terms. It says that you may attach the original documents to the original complaint or to the original declaration, but you may not attach copies of these documents without including a declaration and order to admit the copy.

In other words, you first need to ask for and receive a judge's approval before you can attach the copies to the declaration.

Rather than prepare and file even more paperwork, attach the originals to the declaration if you haven't already attached them to the complaint. That will save you needless work.

If you must prepare a declaration and order to admit the copy of the rental agreement or of the agreement for change in terms, go to Appendix A, study the Application and Declaration for Order of Posting of Summons and the Order for Posting of Summons, and create similar documents. The declaration should state under penalty of perjury that the copies are true copies of the originals. The order should state that the judge accepts the plaintiff's declaration and orders the copies to be treated as originals.

Note that 5b(1), 5e, and 5f in the Declaration for Default Judgment by Court refer to an agreement for change in terms, not to a notice for change in terms. An agreement requires signatures of all affected parties. A notice does not. If you changed a tenant's rent, you likely changed it with a notice, and you would check the following boxes, 5, 5b, 5b(2), 5d, and 18. If you changed a tenant's rent more than once, you would check all of those boxes plus 5a, and you would attach form MC-025, Attachment to Judicial Council Form, and call it Attachment 5a. It would give a history of rent changes.

Look now at section 6, which covers the notice, and 8, which covers the proof of service of the notice. Check box 6d and either of its two subordinate boxes because you must attach the notice or a copy of the notice to the complaint or to the declaration. The same goes for the proof

UD-116

ATTORNEY OR PARTY WITHOUT ATTORNEY *(Name, state bar number, and address):*
Lester Landlord & Leslie Landlord
123 Neat Street
Littletown, CA 91111

FOR COURT USE ONLY

TELEPHONE NO.: 555-123-4567   FAX NO. *(Optional):* 555-123-4568
E-MAIL ADDRESS *(Optional)*:
ATTORNEY FOR *(Name)*: Plaintiff in Propria Persona

SUPERIOR COURT OF CALIFORNIA, COUNTY OF Saddleback
STREET ADDRESS: 100 State Street
MAILING ADDRESS:
CITY AND ZIP CODE: Littletown 91111
BRANCH NAME:

PLAINTIFF: Lester Landlord
Leslie Landlord

DEFENDANT: Richard Renter, Rose Renter

DECLARATION FOR DEFAULT JUDGMENT BY COURT
(Unlawful Detainer—Code Civil Proc., § 585(d))

CASE NUMBER:
1234567890

1. My name is *(specify)*: Lester Landlord
   a. [X] I am the plaintiff in this action.
   b. I am
      (1) [X] an owner of the property   (3) [ ] an agent of the owner
      (2) [ ] a manager of the property (4) [ ] other *(specify)*:

2. The property concerning this action is located at *(street address, apartment number, city, and county)*:
   456 Sweet Street, Littletown 91111, Saddleback County

3. Personal knowledge. I personally know the facts stated in this declaration and, if sworn as a witness, could testify competently thereto. I am personally familiar with the rental or lease agreement, defendant's payment record, the condition of the property, and defendant's conduct.

4. Agreement was [X] written [ ] oral as follows:
   a. On or about *(date)*: 12/14/XXXX   defendant *(name each)*: Richard Renter
      Rose Renter
      (1) agreed to rent the property for a [X] month-to-month tenancy [ ] other tenancy *(specify)*:
      (2) agreed to pay rent of $ 700.00 payable [X] monthly [ ] other *(specify frequency)*:
      with rent due on the [X] first of the month [ ] other day *(specify)*:
   b. [X] Original agreement is attached *(specify)*: [ ] to the original complaint.
      [ ] to the *Application for Immediate Writ of Possession.* [X] to this declaration, labeled Exhibit 4b.
   c. [ ] Copy of agreement with a declaration and order to admit the copy is attached *(specify)*:
      [ ] to the *Application for Immediate Writ of Possession.* [ ] to this declaration, labeled Exhibit 4c.

5. [X] Agreement changed.
   a. [ ] More than one change in rent amount *(specify history of all rent changes and effective dates up to the last rent change)* on *Attachment 5a* (form MC-025).
   b. [X] Change in rent amount *(specify the last rent change)*. The rent was changed from $ 700 to $ 780 , which became effective on *(date)*: 7/1/XXXX and was made
      (1) [ ] by agreement of the parties and subsequent payment of such rent.
      (2) [X] by service on defendant of a notice of change in terms pursuant to Civil Code section 827 *(check item 5d)*.
      (3) [ ] pursuant to a written agreement of the parties for change in terms *(check item 5e or 5f)*.
   c. [ ] Change in rent due date. Rent was changed, payable in advance, due on *(specify day)*:
   d. [X] A copy of the notice of change in terms is attached to this declaration, labeled Exhibit 5d.
   e. [ ] Original agreement for change in terms is attached *(specify)*: [ ] to the original complaint.
      [ ] to the *Application for Immediate Writ of Possession.* [ ] to this declaration, labeled Exhibit 5e.
   f. [ ] Copy of agreement for change in terms with a a declaration and order to admit the copy is attached *(specify)*:
      [ ] to the *Application for Immediate Writ of Possession.* [ ] to this declaration, labeled Exhibit 5f.

Page 1 of 3

Form Approved for Optional Use
Judicial Council of California
UD-116 [New January 1, 2003]

DECLARATION FOR DEFAULT JUDGMENT BY COURT
(Unlawful Detainer—Code Civil Proc., § 585(d))

Code of Civil Procedure, § 585(d)

You will find a blank copy of this form in the FORMS section of this book and in Eviction Forms Creator.

PLAINTIFF: Lester Landlord	CASE NUMBER:
DEFENDANT: Richard Renter	1234567890

6. Notice to quit.
  a. [X] Defendant was served with a
    (1) [X] 3-day notice to pay rent or quit   (4) [ ] 3-day notice to quit
    (2) [ ] 3-day notice to perform covenants or quit   (5) [ ] 30-day notice to quit
    (3) [ ] other *(specify):*
  b. [X] The 3-day notice to pay rent or quit demanded rent due in the amount of *(specify):* $ 730.00   for the rental period
    beginning on *(date)* 9/1/XXXX   and ending on *(date)* 9/30/XXXX
  c. [X] The total rent demanded in the 3-day notice under item 6b is different from the agreed rent in item 4a(2) *(specify history of dates covered by the 3-day notice and any partial payments received to arrive at the balance)* on Attachment 6c *(form MC-025).*
  d. [X] The original or copy of the notice specified in item 6a is attached to *(specify):* [ ] the original complaint.
    [X] this declaration, labeled Exhibit 6d. *(The original or a copy of the notice MUST be attached to this declaration if not attached to the original complaint.)*

7. Service of notice.
  a. The notice was served on defendant *(name each):*   Richard Renter
    (1) [X] personally on *(date):* 9/12/XXXX
    (2) [ ] by substituted service, including a copy mailed to the defendant, on *(date):*
    (3) [ ] by posting and mailing on *(date mailed):*
  b. [ ] A prejudgment claim of right to possession was served on the occupants pursuant to Code of Civil Procedure section 415.46.

8. Proof of service of notice. The original or copy of the proof of service of the notice in item 6a is attached to *(specify):*
  a. [ ] the original complaint.
  b. [X] this declaration, labeled Exhibit 8b. *(The original or copy of the proof of service MUST be attached to this declaration if not attached to the original complaint.)*

9. Notice expired. On *(date):* 9/15/XXXX   the notice in item 6 expired at the end of the day and defendant failed to comply with the requirements of the notice by that date. No money has been received and accepted after the notice expired.

10. The fair rental value of the property is $ 26.00   per day, calculated as follows:
  a. [ ] (rent per month) x (0.03288) *(12 months divided by 365 days)*
  b. [X] rent per month divided by 30
  c. [ ] other valuation *(specify):*

11. Possession. The defendant
  a. [ ] vacated the premises on *(date):*
  b. [X] continues to occupy the property on *(date of this declaration):*   9/23/XXXX

12. [ ] Holdover damages. Declarant has calculated the holdover damages as follows:
  a. Damages demanded in the complaint began on *(date):*
  b. Damages accrued through *(date specified in item 11).*
  c. Number of days that damages accrued *(count days using the dates in items 12a and 12b):*
  d. Total holdover damages *((daily rental value in item 10) x (number of days in item 12c)):* $

13. [ ] Reasonable attorney fees are authorized in the lease or rental agreement pursuant to paragraph *(specify):*
  and reasonable attorney fees for plaintiff's attorney *(name):*   are $

14. [X] Court costs in this case, including the filing fee, are $ 205.00

You will find a blank copy of this form in the FORMS section of this book and in Eviction Forms Creator.

PLAINTIFF: Lester Landlord	CASE NUMBER:
DEFENDANT: Richard Renter	1234567890

15. [X] Declarant requests a judgment on behalf of plaintiff for:
    a. [X] A money judgment as follows:

(1) [X] Past-due rent *(item 6b)*	$	730.00
(2) [ ] Holdover damages *(item 12d)*	$	
(3) [ ] Attorney fees *(item 13)**	$	
(4) [X] Costs *(item 14)*	$	205.00
(5) [ ] Other *(specify):* Interest Special Damages	$	
(6) **TOTAL JUDGMENT**	$	935.00

* [ ] Attorney fees are to be paid by *(name)* only.

    b. [X] Possession of the premises in item 2 *(check only if a clerk's judgment for possession was **not** entered).*
    c. [X] Cancellation of the rental agreement.   [ ] Forfeiture of the lease.

I declare under penalty of perjury under the laws of the State of California that the foregoing is true and correct.

Date: 9/23/XXXX

Lester Landlord	*Lester Landlord*
(TYPE OR PRINT NAME)	(SIGNATURE OF DECLARANT)

Summary of Exhibits

16. [X] Exhibit 4b: Original rental agreement.

17. [ ] Exhibit 4c: Copy of rental agreement with declaration and order to admit the copy.

18. [X] Exhibit 5d: Copy of notice of change in terms.

19. [ ] Exhibit 5e: Original agreement for change of terms.

20. [ ] Exhibit 5f: Copy of agreement for change in terms with declaration and order to admit copy.

21. [X] Exhibit 6d: Original or copy of the notice to quit under item 6a *(MUST be attached to this declaration if it is not attached to original complaint).*

22. [X] Exhibit 8b: Original or copy of proof of service of notice in item 6a *(MUST be attached to this declaration if it is not attached to original complaint).*

23. [ ] Other exhibits *(specify number and describe):*

UD-115 [New January 1, 2003]   **DECLARATION FOR DEFAULT JUDGMENT BY COURT**   Page 3 of 3
(Unlawful Detainer—Code Civil Proc., § 585(d))

You will find a blank copy of this form in the FORMS section of this book and in Eviction Forms Creator.

of service of the notice. Check box 8a or 8b. If you are attaching the notice and the proof to the declaration, also check boxes 21 and 22.

The rest of the declaration is self-explanatory, especially for someone who has already completed a complaint.

Remember that the declaration enables the court to issue a judgment without your appearing in court. It should include enough information for the judge to give you the judgment you want without delay.

Step 9B (Alternatives 1, 2, 3, & 4). If Asked to Do So by the Court Clerk, Prepare and Submit a Declaration of Plaintiff in Support of Writ of Possession.

If there is any discrepancy between the daily rental value as given on the complaint (at item 11) and again on the Writ of Execution (at item 24a.[2a]), you may be asked to complete a Declaration of Plaintiff in Support of Writ of Possession. This is nothing more than a statement of the daily rental value. There is no form for it as such, and I have not included one here because it is so simple and because you likely will never need one.

On the off-chance that you might need one, however, here's what you do.

Make a copy of the blank pleading paper in the FORMS section, and type everything on the upper half of the page to correspond to the declaration shown on the Order for Posting in Appendix A, except that instead of typing "ORDER FOR POSTING OF SUMMONS (CCP 415.45)," type "DECLARATION OF PLAINTIFF IN SUPPORT OF WRIT OF POSSESSION."

Then, beginning on line 15, type the following (double-spaced, of course):

```
PLAINTIFF declares as follows:
The daily rental value on the
date the complaint for unlawful
detainer was filed was $_____.
I declare under penalty of per-
jury that the foregoing is true
and correct.
Executed on _____ at
_____, California.
[Plaintiff's Signature]
```

Step 10 (Alternatives 1, 2, 3, & 4). Mail Request to Tenant.

Mail one copy of the Request for Entry of Default to the tenant. It need only be mailed before the original is entered by the clerk. It need not be received by the tenant before you proceed further.

Step 11 (Alternative 1). Prove Summons Service; File Request.

Whether or not you are able to get into court on the sixth day following service of the summons and complaint, bring the Request for Entry of Default and the Proof of Service of Summons, with you to the courthouse. Show the clerk the proof where the process server has indicated that your summons and complaint have been served. If it indicates that at least five days have passed since service on the defendants, your case will be listed on an upcoming docket calendar. Then the clerk will ask you to hand over the Request for Entry of Default. Having surrendered it, you are ready for your day in court, whenever it is.

Step 11 (Alternatives 2 & 3). Prove Service of 3-Day Notice and Summons; File Request, Judgment, and Writ.

Bring the request, judgment, writ, and written application (if required), as well as the Proof of Service of Summons and the 3-day notice, with you to the courthouse. Tell the clerk that you want a quickie eviction per CCP §1169. Also tell her whether you want to go to court later for a money judgment.

She'll scrutinize your papers with a well-trained eye and tell you whether everything's in order. She'll be looking for consistency primarily. Are all your dates and money amounts correct throughout the paperwork? Is everything legible? If it is, she may make the necessary entries in her books and give you the writ right then and there, or she may ask you to return later. Some clerks are so accommodating that they will let you leave a check with them for the sheriff or marshal and some simple instructions to him to evict your tenant (pick up the proper form from the sheriff or marshal's office or use the one in the FORMS section for this purpose); in that case, you won't have to return at all; the clerk will see that the papers are passed along.

Step 11 (Alternative 4).
Prove Summons Service; File Request; Give Clerk Request, Judgment, and Declaration.

Gather up your papers and take them with you to the courthouse. Tell the clerk that you want to transfer the file to the judge, and show her that you have complied with the requirements regarding service of the summons and complaint, that you have waited five days, and that you have completed a declaration for default judgment.

Give her the request, the judgment, and the declaration. Also, be sure you give her a copy of the rental agreement if you elected to omit it from the complaint as an exhibit. The judge may want to see it to help him determine the merits of your case.

To find out how long the judge will take to examine your case and render judgment, ask when you might expect to hear from him and when you should call back if you fail to hear anything.

Step 12 (Alternatives 1 & 3B).
Appear in Court.

Bring the proper judgment form and the writ with you to court, together with anything pertinent from your files on this particular tenant, especially the rental agreement if you didn't attach it to the complaint. Arrive at least ten minutes before your court time. Generally, the courtroom clerk arrives early to see who is ready to appear, and you may approach her to indicate that you have the proper judgment form partially filled out and would like to have it completed as soon as the judge renders the verdict, so you can proceed with the eviction. The courtroom clerk will usually take the judgment form from you because she will otherwise have to do the whole thing herself, and you can then take a seat to wait for your case to come up.

Now you are in for a surprise, one of the few pleasant surprises that landlords and landladies can ever expect in this whole distasteful process. Unlawful detainers, praise some solon or other, are heard first, before all those other civil cases. You won't have to spend hours in court listening to Mabel and Clarence argue over custody of the family cow; you won't even have to hear the rib-

ald details of how the housewife thought she was paying the plumber with her charms, that is, until she got his bill and learned that she was being charged not only for travel time and work time but for the entire time he was there as well. Evictions take precedence over other civil cases. They are entitled to what the legal world calls "summary proceedings."

When your case comes up, the judge will call you forward and you will have to swear that you will tell no lies. During the oath, the judge will be reading your complaint. Then he will ask you whatever questions come to mind. He may ask to see the rental agreement if it wasn't attached to the complaint as an exhibit; he may ask you why you're praying for such a big judgment; or he may ask what period of time is covered by the sum of money demanded in your complaint. Be prepared to provide him with this information if he should ask for it. Know exactly how much is owed as of the date when you are in court and also as of the date when you can reasonably expect the eviction to be carried out, which is usually six days hence. Consult calendar 3 at the end of this chapter.

Step 12 (Alternatives 2 & 3A).
Skip to Step 15.

Proceed directly to Step 15; lucky you, no appearing in court and no waiting!

Step 12 (Alternative 4). Wait.

By completing your declaration and transferring it to the judge, you have already done the equivalent of appearing in court. Now you'll just have to wait for the judge to reply with the judgment. If you don't like waiting, use another alternative and you'll undoubtedly complete everything a little more quickly.

Step 13 (Alternatives 1 & 3B).
Get the Judgment.

The judge will consider for a time and then indicate the amount of judgment granted. Thank him and go to the court clerk's table in the courtroom to pick up your completed judgment form.

Step 13 (Alternative 4).
Get the Judgment.

The court will send you the judgment by mail. If it doesn't arrive by the time the court clerk told you to expect it, call the clerk and ask about it. Tell her you haven't received it yet, and ask her whether you may come down to the courthouse and pick up a copy so you can proceed with your unlawful detainer.

Step 14 (Alternatives 1 & 3B). Fill in and File the Writ.

Your sweating's over, but don't go home yet. You still have a few things to do. Find a flat spot where you can do a little typing; get out the writs which you've already partially filled out, carbon paper (make two copies), and your portable Smith-Corona.

In item 5 of the writ, put the date when the judgment was entered.

In item 11, put the dollar amount of the judgment which was awarded to you by the court.

In item 12, put the sheriff or marshal's fee for posting the Writ of Possession and the Notice to Vacate, as well as for actually evicting the tenant, unless you already included them under costs in the judgment.

Put the sum of items 11 and 12 on line 13.

In item 14, put any credits not already reflected in the judgment; and on line 15, subtract those credits from line 13.

Skip line 16 unless you are filing a claim for interest by affidavit.

In item 17, include the fee for issuing the writ unless you already accounted for it under costs in the judgment.

Total lines 15, 16, and 17 on line 18.

The legal rate of interest for judgments in California is 10%. Multiply 10% times line 15, and divide by 365 to get the daily interest owed to you on your judgment. Put that in item 19a.

Put nothing in item 19b; it's for the court to use to collect costs waived initially for public agencies and indigents.

Check box 20 only if there's a difference in the amounts owed to you by each of your debtors and attach an explanation if there is.

Date the writ in the "Issued on (date)" box. Now turn the writ over.

If you haven't done so already, enter the names of the lead plaintiff and the lead defendant plus the case number at the top; check boxes 24 and 24a; give the date when the complaint was filed; check either box 24a(1) or 24a(2) as appropriate, and state the daily rental value in 24a(2)(a).

In 24e, if you haven't done so already, put the

street address, unit number, city, state, and zip code. That's it! That's all!

Take the judgment and the writ to the clerk's office and pay the fee to file the writ. Ask the clerk to check your figures. If any of your figures are wrong, use the correction fluid in your lay lawyer's kit to mask the errors and then make the corrections.

Step 14 (Alternative 4). Fill in and File the Writ.

Once you have received the judgment, you'll have to fill out a Writ of Execution so the sheriff or marshal can act. Fill it out following the directions for alternative 1 above. Take it to the court and file it. Then proceed to follow the remaining steps the same as you would have had you appeared in court personally.

Step 15. Set the Eviction and Arrange Service of the Notice to Vacate.

You have now completed all the court-related work to regain possession of your property, but you must do one more thing to carry out the judgment. You must see the sheriff or marshal and give him the authority (that's just what the writ is) to take over your property, evict the inhabitants, and return the property to you. Naturally, you pay for this service, but it's well worth the fee, and it's chargeable to the tenants on the writ, for whatever that may be worth to you.

Visit the sheriff or marshal's office soon after you leave the clerk's office, and hand over the Writ of Execution original as well as your copies. Normally the deputy will hand you a simple form which lists your instructions to the sheriff or marshal, but you probably won't have to fill the whole thing out. A signature and some verbal instructions are usually sufficient to get the eviction set.

At last you're through!

If your court appointment was for 9 a.m., you should now be at this point by 9:30. After what you've been through, since it's hardly martini time, you can decently celebrate at the corner watering hole with a midmorning screwdriver or bloody mary. Light up a big black cigar, too, an expensive one, the likes of which you couldn't afford when your first offspring came into the world. You've earned it.

Step 16. Serve the Notice to Vacate.

The sheriff or marshal should be able to serve and/or post the Writ of Possession and the Notice to Vacate the very same day. At the same time he also leaves a copy of the form, Claim of Right to Possession and Notice of Hearing (more on it in a moment). He will set the eviction date and time, most likely six days later, and he will tell you that you'll have to appear at the designated time fully prepared to change the locks on the doors after the tenants have been evicted and the

the eviction.

In some areas the sheriff or marshal appears automatically on the day set for the eviction, and in other areas he waits for some word from you. Ask what the practice is in your area and do what you must do to get him there.

Step 17. Evict the Tenant.

• THE RECKONING—If your tenants or their possessions are still there when you and the sheriff or marshal arrive, they will be put out bodily, if necessary, and the unit will be posted with an impressive-looking notice (see the front

place has been posted.

According to CCP §715.040, if the sheriff or marshal doesn't serve the Writ of Possession within three normal business days (excluding weekends and legal holidays) after it's turned over to him, you may retrieve it and have it served by a registered process server.

What tenants usually do once they have seen the handwriting on the door is simply move out. Some of the more contrary ones will stay until the very last possible moment and even past it, always testing the limits of the law.

Keep track of your tenant's movements if you can, so you can notify the sheriff or marshal if the tenant does move out before the time set for

cover of this book) saying that it has been returned to your possession and that the tenants may not go inside without your permission. If they do, they will be subject to arrest.

While the sheriff or marshal is posting this notice, you should be changing the locks unless you have any reason to believe that the tenant might break into the place to recover his possessions after you change the locks. In that case, refrain from changing them now. Don't risk broken windows or a broken door just to keep the tenant's possessions. They can't be worth that much. Let him come and get them. Remember that the sheriff or marshal isn't going to remain there guarding the place simply because you have regained full rights to it, and remember that you can always call upon the police to remove the tenant if he tries any funny business after this.

Once the sheriff or marshal posts that notice and escorts the tenant off the premises, your civil action is at an end. His returning to the property after that becomes a criminal matter.

• CLAIM OF RIGHT TO POSSESSION— As mentioned previously, the California Supreme Court's poorly conceived decision in the Arrieta case prevents the sheriff or marshal from evicting any adult who isn't named in the writ and who claims a right to possession on the date you started your unlawful detainer action *unless* you elected to use the prejudgment claim procedure when you served the summons and complaint.

Ordinarily, tenants first learn of their "Arrieta rights" when the sheriff or marshal gives them a blank copy of the Claim of Right to Possession and Notice of Hearing form (the sheriff or marshal supplies the form) at the same time he is serving them with the Writ of Possession and the Notice to Vacate (Step 16).

To some wily tenants this presents still another opportunity to take advantage of the system and remain right where they are at your expense, and there's nothing you can do about it legally. Neither arguing with the tenants nor hollering at the evicting officer will do any good.

If somebody claims to be a "nonparty occupant," that is, a person occupying the premises who was not a party to the unlawful detainer, he has every right to make a claim. He does have to make a formal written claim, however. He can't just sweet-talk the evicting officer and thumb his nose at you.

Here's how the claim procedure works (CCP §715.010 and §1174.3), and here's what you and the claimant do.

The claimant has to complete the claim form and bring it to the court or to the sheriff or marshal's office or, at the very least, present it to the evicting officer on the day set for the eviction. Within 48 hours, the claimant must then submit a filing fee to the court (just as you did when you first filed your complaint) or a *forma pauperis* (a sworn statement that he is too poor to pay the fee) *and* pay the court the equivalent of fifteen days rent. If the court receives all this, the clerk files the claim and sets a hearing not less than five days nor more than fifteen days later.

If the claimant submits nothing to the court within 48 hours of his having presented the claim, the court denies the claim automatically and orders the sheriff or marshal to evict all occupants within five days.

If the claimant submits the filing fee or the *forma pauperis* but not the equivalent of fifteen days rent, the hearing is set on the fifth day following the filing. In either case, the court will notify you of the hearing date. Because time is short, a clerk will usually mail you a notice and phone you.

You must, of course, appear at the hearing prepared to prove that the claimant is a liar and not a nonparty occupant, and the claimant must be there to prove that he is telling the truth. If the court denies the claim (95% are denied), it orders the sheriff or marshal to evict all occupants within five days. If the court grants the claim, it then considers your summons and complaint to have been amended to include the claimant as a defendant, and it also considers the claimant to have been served with the notice which started the action, as well as with the summons and complaint. You don't have to do anything but wait. The claimant then has the usual five days in which to file an answer.

If the claimant fails to file an answer, you must prepare and file a Request for Entry of Default, a Judgment by Default, and a Writ of Execution (Steps 9-11), and then continue through Step 17. When preparing these papers, merely add the claimant's name to those of the other defendants even though the other defendants have already been eliminated. If the tenant does file an answer, you must request a trial and handle the matter as outlined in chapter 10.

By the way, the fifteen days of rent money which the claimant paid to the court goes back to the tenant if the claim is granted. If it is not granted, you will receive that portion of the money which covers the days during which the eviction was delayed, and the tenant gets the rest.

Whereas tenants have little to lose by pressing an Arrieta claim, you have a lot to lose. Just remember, though, that you don't have *everything* to lose in this situation. It is aggravating. It is going to take more of your time and cost you more money in added fees and lost rent. That's for sure. But it's not the end of the world. Don't get discouraged. Don't even think of taking the law into your own hands. Be patient. Let the process run its course.

ATTORNEY OR PARTY WITHOUT ATTORNEY *(Name and Address)*
Lester Landlord & Leslie Landlord
123 Neat Street
Littletown, CA 91111

TELEPHONE NO.: 555-123-4567

FOR COURT USE ONLY

ATTORNEY FOR *(Name)* Plaintiff in Propria Persona

Insert name of court and name of judicial district and branch court, if any:
Saddleback Superior Court

PLAINTIFF/PETITIONER: Lester Landlord
                     Leslie Landlord
DEFENDANT/RESPONDENT: Richard Renter, Rose Renter

REQUEST FOR DISMISSAL
- [ ] Personal Injury, Property Damage, or Wrongful Death
  - [ ] Motor Vehicle   [ ] Other
- [ ] Family Law
- [ ] Eminent Domain
- [X] Other *(specify)*: Unlawful Detainer

CASE NUMBER:
1234567890

— A conformed copy will not be returned by the clerk unless a method of return is provided with the document. —

1. TO THE CLERK: Please dismiss this action as follows:

a. (1) [ ] With prejudice   (2) [X] Without prejudice

b. (1) [X] Complaint   (2) [ ] Petition
   (3) [ ] Cross-complaint filed by *(name)*:   on *(date)*:
   (4) [ ] Cross-complaint filed by *(name)*:   on *(date)*:
   (5) [ ] Entire action of all parties and all causes of action
   (6) [ ] Other *(specify)* :*

Date: 10/15/XXXX

Lester Landlord
. . . .
(TYPE OR PRINT NAME OF __ ATTORNEY [X] PARTY WITHOUT ATTORNEY)

▶ *Lester Landlord*
                                              (SIGNATURE)
Attorney or party without attorney for:
[X] Plaintiff/Petitioner   [ ] Defendant/Respondent
[ ] Cross-complainant

* If dismissal requested is of specified parties only, of specified causes of action only, or of specified cross-complaints only, so state and identify the parties, causes of action, or cross-complaints to be dismissed.

2. TO THE CLERK: Consent to the above dismissal is hereby given.**
Date: 10/15/XXXX

Lester Landlord
. . . .
(TYPE OR PRINT NAME OF [ ] ATTORNEY [X] PARTY WITHOUT ATTORNEY)

▶ *Lester Landlord*
                                              (SIGNATURE)
Attorney or party without attorney for:
[X] Plaintiff/Petitioner   [ ] Defendant/Respondent
[ ] Cross-complainant

**If a cross-complaint--or Response (Family Law) seeking affirmative relief--is on file, the attorney for cross-complainant (respondent) must sign this consent if required by Code of Civil Procedure section 581(i) or (j).

(To be completed by clerk)
3. [ ] Dismissal entered as requested on *(date)*:
4. [ ] Dismissal entered on *(date)*:   as to only *(name)*:
5. [ ] Dismissal **not entered** as requested for the following reasons *(specify)*:

6. [ ] a. Attorney or party without attorney notified on *(date)*:
       b. Attorney or party without attorney not notified. Filing party failed to provide
          [ ] a copy to conform   [ ] means to return conformed copy

Date: Clerk, by _____, Deputy

Form Adopted by the
Judicial Council of California
982 (a)(5) [Rev. January 1, 1997]

REQUEST FOR DISMISSAL

Code of Civil Procedure, § 581 et seq
Cal. Rules of Court, rules 383, 1233

You will find a blank copy of this form in the FORMS section of this book and in Eviction Forms Creator.

When it has run its course, write your state legislators about what you've been through. Explain the unfairness of Arrieta claims and suggest alternatives. What our legislators have come up with so far, the Prejudgment Claim of Right to Possession procedure, is a beginning, but it needs improving. For starters, the prejudgment procedure should allow five rather than ten days for a claimant to file, and it should require that the filing of the claim and the response to the summons and complaint be handled concurrently, not sequentially. Isn't that fair? Sure it's fair. It treats the non-named resident the same as a named resident, and it doesn't penalize those landlords who elect to use the prejudgment procedure by adding ten days to their unlawful detainer. Isn't an unlawful detainer supposed to be a summary action?

• LESSON—A final eviction notice on one door of an apartment building serves as a convincing lesson to other tenants that you know how to evict and that you will evict when necessary. Leave the notice on the door long enough for at least one other tenant to see it and then remove it yourself. The word will spread quickly.

Don't leave the notice up longer than an afternoon because you don't want other owners in the area to see it. They will wonder what's wrong with your building and will depreciate its value in their minds.

The final eviction notice on the door of a single-family dwelling should be removed as soon as the tenant's belongings are cleared out. It serves no useful purpose after that.

• COLLECTING YOUR MONEY JUDGMENT—See chapter 13.

• DISPOSING OF THE REMAINS—See chapter 14.

• FULFILLING ONE VERY IMPORTANT FINAL OBLIGATION—Whenever a tenant moves out, you have a legal obligation to return his entire deposit or provide a written accounting of what you did with it. If you fail to do so within twenty-one days, your tenant has every right to sue you for the deposit and for damages. Your having evicted the tenant does *not* relieve you of this obligation.

The tenant may have trashed your place when you evicted him, and the damages may have cost you a bundle to repair, much more than he ever gave you as a deposit, and you might think, quite naturally, that under these circumstances you shouldn't have to give him a written accounting at all. Wrong! Wrong! Wrong!

The law says that you must give an accounting of deposits to *every* tenant who vacates. "Every tenant" means every tenant, not just the ones you owe money to, not just the ones whose forwarding addresses you have available, not just the ones you hate to lose. Every tenant means the good ones, the bad ones, and the uglies.

Some landlords overlook this obligation because they can't understand why they should have to take the time to account for monies which they have no hope of recovering anyway. Such is the case most of the time, I'll grant you. But a law is a law, and you should comply with this law even when a tenant's departure is the result of an eviction.

Besides, when a tenant moves out and owes you money for damages, this accounting should serve as your itemized bill for what the tenant owes. You should be able to take this bill into small claims court and get a judgment against the tenant. If you haven't provided the tenant with an accounting as required by law, you cannot possibly win a small claims action to recover damages.

One landlord I know failed to give an accounting of deposits to an evicted tenant within twenty-one days because he couldn't assess all the damages within that period of time. When he finally did assess all the damages, he took the co-signer to small claims court. He produced evidence consisting of photos, documents, witnesses, and bills. His was an open-and-shut case, a sure thing, or so he thought. Then the co-signer told the judge that because the landlord had failed to provide a full accounting of the tenant's deposits as required by law within twenty-one days after the tenant vacated, the co-signer shouldn't have to pay a thing. The judge agreed with the co-signer. The landlord got nothing.

The twenty-one-day limitation is crucial in providing the accounting. Don't delay beyond the twenty-one days. If you can't complete the repairs within twenty-one days, make a reasonable estimate of what the costs should turn out to be and send the accounting off to the tenant. You can always quibble about the costs later if they become an issue.

Once you have prepared the accounting, send one copy to the tenant at his last known address, which may be the place you've evicted him from, and keep one copy for your files.

Dismissal

Every so often tenants will vacate shortly after you file the summons and complaint, that is, before you've had a chance to request a default judgment. What you do next will depend upon whether they still owe you any money after you deduct what they owe you from their deposits.

If they owe you any money, you should forge ahead and get the default judgment so you'll have some legal entitlement to this money and can try to collect it in the future or at the very least ding their credit. If they wind up owing you nothing, you should file a Request for Dismissal form to advise the court that it can close its books on the case.

Fill out the request as shown. Note that you have the option of dismissing with or without prejudice. You should dismiss "without prejudice." If you dismiss "with prejudice," you cannot file another complaint based on the same facts as the dismissed complaint. If you dismiss "without prejudice," you are free to file another complaint later based upon the same facts. Don't limit yourself. You never can tell what might happen when you're dealing with wily tenants.

Settlement Before Judgment

See chapter 10 for a discussion of "Settlement Before Trial." That discussion concerns how you might settle with your tenant after he files an answer to your complaint and before you go to trial.

What should you do if your tenant hasn't filed an answer to your complaint and he approaches you with an offer to settle before you get the default judgment?

First, listen to everything the tenant has to say. In filing an unlawful detainer lawsuit against him, you might just have awakened him out of his complacency, and he might now be ready to agree to terms which meant little to him before.

Second, understand that you and your tenant might each have something to gain by settling now. You might get everything or almost everything you wanted in the first place, and your tenant might get to stay right where he is without having to deal with a money judgment on his credit record.

Third, agree to nothing unless it is in writing and signed by both of you.

The settlement you reach may be expressed as an ordinary written agreement in plain English or as a Stipulation for Entry of Judgment, which may or may not be filed with the court (see chapter 10). A filed stipulation is better for you. It's "official."

If your tenant fails to comply with your settlement and you have a stipulated agreement, you don't have to go back into court to get him evicted. You can get the judgment and writ immediately and have him evicted in short order.

If your tenant fails to comply with your settlement and you have a plain English agreement, you will have to go into court to get a judgment, and then you may find that you cannot get a judgment because you have accepted partial payments. You may have to start all over again.

Whereas you should consider initiating an effort to settle when a tenant answers your complaint, you should not initiate an effort to settle when a tenant has failed to answer. Let your tenant do it. In filing the summons and complaint, you have already fired a salvo at your tenant. Now it's his turn to respond. If you initiate an effort to settle, you may hurt yourself in two ways—1) by appearing too eager and thereby weakening your bargaining position and 2) by calling his attention to the whole unlawful detainer matter and thereby increasing the likelihood that he will answer the complaint. Play your hand right.

If you do settle amicably with the tenant, file a Request for Dismissal.

- Study the entire eviction procedure carefully.
- Proceed with each step cautiously.
- Fill out each required form painstakingly.
- Observe the time restraints attentively.
- Pursue the eviction relentlessly.
- When the smoke clears, fulfill your obligations religiously.

AN UNCONTESTED UNLAWFUL DETAINER FOR NONPAYMENT OF RENT

(Step-by-Step Procedure, Alternative 1)

Step	Person	Place	Time
1. Prepare 3-Day Notice	You	Home	Anytime
2. Serve 3-Day Notice	You or third party	Tenant's dwelling or place of business	Same day as step 1
3. Prepare Summons and Complaint	You	Home	Late on 3d day after step 2
4. File Summons and Complaint	You	Court clerk's office	Early on 4th day after step 2*
5. Arrange service of Summons and Complaint	You	Sheriff or marshal's office	Same as step 4
6. Serve Summons and Complaint	Process server	Tenant's dwelling or place of business	Same day as step 4
7. Inquire about a response	You	Home (by phone to court clerk's office)	Late on 5th day after step 6**
8. Set court hearing time	You	Home (by phone to court clerk's office)	Same day as step 7
9. Prepare Request, Judgment, and Writ	You	Home	Same day as step 7
10. Mail Request to tenant	You	Mailbox	Same day as step 7
11. Prove Summons service; give clerk Request	You	Court clerk's office	Early on day after step 7
12. Appear in court	You	Courtroom	Same as step 11
13. Get Judgment	You	Courtroom	Same as step 11
14. Fill out and file Writ	You	Court clerk's office	Same as step 11
15. Set eviction date with sheriff or marshal; arrange service of Notice to Vacate	You	Sheriff or marshal's office	Same as step 11
16. Serve Notice to Vacate	Sheriff or marshal	Tenant's dwelling	Same as step 11
17. Evict tenant	Sheriff or marshal and you	Tenant's dwelling	6th day after step 16

*The third day following service of a 3-Day Notice to Pay Rent or Quit must be a "business day," that is, neither a weekend day nor a holiday. If it is not a business day, you must give the tenant a business day to pay before you file the Summons and Complaint.

**The fifth day permitted for the tenant to file an answer must be a day when the courts are open. When counting the five days, you may count Saturdays and Sundays *but not court holidays.*

Calendars for Determining the Important Days in an Uncontested Unlawful Detainer Which Begins with a 3-Day Notice to Pay Rent or Quit (Best Case)

Instructions

Find the day of the week when you served the 3-Day Notice to Pay Rent or Quit, and note the number which appears next to the "N." For Tuesday in calendar 1, it's a 3 (enlarged for easy identification). Then look for the next time a 3 appears. It's on Monday of the next week, and there's an "S" by it (it's enlarged, too). Being where it is, this "S3" means that if you serve a 3-Day Notice to Pay Rent or Quit on a Tuesday, you cannot file the Summons and Complaint until the following Monday. If you do file the Summons and Complaint on that Monday and have the tenant served the very same day, then the earliest you can get into court is on the following Tuesday, which is where the next 3 appears. It's by a "J" this time. If you go to court that day and you take care of all the paperwork afterward, including arranging with the sheriff or marshal for service of the Notice to Vacate, then the eviction will be set when the last 3 appears. It's by an "E," and it's on the following Monday. All together, then, the eviction will be completed on the twentieth day after the Tuesday when you served the 3-Day Notice to Pay Rent or Quit.

Now try following the 2's on calendar 1 to see what advantage there is in serving the notice on Monday. You save a few days, don't you? In fact, you save four days.

This first calendar should help you visualize the relationship of all the important days in an unlawful detainer action so long as everything goes according to schedule and there are no delays. You won't often be able to evict a tenant in a total of sixteen days from service of the 3-Day Notice to Pay Rent or Quit to the actual eviction, but you *can*. I know. I've done it. It does take some cooperation from the court clerk and some good luck. That I'll admit. But it can be done.

Do remember when you're thinking about the timetable for a nonpayment-of-rent eviction that the third day after service of the notice must be a business day. It may not be a weekend day or a holiday. If the third day falls on a Saturday, for example, you must give the tenant through the following Monday to pay up. You must not file your Summons and Complaint until Tuesday. If the third day falls on a Friday, though, you may file your Summons and Complaint on the following Monday.

Also remember that you may count Saturdays and Sundays *but not court holidays* among the five days you must wait for the tenant to file an answer to the Complaint, and the final day permitted for the answer must be a day when the courts are open.

Refer to calendar 2 if, for some reason, there is a delay in the procedure. For example, if the process server tried to serve the tenant with the Summons and Complaint on Monday but couldn't do it until Thursday, switch from calendar 1 to calendar 2 and follow the 5's to see what the next important days are. The court day would be the following Wednesday, and the eviction day would be the Tuesday after that.

Refer to calendar 3 if there is a delay in getting the Writ of Execution to the sheriff or marshal after the court hearing. If the writ is issued on Wednesday (J3), but you can't get it to the sheriff or marshal until Thursday (J4), follow the 4's, and you'll see that the eviction will be set for the following Wednesday. Simple, eh?

1. Calendar for Determining Summons Days, Judgment Days, and Evictions According to Notice Days

Sun	Mon	Tues	Wed	Thurs	Fri	Sat
N1	N2	**N3**	N4	N5; S1	N6; S2	N7
N8	N9; **S3**	S4-6	S7; J1	S8; J2	S9	●
●	●	**J3**-7; E1	J8; E2	J9	●	●
●	**E3**-7	E8	E9	●	●	●

Abbreviations:
N = Day of service of 3-Day Notice to Pay Rent or Quit
S = Day of service of Summons and Complaint
J = Judgment day (Judgment [Default] entered; Writ of Execution issued)
E = Day set for the eviction

Summons days on this calendar assume that the filing and service of the Summons and Complaint occur on the same day. You cannot, of course, file on either Saturday or Sunday although you may serve the Summons and Complaint on weekends. If service is completed on a weekend day, see Calendar 2 for the followup.

If you want to complete an unlawful detainer in the shortest possible time, you will find that Sunday (here represented by N1) and Monday (here represented by N2) are the best days for serving a 3-Day Notice to Pay Rent or Quit, and Tuesday (N3) and Wednesday (N4) are the worst days. Don't wait for a Sunday or a Monday to come around just because they're the best, though. Serve the notice any day you're ready to, because there may be some delays in the process somewhere, and the earlier you serve it, the better off you'll be. Even though Tuesday (N3) through Saturday (N7) are poor notice days when compared with the previous Sunday (N1) and Monday (N2), they still wind up with a one-day advantage in this whole streamlined eviction process over the following Sunday (N8) and Monday (N9). Don't delay the eviction by even one single day!

2. Calendar for Determining Judgment Days and Evictions According to Summons Days

Sun	Mon	Tues	Wed	Thurs	Fri	Sat
S1	S2	S3	S4	**S5**	S6	S7
●	J1	J2-4	**J5**	J6	J7	●
●	E1-4	**E5**	E6	E7	●	●

Sheriffs and marshals do not serve Summons and Complaints on Saturday or Sunday, but private process servers do, so all seven days of the week are included here. Naturally, you may file the Summons and Complaint only on a business day when the courts are open.

3. Calendar for Determining Evictions According to Judgment Days

Sun	Mon	Tues	Wed	Thurs	Fri	Sat
●	J1	J2	J3	**J4**	J5	●
●	E1-2	E3	**E4**	E5	●	●

Please note that all evictions are set by the sheriff or marshal as soon as you bring him the Writ of Execution. If you do so early in the day, he may be able to post the writ and the Notice to Vacate that very same day, and the tenant will then be evicted within the timeframe indicated on all three calendars. Otherwise, the eviction will be delayed. A Monday court day, as the calendar above shows, is the one exception. Since evictions are set the same for both Monday and Tuesday judgment days, bringing the writ to the sheriff or marshal late Monday won't make any difference.

6
Handling an Eviction for Breach of Contract

Your tenant in Apartment 6 has had a noisy party every night for the last four nights, and all the neighbors are on the warpath, complaining to you every chance they get and urging you to get rid of him right away. You can't even watch the nightly news without hearing the telephone ring, without having to listen to a tenant complain and inform you of more pressing news on the local scene.

Your tenant in that little bungalow on Bissell has just acquired an Irish Setter from a friend who's dying of AIDS, and he has resisted your every reasonable request to get rid of the dog, which is specifically forbidden in the rental agreement.

Your tenant in that sunny studio now has three people living with her who aren't listed on the rental agreement, and she has informed you defiantly that they're all staying because she needs them to help her pay the rent.

What are you going to do about these problems, landlord? Huh? Huh? You have to do something. You can't expect them to cease if you overlook them. They will only get worse. If you don't get that noisy tenant out, all of your good tenants are going to be leaving. If you don't get rid of the one tenant who has the dog, you're going to find that a second and a third tenant will be acquiring pets of their own without ever consulting you. After all, why should they? You don't seem to care. Let that mass of humanity stay in the one-room dwelling you rented to a single woman, and you will be paying considerably higher maintenance costs.

Before your building empties or deteriorates, you are going to have to do something about these problems, each of which is known in legal circles as a breach of contract and can be dealt with legally through the courts. "Breach of contract" means simply that the tenant is breaking the agreement outlining those terms which the two of you agreed would govern your relationship when it all began.

Other breach-of-contract evictions might be for installing a wood-burning stove without getting your permission, painting the walls without getting your permission, working on cars at all hours of the day and night, parking cars on the lawn, cluttering the yard, letting the landscaping deteriorate, denying you access to inspect or work on the premises, changing the locks without getting your permission and without giving you copies of the new keys, subletting to others, or anything else which was legitimately prohibited in the agreement.

As you might imagine, breaches of contract involve interpretations and misunderstandings, and they generally involve some personality conflicts and hard feelings, too. The landlord wants to maintain some semblance of order on the premises while the tenants naturally want to exercise their independence by testing the rules and doing as they please.

These situations are different from those as clear-cut as nonpayment of rent, unlawful acts, and failure to vacate. Consequently, many landlords will forego the quicker dispatch of an unlawful detainer for breach of contract because it will sometimes cause protracted and costly complications in court, and they will seek to evict their breachers by using a Notice to Terminate Tenancy instead. This tactic enables the tenant to save face. He doesn't feel obligated to marshal his forces to fight the eviction. He has more time to think things over and come to understand that he can't continue living where he is under the circumstances. He must find another place, and so he usually just leaves.

Because evictions for failure to vacate, which are explained in chapter 8, have become subject to certain limitations in those localities with rent control (see chapter 4), you may not have a good alternative. You may have to evict for breach of contract, knowing full well that such an action may precipitate opposition every step of the way. Don't despair. Do it and get the breacher out. You'll have little peace from your other tenants until you do.

You should know that an unlawful detainer action for breach of contract will involve your having to prove that the tenant is, in fact, breaching the contract, and you would be wise to gather as much evidence as you can to support your case later on. It will likely be needed. This evidence

that you are recording the noise as evidence for the court case you are preparing. They will respond much differently to that approach, I can assure you, than they would if you were there all by yourself without your electronic monitoring gear.

If it's a messy yard or the presence of a pet which constitutes the breach, get out your camera and snap away when you think you might arouse the interest of the offending tenant. Tell him what you are doing and why. You might find that the tenant will be more cooperative after that, and then again he might not be. Even if your evidence-gathering activity does not serve to in-

may be a sound recording, a video recording, a photograph, or the testimony of witnesses.

Gather the evidence openly if you can. If possible, try to be seen in the act of speaking into the microphone of your hand-held recorder: "This recording is being made at 11:32 p.m. on the 12th of April outside the front door of 1128 Sutter Street, Apartment 6, residence of Tom Twit, to be kept as evidence of the noise level which his neighbors have been complaining about, noise disturbing to the general peace and quiet." Then hold up the microphone ostentatiously. Perhaps you might even knock on the door and mock-innocently inform the occupants

timidate the tenant into mending his ways, you still have great evidence to introduce in court. Judges love to see things such as pictures and videos entered into evidence and generally give great credence to them.

We're supposing here that you have already tried to handle the matter with either a direct approach or a well-calculated psychological approach or both. If you haven't tried these approaches fully yet, go back to chapter 2 and mine it for any ideas pertinent to your situation. Try them first.

Whatever you do, do not set up your own amplifier and blast the noisemakers with Beatles or Bach. Do not poison the dog. Do not go for your six-shooters. Use your head. Don't get angry yourself, and don't get your tenants angry. Keep cool. Understand what you want and what they want, and try to come to some compromise that suits all of you. Be diplomatic, tough as that can be at times. Finally, if you cannot come to a mutual understanding and if you believe you have given the tenant every opportunity to mend his ways, go about using the legal means available to you to get him out.

Before handling any eviction for breach of contract, familiarize yourself with the basic procedure of an eviction for nonpayment of rent in

Step 1. Prepare a Notice to Perform Covenant.

The first step in an eviction for breach of contract is the preparation of a notice stating precisely which covenants the tenant has broken in your rental agreement. State one or more, but make certain you can *prove* each one you mention with evidence sufficient to convince a judge or a jury that your tenant is not living up to the agreement you made with him and that you are telling the truth about the situation. Fill out your notice like the sample shown on the next page, quoting chapter and verse from the rental

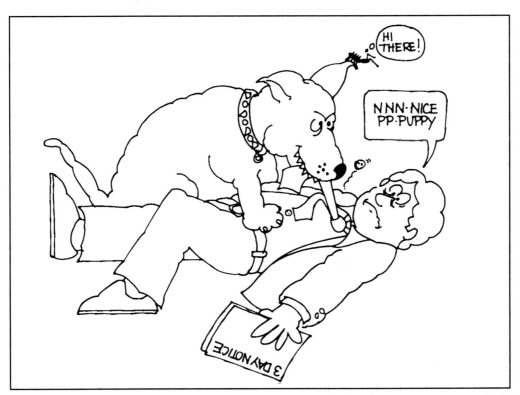

chapter 5, for there are many similarities between these two basic unlawful detainer procedures. Once you are familiar with how you go about evicting a tenant who doesn't pay, you will have a better understanding of how you go about evicting a tenant who doesn't comply with the rental agreement.

Now that you have been introduced to evictions for breach of contract, and you know what they're all about, let's look at the steps involved in handling this particular kind of an eviction. (The step numbers correspond exactly to the ones used in chapter 5 for handling an eviction for nonpayment of rent.)

agreement's pertinent covenants and giving the tenant three days to "clean up his act" or clear out.

Note that this notice states specifically that it does not terminate or forfeit the rental agreement. If the tenant has a long-term lease or certain obligations stated in the agreement which you do not want canceled just because he was evicted for breach of contract, then those terms can still be enforced. His obligation to pay rent under an unexpired lease, for example, would continue just as if he had moved out prematurely of his own volition.

As the notice states, "If, after legal proceed-

NOTICE TO PERFORM COVENANT

TO: Richard Renter

Rose Renter

_____

_____

and all other tenants in possession of the premises described as:

456 Sweet Street
(Street Address)

Littletown   California   91111
(City)   (State)   (Zip)

PLEASE TAKE NOTICE that you have violated the following covenant(s) in your Lease or Rental Agreement:

Only the following persons and pets are to live on said premises: Richard and Rose Renter. No other persons or pets are to live there without plaintiff's prior written permission.

You are hereby required within <u>THREE (3)</u> days to perform the aforesaid covenant(s) or to deliver up possession of the above-described premises which you currently hold and occupy.

If you fail to do so, legal proceedings will be instituted against you to recover said premises and such damages as the law allows.

This notice is intended to be a <u>THREE (3)</u>-day notice to perform the aforesaid covenant(s). It is not intended to terminate or forfeit the Lease or Rental Agreement under which you occupy said premises. If, after legal proceedings, said premises are recovered from you, the owners will try to rent the premises for the best possible rent, giving you credit for sums received and holding you liable for any deficiencies arising during the term of your Lease or Rental Agreement.

Dated: 9/10/XXXX   _Lester Landlord_
                              Owner/Manager

PROOF OF SERVICE (Server should complete this proof of service only AFTER serving tenants.)

I, the undersigned, being at least 18 years of age, declare under penalty of perjury that I served the above notice, of which this is a true copy, on the following tenant(s) in possession in the manner(s) indicated below: _Richard Renter_

☒ On 9/12/XXXX, I handed the notice to the tenant(s) personally.

☐ On _____, after attempting personal service, I handed the notice to a person of suitable age and discretion at the residence/business of the tenant(s), AND I deposited a true copy in the U.S. Mail, in a sealed envelope with postage fully prepaid, addressed to the tenant(s) at his/her/their place of residence (date mailed, if different _____).

☐ On _____, after attempting service in both manners indicated above, I posted the notice in a conspicuous place at the residence of the tenant(s), AND I deposited a true copy in the U.S. Mail, in a sealed envelope with postage fully prepaid, addressed to the tenant(s) at his/her/their place of residence (date mailed, if different _____).

Executed on 9/12/XXXX, at _Littletown_, California.
                    Served by _Lester Landlord_

You will find a blank copy of this form in the FORMS section of this book and in Eviction Forms Creator.

ings, said premises are recovered from you, the owners will try to rent said premises for the best possible rent, giving you credit for sums received and holding you liable for any deficiencies arising during the term of said Lease or Rental Agreement."

In other words, even though you intend to force the tenant to move because he has violated his contract, you are still not releasing him from his original obligations to you. Those obligations might include the fulfillment of a one-year lease which still has eight months to run. If an eviction for breach of contract were to release tenants from their original obligations, then they would try to get their landlord to evict them for breach of contract when what they really wanted to do was to terminate their lease prematurely and not be obligated to pay any more rent.

Like the notices used to initiate the other types of unlawful detainers described in this book, this form combines both the notice and the proof of service because combining them saves paper and copying costs. Complete the proof of service after you hand a copy of the notice to the tenant, not before. The tenant's copy should not have the lower section filled in when it's served because that section tells how the notice was served (past tense). Complete it following service.

Step 2. Serve the Notice.

In aggravating, but otherwise tranquil, situations which require a notice for breach, the best time to serve a Notice to Perform Covenant, stating that the tenant is doing something he agreed he would not do or that he isn't doing something he agreed he would do, is shortly after he pays his rent, for you must consider that the tenant won't be too eager to pay you any further rent monies after he receives the notice if he expects to be, and intends to be, evicted. If the case goes to court and all goes well, you might be rid of the tenant before the next rent payment falls due, thereby losing no rent whatsoever.

In those crisis situations which require immediate attention, the best time to serve the notice is *now, this very minute.* Do not even consider whether you might lose a month's rent if you serve the notice at an inopportune time of the month. Rather, consider whether you might lose your property, your good tenants, your health, or your sanity by waiting. What are they worth to you? If they're worth more than a few days of rent, serve the notice right now. Do not wait.

Try repeatedly to serve the notice directly to the person you're evicting, and when you serve it, be friendly, even if you encounter a grumpy tenant who'd rather not see you standing on his doorstep.

If you can't find the tenant, you'll have to resort to one of the other legal methods for serving a 3-day notice. See the bottom of the notice itself for the choices.

Having served the notice, you must wait three days for the tenant to perform the covenant you identified in the notice. Begin counting the days with the one following the date of service. Let's say you served the notice on a Wednesday. You'd count Thursday, Friday, and Saturday as the three days, and you could then file your paperwork with the court on Sunday. Well, you could if the courts were open. Since they're not, the first day you could file would be Monday.

Because the tenant doesn't need access to money to cure his breach, the final day for him to comply with the notice does not have to be a day when the banks are open as it does for a 3-Day Notice to Pay Rent or Quit. He gets three days, not four or five or six. Give him more time only if you want to give him more time. If you serve him a Notice to Perform Covenant on a Wednesday and you're giving him three days to perform and he doesn't, you may file the summons and complaint on the following Monday. If you serve him on a Monday, you could file your court paperwork on the following Friday.

Step 3. Prepare the Summons, Complaint, and Cover Sheet.

Use the same summons form for this kind of unlawful detainer as you would if you were evicting the tenant for nonpayment of rent, and fill it out the same way, too.

Your complaint form will be the same as the one used for nonpayment of rent, but you must fill it out a little differently. The differences begin with item 7. Check the box after 7; put the defendant's name after the word "names" which appears in parenthesis; and under 7a, check box 4 to indicate that you served the defendants a "3-day notice to perform covenants or quit."

Complete 7b by giving the date when the notice expired. In this case, the date of expiry is three days after service. If you served the notice on the twelfth, it would expire on the fifteenth.

MC-025

SHORT TITLE:	CASE NUMBER:
LANDLORD VS. RENTER	

ATTACHMENT *(Number):* ____15____   **Page** 4 **of** 4
(This Attachment may be used with any Judicial Council form.)   *(Add pages as required)*

1

2   By the terms of said agreement, defendant covenanted and agreed to have only

3 the following persons and pets live on said premises: Richard and Rose Renter, and

4 to have no other persons or pets live there without plaintiff's prior written

5 permission.

6   Defendant does now harbor a pet dog on said premises, and plaintiff has never

7 given permission to defendant to harbor a dog on said premises.

8

9

10

11

12

13

14

15

16

17

18

19

20

21

22

23

24

25

26

27 *(If the item that this Attachment concerns is made under penalty of perjury, all statements in this Attachment are made under penalty of perjury.)*

Form Approved for Optional Use
Judicial Council of California
MC-025 [New July 1, 2002]

ATTACHMENT
to Judicial Council Form

Cal. Rules of Court, rule 982

You will find a blank copy of this form in the FORMS section of this book and in Eviction Forms Creator.

Do not check box 7d, whatever you do. You did not ask for forfeiture of the tenant's rental agreement in the notice. Remember?

Check 7e because you must attach a copy of the notice whenever you are proceeding against a residential tenant. Read 7f carefully and decide whether it applies. If it does, check it and 8c, and attach a statement labeled 8c with the required information.

Fill in items 8, 11, 12, 13, and 14 as appropriate, and omit items 9 and 10 completely. Check item 15 for sure because you'll have to attach a description of the particular kind of breach the tenant is committing, and you'll be calling it Attachment 15.

Under item 17, sometimes referred to as "the prayer," check box "f" to request damages and give a date when they should begin. If the tenant owes you any rent following the expiration of the notice, that rent is known as damages, and the judge or court clerk, at your direction, will determine what it is from the per-diem rate you put in item 11. If you have any other requests, such as charges other than rent which the tenant still owes you, check box "h" and specify what they are.

Check box 18 because you will be attaching a number of pages, and put the number of pages attached after "specify." Your count of pages attached should include at least the following: the agreement, the notice, the proof of service of notice, and the statement.

Finally, check the first box in item 19 to indicate that you did not use an unlawful detainer assistant.

Attachment 15 should follow the format of the sample shown here referring to a breach involving an unauthorized pet. Attachments for other kinds of breaches might be worded as follows in these examples:

For a breach regarding messiness or filth—"By the terms of said agreement, defendant covenanted and agreed to keep yards and garbage areas clean; defendant does now maintain the aforesaid premises in an unclean and unsanitary condition."

For a breach regarding subletting—"By the terms of said agreement, defendant covenanted and agreed that only Richard Renter and Rose Renter would live on said premises and that no other persons would live there without written permission; defendant has sublet the premises to a third party now occupying same; and plaintiff has never given permission to defendant to sublet the premises."

For a breach regarding alterations—"By the terms of said agreement, defendant covenanted and agreed not to alter the dwelling; defendant has constructed or caused to be constructed a metal storage shed in the front yard of the demised premises; plaintiff has never given permission to defendant for construction of said shed."

For a breach regarding noise—"By the terms of said agreement, defendant covenanted and agreed to keep from making loud noises and disturbances and to play music and broadcast programs at all times so as not to disturb other people's peace and quiet; defendant has deliberately disturbed other people's peace and quiet on various occasions so as to cause complaints from neighbors about said noise."

Surely from these examples you can devise your own attachment sufficient to describe your tenant's particular breach, whatever it is. Couch your description in typical legalese if you possibly can. Use at least one "aforesaid," "plaintiff," "defendant," or "covenanted" in the wording to make it all sound reasonably consistent with the gobbledygook an attorney might use.

Complete a cover sheet to accompany your summons and complaint, following the instructions for doing so in chapter 5.

Steps 4-17. (Follow those given in chapter 5.)

• • • • • • • • •

Should you, in the course of your unlawful detainer for breach, encounter any response to your complaint, turn to chapter 10 for information about what to do next.

If you go to court for your default judgment, you won't have to bring any witnesses to testify, but you should consider bringing either audio or visual evidence of the breach. Although the judge will take your sworn testimony as sufficient evidence that your tenant has indeed breached the contract, he will be all the more convinced by a recording and some photographs.

The one big difference between nonpayment and breach cases is that in a breach-of-contract case you would be approximately even with the tenant in terms of money, especially if you gave him his notice shortly after he paid the rent. He may owe you some money, or you may owe him some.

Once he moves, rejoice and heave a sigh of relief that he has actually departed. Then treat him like any other tenant who has moved out of your rental property. Settle up with him according to the terms of his lease or rental agreement, making sure that you give him the required written accounting of his deposits within the time the law allows.

- Gather concrete evidence of the breach of contract if you can.
- Use a Notice to Terminate Tenancy and the entire procedure explained in chapter 8 if that option is available in your area, if you believe the tenants might feel challenged by your proceeding against them and might be tempted to contest the case, and/or if the breach can wait that long.
- Serve the Notice to Perform Covenant shortly after the tenants pay their rent so you will have plenty of time to conduct your court case and incur the least loss of rent possible.

7
Handling an Eviction for Waste, Nuisance, or Unlawful Acts

In the course of everyday landlording, you may have the misfortune to happen upon some tenants who have more personality disorders than Dr. Jekyll, more faces than Eve, more sinister pals than the Godfather, more marijuana than a Mendocino pot grower, more cocaine customers than a Colombian cartel, more delusions than a Watergate burglar, more armaments than an American Nazi, more gentlemen callers than Sally Sanford, more corn whiskey than a Kentucky moonshiner, or more problems of some other sort than even a soap opera could dramatize or a Pollyanna could handle.

For whatever reason, these people are not what they seem, and you unfortunately do not discover what they are truly like until after they have managed to gain possession of your rental dwelling.

They may have convinced you to rent to them by appearing quite normal when they made an application to rent or by resorting to some form of deception, such as renting through the personal appearance of a comely friend. How they gained possession doesn't matter now. The fact is that they have possession. They are living in one of your rentals, and you want them out. You have to get them out before they damage your property any more, hurt somebody, involve you in a lawsuit, alienate every neighbor within two stones' throws, or provoke a police raid.

You can't really evict them using any of the other three types of evictions because they are current in their rent, they haven't specifically broken any provision in the rental agreement, and they must be dealt with before thirty or sixty days have elapsed. So how do you deal with them?

You evict them on the grounds that they are committing waste, committing a nuisance, or committing unlawful acts. The law is reasonably specific about these grounds. Here are the definitions: "waste" is abusing or destroying property; "nuisance" is "anything which is injurious

to health, or is indecent or offensive to the senses, or an obstruction to the free use of property, so as to interfere with the comfortable enjoyment of life or property..."; and "unlawful acts" are any acts committed in violation of the law.

The problem you face in trying to evict a tenant on any of these grounds, of course, is that you have to prove that he is guilty. You have to be the first judge of whether the bothersome behavior is substantial enough and whether the evidence you have gathered to prove your allegations about this tenant's bothersome behavior is good enough to convince a real judge, and perhaps a jury, that the tenant should be evicted. In a way, you are like the wife who is afraid that her husband is going to kill her, but she's unable to prove to the police or the courts just how great the danger is in order to get protection. No one quite believes her until she turns up dead.

You may be damned if you do try to evict a tenant who you feel is destructive, dangerous, troublesome, or law-breaking, and you may be damned if you don't. Yes, I said "damned if you don't." That Dr. Jekyll who has laid your property waste already by kicking holes in the doors and uprooting the wall heater will keep right on destroying the place if you ignore him, and he'll no doubt accelerate his demolition if you attempt to evict him. That naughty lady who's a nuisance to her neighbors because she parades about the hallways in her boa, mules, and birthday suit soliciting tricks is going to drive your good tenants to vacate if you don't force her to vacate first, and she'll undoubtedly rail at you and charge you with unmentionable sins if you try to force her out. That drug dealer who brazenly peddles cocaine out of his apartment at all hours will attract more criminal elements to your property if you look the other way when you discover what's going on, and he'll likely threaten you with foul play if you dare to begin eviction proceedings

109

3-DAY NOTICE TO QUIT
FOR WASTE, NUISANCE, OR UNLAWFUL ACTS

TO: Boom Boom Suess

and all other tenants in possession of the premises described as:

456 Sweet Street
(Street Address)

Littletown   California   91111
(City)   (State)   (Zip)

PLEASE TAKE NOTICE that you are hereby required within three (3) days to deliver up possession of the above-described premises which you currently hold and occupy because you have committed the following waste, nuisance, or unlawful act(s):

Committing acts of prostitution on the premises on at least two occasions, August 6th and August 15th, as evidenced by police reports.

As a consequence of your having committed the foregoing acts, your Lease or Rental Agreement is hereby declared canceled under California law (CCP §1161.4).

Should you fail to comply with this notice, legal proceedings will be instituted against you to recover said premises and such damages as the law allows.

Dated: August 16, XXXX   *Lester Landlord*
                                          Owner/Manager

PROOF OF SERVICE (Server should complete this proof of service only AFTER serving tenants.)

I, the undersigned, being at least 18 years of age, declare under penalty of perjury that I served the above notice, of which this is a true copy, on the following tenant(s) in possession in the manner(s) indicated below: *Boom Boom Suess*

☒ On 8/16/XXXX , I handed the notice to the tenant(s) personally.

☐ On _____, after attempting personal service, I handed the notice to a person of suitable age and discretion at the residence/business of the tenant(s), AND I deposited a true copy in the U.S. Mail, in a sealed envelope with postage fully prepaid, addressed to the tenant(s) at his/her/their place of residence (date mailed, if different _____).

☐ On _____, after attempting service in both manners indicated above, I posted the notice in a conspicuous place at the residence of the tenant(s), AND I deposited a true copy in the U.S. Mail, in a sealed envelope with postage fully prepaid, addressed to the tenant(s) at his/her/their place of residence (date mailed, if different _____).

Executed on 8/16/XXXX , at *Littletown* , California.

                    Served by *Lester Landlord*

efc

You will find a blank copy of this form in the FORMS section of this book and in Eviction Forms Creator.

against him.

You are trapped in a no-win situation. You probably won't turn up dead if you attempt to evict the tenant who discharges his arsenal in the backyard of your rental property, and you probably won't turn up dead if you actually evict him, but you might find yourself involved in a costly and protracted lawsuit if you do nothing.

Remember, landlord, that you have what attorneys call "deep pockets," and you are constantly being pickpocketed in suits which blame you whenever something actionable happens which is remotely connected with your property,

short and cheap. If you are particularly fearful, consider one or more of a variety of defensive measures to enhance your physical safety. Consider making yourself scarce around the property all the while you are involved in this kind of an eviction. Consider hiring a bodyguard and wearing a bulletproof vest wherever you go. Consider hiring an attorney to handle all the legal work for you, although even then you may face danger if the tenant knows where to find you and wants his revenge.

At the very least, keep someone else informed of your whereabouts to increase the chances that

regardless of whether you were directly responsible or not. You may have been nowhere near the backyard of your property when a tenant fired the bullet which paralyzed a neighbor, but if you were aware that your tenant might discharge a weapon in the yard, then you, along with the gun-slinger would likely be held accountable for the injury. Why you? You got the bucks, dearie. You may not want to do anything, but you have to. There's no sensible alternative.

You cannot be idle in these situations. You have to act.

You may be putting your own life in danger when you initiate this kind of an eviction, for some of these people live in a netherworld where life is

the tenant will be caught if he tries to harm you physically, and program your cellphone so that you can call for help by pushing just one or two buttons. Keep the cellphone on your person, and keep it turned on.

Step 1. Prepare the Notice.

State law allows you to evict a tenant on grounds of waste, nuisance, or unlawful acts without offering him the opportunity to reform his behavior. In other words, the 3-Day Notice to Quit which is used in this situation does not have to include an alternative. It may have one, but it doesn't have to, and you will notice that the one provided here does not (in some rent-control areas, this kind of notice must include an alternative; check your local rent-control ordinances).

This is serious business. You are saying, by not providing an alternative, that the tenant cannot remain even if he does mend his ways. He has squeezed the toothpaste out of the tube, and he can't force it back in. The notice informs the tenant why he is being evicted, and it gives him three days to leave. That's all. No alternatives, no and's, no if's, no but's, no maybe's.

You should take advantage of your opportunity to be tough here, for nobody, not even a psychic psychiatrist, could possibly determine whether a tenant has reformed enough within three days to be a suitable tenant again. Besides, you would still be held accountable if he lapses back into his errant ways in the future, and you would still have to answer to the other tenants for allowing him to stay. They tend to be unforgiving of people with a past. You have to get that bad-acting tenant out!

When you prepare the notice, be careful to list only those grounds which you feel confident you can prove in court. If you can't prove them to be utterly and undeniably true, use some other pretext to evict the tenant. Don't bother listing all the derogatory tidbits you can possibly remember about the tenant. List the most flagrant ones only, the ones you can photograph, tape-record, or get witnesses to verify.

On the notice itself, describe the grounds for the eviction something like this: Discharging a gun through the floor of Apartment 212 at 11:35 on the night of September 12; growing marijuana plants on the balcony of the tenant's domicile in violation of state and federal laws; dealing drugs on the premises, resulting in an arrest on October 11; committing acts of prostitution on the premises on at least two occasions, per police reports dated August 6th and August 15th; violating City Fire Ordinance 112.3 regarding the operation of a kerosene heater inside a living area; disturbing the neighbors with loud quarreling, loud music, obscene language, drunken disturbances, all of which required a police visit on January 6; storing and fencing stolen goods on the premises; harboring two illegal aliens in a storeroom on the premises; dismantling stolen automobiles in a garage on the premises; operating a bookmaking business on the premises.

Don't try to evict a tenant on these grounds unless the incident or activity which you are citing in the notice occurred recently or continues to occur. If a tenant used to commit acts of prostitution on the premises months ago but has obviously reformed since then, and you did nothing earlier to evict her, don't try to evict her now on those old grounds. Your case would be thrown out of court. She'd be given the benefit of the doubt if she claimed that she had reformed and was a new woman now, that she had regained custody of her children and was about to be married to a good man who had gone to the trouble of taking the day off from his job to testify on her behalf in court. Stories like this tug at judges' heartstrings. Judges like to give second chances to anybody who is trying to reform, and you should as well. Take a wait-and-see attitude. See whether she actually has reformed, and if she has, you'll want to keep her as a tenant. If she hasn't, you'll want to get rid of her.

In any case such as this and the others in this chapter, the "punishment" should follow the errant behavior promptly.

Step 2. Serve the Notice.

If you consider the tenant to be dangerous, do not serve the notice yourself. Hire a sheriff, marshal, off-duty peace officer, security guard, or professional process server to serve it for you.

If the tenant has always been friendly to you and isn't somebody you'd consider dangerous, screw up your courage and approach him directly with notice in hand, when he might think you have come merely to reprimand him.

Don't just hand him the notice and leave. Talk with him. Try to convince him that his moving would be in your mutual best interest. Tell him he should begin looking immediately for other accommodations where he'll be able to live more freely according to the life-style he has chosen for himself. If he wants to be destructive, tell him to rent a dilapidated place which the owner wants to tear down anyway. If she wants to peddle her favors, tell her to look for a place in that part of town where such assignations are commonplace. If he wants to discharge weapons any time of the day or night, tell him to look for a place with fewer neighbors.

Be polite, yet firm. Tell him you have to get him out so all the neighbors will quit bugging you. Tell him you don't want to have to call the police about his marijuana, but you will if you have to. You are challenging the tenant directly, so expect to be yelled at, perhaps even threatened, if he's in a bad mood.

The best time to serve one of these notices is when the tenant is committing the waste, nuisance, or unlawful act. That establishes a one-to-one causal relationship between what he is doing and what you are doing. Your approach becomes a kind of just retribution, prompt and exacting. If you can't serve it then, serve it anytime. Because the bad-acting, nuisance, or law-breaking tenant tends to keep irregular hours and may be difficult to catch, however, you may have to lie in wait behind a good book until he appears or else ask a cooperative neighbor to alert you when he returns.

Step 3. Prepare the Summons, Complaint, and Cover Sheet.

Should your tenant refuse to heed the 3-day notice, you must proceed against him in court. As in other kinds of evictions, that necessitates preparing a summons, complaint, and cover sheet. The forms themselves are the same ones used for every unlawful detainer involving residential property, no matter what the reason behind it happens to be.

Begin preparing the forms with the summons and cover sheet, and fill them out exactly as instructed in chapter 5.

When filling out the complaint form, under "Jurisdiction," check the box preceding "ACTION IS A LIMITED CIVIL CASE," and check the box "does not exceed $10,000," so you may claim whatever might be due you.

Complete the rest of page 1 as instructed in chapter 5.

Check the box after 7 on the form, and put the defendant's name or their names after the word "names." Under 7a, check "3-day notice to quit," since that is the kind of notice you should have served to initiate this kind of eviction. Indicate when that notice expired in 7b, and check 7d to confirm that the notice included an election of forfeiture (really a declaration of cancellation). Check 7e because you must attach a copy of the notice whenever you are proceeding against a residential tenant. Read 7f carefully and decide whether it applies. If it does, check it and 8c, and attach a statement labeled 8c with the required information.

Fill in items 8, 11, 12, 13, and 14 as appropriate. Omit items 9 and 10 completely. Check

item 15 to indicate that you are attaching a statement about the tenant's wrongdoing.

Under item 17, check box "e" because you are canceling the agreement. Check box "f" to make yourself eligible to receive any damages. If you have any other requests, such as charges other than rent which the tenant still owes you, check box "h" and specify what they are.

Check box 18 because you will be attaching a number of pages, and put the number of pages attached after "specify." Your count of pages attached should include all of the following: the agreement, the notice, the proof of service of notice, and the statement.

Finally, check the first box in item 19 to indicate that you did not use an unlawful detainer assistant, and complete the last thing on the complaint, the verification.

In your Attachment 15, which ought to use Judicial Council form MC-025 (see sample in chapter 6), you needn't try to be creative. In fact, you shouldn't be. State the facts as you know them, simply and directly, following the description of the grounds for the eviction which you stated originally in the tenant's notice. Refer to the tenant in the attachment as the defendant rather than as your tenant, and refer to yourself as the plaintiff. This attachment is not supposed to prove that the tenant did what you say he did. It can't do that. You are merely stating in it what the tenant is doing or has done to commit waste, nuisance, or unlawful acts.

Here's a sample of the wording you might use in your case against Boom Boom Suess, who's turning tricks in her apartment all night long:

```
Defendant has committed acts of
prostitution on at least two oc-
casions, per police reports dated
August 6th and August 15th.

Defendant's downstairs neigh-
bors have called the Plaintiff
three times (August 9, August 20,
and August 22) at approximately 2
a.m. to complain of boisterous
activity in Defendant's apart-
ment.

Plaintiff has investigated com-
plaints, has witnessed the commo-
tion, has talked with the Defen-
dant about it, and has received
promises that the activity would
stop. The activity has continued
```

in spite of the promises.

The activity has brought strange people onto the premises at unusual hours and has resulted in police visits. Defendant's activity infuriates other tenants and endangers the children who live on the premises.

Steps 4-17. (Follow those given in chapter 5.)

• • • • • • • • •

Once you have endured this kind of an eviction, you will have earned your landlord's hard nose, pitchfork, and pointed tail. You may appear autocratic and even devilish to the meek souls you know socially because you'll be all the more suspicious of people and especially of anyone who applies to rent from you. You'll have changed.

Churchill is credited with having said, "If you're not a liberal by the time you're twenty, you have no heart, and if you're not a conservative by the time you're forty, you have no brains." We landlords are on an accelerated schedule. We become conservative soon after assuming the "Landlord" mantle, regardless of our age.

This kind of an eviction makes us so.

- Recognize that this kind of eviction is the most trying of all.
- Understand that you may be damned if you don't evict and damned if you do.
- Document your case carefully.
- Keep your loved ones informed of your whereabouts at all times during one of these evictions.
- Keep good help in the wings, an attorney and a process server.

8
Handling an Eviction for Failure to Vacate

You are planning to renovate a rental dwelling, and you can't do the work you want to do while tenants are occupying the place.

You are selling a rental house, and the new owner wants to move in but insists that you get the current tenants out before escrow closes.

Your father and his ladylove want to move into one of your rentals, and unless you have a rental available for them to move into within a month, they're going to be moving in with you.

You are tired of having to chase after a tenant who insists upon paying his rent in cash and wants you to pick it up in person every month.

Your tenant always pays one day late and refuses to pay the late fee he owes.

Your tenant has already caused one small fire with his careless smoking, and you're afraid that the next time he lights up, he may burn down the whole building.

Your tenants have some destructive monsters masquerading as innocent babes, and they have broken everything from faucets to windows to doors and what they haven't broken, they've defaced.

Your tenant won't use the "pooper-scooper" you gave him last Christmas, and every time he walks his dog, the animal poops on the walkway near the entrance to the apartment house.

Your tenants have noisy parties every weekend, all weekend, and the other tenants are threatening to move.

You've had it up to your eye sockets with two chronic complainers because you can't do enough for them, and still they complain, complain, complain.

In any of these situations involving tenants who are paying their rent regularly and may or may not be breaching their rental agreement, the best way for you to get rid of them is to give them a Notice to Terminate Tenancy. Then you add crossed fingers to your already crossed eyes, and you hope that they move before the 30-day period is up so you don't have to spend the time and money necessary to evict them through the courts.

Before you begin passing out notices to all of your tenants who are in situations like the ones above, though, you must consider three important questions:

1) Are these tenants leasing from you rather than renting; that is, do they have a fixed-term agreement which permits them to occupy your rental dwelling for a certain period of time, a period which has not yet expired?

If they have such an agreement, you may not serve them with a Notice to Terminate Tenancy because you may not terminate their lease on your own initiative until it expires. The lease may be terminated prematurely only if you and the tenants together agree to terminate it or if you can show cause.

Ah, but if the lease has expired and you have not yet signed a new one and you have continued accepting rent from the tenants, then you may use a Notice to Terminate Tenancy because the tenancy has automatically become a month-to-month tenancy.

So what do you do if you have a valid lease with the tenants which precludes your evicting them with a Notice to Terminate Tenancy, yet you still want to get them out?

You have a number of options. You may try to buy them out of their lease. You may find a significant breach which they're committing and evict them on that ground. You may pounce on them with a 3-Day Notice to Pay Rent or Quit as soon as their rent first becomes delinquent and hope that they don't pay within the three days so you can evict them for nonpayment of rent. Or you may wait until their lease expires and give them notice beforehand that you will not be renewing it.

NOTICE TO TERMINATE TENANCY

TO: Herman Lockyear

Preston Lockyear

_____

_____

and all other tenants in possession of the premises described as:

458 Sweet Street
(Street Address)
Littletown   CA   91111
(City)   (State)   (Zip)

PLEASE TAKE NOTICE that you are hereby required within THIRTY (30) days to remove from and deliver up possession of the above-described premises, which you currently hold and occupy.

This notice is intended for the purpose of terminating the Lease or Rental Agreement by which you now hold possession of the above-described premises, and should you fail to comply, legal proceedings will be instituted against you to recover possession, to declare said Lease or Rental Agreement forfeited, and to recover rents and damages for the period of the unlawful detention.

This notice is being given for good cause as follows:
In compliance with local housing ordinance (LMC-TX 13.76), owners desire to move into this dwelling.

Dated: June 5, XXXX   *Lester Landlord*
                                        Owner/Manager

PROOF OF SERVICE   (Server should complete this proof of service only AFTER serving tenants.)
   I, the undersigned, being at least 18 years of age, declare under penalty of perjury that I served the above notice, of which this is a true copy, on the following tenant(s) in possession in the manner(s) indicated below: ___*Preston Lockyear*___

☒ On *June 5, XXXX*, I handed the notice to the tenant(s) personally.

☐ On _____, after attempting personal service, I handed the notice to a person of suitable age and discretion at the residence/business of the tenant(s), AND I deposited a true copy in the U.S. Mail, in a sealed envelope with postage fully prepaid, addressed to the tenant(s) at his/her/their place of residence (date mailed, if different _____).

☐ On _____, after attempting service in both manners indicated above, I posted the notice in a conspicuous place at the residence of the tenant(s), AND I deposited a true copy in the U.S. Mail, in a sealed envelope with postage fully prepaid, addressed to the tenant(s) at his/her/their place of residence (date mailed, if different _____).

☐ On _____, I sent by certified mail a true copy of the notice addressed to the tenant(s) at his/her/their place of residence.

Executed on ___*6/5/XXXX*___, at ___*Littletown*___, CA.

                    Served by ___*Lester Landlord*___

efc

You will find a blank copy of this form in the FORMS section of this book and in Eviction Forms Creator.

Incidentally, if they refuse to move at the expiration of a fixed-term lease which you have chosen not to renew and if you do not accept any rent from them beyond the lease's expiration date, you may have them served with a summons and complaint without first serving them a notice. In that case, fill out the Judicial Council complaint form as appropriate, omitting any reference to a "notice" and to service of the notice because there is no notice required in such cases. Make sure you check box 9 on the complaint, which refers to demanding possession at the end of a fixed-term lease.

Although giving them some kind of notice that you aren't going to renew their lease is not obligatory unless called for in the lease, you would be wise to do so. You want the tenants to know what your intentions are in plenty of time for them to move. Giving them advance notice will avoid any misunderstandings. You won't have to argue with them when the lease ends and you find that they want to renew the lease, while you want them to vacate.

The lease agreement in the *Landlording* book says this about the end of the lease: "Upon expiration, this Agreement shall become a month-to-month agreement AUTOMATICALLY, UNLESS either Tenants or Owners notify the other party in writing at least thirty days prior to expiration that they do not wish this Agreement to continue on any basis."

In other words, landlords using this lease must give their tenants notice at least thirty days before the lease expires informing them that the tenancy will be ending when the lease ends. If they don't, the fixed-term lease becomes a month-to-month agreement.

2) Is the rental dwelling located in any rent-control/eviction-control area which requires that you have a "just cause," otherwise known as a "good cause," for an eviction? (See chapter 4.)

Even in eviction-control areas, you may certainly evict for nonpayment of rent or for a legitimate breach of contract if you want to, but you may evict for failure to vacate only if you have a so-called "just cause," and some of the situations given at the beginning of this chapter do not constitute such a cause. Check your local ordinances. You'll find that they vary quite a bit. Habitually paying late, for example, may be a just cause in one eviction-control area but not in another.

3) Does this particular rental dwelling fall under any special category which exempts it from eviction controls in an eviction-control area?

Four factors generally dictate whether a particular rental dwelling is exempt from eviction controls and thus whether you would likely not have to provide a just cause on a Notice to Terminate Tenancy.

The first factor is the number of rental units in the building, that is, whether it's a single-family dwelling, a duplex, a fourplex, or a twenty-unit building. The smaller the building, the less likely it is to be subject to eviction controls.

The second factor is the date of construction. Older buildings may be subject to eviction controls, whereas newer buildings may be exempt. Find out when your building was constructed and keep that date in mind when you look through your eviction-control ordinances.

The third factor is whether the owner is also an occupant of the building. Owner-occupied buildings are less likely to be subject to eviction controls than non-owner-occupied buildings.

The fourth factor is whether the building is under a government subsidy program of some sort, either a loan subsidy or a rent subsidy. Owners who participate in the HUD Section 8 program must give their Section 8 tenants a just cause to terminate midterm. If you have Section 8 tenants whom you want to evict, contact your local housing authority for guidance. The rules you must follow to evict a tenant under Section 8 keep changing.

Check the ordinances applicable to your building and your tenants. Find out for yourself what you can and cannot do.

Once you have determined that you may legally use a Notice to Terminate Tenancy, you may follow the steps given here and in chapter 5 to evict your tenant.

Step 1. Prepare the Notice.

Fill out the notice by following the sample shown in this chapter.

Ignore the Proof of Service section entirely on the original notice served to the tenant. Complete it only after the notice has been served.

Note that there's one blank on the notice where you're supposed to enter the number of days allowed for the tenant to move. "Thirty" is the most common number entered here, but it's not the only number you might enter.

If you specified in your rental agreement another number of days as the advance notice you have agreed to give for changes in terms of tenancy, including notices of termination, you may use that number. It may be as little as seven. It will automatically be seven for a week-to-week rental agreement unless a larger number has been agreed upon because the notice period is supposed to correspond to the frequency of the rent payments.

In any case, give the tenants the length of time they're legally entitled to, more if you choose, but no less.

In those situations where just-cause requirements apply, indicate on the notice itself your "just" cause(s) for giving the notice. What you consider a "just" cause must, of course, correspond to what HUD or your rent control ordinances consider a "just" cause. Type or print the following on the notice in the space above the date: "In compliance with local housing ordinances [or HUD requirements], this notice is being given for just cause as follows: [describe your reason briefly]."

Unless you are required to give a "just" cause, you need give no reason at all for your notice, and you shouldn't give a reason because a reason will only antagonize the tenant, and an antagonized tenant may be more inclined to fight the eviction every step of the way. You don't want an antagonized adversary battling you in court. That's Misery with a capital M, and you don't need any more misery in your life.

Step 2. Serve the Notice.

• THE SERVICE—You may serve a Notice to Terminate Tenancy in any of four ways. The first three are the same as those prescribed for serving a 3-Day Notice to Pay Rent or Quit. The fourth way is different. It's specific to this kind of notice primarily because this kind of notice allows more than just a few days for compliance.

1) You may serve it in person directly to the tenant at his residence or place of business, although these are not the only places where you may serve the notice, or you may serve it to him wherever you happen to find him.

2) You may serve it in person to someone "of suitable age and discretion" other than the tenant who is found at the tenant's residence or place of business *and* send a copy by first-class mail to the tenant at his residence.

3) You may post a copy in a conspicuous place at the tenant's residence *and* send a copy by first-class mail to the tenant at his residence.

4) You may send a copy by certified or registered mail. You needn't secure a return receipt. That's up to you. I don't secure a receipt because I know that tenants who have to sign a receipt for mail tend to avoid doing so. They know instinctively that the mail is bad news, and they may decide never to sign for it.

While we're on the subject of certified and registered mail, let's consider the differences, and you'll understand why you should always use certified rather than registered mail for tenant notices and other commonplace, intrinsically worthless documents, that is, when you have a choice between the two.

Certified mail enables the user to trace something as it makes its way through the postal system. It provides a record of mailing and a record of delivery. The sender receives a record of mailing upon entrusting the item to the postal service, and there's a record of delivery kept at the other end, at the recipient's post office, for a full two years. The sender pays extra to receive a record of delivery.

Registered mail enables the user to trace something as it makes its way through the postal system, too, but what is sent by registered mail is generally something of value to anybody, such as cash or transferable securities, or something of great value to somebody, such as a one-of-a-kind grant deed or a signed last will and testament. Registered mail gives users confidence that the contents of the envelope will arrive intact. No other mailing option is more secure. Registered mail is always kept under lock and key, and everyone who handles it must sign for it. The sender pays extra to receive a record of delivery.

As you might imagine, the security provided by registered mail comes at a price. It costs almost four times more than certified mail, and it tends to be slower.

Naturally, personal service is still the best type of service for this kind of notice as it is for all the others. Try to serve the notice personally if you can.

• CONFUSING TWO NOTICE TYPES—I have heard some landlords say that the only time to serve a Notice to Terminate Tenancy is on the rent due date. That's piffle! It's a good time to serve the notice, but it's not the only time or even the only good time to serve the notice.

They're probably confusing the Notice of Change in Terms of Tenancy (used primarily for increasing rent), which is a 30-day notice except when the rent increase is over 10% per year (CC §827), with the Notice to Terminate Tenancy, which is a 30-day notice as well. The two notices have only their time frames in common. Otherwise, they're completely different. Don't confuse the two.

You may serve a Notice to Terminate Tenancy any old time, and it expires in a certain number of specified days from when it was served (a Notice of Change in Terms of Tenancy may be served anytime, too, but it is generally served on or before the rent due date, to give the tenant at least the indicated days' notice before there's a rent increase).

• BEST TIME TO SERVE—The best time to serve a Notice to Terminate Tenancy is shortly *after* the rent has been paid. You should know that as soon as you serve the notice, the tenant's desire to pay any more rent diminishes dramatically, even though he is legally liable to pay rent for every day he remains. You may lose some rent if the tenant does prove to be recalcitrant and remains for the entire time allowed and on into the eviction proceedings, but it will be the least amount you could possibly lose.

If at any time during the waiting period the tenant becomes delinquent in his rent, serve him with a 3-Day Notice to Pay Rent or Quit. That way you can evict him all the more quickly, and you can sue for back rent in your complaint as well.

• TWO MISUNDERSTANDINGS—Now take note of two important things which people often misunderstand because they fail to think through what happens when an eviction for failure to vacate becomes, or ought to become, an eviction for nonpayment of rent.

First, take note that a Notice to Terminate Tenancy demands possession only. It does not demand rent. Should you fail to serve a 3-Day Notice to Pay Rent or Quit when the tenant becomes delinquent in rent during the thirty-day period of time when you're waiting for a Notice to Terminate Tenancy to expire, you might find yourself in an unfortunate position where you have evicted the tenant successfully without at the same time receiving a judgment for his unpaid rent [*Castle Park No. 5 v. Katherine* (1979)

91 CA3d Supp 6, 154 CR 498]. Naturally, you could sue the tenant for the back rent in small claims court if you wanted to, but that's just another hassle. You want to get the tenant out of your life in one legal action, not two.

Second, take note that if you do serve a 3-Day Notice to Pay Rent or Quit to a tenant who becomes delinquent during a thirty-day period of waiting for a Notice to Terminate Tenancy to expire, the 3-day notice takes precedence over the 30-day notice. The 30-day notice might as well have been voided or torn up and thrown away. It's no longer of any consequence. The only notice which matters then is the 3-day notice.

If you have served a 3-day notice to a tenant who becomes delinquent while you're waiting for his 30-day notice to expire, stop right here in this chapter, go to Chapter 5, and begin following the procedure outlined there for evicting a delinquent tenant.

If you have had no reason to serve a 3-day notice and are relying upon the Notice to Terminate Tenancy to evict your tenant, continue your reading in this chapter and follow the procedure outlined here.

• ADDING AN EXTRA FIVE DAYS—If you serve a Notice to Terminate Tenancy using the fourth method, mailing by certified or registered mail, you ought to wait an extra five days before filing the summons and complaint because you're actually serving the notice according to CCP §1013, which covers civil actions generally and extends the notice period by five days. Don't change the notice itself to make it a thirty-five-day notice. On its face, it should remain a thirty-day notice. Merely allow the tenant an extra five days to vacate before you file the summons and complaint.

If you serve the notice according to CCP §1162 (personal service or substituted service *and* service by mail), which covers evictions specifically, you need wait only the thirty days. That's the essence of a court decision on the subject [*Losornio v. Motta* (1998) 67 CA4th 110, 115, 78 CR2d 799, 801].

• COUNTING THE DAYS—If you serve your tenants a Notice to Terminate Tenancy on June 16th and give them thirty days to comply, begin counting with the 17th as the first day and stop counting with July 16th as the thirtieth day. On the following day, July 17th, you could file the summons and complaint. If you serve it January 10th, February 9th is the thirtieth day. On the following day, February 10th, you could file the summons and complaint. Remember that you are counting thirty days rather than one month.

• PITFALLS—There are three primary pitfalls you face after serving a Notice to Terminate Tenancy.

The first pitfall is accepting rent beyond the notice period. Doing so invalidates your notice, requiring you to start all over again. You know what that means. You have to serve another notice and bide your time until the lengthy notice period ends. Remember, this notice period is not a mere three days like the one for nonpayment of rent. It's ten times that, a whopping thirty days! That's a long time to have to wait for making the simple mistake of accepting rent beyond the notice period.

The tenant may offer you rent money beyond the notice period, but so long as you refuse it, you can follow up on your notice in court with confidence. Accept rent money only through the end of the notice period. Period!

To avoid this pitfall of accepting rent beyond the notice period, try to make the notice period end on the same day as the tenant's rental period, but be careful when you do. You could be creating additional trouble for yourself.

Here's an example. Say that the tenant's rental period begins on the first day of the month and ends on the last day of the month, and he pays you his August rent in person on the 28th of July. You know you want to serve him a 30-day notice. When should you serve it?

If you served the notice to him in person when he pays his rent, it would expire on the 27th of August, but it would not be valid because you already accepted rent through August 31st, which is beyond the expiration date of the notice.

You could wait until the first of August to give him the notice because you know that August has thirty-one days, and the notice period would end on the 31st of the month, the same date he has paid his rent through. That would work.

Ah, but what if you can't find him on the first of August to serve him? You'll have to wait until a later date to serve him in person or else resort to substituted service, and that will surely result in a loss of rent for you.

Let's say that you can't find him until the fifth of August and you serve him the notice then. The notice will expire on the fourth of September.

ber, and he ought to pay you rent for those four days in September if he complies with the notice and moves out on the fourth. Will he? Don't bet on it.

There's a better way to handle serving a Notice to Terminate Tenancy to a tenant who pays his rent early, one which avoids this first pitfall in a way which insures that you will receive your rent through the end of the notice period. It's simple. You lengthen the notice period so that the expiration date of the notice coincides with the date his rent is paid through.

Rather than giving a 30-day notice to the tenant who pays you his August rent in person on the 28th of July, you give him a thirty-four-day notice. You lengthen the notice period by four days, so that the notice expiration date falls on the same day as his "rent paid through" date.

You see, you can always add days to a 30-day notice. You cannot subtract days. You can turn a 30-day notice into a 34-day notice or a 40-day notice, but you cannot turn it into a 29-day notice or a 25-day notice.

Be aware of this first pitfall, and make adjustments as necessary to avoid accepting rent beyond the notice period.

The second pitfall is taking the tenant's last month's rent (security and cleaning deposits have no bearing on the situation) into account. A last month's rent is supposed to be used for, what else, the last month's rent. When you give a tenant thirty days to terminate tenancy, you are, in effect, telling him that this is his last month, so the last month's rent you have been holding should be applied. Make sure that the expiration date of your notice does not occur before *all* of the tenant's prepaid rent has been used up, whether that prepaid rent was paid to you recently or some time ago, when he moved in.

When you give a Notice to Terminate Tenancy to a tenant who paid you his last month's rent when he moved in, you want to give him the notice when he makes his normal rent payment. Then he will have paid you all his rent through the end of the 30-day notice period. Again, you must make sure that you don't inadvertently accept rent beyond the notice period. Adjust the period upward, increasing the days, if you have to.

The third pitfall is not waiting the full number of days following service of the notice before filing the summons and complaint. Remember that you must wait at least thirty days following actual service of the notice, not thirty days after the date appearing on the notice. The date appearing on the notice is nothing more than the preparation date. It may or may not be the same as the date of service. Whatever it is, it does not mark the beginning of the notice period. The date of service marks the beginning of the notice period. That's the important date. That's the date from which you begin your counting of the days.

Remember that there are only four 30-day months in any calendar year. The other eight have more or fewer than thirty days. Be careful with your counting. You are giving thirty days' notice, not one month's notice.

Begin with the right date, the date when the notice was served, count off the days on a calendar, and you will avoid this third pitfall.

Step 3. Prepare the Summons, Complaint, and Cover Sheet.

Use the same summons, complaint, and cover sheet forms as those referred to in chapter 5, but prepare the complaint somewhat differently to reflect the special nature of this kind of unlawful detainer.

Follow the explanation in chapter 5 to complete the top part and the first six items of the complaint. Under "Jurisdiction," check "ACTION IS A LIMITED CIVIL CASE," and check "does not exceed $10,000" for "Amount Demanded."

Name the defendants in 7a. Check box 7a2 to indicate that the tenants were served with a 30-day notice to quit, which is the same as a Notice to Terminate Tenancy. Check box 7d because the notice included an election of forfeiture. Check box 7e to indicate that you are attaching a copy of the notice to the complaint.

Report how the notice was served in item 8, and complete items 8b-d, 11, 12, 13, and 14 as appropriate. Omit items 9 and 10, and unless you feel compelled to make other allegations, omit 15 as well. Check item 18 and indicate how many pages you are attaching. They would include the rental agreement, the notice you served, and the proof of service of the notice if it's on a separate page.

Check 17e and f. You are entitled to "damages" equivalent to per-diem rent for all the days the tenant refuses to vacate following the expiration of the notice. Check 17h if the tenant owes you for anything other than rent.

Finally, check the first box in item 19 to indicate that you did not use an unlawful detainer assistant.

Steps 4-17. (Follow those given in chapter 5.)

Should you be following the fourth alternative under step 8 as described in chapter 5, namely a default in lieu of personal testimony, involving no court appearance, while providing judgment for both restitution and money, you will have to submit a Declaration for Default Judgment by Court (UD-115), another Judicial Council form.

It's easy to follow and fill out until you get to item 7, service of notice, where there are three choices, not four. If you served the Notice to Terminate Tenancy according to the fourth method mentioned here, service by certified or registered mail, you will have to change the form somewhat to indicate how you served the notice. To do so, cross out the words "posting and" in 7a3, so that it reads "by mailing on (date mailed)."

Note that the declaration form says you MUST attach the notice and the proof of service of the notice to the original complaint or to the declaration. The judge wants to see them, and since you won't be appearing in court to show them to him if you use this form, you will want to attach them.

If you have any other relevant paperwork which you did not attach to the complaint, attach it to the declaration here because the judge will want to see it. You can be sure of that, and when you're pursuing an unlawful detainer, you want to be sure of everything you can be sure of.

• • • • • • • • •

The major advantage of this kind of unlawful detainer is that there are really only two substantial defenses a tenant might raise against it, and the burden of proof is on the tenant. He might say, "My landlord is discriminating against me," or "My landlord is retaliating against me." Discrimination according to the Unruh Civil Rights Act is illegal when you are selecting tenants, when you are managing tenants, and when you are evicting tenants. Don't do it!

The retaliation referred to here involves your evicting a tenant arbitrarily within 180 days after he has exercised, or attempted to exercise, some legal right which is considered by the court to be of substantial importance. This would include a complaint to a governmental agency about conditions of the dwelling which violate housing or safety code requirements. It would also include the tenant's good-faith use of his right to "repair and deduct."

If you're interested in examining the law regarding retaliatory evictions, look at Civil Code §1942.5.

- Know your local housing ordinances well enough to understand how they relate to a Notice to Terminate Tenancy.
- Don't accept any rent money from your tenant for the period following the expiration of the notice.
- Wait a full thirty days after serving the notice before filing your summons and complaint.

9
Handling an Eviction of Holdover Owners

You have just acquired a property, and you would like to move into it yourself or rent it out to somebody else, except that the former owners still occupy the place and don't appear to be in any hurry to vacate. In fact, they appear determined to stay there as long as they can without paying anybody anything and without lifting two fingers to take care of the overgrown yard. The place could fall down around them, and they wouldn't care. Why should they? They don't own it anymore. To them it's nothing more than a free roof over their heads.

Whether the sale occurred voluntarily (with the owners' cooperation) or involuntarily (without the owners' cooperation as the result of a foreclosure, an IRS sale, a writ of execution, a trust deed default sale, or a default sale under a conditional sales contract) doesn't matter. What does matter is that you hold title to the property and that you want to take possession now.

What should you do?

The very first thing you should do is communicate with the firmly ensconced former owners and try to persuade them to vacate.

Persuading Holdover Owners to Vacate

Persuading holdover owners to vacate is no different from persuading ordinary tenants to vacate.

You assess the situation, including how much you're hurting, how much they're hurting, how much you'll have to pay in costs to evict them, how much time an eviction will require, and how immediate is your need to gain possession. Then you approach them, discuss their options and yours, reason with them, make them an offer, come to an agreement, and help them follow through. At least you hope they are reasonable people who can understand your position and theirs without becoming too emotional about

moving out of the place they have owned and called home.

You will get the best results if you take the time to learn why they haven't vacated and consider how to address their most pressing needs. When you ask them why they haven't vacated, you may find that they need guidance from you more than they need money. Perhaps they had plans to vacate prior to the sale, and those plans fell through for reasons beyond their control, and now they need help in assessing their options and formulating new plans.

Try talking with them. Try reasoning with them. Try helping them.

Owners whose property you acquired without their cooperation may require lots of persuading. You may have to pull out all the stops. Go ahead and pull them out. Don't be cheap, either. Bribery does work, you know. A little money offered to people who have recently lost all legitimate claims to their home, people who could be both despondent and obstinate, might work wonders. When you tally the overall costs of evicting the former owners—the legal fees, the loss of use, and the repair of all the damage they could do to the property—even if you do handle the eviction and all the repairs yourself, you'll still find that the dollars add up in a hurry. You might offer them $500 to leave within three days and find that you're much better off than you'd ever be if you'd "gone all the way" through the courts and had the sheriff evict them in due course.

If your holdover owners won't vacate in spite of your best efforts to get them out, you'll have to force them out legally, of course. There is a way (CCP §1161a), and you can do it yourself. It's a straightforward unlawful detainer procedure requiring, most importantly, some proof that you hold the title and actually are the legitimate owner of the property.

Keep in mind that you may use this particular

NOTICE TO QUIT

TO: Allen Barnes
    Marion Barnes

and all other persons in possession of the premises described as:

456 Sun Valley Road
(Street Address)
Dallasville   California   95555
(City)   (State)   (Zip)

PLEASE TAKE NOTICE that your possession of the above-described premises is without the consent of the owner and is in violation of California law regarding

PLEASE TAKE NOTICE that your possession of the above-described premises is without the consent of the owner and is in violation of California law regarding holdover after foreclosure or execution (CCP Section 1161a).

You are hereby required to remove from and deliver up possession of said premises within three (3) days, or legal proceedings will be instituted against you to recover said premises and such damages as the law allows.

Dated: March 4, XXXX   *Bruce Bunger*
                                        Owner/Manager

PROOF OF SERVICE (Server should complete this proof of service only AFTER serving tenants.)
  I, the undersigned, being at least 18 years of age, declare under penalty of perjury that I served the above notice, of which this is a true copy, on the following person(s) in possession in the manner(s) indicated below: ALLEN BARNES

☒ On 3/4/XXXX , I handed the notice to the person(s) in possession personally.

☐ On _____, after attempting personal service, I handed the notice to a person of suitable age and discretion at the residence/business of the person(s) in possession, AND I deposited a true copy in the U.S. Mail, in a sealed envelope with postage fully prepaid, addressed to the person(s) in possession at his/her/their place of residence (date mailed, if different _____).

☐ On _____, after attempting service in both manners indicated above, I posted the notice in a conspicuous place at the residence of the person(s) in possession, AND I deposited a true copy in the U.S. Mail, in a sealed envelope with postage fully prepaid, addressed to him/her/them at his/her/their place of residence (date mailed, if different _____).

Executed on 3/4/XXXX , at DALLASVILLE , California.

                    Served by *Bruce Bunger*

                                                            efc

procedure only when you're evicting an owner who is holding over, an owner who has not become a tenant.

If the property you acquired is occupied by the previous owner's tenant or if you turned the holdover owners into tenants yourself by executing a rental agreement with them or by accepting rent from them, then you should be using the normal tenant eviction procedure outlined in earlier chapters, for you are bound by whatever contract the previous owner had with his tenants or whatever expressed or implied contract you have now with the owners-turned-tenants.

Tenants who have a legitimate two-year lease on the property which still has six months to run, for example, cannot be evicted until the lease expires unless the tenants break the lease or the lease provides for cancellation upon notice that there has been a change of ownership.

Let's say that there's no doubt about your holdover owners. They definitely are the former owners of the property. They are still living there. You haven't turned them into tenants by accepting rent from them, and you want them out. You want possession for yourself. You have tried reasoning with them and you have tried persuading them, all to no avail. They're standing their ground, protecting what they still think of as "their castle." What's next?

Next is an eviction through the courts.

Study the procedure you must follow when evicting holdover owners. Then get busy and evict them as soon as possible.

Five Things You Should Know About Holdover Cases

The eviction procedure for holdover owners is a little different from any other eviction, and there are five things you should know before you begin the procedure.

First of all, you should know about and understand the difference between "holdover tenants" and "holdover owners."

I cannot emphasize enough how important this difference is in holdover cases. The term "holdover tenants" refers to those tenants who have given notice that they plan to move as of a certain date, and then they "hold over" after that date. "Holdover tenants" also refers to those tenants whose long-term lease has expired and who are "holding over" following the expiration of

their lease.

The term "holdover owners" refers to occupants who used to be the owners of a property but no longer are. They have neither property rights nor tenancy rights, but they continue in possession of the property.

Evict holdover owners using the procedure explained in this chapter. Evict holdover tenants using the procedures explained in other chapters.

Second, you should know that you must serve a notice to begin the eviction of holdover owners. You should serve the notice as soon as possible because you cannot ask for any rent from holdover owners in your complaint. You cannot ask for rent because the holdover owners are not tenants, but you can ask for damages to begin on a per-diem basis once the notice expires.

Third, you should know that you cannot use the Judicial Council's complaint form in holdover cases. You may have noticed that the Judicial Council complaint form even has a note at the bottom of the first page which states specifically: "Do not use this form for evictions after sale."

Fourth, you should know that you must attach a verification to your holdover complaint. Look at the end of the Judicial Council complaint form for unlawful detainer, and you'll see that a plaintiff's verification is part of the complaint. A holdover complaint must include a similar verification. The verification needs to be on a separate sheet of pleading paper and attached to the complaint. You may use the verification form included in the FORMS section of this book.

Fifth, in case there are any local eviction controls in your area (see chapter 4 and study your local ordinance) which might prevent a new owner from filing an unlawful detainer against holdover owners following a sale, you may still file an action against them to get them out, but it'll have to be some other kind of action, such as an ejectment, and you won't get to take advantage of the summary nature of an unlawful detainer. (Should you have to file an ejectment, consult the *California Practice Guide: Landlord-Tenant* for details.)

Step 1. Prepare the Notice.

Use the Notice to Quit form which refers specifically to the holdover owners as occupants and not as tenants. Identify the holdover situation right on the notice, and give the holdover own-

```
1 │ Bruce Buyer
  │ 1223 Pinehurst Ct.
2 │ Dallasville, CA 95555
  │ 555-555-5555
3 │ Plaintiff in Propria Persona
4 │
5 │
6 │
7 │
8 │     IN THE SUPERIOR COURT OF _____DALLASVILLE_____ JUDICIAL DISTRICT,
9 │     COUNTY OF _____BACKBONE_____, STATE OF CALIFORNIA
10│
11│ BRUCE BUYER_____,)
  │                 Plaintiff,)
12│         vs.               )        NO.
  │ ALLEN BARNES              )
13│ MARION BARNES_____,)        COMPLAINT FOR
  │             Defendant.)             UNLAWFUL DETAINER
14│ _____)        (CCP §1161a)
15│ Plaintiff alleges as follows:
16│      1. At all times mentioned herein, plaintiff was and now is a
17│ competent adult residing in the City of _____Dallasville_____, County of
18│ _____Backbone_____, State of California.
19│      2. Plaintiff is the owner of the premises located at
20│ _____456 Sun Valley Road_____ in the City
21│ of _____Dallasville_____, County of _____Backbone_____, State of
22│ California.
23│      3. Plaintiff believes that defendants are competent adults
24│ residing in the City of _____Dallasville_____, County of
25│ _____Backbone_____, State of California.
26│      4. The true names and capacities of defendants sued as Does are
27│ unknown to plaintiff. Plaintiff will seek leave of court to amend this
28│ complaint when said true names and capacities have been determined.
29│      5. At all times mentioned herein, each of the defendants,
```

You will find a blank copy of this form in the FORMS section of this book.

ers three days to move out.

Step 2. Serve the Notice

Since the notice used to evict holdover owners is a three-day notice, you should serve it the same way you serve other three-day notices (see chapter 5). Be diligent in trying personal service first before you resort to one of the other two methods.

Don't be so naive as to expect the holdover owners to move out within the three days. Be realistic. Spend this interval preparing to file the required legal papers rather than preparing to clean up the mess they leave behind when they vacate.

Count the days correctly. If you were to give the holdover owners their notice on Friday, the 9th, the date when the notice expires would be the 12th. The 9th doesn't count. The count begins with the 10th and ends with the 12th, which is the third day following the 9th and the last day for them to comply with your 3-day notice. The expiry date need not be a day when the courts are open, but the day following the expiry date must be a day when the courts are open. If it isn't, you'll just have to wait to file your summons and complaint until a day when the courts are open.

Step 3. Prepare the Summons and Complaint.

You already know that you cannot use the Judicial Council's complaint form in holdover cases. You must use a complaint especially drafted for a holdover case, and it must be printed on pleading paper (paper with line numbers down the left side). There's nothing magical about the verbiage except that it must include a certain few things, such as the exact relationship between the plaintiff and defendants which entitles the plaintiff to possession, the method used by the plaintiff to obtain title, and an allegation that the title was perfected through compliance with all legal requirements.

The sample complaint form shown here (only the first page of the three-page form appears here; you'll find all three pages in the FORMS section) may be used in any holdover-owner case. For example, let's suppose that you want to evict holdover owners who sold you their house and now won't vacate the place after you have paid them for it. You would need to fill in the blanks

on the complaint and select the first of the choices in paragraph 7. That choice identifies you as the owner of record, holding legal entitlement to the premises as purchaser from the defendants through a voluntary sale.

Note that paragraphs 8 and 10 refer to two exhibits, A and B. Exhibit A is whatever evidence you have to show that you are the legal owner. For the court to take it seriously, it should be a recorded document. Attach a copy and label it "Exhibit A." Exhibit B is the proof of service of the notice. Attach a copy of the notice and the proof of service and label them "Exhibit B."

Be sure that you indicate the proper date when damages begin. That date is four days following service of the Notice to Quit. In other words, the holdover owners have three days to vacate following service of the notice. If they don't vacate by then, one day later damages begin.

Per-diem "damages" amount to a rental equivalent for every day the owner holds over following expiration of the notice period. Since the property hasn't been rented, there is no established rent, and you must determine what the fair rental value would be if the property were available for rent.

You can determine a fair rental value for the premises by checking the classified ads for similar properties and phoning the landlords of those properties. Discuss the size, condition, amenities, location, and rent of their property. Compare that information with everything you know about your property, and come up with a fair rental value. When you pick a figure, make sure it's reasonable and be prepared to justify it. You don't want to pick a figure which is so unreasonable that the holdover owners will want to answer the complaint only to dispute your damages figure.

Along with the complaint, you must prepare a verification. A self-explanatory verification form for this very purpose appears in the FORMS section. It's a versatile form. You as the defendant may use it. Any other defendant may use it. Even the attorney who is representing you may use it. It requires that you identify your role in the action, date it, and sign it.

Steps 4-17. (Follow those given in chapter 5.)

Because holdover owners are not tenants, they cannot raise the normal tenant defenses, such as warranty of habitability or retaliation. You prevail against them merely by proving to the court that you, not they, are now the undisputed owner of record and hence are entitled to possession. Go to it!

- Find out why the holdover owners haven't vacated.
- Persuade them to vacate as best you can.
- Once you realize the futility of persuasion, follow the legal procedure to evict them.
- Serve the Notice to Quit promptly to start the "damages" clock the day after it expires.
- Check the rents for similar properties to determine a realistic figure for per-diem "damages."

10
Handling the Contested Case

Your tenant has chosen to file a response to your complaint, and you are absolutely livid that he would dare to use a legal means to oppose your efforts to evict him. He's a scumbag, an absolute scumbag. He lies and cheats, and he uses the "system" whenever he can to further his own ends. You know that you are entirely in the right, that his claim against you is on a par with Iraq's claim against Kuwait before the Gulf War, but you are also uncertain about what you ought to do next.

Calm down first. A response to one eviction complaint doesn't portend the end of the world. It doesn't even portend the end of your rental property business. It means only that the eviction will be delayed somewhat. That's all. Worse things could happen, and in this business, you can be sure that they will.

Once you have calmed down and your blood pressure has returned nearly to normal, read the response your tenant has made. Read it over and over until it makes good sense to you, eighty-three times if need be. Only then will you be in any position to decide what you should do next. Don't despair. You have plenty of options, and you are going to prevail. Take some time while you're reviewing your options to consider again what your primary objective is and how you might best achieve it now that you know your tenant is trying to use the law to stymie your best efforts to get him out. That objective of yours should still be to evict your tenant as quickly and as cheaply as possible.

How you can evict him quickly and cheaply under these changed circumstances is the subject of this chapter.

Let an Attorney in Your Life?

Earlier I tried to dissuade you from paying an attorney to crank up his eviction mill and have his secretary fill out a few forms in order to per-

form a perfunctory eviction for you, especially when the chances are slim that you will encounter any opposition.

Once a response has been filed, however, the chances are good that you will encounter further legal complications which may require the expertise of an attorney. Understand that a wily attorney for the tenant can create a flurry of paperwork which can delay your case a month or more. Ask yourself whether you can afford these delays. Your securing the services of an attorney now will cost you some bucks, that's for sure, but it may save you many in the long run. Weigh your alternatives.

Naturally you don't have to hire an attorney to represent you at this point, but you may if you want to. You may hire him to take the case over completely or you may elect to buy half an hour of his time and ask him to review your case and offer you some advice about what you should do next. You should seriously consider hiring an attorney if your tenant has hired one, though, and you'll know whether he has when you see the words "Attorney at Law" somewhere on the written response.

Read further in this chapter to learn what's in store for you whether you hire an attorney or not, and if you think then that it all sounds too complicated for you to do by yourself, get help. Remember that you may secure legal counsel whenever you think you need it.

The Various Responses

Having read the tenant's response carefully to understand what it says, you should know whether it's a motion to quash service, a demurrer, a motion to strike, or a straightforward answer to your complaint. It could be any of these four responses, and it could be totally groundless, filed for no reason other than to gain some additional rent-free possession of your rental

ATTORNEY OR PARTY WITHOUT ATTORNEY *(Name and Address)*   TELEPHONE NO. (415) 123-4567   FOR COURT USE ONLY

LESTER LANDLORD AND LESLIE LANDLORD
123 NEAT STREET
LITTLETOWN, CA 91111

ATTORNEY FOR *(Name):* Plaintiff in Pro Per

NAME OF COURT: SADDLEBACK MUNICIPAL COURT
STREET ADDRESS: 110 STATE STREET
MAILING ADDRESS:
CITY AND ZIP CODE: LITTLETOWN, CA 91111
BRANCH NAME:

PLAINTIFF: LESTER LANDLORD AND LESLIE LANDLORD

DEFENDANT: DANA CHEEP AND MURETTA SHODDI

ANSWER—Unlawful Detainer   CASE NUMBER: 987654

1. Defendant *(names):* DANA CHEEP AND MURETTA SHODDI

answers the complaint as follows:

2. *Check ONLY ONE of the next two boxes:*
   a. ☐ Defendant generally denies each statement of the complaint. *(Do not check this box if the complaint demands more than $1,000).*
   b. ☒ Defendant admits that all of the statements of the complaint are true EXCEPT
      (1) Defendant claims the following statements of the complaint are false *(use paragraph numbers from the complaint or explain):*

      6a; We did not receive the 3-day notice.

      ☐ Continued on Attachment 2b(1).
      (2) Defendant has no information or belief that the following statements of the complaint are true, so defendant denies them *(use paragraph numbers from the complaint or explain):*

      ☐ Continued on Attachment 2b(2).

3. AFFIRMATIVE DEFENSES   *(NOTE: For each box checked, you must state brief facts to support it in the space provided at the top of page two (item 3j).)*
   a. ☐ *(nonpayment of rent only)* Plaintiff has breached the warranty to provide habitable premises.
   b. ☐ *(nonpayment of rent only)* Defendant made needed repairs and properly deducted the cost from the rent, and plaintiff did not give proper credit.
   c. ☐ *(nonpayment of rent only)* On *(date):* _____ , before the notice to pay or quit expired, defendant offered the rent due but plaintiff would not accept it.
   d. ☐ Plaintiff waived, changed, or canceled the notice to quit.
   e. ☐ Plaintiff served defendant with the notice to quit or filed the complaint to retaliate against defendant.
   f. ☐ By serving defendant with the notice to quit or filing the complaint, plaintiff is arbitrarily discriminating against the defendant in violation of the Constitution or laws of the United States or California.
   g. ☐ Plaintiff's demand for possession violates the local rent control or eviction control ordinance of *(city or county, title of ordinance, and date of passage):*

      (Also, briefly state the facts showing violation of the ordinance in item 3j.)
   h. ☐ Plaintiff accepted rent from defendant to cover a period of time after the date the notice to quit expired.
   i. ☐ Other affirmative defenses are stated in item 3j.

(Continued on reverse)

Form Approved by the
Judicial Council of California
982.1(95) [Rev. January 1, 1997]

ANSWER—Unlawful Detainer

Civil Code, § 1940 et seq.
Code of Civil Procedure, § 425.12

For obvious reasons, you will not find a blank copy of this form in the FORMS section of this book or in Eviction Forms Creator.

dwelling. Don't suppose that simply because your tenant has filed a response that there is any merit in it. There probably isn't, no, not in the least.

Let's examine the most likely responses in some detail so that you will know what each one of them is all about.

A *motion to quash service* is used to seek dismissal of a case by alleging that there was some defect in the summons. The defect might be that you as a party to the suit served the summons, that the wrong person was served, that the summons failed to mention the five-day period available for responding, that the summons mentioned the wrong court or judicial district, that the wrong kind of summons was used, or even that the summons was never served. You can avoid this kind of a response by using the proper summons form and by seeing that it is filled out and served correctly. Remember, all the same, that even if you do everything properly, the tenant may still file a motion to quash just to be obstinate and gain time, knowing full well that he will lose the motion when you come forward to prove that you did handle the summons and service correctly.

A *demurrer* is used to delay or seek dismissal of a case by alleging that whereas the matters of fact may be true as stated, the plaintiff really has no case at all. It may allege that either the notice or the complaint was inadequate. The inadequacy might be that the notice wasn't in writing, that it wasn't signed by the right person, that it wasn't dated, that it didn't give the right address, that it was served before the tenant was delinquent, that it was improperly served, that it wasn't specific enough, that it wasn't in the alternative if it was supposed to be, that it requested rent which was higher than it should have been according to the complaint, or that it requested money other than rent. A demurrer filed concerning the complaint might mention that the complaint failed to indicate whether the rental agreement was oral or written, that the complaint was vague or inconsistent, that it failed to mention whether the required notice was served, that it failed to indicate whether the plaintiff was either the owner or the authorized agent, that it was filed before it should have been, or that it revealed a defect in another relevant notice such as one given for a rent increase. (You might want to know that there is some controversy in legal circles about what constitutes proper grounds for a demurrer in an

unlawful detainer action [*Delta Imports, Inc. v. Municipal Court*, 146 CA3d 1033, 1036 194 CR 685, 687 (1983)]. Look at this case should someone file a demurrer against you.)

A *motion to strike* is used to seek a delay or dismissal of a case by alleging that the complaint contains irrelevancies, redundancies, or some other defect. These might say that the complaint includes much about the tenant which is irrelevant or repetitious, that it is not verified, that it asks for a reasonable rental value but fails to mention what a reasonable rental value is, that it asks for extra damages but fails to indicate maliciousness on the tenant's part, that it asks for attorney fees but fails to say whether the rental agreement authorized them, that it asks for damages but fails to support the claim sufficiently, or that it asks for damages beyond the holdover period.

An *answer* to the complaint is used to defend the tenant on any of a variety of grounds, some of which are the same as those allowed under the responses already mentioned. For example, an answer might allege that the tenant never received a notice, that the notice didn't give the correct rent owed, that the notice was unclear, that the notice failed to offer an alternative when it should have, that either the notice or the complaint was served prematurely, that the landlord refused to accept rent within the three days after serving the notice, that the rent demanded was different from what was agreed upon, that the complaint failed to specify which rental agreement provision was broken, that rent was accepted when it shouldn't have been, that the tenant was not guilty of bad faith in holding over and shouldn't be charged treble damages, that the eviction is retaliatory, that the eviction is racially motivated, that the landlord breached the warranty of habitability and isn't owed any rent, that the landlord violated local rent control or eviction ordinances, or that some other reason should be considered.

Take a look at the answer form shown here which the Judicial Council of California in its evenhandedness made available to tenants at the same time it made its complaint form available to landlords. You can see that it's much the same as the complaint form you're already familiar with, even to the point of referring to specific items in the complaint.

Now that you know what kinds of responses your tenant might make and the likely grounds

PLAINTIFF *(Name)*: LESTER LANDLORD AND LESLIE LANDLORD	CASE NUMBER
DEFENDANT *(Name)*: DANA CHEEP AND MURETTA SHODDI	987654

3. AFFIRMATIVE DEFENSES *(cont'd)*

j. Facts supporting affirmative defenses checked above *(identify each item separately by its letter from page one)*:

(1) ☐ All the facts are stated in Attachment 3j.   (2) ☐ Facts are continued in Attachment 3j.

4. OTHER STATEMENTS

a. ☐ Defendant vacated the premises on *(date)*:

b. ☐ The fair rental value of the premises alleged in the complaint is excessive *(explain)*:

c. ☐ Other *(specify)*:

5. DEFENDANT REQUESTS

a. that plaintiff take nothing requested in the complaint.

b. costs incurred in this proceeding.

c. ☐ reasonable attorney fees.

d. ☐ that plaintiff be ordered to (1) make repairs and correct the conditions that constitute a breach of the warranty to provide habitable premises and (2) reduce the monthly rent to a reasonable rental value until the conditions are corrected.

e. ☐ other *(specify)*:

6. ☐ Number of pages attached *(specify)*:

UNLAWFUL DETAINER ASSISTANT (Business and Professions Code sections 6400-6415)

7. *(Must be completed in all cases)* An **unlawful detainer assistant** ☒ did not ☐ did for compensation give advice or assistance with this form. *(If defendant has received any help or advice for pay from an unlawful detainer assistant, state)*:

a. Assistant's name: b. Telephone No.:

c. Street address, city, and ZIP:

d. County of registration: e. Registration No.:   f. Expires on *(date)*:

DANA CHEEP	▶ *Dana Cheep*
(TYPE OR PRINT NAME)	(SIGNATURE OF DEFENDANT OR ATTORNEY)

MURETTA SHODDI	▶ *Muretta Shoddi*
(TYPE OR PRINT NAME)	(SIGNATURE OF DEFENDANT OR ATTORNEY)

*(Each defendant for whom this answer is filed must be named in item 1 **and** must sign this answer unless his or her attorney signs.)*

VERIFICATION

(Use a different verification form if the verification is by an attorney or for a corporation or partnership.)

I am the defendant in this proceeding and have read this answer. I declare under penalty of perjury under the laws of the State of California that the foregoing is true and correct.

Date: August 10, XXXX

DANA CHEEP	▶ *Dana Cheep*
(TYPE OR PRINT NAME)	(SIGNATURE OF DEFENDANT)

For obvious reasons, you will not find a blank copy of this form in the FORMS section of this book or in Eviction Forms Creator.

for each, you should know something about handling them.

Handling Responses

No matter what response the tenant has made, you will have to participate in a court hearing, but unless you opted to file a Declaration for Default Judgment by Court or to have the court clerk enter a default judgment for restitution only, you would have had to appear in court anyway for the prove-up trial even if the tenant failed to respond, so it's nothing out of the ordinary, and it's certainly nothing to fear. The only difference here is that there will be an adversary facing you in court, your tenant.

If the tenant files a motion to quash, a demurrer, or a motion to strike, the court hearing will be set automatically, and you should plan to be there well prepared to substantiate your position. You will get a notice in the mail, of course, but you should ask the court clerk about the hearing date before the notice reaches your mailbox.

If the tenant files an answer, you will have to take the initiative and request a trial date.

If the response is a demurrer or a motion to strike and it alleges some deficiency which might be corrected, you would have an opportunity to correct the deficiency after the hearing. If the response is a motion to quash or an answer, and either were judged in the tenant's favor, you would lose your case and you would have to begin anew by serving the tenant with another notice in order to pursue the eviction.

Remember, the notice you serve to begin your unlawful detainer action is extremely important to your case. It must be correct, absolutely correct. Once you file the complaint, anything found to be deficient in your notice cannot be corrected. That's why you must be certain that your notice is absolutely correct *before* you file the complaint. Before you file, you may "correct" an incorrect notice by serving a new one (see chapter 5, "Correcting" the Notice). After you file, forget it. The notice might as well have been cast in concrete. Your unlawful detainer is dependent upon that notice's correctness for its very life.

Two Defendants, One Response

Whenever you serve more than one tenant with a summons and complaint, each becomes a defendant, and each must respond to your complaint. Sometimes only one will make a response; the other doesn't bother. When that happens, be sure you get a default judgment against the one who did not respond (follow the steps described in chapter 5, beginning with step 8), or you will not be able to evict that person even when you do get a judgment against the party who responded. Get the non-responding party out of the picture as soon as possible.

Settlement Before Trial

Even though your case is working its way into court at this point, you may still want to work something out with your tenant before actually going to trial in order to resolve everything more quickly and to leave nothing to chance. After all, you're still looking at a delay of at least twenty-five days before the tenant is evicted if you do prevail in court, and you can't know for sure whether you will prevail in court until the judge gives judgment. No matter how good your case is, the judge may show your raggedy tenant some leniency or even rule against you entirely because your tenant cries bigger tears than you do.

A settlement now may be to your advantage and to your tenant's advantage as well, a bona-fide win-win arrangement.

Should your tenant or his attorney call you to suggest a settlement before trial, listen to the suggestion and give it some serious consideration as an alternative to going to trial. You may even want to contact the tenant or his attorney yourself with your own suggestions for settling your differences before trial.

In determining whether you ought to settle, you must understand what your primary objectives are. Do you want your rent money more than you want the tenant to vacate? Do you want the tenant to vacate more than you want the rent money? Do you want to minimize the hassle in continuing the eviction through the courts? In these cases and in any number of others, you may want to reach a settlement before trial because a settlement will likely save you money and time and hassles.

Remember that in most contested nonpayment cases, no matter how favorable the judgment is to you, you can't win. All you can do is try to control your losses. Forget fairness, forget ego, forget pride, but don't forget money. Don't forget that you are a business person. Don't forget that you are in the landlording business to make money. You must always keep your mind

UD-115

ATTORNEY OR PARTY WITHOUT ATTORNEY *(Name, state bar number, and address):*	FOR COURT USE ONLY
Lester Landlord & Leslie Landlord 123 Neat Street Littletown, CA 91111 TELEPHONE NO.: 555-123-4567 FAX NO *(Optional)*: 555-123-4568 E-MAIL ADDRESS *(Optional)*: lesterlandlord@wazoo.com ATTORNEY FOR *(Name)*: Plaintiff in Propria Persona	

SUPERIOR COURT OF CALIFORNIA, COUNTY OF **Saddleback**
STREET ADDRESS: 100 State Street
MAILING ADDRESS:
CITY AND ZIP CODE: Littletown 91111
BRANCH NAME:

PLAINTIFF: Lester Landlord
         Leslie Landlord

DEFENDANT: Richard Renter, Rose Renter

STIPULATION FOR ENTRY OF JUDGMENT (Unlawful Detainer)	CASE NUMBER: 1234567890

1. IT IS STIPULATED by plaintiff *(name each):* Lester Landlord, Leslie Landlord   and
defendant *(name each):* Richard Renter, Rose Renter

2. [X] Plaintiff [ ] Defendant *(specify name):* Lester Landlord, Leslie Landlord   is awarded
  a. [X] possession of the premises located at *(street address, apartment number, city, and county):*
        458 Sweet Street, Littletown 91111, Saddleback County

  b. [X] cancellation of the rental agreement. [ ] forfeiture of the lease.
  c. [X] past due rent $ 730.00
  d. [ ] total holdover damages $
  e. [ ] attorney fees $
  f. [X] costs $ 317.00
  g. [ ] deposit of $ [X] See item 3.
  h. [ ] other *(specify):*   Interest   Special Damages
  i. Total $ 1,047.00 to be paid by [ ] *(date):*   [ ] installment payments (see item 5)

3. [X] Deposit. If not awarded under item 2g, then plaintiff must
  a. [X] return deposit of $ $500.00   to defendant by *(date):* October 21, XXXX
  b. [X] give an itemized deposit statement to defendant within three weeks after defendant vacates the premises
      (Civ. Code. § 1950.5).
  c. [X] mail the [X] deposit [X] itemized statement   to the defendant at *(mailing address):*

4. [X] A writ of possession will issue immediately, but there will be no lockout before *(date):*   September 30, XXXX

5. [ ] AGREEMENT FOR INSTALLMENT PAYMENTS
  a. Defendant agrees to pay $ on the *(specify day)*   day of each month beginning
    on *(specify date)*   until paid in full.
  b. If any payment is more than *(specify)*   days late, the entire amount in item 2i will become immediately due and
    payable plus interest at the legal rate.

6. a. [ ] Judgment will be entered now.
  b. [X] Judgment will be entered only upon default of payment of the amount in item 2i or the payment arrangement in item 5a.
    The case is calendared for dismissal on *(date and time)*   October 5, XXXX; 9A   in
    department *(specify)*   27   unless plaintiff or defendant otherwise notifies the court.
  c. [ ] Judgment will be entered as stated in Judgment—Unlawful Detainer Attachment (form UD-110S), which is attached.
  d. [X] Judgment will be entered as stated in item 7.

Page 1 of 2

Form Approved for Optional Use Judicial Council of California UD-115 [New January 1, 2003]	STIPULATION FOR ENTRY OF JUDGMENT (Unlawful Detainer)	Code of Civil Procedure § 664.6

You will find a blank copy of this form in the FORMS section of this book and in Eviction Forms Creator.

open to the many different ways there are in this business to make money and if not to make money, then to control losses.

Settlement before trial could be one of those ways to control losses.

Remember that there's now a certain amount of pressure to settle which didn't exist before you filed your unlawful detainer. You have put some pressure on the tenant by filing the unlawful detainer, and your tenant has put some pressure on you by filing an answer. As a result, both of you are likely to be more agreeable to coming up with a settlement you can live with. You may agree to terms that you wouldn't have agreed to before, and your tenant may do the same.

You both know what you're facing if you don't come to a settlement yourselves. You're facing uncertainty, and uncertainty means nail-biting, sleeplessness, butterflies in the tummy, cold sweat, extra knee time, maybe even some chain smoking and an extra shot of Scotch.

Face it, you have nothing to lose by trying to settle before trial, that is, if you believe that you are dealing with someone who can be dealt with, someone who is neither a professional deadbeat nor a genuine ignoramus nor a certifiable incompetent.

Should you decide that you might be able to settle with your tenant, rehearse what you're going to say to him. Stress the advantages of settling over the disadvantages of not settling.

Start by asking something like this, "Do you have any idea what's really going to happen to you as a result of your being evicted through the courts? Well, let me tell you. I know." Most tenants don't have a clue.

"First of all, I'm going to get a judgment against you which will go down on your credit report immediately and remain there for seven years. Second, the sheriff is going to come out here and humiliate you in front of your neighbors by throwing you out on the street and locking the door behind you. Third, I'm going to inventory your belongings, move them into storage, and dispose of them legally. Fourth, I'm going to hire a bill collector to hound you for the money you owe me from now until kingdom come. Fifth, you're going to have trouble renting from any other landlord in the future, for all of them will know that I have evicted you. Sixth, I'm going to tell the IRS that you had income equal to the amount of the judgment against you,

and you're going to have to pay taxes on it. Do you want all these things to happen to you?"

Finish up by saying, "Consider what you stand to gain by fighting this eviction. There is one thing and one thing only, and that is a few extra days of living under this roof. That's all. There's nothing more. Just remember, once you've been evicted from here, your eviction is going to haunt you long after you leave. Ask anybody you know who's been evicted through the courts whether they'd ever go through another eviction. They'll tell you. They'll tell you they wouldn't. They'll tell you that the loss outweighs the gain."

Next, try to figure out what the tenant's concerns really are. Does he need a little more time to find another place? Does he need a little more time to raise the money to pay you off? Would he be ready to move today if you were to agree not to seek a judgment against him? Does he need some help of one sort or another that wouldn't cost you much, perhaps some help with moving or paying for a storage unit? What can the two of you do right now to settle the case?

If you can establish some terms agreeable to both of you, write them down and sign them. You could summarize them in a simple agreement, something like this:

```
Lester Landlord agrees to drop
his unlawful detainer action
against Richard Renter provided
that Richard Renter vacates the
premises known as 456 Sweet St.,
Littletown, CA, completely as of
tomorrow, March 12, xxxx.

Richard Renter agrees to leave
the premises clean and undamaged.

Richard Renter agrees to allow
his entire security deposit to be
applied to his past-due rent and
other charges.

Once Richard Renter has vacated,
Lester Landlord will ask the
court to dismiss the case without
prejudice and will send a copy of
the dismissal to Richard Renter.

Dated:       Signed: [both parties]
```

A tenant may be more willing to sign a simple agreement like this than an official-looking Judicial Council form called a Stipulation for Entry of Judgment, but you may use the Judicial Coun-

PLAINTIFF: Lester Landlord	CASE NUMBER:
DEFENDANT: Richard Renter	1234567890

7. [X] Plaintiff and defendant further stipulate as follows *(specify):*

Plaintiffs and Defendants agree to drop any and all other claims they may have made against one another as landlords and tenants.

Plaintiffs and Defendants agree that this stipulation makes no conclusion as to which side has prevailed in this legal action.

8. a. **The parties named in item 1 understand that they have the right to (1) have an attorney present and (2) receive notice of and have a court hearing about any default in the terms of this stipulation.**

   b. Date: 9/23/XXXX

   Lester Landlord
   _____
   (TYPE OR PRINT NAME)

   ▶ *Lester Landlord*
   _____
   (SIGNATURE OF PLAINTIFF OR ATTORNEY)

   Leslie Landlord
   _____
   (TYPE OR PRINT NAME)

   ▶ *Leslie Landlord*
   _____
   (SIGNATURE OF PLAINTIFF OR ATTORNEY)

   [ ] Continued on *Attachment* 8b (form MC-025).

   c. Date: 9/23/XXXX

   Richard Renter
   _____
   (TYPE OR PRINT NAME)

   ▶ *Richard Renter*
   _____
   (SIGNATURE OF DEFENDANT OR ATTORNEY)

   Rose Renter
   _____
   (TYPE OR PRINT NAME)

   ▶ *Rose Renter*
   _____
   (SIGNATURE OF DEFENDANT OR ATTORNEY)

   _____
   (TYPE OR PRINT NAME)

   ▶
   _____
   (SIGNATURE OF DEFENDANT OR ATTORNEY)

   [ ] Continued on *Attachment* 8c (form MC-025).

9. IT IS SO ORDERED.

Date:

_____
JUDICIAL OFFICER

| UD-115 [New January 1, 2003] | **STIPULATION FOR ENTRY OF JUDGMENT**
(Unlawful Detainer) | Page 2 of 2 |

You will find a blank copy of this form in the FORMS section of this book and in Eviction Forms Creator.

cil form rather than a simple agreement if you wish because you have already filed an action against the tenant, and the form does fit a variety of circumstances.

Use a simple agreement only if the tenant agrees to pay you in full immediately or vacate immediately. Do not use a simple agreement to spell out a payment scheme, for if the tenant makes only one payment and refuses to make any more, you will have to start the eviction from scratch.

Using a Stipulation for Entry of Judgment, you and your tenant may stipulate that you will drop the case if one or both of you meet certain conditions. The conditions might be paying all of what is owed by a certain date, vacating by a certain date, or making installment payments promptly as agreed. If the conditions are not met, you agree that the lawsuit will continue to its conclusion. A stipulated agreement keeps your unlawful detainer alive while still giving your tenant a chance to perform whatever terms you agree upon.

Keep in mind the difference between a simple agreement and a stipulated agreement. It's a major difference.

Whereas you may create a simple agreement anytime (the payment pledge introduced in chapter 1 is one example of a simple agreement), you cannot create a stipulated agreement without first having filed a lawsuit. It's part of the lawsuit. It's legal paperwork, and it has legal consequences. If a tenant does not abide by a stipulated agreement and you have submitted it to the court and had it approved by a judge, you can have the tenant evicted legally in short order.

You may submit a Stipulation for Entry of Judgment to the court straightaway, or you may choose to wait until later, even until your court date arrives. In the end, you may never submit one at all if the tenant performs as agreed prior to the court date and if you elect to have the case dismissed using a Request for Dismissal form (an example of the form appears at the end of chapter 5).

What you do about settling the case before trial depends mostly upon how the tenant views his credit rating and future trouble. He may understand how bad a judgment will look on his credit report and want to make certain concessions to you so you won't file a judgment against him. Hope that he does.

Preparing for Trial—The Judge

You may think that your case is so one-sided in your favor that you needn't be concerned about which judge will hear your case. You may think that nobody could possibly side with your tenant once you have an opportunity to present your case in court. You may think, too, that judges are completely impartial, or else they wouldn't be sitting on the bench.

Think again.

Judges are human, and no human is completely impartial. Everybody has prejudices. Whenever there's a doubt or an issue which could go either way, some judges tend to side with tenants, and some judges tend to side with landlords. You certainly don't want to appear before a judge who tends to side with tenants, not if you have a choice in the matter.

You may indeed have a choice in the matter, and you may want to do a little sleuthing down at the courthouse to learn whatever you can about the judges you could get.

Randomly visiting different courtrooms where unlawful detainers are being heard is one way to do your sleuthing, but there is another, quicker way to find the right judge. Ask the clerk which attorney handles more unlawful detainers than anybody else in the jurisdiction and then ask whose courtroom that attorney is appearing in today. That courtroom will likely have the judge who's most favorable to landlords because that attorney knows who that judge is and how to get into his courtroom.

Try to get your unlawful detainer scheduled into his courtroom.

Without telling the clerk that you're trying to get into the courtroom of the judge who is most favorable to landlords, you might simply tell her that you'd like to go before a judge who has lots of experience with unlawful detainers. She may accept your reasoning and schedule you into that courtroom.

If you can't get into that courtroom by asking directly, try asking when that particular judge hears unlawful detainers and then asking the clerk to schedule your case for trial then.

Of course, you may find that the judge you think would be most favorable to landlords is not at all favorable to landlords who appear *in pro per*, and the whole effort to find the right judge may be a waste of your time. That's just a risk you have to take.

UD-150

ATTORNEY OR PARTY WITHOUT ATTORNEY *(Name, State Bar number, and address):*
Lester Landlord & Leslie Landlord
123 Neat Street
Littletown, CA 91111

TELEPHONE NO.: 555-123-4567   FAX NO. *(Optional):* 555-123-4568
E-MAIL ADDRESS *(Optional):* lesterlandlord@yahoo.com
ATTORNEY FOR *(Name):* Plaintiff in Propria Persona

FOR COURT USE ONLY

SUPERIOR COURT OF CALIFORNIA, COUNTY OF Saddleback
STREET ADDRESS: 100 State Street
MAILING ADDRESS:
CITY AND ZIP CODE: Littletown 91111
BRANCH NAME: Creekside

PLAINTIFF: Lester Landlord
Leslie Landlord
DEFENDANT: Richard Renter, Rose Renter

[X] REQUEST [ ] COUNTER-REQUEST	CASE NUMBER:
TO SET CASE FOR TRIAL—UNLAWFUL DETAINER	1234567890
[X] **Plaintiff** [ ] **Defendant**	

1. [X] **Plaintiff's request.** I represent to the court that all parties have been served with process and have appeared or have had a default or dismissal entered against them. I request that this case be set for trial.

2. **Trial preference.** The premises concerning this case are located at *(street address, apartment number, city, zip code, and county)*
   123 Neat Street, Littletown 91111, Saddleback County

   a. [X] To the best of my knowledge, the right to possession of the premises is still in issue. This case is entitled to legal preference under Code of Civil Procedure section 1179a.

   b. [ ] To the best of my knowledge, the right to possession of the premises is no longer in issue. No defendant or other person is in possession of the premises.

3. **Jury or nonjury trial.** I request [ ] a jury trial [X] a nonjury trial

4. **Estimated length of trial.** I estimate that the trial will take *(check one):*

   a. [ ] days *(specify number):*   b. [X] hours *(specify if estimated trial is less than one day):*   1/2 hour

5. **Trial date.** I am not available on the following dates *(specify dates and reasons for unavailability):*
   October 8-10, XXXX - My work takes me out of town then.

UNLAWFUL DETAINER ASSISTANT (Bus. & Prof. Code §§ 6400-6415)

6. *(Complete in all cases.)* An unlawful detainer assistant [X] did **not** [ ] did for compensation give advice or advice with this form. *(If declarant has received any help or advice from an unlawful detainer assistant, complete a-f:)*

   a. Assistant's name: c. Telephone no.:
   b. Street address, city, and zip code: d. County of registration:
                                                  e. Registration no.:
                                                  f. Expires on *(date):*

I declare under penalty of perjury under the laws of the State of California that the foregoing is true and correct.
Date: 9/23/XXXX

_____   ▶ *Lester Landlord*
Lester Landlord
(TYPE OR PRINT NAME)   (SIGNATURE OF PARTY OR ATTORNEY FOR PARTY)

NOTICE

- An unlawful detainer case must be set for trial on a date not later than **20 days after the first request** to set the case for trial is made (Code Civ. Proc., § 1170.5(a)).
- If a jury is requested, $150 must be deposited with the court 5 days before trial (Code Civ. Proc., § 631).
- Court reporter and interpreter services vary. Check with the court for availability of services and fees charged.
- If you cannot pay the court fees and costs, you may apply for a fee waiver. Ask the court clerk for a fee waiver form.

Page 1 of 2

Form Approved for Mandatory Use
Judicial Council of California
UD-150 [New January 1, 2005]

**REQUEST/COUNTER-REQUEST TO SET CASE
FOR TRIAL—UNLAWFUL DETAINER**

Code of Civil Procedure §§ 631,
1170.5(a), 1179a
www.courtinfo.ca.gov

Preparing for Trial—The Paperwork

When a tenant files an answer to your complaint, you must request a trial date using a two-page form called Request/Counter-Request to Set Case for Trial–Unlawful Detainer (UD-150) (you'll need an original and two copies, plus a copy for each additional defendant who answered). Either you or the tenant may request a jury trial, but whoever requests one will have to pay more costs, and generally nobody wants to pay, unless the tenant is willing to gamble on still another delaying action. Don't you request one.

days following the filing of a request to set. The sooner you file the request, the sooner you will get into court. When you get your date, make sure that it's within the legal limits.

Sometime before the trial, you should prepare a Judgment–Unlawful Detainer and a Writ of Execution, which are Judicial Council forms introduced in chapter 5. You are an optimist, aren't you? You know you're going to prevail, don't you?

You cannot complete these forms entirely because you don't know yet all the particulars about how your case fared in court. Once you do, you may complete them. Ask the clerk whether you

Note that the instructions on page 2 of the request (see page 232), which is really just the proof of service by mail, say that somebody other than you must mail *both* pages of the form to the defendant. Both pages should be completed except that the second page should not be signed. After mailing the form, the person who mailed it to the defendant should sign the second page of the original and a copy where indicated, take them to the court clerk's office, and ask that the trial be set for the earliest possible date.

Fortunately for us landlords, there's an important law, CCP §1170.5(a), which requires courts, except under unusual circumstances, to schedule unlawful detainer trials within twenty

may print the particulars legibly in ink or whether you must use a typewriter or computer. If you complete the forms yourself, you may submit them immediately for the judge's signature, and you'll save time. Avoid having the clerk complete them unless she says she can do so that very day.

Both you and the tenant have the right before trial to try to discover certain things about the other's case which might help your own, and for that the Judicial Council has prepared a form called Form Interrogatories–Unlawful Detainer (FI-128). Because it's seven pages long and doesn't require any explanation to complete for someone who has come this far in handling his own unlawful detainer, you won't find it reproduced here, and because it is seldom used due to time limitations, you will not find a blank copy in the FORMS section. It's available on the Judicial Council website (courtinfo.ca.gov).

Both discoveries and the form itself would appear to benefit the tenant more than the landlord, for there are many more things a tenant might discover about your case against him than you might discover about his defense. Still, you might want to use the form for a few things under exceptional circumstances, such as for discovering the names and tenancy dates of unknowns who are living on your property, discovering the basis for a tenant's warranty of habitability de-

tories no sooner than five days following service of the summons and complaint. Normally an opponent has thirty days to respond, but since an unlawful detainer trial must be set no more than twenty days following the filing of the request to set, answers to unlawful detainer interrogatories must be returned within five days following service (CCP §2030[h]).

As your trial date nears, review your complaint and the tenant's answer before you go to trial, make notes about what you're going to say, and arrange to bring along whatever witnesses, documents, photographs, and tapes might be helpful to your case. Don't suppose that you will win simply because your cause is just or because you've

fense, and discovering various facts involved in any affirmative defense the tenant might claim to be making. Don't use the form to harass the tenant, that is, don't check off every conceivable question. That kind of harassment could backfire on you if the tenant were to call it to the judge's attention. Use the form strictly to discover relevant information.

If you are going to use your discoveries at the trial, you must receive the answers to your interrogatories before the trial, so you'll need to serve them as soon as possible. Much as you'd like to serve them right away, you may serve interroga-

kissed the Blarney Stone. You have to convince the judge that your cause is just, and you must have the proof on hand to do it. Otherwise it's your word against your tenant's, and he may have kissed the Blarney Stone more passionately than you did.

Remember, that judge you're appearing before doesn't know you or your tenant from Eve or Adam. If he did know either of you, he'd have to disqualify himself. For all he knows, your tenant might be a good Samaritan, and you might be an ogre of a landlord who is accustomed to exacting pints of blood from tenants just for late fees. If you are that predatory, don't look it in court at least. Look honest, hard-working, tolerant, long-suffering, and maybe even a little oppressed.

Every successful trial lawyer spends some pretrial time grooming his clients for court. A client may be as guilty as a hit man caught with a smoking gun in his hand, but in court he shouldn't look guilty. You should pay attention to what you look like in court, too. Don't prejudice your case by looking like an unscrupulous, filthy-rich landlord. Leave your pinkie rings, your gold chains, your monogrammed shirts, your designer jeans, your Rolex watch, and your Gucci shoes at home. Put on your plain pockets jeans, your Penney's work shirt, your Timex wrist watch, and your well-worn jogging shoes. Look like the salt of the earth. Justice may be blind, but judges are not, and the judge is the law in that courtroom where you'll be appearing. Judges are only human, and they will be scrutinizing you and your tenant in court for clues which will sway their judgment one way or the other.

One thing which will sway a judge is organization. Organize your evidence and your remarks well for your court appearance. Understand what you need to do in court, and then do it.

If your complaint is for nonpayment of rent, you will have to prove that your notice was served properly, that it accurately stated the amount of rent due, and that the rent was not paid.

If your complaint is for breach of contract, you will have to prove both that the tenant has breached the contract and that he has been properly served.

If your complaint is for waste, nuisance, or unlawful acts, you must prove that the tenant committed the acts you allege and that you served him proper notice.

If your complaint is for termination of tenancy and you're not in a rent-control area, you need prove only that the notice was properly served. The burden is on the tenant to show that the eviction is discriminatory or retaliatory.

In the Courtroom

Should you feel especially apprehensive about appearing in court, find out when other contested unlawful detainer cases are scheduled to be heard. Attend one and observe what goes on. Imagine yourself appearing and speaking on your own behalf. You'll find that what goes on in your lo-

cal court isn't so very different from the courtroom television programs like "Judge Judy" you have seen. The only difference is that attorneys are allowed in the courtroom where you'll be appearing.

To free your stomach's butterflies on your big day, rehearse what you're going to say before you walk into the courtroom. When the judge calls upon you to present your case, speak up and tell the truth, the whole relevant truth. Don't waste the court's time with irrelevancies. You and your tenant together have twenty minutes. That gives you less than ten minutes to tell your side of the story. Don't try to tell the history of the world in that amount of time. You can't. Be brief in your remarks. Address yourself to the judge, and don't argue with the defendant.

Also, remember what every experienced courtroom lawyer says about questioning witnesses, "Don't ask any question unless you already know what the witness's answer is going to be." Unanticipated answers have a way of blindsiding you and demolishing your case.

Your courtroom dialogue might go something like this:

Judge:　All right, Lester Landlord, what do you have to say for yourself?

Lester:　Your honor, my name is Lester Landlord, and I am the plaintiff in this case. I am the owner of a little duplex at 456 Sweet Street right here in town and am entitled to possession of the premises. In order to save the court's time, I would like to call the defendant, Richard Renter, to the stand now and ask him to testify to certain facts in this case. May I do that, your honor?

Judge:　You may. Call Richard Renter to the stand.

Bailiff:　Richard Renter, do you swear to tell the truth, the whole truth, and nothing but the truth, so help you God?

Richard: I do.

Lester:　Please state your name.

Richard: My name is Richard Renter.

Lester:　Where are you currently living?

Richard: I live at 456 Sweet Street, Littletown.

Lester:　Did you rent 456 Sweet Street from me for $895 on December 16th, XXXX, and did you sign this written agreement to that effect?

Richard: Yes, I did, but you raised my rent last month.

Lester:　Is the rent there now $980 per

month?

Richard: Sure is.

Lester: And did I serve you with a notice like this one on January 12th, more than a month and a half in advance, that your rent was going to go up on the first of March?

Richard: You did, but I told you then that I was going to be laid off and that I wouldn't have any money to pay you the rent for a while.

Lester: Did you pay me the rent on March first?

Richard: No, I didn't. I just told you I got laid off and didn't have the money to pay my rent.

Lester: Your honor, I would like to ask the court to disregard the defendant's reason for not paying his rent. That was not part of my question.

Judge: Sustained. Do you have any further questions?

Lester: Yes, your honor. Richard Renter, were you served on March 12th with a 3-Day Notice to Pay Rent or Quit like this one?

Richard: Yes, I was.

Lester: I have no further questions, your honor.

Judge: You may step down.

Lester: Would you like me to take the stand and testify to these same facts that Richard Renter has already testified to, your honor?

Judge: No, that won't be necessary. Richard Renter, would you like to testify now on your own behalf?

If Richard does testify, write down any points he makes which you feel should be dealt with in a cross-examination, especially if he is lying about something crucial to the case, like not receiving the notice. Don't worry if he tells his hard-luck story to the court, even if he embellishes it enough to move the entire courtroom to tears, yourself included. His being out of work is not relevant to the case, and while it may gain him the sympathy of the court, it's not enough to gain him the right to live rent-free in your rental dwelling. The court is concerned only about whether he rented the place from you at an agreed-upon rent, whether he paid the rent when it was due, whether you gave him notice that the rent was delinquent, whether you have taken any rent money from him since giving him the notice, and whether he still lives there. If he says

anything to refute what you establish about those concerns, then you should make note of them and attempt to prove he is wrong.

The judge may or may not render his verdict as soon as he has heard both sides. If he does, and it's in your favor, submit your judgment form to the courtroom clerk for approval and signing. Then follow the same procedure for filing the writ, etc. as it's explained in chapter 5 for a default hearing. If the judge decides to take the matter "under submission," he will have the judgment form mailed to you, and you will have to wait before proceeding any further.

If the judge's verdict is not in your favor, figure out exactly what you need to change in order to be assured of success before you make another attempt to evict the tenant. Waste no time. Go right ahead and begin the process all over again. Do it right this time.

By the way, every time I have had to begin the process all over again with the same tenants, and I've had to do so only twice, they vacated in short order. They knew that I was serious, that I knew what I was doing, and that I wouldn't make the same mistakes twice. They understood that they wouldn't stand a chance using the same arguments again in court, and they didn't even wait until I had to file a summons and complaint. They were gone shortly after they received their notices.

- Make every effort to understand any response your tenant files.
- Consider hiring an attorney more seriously if your tenant responds to your complaint and is himself represented by an attorney.
- Consider the advantages of settling before trial using a stipulated agreement.
- Be well prepared to prove your case in court.

11
Handling the Bankruptcy Case

For some time, declaring bankruptcy was a popular last-ditch measure which unscrupulous tenants would take to delay their inevitable eviction. Just by filing bankruptcy they'd get an automatic stay. The stay would put the brakes on the landlord's every effort to evict them until the bankruptcy court allowed the eviction to proceed. In the meantime, the tenants stayed put.

One bankruptcy judge and a majority of California's lawmakers came to recognize that these tenants, prodded by unscrupulous eviction-delay services, were declaring bankruptcy for one reason and one reason only—to beat their landlords out of as much rent as they possibly could.

That judge and the lawmakers tried to put a stop to this practice, and statistics show that they were successful. Back in 1991 the percentage of bankruptcy cases filed primarily to stop evictions was a whopping 16.9%. By 2004, it had dropped to a minuscule 1%!

Nowadays there's little likelihood that you will find yourself stymied by a tenant who declares bankruptcy primarily to keep you from evicting him in a timely manner, especially since The Bankruptcy Abuse Protection and Consumer Protection Act of 2005, which imposes numerous hurdles for a bankruptcy filer, took effect on the 17th of October, 2005.

Still, you ought to know what happened to curb this abuse and what you need to do today to see an eviction through to completion if a good-for-nothing tenant of yours does declare bankruptcy before you try to evict him or even after you receive a judgment to evict him.

The Judge and *In Re Smith*

After hearing hundreds of patently frivolous cases where tenants were trying to delay their eviction by filing bankruptcy, Vincent Zurzolo, a bankruptcy judge in the Central District (see p. 145 for a list of the bankruptcy court districts) wrote a candid opinion about the practice *(In re Smith* 105 B.R. 50 (Bkrtcy.C.D.Cal. 1989). In it, he concluded that a month-to-month residential tenancy itself has inconsequential monetary value, and therefore, an unlawful detainer which terminates such a tenancy should not be stayed at all by a bankruptcy filing. Only the money judgment should merit the concern of a bankruptcy court, not the judgment for possession.

Judge Zurzolo wrote this opinion back in 1989. It made perfect sense then. It makes perfect sense now. Why in the world should a bankruptcy, of all things, allow a tenant to continue living in your rental dwelling rent free when you already have a judgment entitling you to reclaim possession?

That's a travesty of justice. A bankruptcy is supposed to insure that justice is done, not frustrated. It's supposed to help both debtors *and* creditors settle their affairs in an organized fashion. The bankruptcy court identifies all the debtor's assets, liabilities, and creditors and then determines who should get what. That's the way the system is supposed to work. Identify everything of value, identify everybody involved, distribute the assets in some equitable fashion, and get on with life. Well and good! So where does the tenancy fit in?

What Judge Zurzolo said in his opinion is that the *tenancy* which the debtor wants to prolong with a bankruptcy filing *is not an asset.* It has no monetary value whatsoever. It's more of a condition, like an ability or an achievement or an illness or a job at Burger King. What're they worth? Nothing, really. Can they be pawned or auctioned or sold? Nope. As a consequence, none of them warrants protection from a bankruptcy court. A bankrupt tenant's eviction shouldn't be held up by his bankruptcy filing at all.

This is heady stuff for any landlord confronted with tenants who think they're going to "pull a fast one" at the very last minute and enjoy still more rent-free living! The tenants might think they're entitled to an automatic stay by filing bankruptcy, but they are in for a big surprise when they discover that you are entitled to get automatic relief! At least you would be entitled to automatic relief if Judge Zurzolo had his way.

The trouble is that Judge Zurzolo's decision is not binding in other bankruptcy courts, and it may not get you anywhere if you try to use it to your benefit wherever in California you happen to be. Nonetheless, here's what he says in his conclusion:

"I further observe that this opinion will have absolutely no effect on this problem unless residential landlords, and the attorneys who represent them, call it to the attention of the state courts that issue unlawful detainer judgments and convince those state courts to order the proper state law enforcement officials to evict debtor/tenants without first requiring residential landlords to obtain relief from the Stay. If this chain of events results, there is a chance that this widespread and daily abuse of the Bankruptcy Court system and the shameless defrauding of thousands of tenant victims will cease."

Judge Zurzolo urges us to avoid taking our cases to bankruptcy court unless our superior courts absolutely refuse to allow enforcement of the judgment. He goes on to state emphatically at the end of Section VI. The Scope of the Stay:

"I conclude that the Stay does not enjoin a landlord from regaining possession of residential premises from a wrongfully holding-over bankruptcy debtor/tenant, as long as the landlord seeks only to repossess the property and not to enforce any other portion of his unlawful detainer judgment against the debtor and the bankruptcy estate, such as collecting money damages."

CCP §1161.2 and §715.050

No doubt mindful of the thinking behind *In re Smith*, California's legislators tried to help those unfortunate landlords whose tenants declare bankruptcy in order to delay an eviction. They passed two laws for this express purpose.

The first one, CCP §1161.2, already referred to in chapter 5, delays public access to unlawful detainer paperwork for sixty days. As a consequence, unscrupulous eviction defense services which used to be able to access court documents to learn the names of tenants being evicted so they could solicit them as clients, can no longer find the tenants so easily. Since they can't find the tenants, they can't use their bag of tricks, including the filing of bankruptcy, to delay evictions.

The second law is CCP §715.050, and here's what it says:

"Except with respect to enforcement of a judgment for money, a writ of possession issued pursuant to a judgment for possession in an unlawful detainer action shall be enforced pursuant to this chapter without delay, notwithstanding receipt of notice of the filing by the defendant of a bankruptcy proceeding."

State Law and Federal Law

Before you try using this second law to your advantage, you should know that it is a state law. Bankruptcy law is federal law. Wherever there is a conflict between state and federal law, federal law takes precedence. At least, such is the case if somebody can prove there is a conflict.

Some say there is no conflict between CCP §715.050 and federal law (*Lee v Baca* (1999) 73 CA4th 1116, 1118-1120, 86 CR2d 913, 914-916, cert. den. (2000) 529 US 1020; *In re Smith* (BC CD CA 1989) 105 BR 50, 53-54).

Some say there is a conflict (*In re DiGiorgio* (CD CA 196) 200 BR 664, 675) (*In re Butler* (BC CD CA 2002) 271 BR 867, 875-876).

If your court will allow you to use CCP §715.050 to proceed with an eviction against a tenant who has declared bankruptcy, use it. If not, you will have to go to bankruptcy court.

New Hurdles for Filers

The Bankruptcy Abuse Protection and Consumer Protection Act of 2005, which was sponsored primarily by credit card companies that lost billions through the discharge of debts in personal bankruptcies, is a boon to landlords because it imposes some high hurdles for bankruptcy filers. They must get credit counseling before filing. They must pay higher filing fees and higher attorney fees. They must submit to a means test. They cannot file for bankruptcy as often as they could in the past, and they do not get the generous automatic stays they used to get.

As a result, there are few tenants today who find bankruptcy to be a good countermeasure to being evicted, that is, unless they also have a heavy burden of consumer debt weighing them down.

Provisions of the New Act

There are some important provisions in this new act which you as a landlord should know about. First, you should know that a residential tenant who files for bankruptcy after a landlord obtains an unlawful detainer judgment, gets an automatic stay of only thirty days after the filing. So long as the tenant does nothing to certify "cure" rights during the thirty days, the landlord needn't seek relief from the automatic stay but may continue with the eviction after the thirty-day wait.

Second, you should know that a residential tenant who files for bankruptcy after a landlord obtains an unlawful detainer judgment seeking possession because of endangerment of the property or the illegal use of controlled substances on the property, gets an automatic stay of only fifteen days after the landlord files a certification with the court attesting to one or the other of these causes of action.

In either of these situations, you may, of course, file to lift the automatic stay in less than the fifteen or thirty days.

Possession, Money, and Timing

Remember this: Whereas bankruptcy laws have changed to enable landlords to execute judgments for possession more easily, they haven't changed to enable landlords to execute money judgments more easily. In order for you to collect your money judgment, you must still file the appropriate papers which creditors file with the bankruptcy court.

Remember, too, that landlords get automatic stays lifted automatically in bankruptcy court only if they already have a judgment when the tenant files for bankruptcy. If they are unfortunate enough to have bad timing and get the judgment after the tenant files for bankruptcy, they will have to petition the bankruptcy court to lift the stay. It won't be lifted automatically.

Bankruptcy Courts

There aren't nearly as many bankruptcy courts as there are state courts. In all, California has only thirteen bankruptcy courts spread throughout the state. They're organized by region into four districts.

BANKRUPTCY COURTS NORTHERN DISTRICT
canb.uscourts.gov
235 Pine St., 19th Floor
San Francisco, CA 94104
415.268.2300, ext. 0

1300 Clay St., Suite 300
Oakland, CA 94612
510.879.3600

280 S. First St., Rm. 3035
San Jose, CA 95113
408.535.5118

99 S. "E" St.
Santa Rosa, CA 95404
707.525.8539

EASTERN DISTRICT
caeb.uscourts.gov
501 "I" St., Suite 3-200
Sacramento, CA 95814
916.930.4400

1130 "O" St., Suite 2656
Fresno, CA 93721
559.498.7217

1130 12th St., Suite C
Modesto, CA 95354
209.521.5160

CENTRAL DISTRICT
cacb.uscourts.gov
255 E. Temple St.
Los Angeles, CA 90012
213.894.3118

3420 Twelfth St.
Riverside, CA 92501
951.774.1000

411 West Fourth St.
Santa Ana, CA 92701
714.338.5300

1415 State St.
Santa Barbara, CA 93101
805.884.4800

21041 Burbank Blvd.
Woodland Hills, CA 91367
818.587.2900

SOUTHERN DISTRICT
casb.uscourts.gov
325 West "F" St.
San Diego, CA 92101
619.557.5620

The Northern District covers the counties of Del Norte, Mendocino, Humboldt, Napa, Sonoma, Marin, and Lake out of its Santa Rosa division. It covers the counties of San Francisco and San Mateo out of its San Francisco division. It covers the counties of Alameda and Contra Costa out of its Oakland division, and it covers the counties of Santa Clara, Santa Cruz, Monterey, and San Benito out of its San Jose division.

The Eastern District covers the counties of Alpine, Amador, Butte, Colusa, El Dorado, Glenn, Lassen, Modoc, Mono, Nevada, Placer, Plumas, Sacramento, Shasta, Sierra, Siskiyou, Solano, Sutter, Tehama, Trinity, Yolo, and Yuba and parts of San Joaquin County out of its Sacramento division. It covers the counties of Calaveras, Stanislaus, and Tuolumne and certain parts of San Joaquin County out of its Modesto division, and it covers the counties of Fresno, Inyo, Kern, Kings, Madera, Mariposa, Merced, and Tulare out of its Fresno division.

The Central District covers the counties of Los Angeles, Orange, Riverside, San Bernardino, San Luis Obispo, Santa Barbara, and Ventura out of its five division offices. Zipcodes determine which one handles the bankruptcies in a particular area.

The Southern District covers the counties of Imperial and San Diego.

Sympathy in Bankruptcy Court

When you have to go into bankruptcy court to petition for early relief in order to evict a tenant in superior court, you are going to feel pretty hostile toward your no-good tenant who is costing you all this extra time and money. Grit your teeth and press on, knowing that the tenant is going to get his comeuppance eventually and knowing that you are going to find at least a modicum of sympathy in bankruptcy court.

Bankruptcy courts are fed up with tenants who file for bankruptcy primarily to frustrate their landlords, and they look favorably upon landlords' petitions to proceed with evictions. The bankruptcy ploy, which used to gain tenants a delay of at least sixty days, is now gaining them as little as seven days, and it's costing them far more than they realize when they resort to it. It scars their credit and haunts them for years.

As Judge Zurzolo remarked in *In Re Smith*, "These relief from Stay motions are rarely contested and are never lost, as long as the moving party provides adequate notice of the motion and competent evidence to establish a *prima facie* case."

Website Help

Bankruptcy courts have embraced the internet wholeheartedly. Every district has its own website (see sidebar on previous page), where it provides information, assistance, and forms. Visit the website of the district where your tenant has filed for bankruptcy before you make your first contact with the court. You may find that the website

```
 1  Lester Landlord
    Leslie Landlord
 2  123 Neat Street
    Littletown, CA 91111
 3  (510) 123-4567
    Movant in Propria Persona

 4

 5              IN THE UNITED STATES BANKRUPTCY COURT
                  FOR THE XXXX DISTRICT OF CALIFORNIA
 6                          XXXX DIVISION
                [use the appropriate court identification]

 7
    IN RE:                             )   CASE NO. XXXXX
 8                                     )   CHAPTER XX
    RONALD E. ROTTER and              )   RS NO. [number stamped by clerk]
 9  HAZEL C. ROTTER                    )   HEARING TO BE HELD
                                       )   DATE:   XXXX
10  DEBTORS                            )   TIME:   XXXX
                                       )   PLACE:  COURTROOM XX
11
                NOTICE OF MOTION FOR RELIEF FROM THE AUTOMATIC STAY
12                      [use the appropriate title]
```

has everything you need to know and everything you need to have in order to file your motion electronically, pay the correct fees, calendar your motion, give notice to the tenant and everybody else involved, and prepare the order for relief from stay.

If you don't know your way around the internet well enough to take advantage of the website help provided by the courts, find somebody who does and ask for guidance. You may save yourself hours of driving time and frustration and achieve your objective of getting a relief from stay all the more quickly.

The Basic Procedure

Whether you take advantage of the court's website help or not, you ought to know the basic procedure for working your way through bankruptcy court to get relief. You may have to use some of the basic procedure or all of the basic procedure, depending upon the local rules of the court.

To get into the correct bankruptcy court, you'll need to find the physical location and the telephone number of the court where your tenant filed bankruptcy. Call that court, ask for the clerk who handles motions, explain to her that you that you are trying to evict an incorrigible tenant who has filed for bankruptcy, and answer any questions she might have. You'll find that bankruptcy clerks are generally quite helpful, and they know what they're doing because they handle stays all the time. In fact, most bankruptcy litigation consists of motions for relief from stay. She will tell you that in order to get relief, you will need to get a hearing date directly from the calendar clerk first. Go ahead and get the earliest possible date.

Next, you prepare and file a Relief from Stay Cover Sheet, a Notice of Motion for Relief from the Automatic Stay, a Motion for Relief from the Automatic Stay (Unlawful Detainer), and a Declaration in Support of Motion for Relief. Then you pay a filing fee and serve the papers as directed.

Tell the clerk that you live some distance from the court and that you would like to keep your trips there to a minimum. Ask her whether she has any suggestions. You might be able to minimize your trips by having her mail you whatever you need to file with the court along with instructions so you can complete everything at home and send it in, or you might take a portable typewriter with you on your very first visit, so you can fill out all the paperwork right then and there and file it immediately.

Make sure that you have a copy of the tenant's paperwork with you when you prepare your own paperwork. You'll need it for reference, and you'll need your checkbook for funds to pay the filing fee. As for the paperwork, the clerk will supply you with the Relief from Stay Cover Sheet, and she may have forms similar to Judicial Council forms for the Notice of Motion and the Motion itself. Use what forms she has available. In some courts, certain forms are mandatory. Make sure you use them.

If you have to make up the documents from scratch yourself, ask the clerk whether you should use pleading paper (there's a blank in the FORMS section of this book) or ordinary typing paper. You can't go wrong using pleading paper, of course.

No matter what kind of paper you use, you must follow a particular format in the upper section of the first page of each document (see sample on facing page). This particular format enables the court's paper shufflers to identify each case's paperwork readily.

You should double-space the text, which appears next in the document, and number each page at the bottom.

Incidentally, in all of this paperwork, you refer to yourself as the "movant." You're akin to somebody who makes a motion at a meeting, saying, "I move that we adopt the resolution." This person in legalese would be a "movant." Because you are making a motion before the bankruptcy court in this case, you are the "movant."

The Notice of Motion for Relief from the Automatic Stay should read something like this:

NOTICE IS HEREBY GIVEN that on [date] at [time], the above-entitled Court, located at [street address, including city], Movant in the above-captioned matter will present a motion to have the automatic stay terminated, conditioned, modified, and/or annulled. The particulars of said motion are described in the accompanying Motion, Declaration, and other such evidence as may be

presented to the Court on the
above date. Debtors and trustee,
if any, are hereby informed that
no written response is required
to oppose this motion. Further,
no oral testimony will normally
be presented at the above-described hearing. However, the
debtors and/or the debtors' attorney and the trustee must appear at said hearing, or the relief requested by the Movant will
be granted. The applicable law is
United States Bankruptcy Code 11
U.S.C. 362 and Bankruptcy Rules
of Procedure 4001 and 9014.

Dated this [day] of [month and
year].

Respectfully submitted,
[Movant's Name]
Movant

The Motion for Relief from the Automatic
Stay (Unlawful Detainer) should read something
like this (remember that this motion is a separate
document all its own and that its first page should
include a properly formatted first-page heading):

MOTION FOR RELIEF FROM THE AUTO-
MATIC STAY (UNLAWFUL DETAINER)
[use the appropriate title]

1. Movant in the above-captioned matter moves this Court
for an Order granting relief from
the automatic stay on the grounds
set forth herein.

2. A Petition under Chapter
[Chapter number of Debtor's filing; either 7, 11, 12, or 13] was
filed on [date].

3. Movant alleges the following
in support of its motion:
a. Debtor occupies the premises
commonly known as [street address, including city].
b. Debtor occupies the premises
[select one of the following: on
a month-to-month tenancy; on a
holdover tenancy; pursuant to a
lease in default; on a tenancy at
will; after a foreclosure sale;
or pursuant to a terminated
lease].
c. Debtor last paid the monthly

rent of $[amount] on [date],
which paid for the period through
[date], and has paid no rent
since.
d. The procedural status of
Movant's case against debtor in
state Court is as follows [in-
clude only those which are appli-
cable]:
i. On [date], Movant served a
Notice to Pay Rent or Quit on the
Debtors.
ii. On [date], Movant filed a
Complaint for Unlawful Detainer
in State Court.
iii. On [date], a Judgment was
entered on said Complaint by the
State Court.
[THIS ENTIRE SECTION IS OP-
TIONAL] 4. Movant alleges that
Debtor filed this bankruptcy case
in bad faith based upon the following [include only whatever is
appropriate]:
a. The Debtor filed what is commonly referred to as a "face
sheet" filing of only a few pages
consisting of the Petition and a
few other documents. No Schedules
or Statement of Affairs accompa-
nied the Petition.
b. The landlord and/or the
landlord's attorney was the only
creditor listed on the master
mailing matrix.
c. Movant is informed and believes
that the Debtor filed the Petition herein for the sole purpose
of attempting to obstruct a State
Court unlawful detainer proceeding and without intending to seek
a fresh start as provided under
the Bankruptcy Code. Debtor's use
of the bankruptcy system for such
purpose is an abuse of such system.

5. Movant attaches the following supporting evidence pursuant
to Local Bankruptcy Rule
112(3)(a) [include only whatever
is appropriate]:
a. Declarations under penalty of

perjury which include any material to which the declarant would be allowed, under Federal Rules of Evidence, to testify if called as a witness at the hearing.
b. Copy of State Court Unlawful Detainer judgment.
c. [Other evidence].

6. There are [number] attached pages of supporting documentation.

WHEREFORE, Movant prays that this Court issue an Order granting the following [include only whatever is appropriate]:

Relief from the automatic stay, or alternatively, for adequate protection.

Prospective relief and findings under Bankruptcy Code §109(g).

Attorney's fees and/or sanctions as requested in the supporting Declaration and Order.

Dated this [day] of [month and year].

Respectfully submitted,
[Movant's Name]
Movant

The Declaration in Support of Motion for Relief, which you have to make up to accompany the other paperwork, should read something like this (use an appropriate first-page heading):

I, [give your full name], am over eighteen (18) years of age, and declare as follows:

1. I am the Movant in this action and have personal knowledge of the facts stated herein and am competent to testify about them.

2. Judgment was entered for the Movant in [name and address of municipal court] on [date] for possession of the premises located at [address] and for $ [amount of judgment].

3. Movant is owner of and entitled to possession of said premises.

4. Debtor remains in possession of said premises.

5. There is a need for this stay to be lifted because Movant is incurring additional costs on a daily basis as a result of Debtor's continuing possession.

6. To the best of my knowledge, information and belief, the Debtor has no equity in the property, and the property is not necessary to any effective reorganization by the Debtor.

I declare under penalty of perjury under the laws of the State of California that the foregoing is true and correct.

[Dated] [Signed]

You need an original plus two copies of all this paperwork.

You also need to provide a Proof of Service. Word it as follows (because it is a part of other documents, the proof need not include a first-page heading):

PROOF OF SERVICE

I, the undersigned, do hereby certify that a true and correct copy of the Notice of Motion for Relief from the Automatic Stay and Motion for Relief from the Automatic Stay and the Declaration in Support of Motion for Relief was forwarded to all interested parties at their last known address in this action by placing a true and correct copy thereof in a sealed envelope with postage thereon fully prepaid in the United States Mail at [city], California, addressed as set forth below on this [date].
[Type your name below this statement and sign it.]
[Give the names and addresses of everyone to whom you sent these documents, and also indicate how you sent them.]

Send copies of the documents to the debtors, their attorney, and to the trustee, if any. To make sure that there is no argument over whether they were ever sent, send them by first-class mail and get a proof of mailing. If you want better proof, send them by certified mail as well, return receipt requested.

Ask the calendar clerk about the time frame for sending these documents, and make absolutely certain that you send them in plenty of time to comply.

Then prepare the Order for Lifting the Automatic Stay, the paper you need from the bankruptcy court to show the superior court that you have had the stay lifted. Take the original and three copies of it with you into court. It should read something like this (use an appropriate first-page heading):

```
    Upon reading the Movant's MO-
TION FOR RELIEF FROM THE AUTO-
MATIC STAY and the DECLARATION IN
SUPPORT OF MOTION FOR RELIEF and
hearing this matter, the Court
appears satisfied therefrom that
there exists no reason to stay
the Movant's action for unlawful
detainer against Debtor.

    IT IS HEREBY ORDERED therefore
that Movant is authorized, to the
extent that such authority is re-
quired, [to continue the unlawful
detainer in state court] [to en-
force the judgment] to regain
possession of the premises from
Debtor.

    [Dated] [Signed, Judge of the
Bankruptcy Court]
```

At your hearing, you ask the court to remove the automatic stay so you can get the tenant out. In order to receive approval, you'll have to establish that the lease rate is not substantially less than the fair rental value for the property, that your getting the property back will in no way harm either the tenant's other creditors or the reorganization plan itself, and what's more, that you will suffer irreparable damages if you don't get the property back doggone soon.

Come prepared with everything you need to support your position. Gather every scrap of paper you have on the tenant, including the rental application, rental agreement, and rent receipts. Come up with some evidence, perhaps current rental listings, that the property's rental value is at or near market level, and put together a listing of the expenses you normally pay out of your rental income, so you can show that you are suffering damages from the tenant's continuing to stay without paying any rent.

Chances are good that you won't have to say much in court because the tenants are unlikely even to show up.

As soon as you have proof from the bankruptcy court that the automatic stay has been lifted, go back to superior court and continue your unlawful detainer from where you left off.

You may be detoured, but you will prevail!

- Become familiar with *In re Smith* in order to understand the frustration bankruptcy judges feel when tenants file a bogus bankruptcy for the sole purpose of delaying an unlawful detainer.
- Take note of the provisions in The Bankruptcy Abuse Protection and Consumer Protection Act of 2005 as they apply to evictions of residential tenants.
- Should your tenant declare bankruptcy while you're trying to evict him, proceed without delay to do what you must to get the automatic stay lifted.
- Visit the website of the district where your tenant has filed for bankruptcy before you make your first contact with the court, and mine it for information, assistance, and forms.
- Learn the basic procedure for working your way through bankruptcy court to get relief.

12
Handling Non-payment & Non-compliance in a Mobilehome or RV Park

The laws governing residency in mobilehome (MH) and recreational vehicle (RV) parks, both of which used to be lumped together under the term "trailer parks," have expanded right along with the length and width of the coaches being manufactured (the term "coach" here refers to mobilehomes and recreational vehicles of all sizes).

As you might imagine, this proliferation of laws would tend to restrain park management and unshackle park residents. It has. Management used to be able to hitch the park's pickup truck up to a coach occupied by deadbeats, haul them out into the street while they were having dinner, and put a lien on the coach to boot.

Today that's no longer possible. First of all, a park's itty-bitty pickup truck couldn't begin to budge most residents' yacht-sized coaches from their moorings; second, management must meet all sorts of conditions before evicting anybody at all; and third, even when those conditions have been met, there are still further limitations to the remedies available.

So how do you proceed against a problem resident today? To begin with, you must determine who is the registered owner of the problem resident's coach, who is the legal owner, what type of space it occupies, whether the coach is classified as an RV or a mobilehome, and how long it's been where it is.

If you own the coach and you rent it out as a residence on a month-to-month tenancy, regardless of where it sits or who owns the real property beneath it or what type of coach it happens to be, so far as you and that resident are concerned, the laws governing conventional rental dwellings apply. The resident might as well be renting an apartment or a house from you. If this is the case and your resident should give you trouble, go ahead and use the appropriate procedures as outlined in previous chapters.

If the coach is situated on a space designated for RV's, and it is, in fact, an RV, how you proceed against the occupants will be determined by how long it's been parked where it is. If it's been there less than thirty days, its occupants are entitled to get a 72-hour notice (see notice next page) before you can act to have it moved out; if it's been there for at least thirty days but less than nine months, they're entitled to get a 30-day notice (see page 200) before you can take action; and if it's been there longer, they're entitled to the same treatment as mobilehome occupants.

To be considered an RV (included are motor homes, truck-mounted campers, fifth wheelers, travel trailers, camping trailers, and the like), the coach must not require a special moving permit to be out on the highway. If it does require a permit, then it's a mobilehome.

This distinction between RV's and mobilehomes is an important one because each is governed by a separate set of laws. RV's can travel about the highway as readily as prairie schooners, so they're governed by laws more like innkeeper statutes and vehicle codes. Mobilehomes may be called "mobile," but once set up with awnings, skirting, landscaping, and fencing, they aren't much more mobile than tract houses, so they're governed by laws more like those for conventional housing, to be specific, §§798, et seq., of the Civil Code, commonly referred to as the "Mobilehome Residency Law" (MRL). Recreational vehicle parks, on the other hand, are governed specifically by the "Recreational Vehicle Park Occupancy Law," which is §§799.20, et seq., of the Civil Code.

The MRL has become a kind of accounting of the battles enjoined by the opposing mobilehome-related associations—in the one corner, the Golden State Mobilehome Owners League (GSMOL), representing park residents, and in the other, the Western Manufactured

151

72-HOUR NOTICE TO VACATE

(Recreational Vehicles)

TO: Dennis Sampson
Vernagae Sampson

and all other occupants in possession of the premises described as:
2020 Cherry Hill Rd., Space 26
(Street Address)
Lemon   California   91222
(City)   (State)   (Zip)

PLEASE TAKE NOTICE that you have failed to pay for your occupancy or failed to comply with the reasonable written rules and regulations of the park provided to you upon registration. You are hereby required within seventy-two (72) hours to remove from and deliver up possession of the above-described premises which you currently hold and occupy.

Should you fail to comply with this notice, your recreational vehicle will be removed from the park pursuant to the procedure described in that part of the California Civil Code (CCC §799.20 et seq.) commonly known as the Recreational Vehicle Park Occupancy Law.

Dated: 2/8/XXXX   *Dan Coffey*
                                              Owner/Manager

PROOF OF SERVICE (Server should complete this proof of service only AFTER serving tenants.)

I, the undersigned, being at least 18 years of age, declare under penalty of perjury that I served the above notice, of which this is a true copy, on the person(s) indicated below and in the manner(s) indicated below: DENNIS SAMPSON

☒ On 2/8/XXXX   , I handed the notice to the occupant(s) personally.

☐ On _____, after attempting personal service, I handed the notice to a person of suitable age and discretion at the address above or at the place of business of the occupant(s), AND I posted a true copy in a conspicuous place at the address above, AND I deposited a true copy in the U.S. Mail, in a sealed envelope with postage fully prepaid, addressed to the occupant(s) at the address above. I also deposited a true copy in the U.S. Mail, in a sealed envelope with postage fully prepaid, addressed to the occupant(s) at the following address given on their registration agreement:

_____

☒ On 2/8/XXXX   , I [cross out one] ~~(sent by certified mail)~~ (hand-delivered) a true copy of the notice to the police or sheriff's department serving the area where the premises are located.

Executed on 2/8/XXXX   , at LEMON   , California.
                    Served by Dan Coffey

efc

You will find a blank copy of this form in the FORMS section of this book and in Eviction Forms Creator.

Housing Communities Association (WMA) and the California Mobilehome Parkowners Alliance (MPA), representing park owners and managers. Each of them has its lobbyists in Sacramento vying for legislators' ears.

Whereas mobilehomes are always governed by the MRL, RV's are not always governed by laws written for RV's. RV's are chameleon-like. They become mobilehomes when they act like mobilehomes, that is, when they occupy a space designated for mobilehomes or when they occupy a space designated for RV's for more than nine continuous months or more (Civil Code

ferred to as "residents" if they occupy the coach) and rent space in a mobilehome park tend to be more responsible about paying their bills than other renters and because moving a mobilehome is such an expensive proposition nowadays, park owners and managers tend to use what may seem to apartment owners and managers to be a lenient approach to collecting delinquent rents. They operate more on the premise that mobilehome residents will pay their rent if given proper notice and a reasonable period of time in which to pay it.

Here's the collection routine followed by one

§798.3.b.2). Then they, too, are governed by the MRL, unless, that is, they are motor homes, truck campers, or camping trailers, which are always RV's no matter what.

Before outlining the eviction procedure dictated by the MRL, I'd like to describe a pragmatic collection procedure which you might use yourself for handling those residents whose rent doesn't arrive when it's supposed to. Some sort of collection procedure should always precede an eviction for nonpayment.

Nonpayment

Because those who own their own coaches (called "homeowners" in the MRL but also re-

experienced mobilehome park manager, a manager who has never had to resort to the courts to evict a resident for nonpayment and has never failed to collect all the rent owed to his park in more than a dozen years as manager of a 113-space park. That's quite a record. He's doing something right. His routine provides the resident with informal notice and then proper legal notice, and it allows him plenty of time to pay.

Central to this collection routine are consistency, persistence, reasonableness, and four informal notices, written on imprinted, half-sheet, two-part park stationery and sent to the resident by first-class mail. At the bottom of each notice the manager puts the following verbiage:

WARNING: This notice is the ___first___ three-day notice for nonpayment of rent, utility charges, or other reasonable incidental services that has been served upon you in the last 12 months. Pursuant to Civil Code Section 798.56(e)(5), if you have been given a three-day notice to either pay rent, utility charges, or other reasonable incidental services or to vacate your tenancy on three or more occasions within a 12-month period, management is not required to give you a further three-day period to pay rent or vacate the tenancy before your tenancy can be terminated.

3-DAY NOTICE TO PAY RENT OR QUIT

TO: Peter Romstead   Roseanne Romstead

_____and all other residents or occupants in possession of the premises described as: 2020 Cherry Hill Rd., Space 14, Lemon California 91222

PLEASE TAKE NOTICE that the rent is now due and payable on the above-described premises which you currently hold and occupy. Your rental account is delinquent in the amount itemized as follows:
Rental period ___3/1/XXXX___ through ___3/31/XXXX___

RENT DUE $	285.00
less partial payment of $	0.00
equals TOTAL RENT DUE of $	285.00

YOU ARE HEREBY REQUIRED to pay said rent in full within three (3) days or to deliver up possession of the above-described premises to the park manager, who is authorized to receive same, or legal proceedings will be instituted against you to recover possession of said premises, to declare the forfeiture of the Lease or Rental Agreement under which you occupy said premises and to recover rents and damages, together with court costs and attorney's fees, according to the terms of your Lease or Rental Agreement.

RENT MUST BE PAID IN FULL AND IN PERSON TO THE FOLLOWING PERSON OR ENTITY:
Name Dan Coffey   Phone 555-987-6543
Address where rent is to be paid 123 Lime Street, Lemon, California
Usual days and times for payment of rent Mon.-Fri., 1P-5P; Sat., 10A-5P; Sun., 3P-5P
Please phone in advance to make sure that someone will be available to accept payment.

3-DAY NOTICE TO PERFORM COVENANT OR QUIT

PLEASE TAKE NOTICE that you have also failed to perform that covenant in your Lease or Rental Agreement requiring that certain other charges be paid along with your rent. These charges are itemized as follows:
Other charges ___Water___   TOTAL other charges due $ ___12.29___

You are hereby required to perform this covenant within three (3) days or to deliver up possession of the above-described premises to the park manager. If you fail to do so, legal proceedings will be instituted against you to recover said charges and to recover said premises and such damages as the law allows.

PLEASE NOTE: If you fail to pay the total amount of rent and other charges due and owing within three days, your tenancy is terminated. The additional time period allowed in the "60-Day Notice" which accompanies this three-day notice is strictly to give you time to locate a place to move your mobilehome or to find a qualified buyer. It does not extend the time you have to pay what you owe.

Should you sell or transfer the mobilehome, you must pay what you owe upon the sale or transfer.

Whoever resides in the mobilehome after service of this notice shall continue to be subject to the Mobilehome Residency Law and park rules and regulations, including rules regarding space maintenance.

Dated: 4/15/XXXX _____   _____Dan Coffey_____
                                                              Owner/Manager

PROOF OF SERVICE   (Server should complete this proof of service only AFTER serving residents.)
I, the undersigned, being at least 18 years of age, declare under penalty of perjury that I served the above notice, of which this is a true copy, on the above-mentioned resident(s) in possession in the manner(s) indicated below:

☒ On _4/17/XXXX_, I handed the notice to the resident(s) personally.

☐ On _____, after attempting personal service, I handed the notice to a person of suitable age and discretion at the residence/business of the resident(s), AND I deposited a true copy in the U.S. Mail, in a sealed envelope with postage fully prepaid, addressed to the resident(s) at his/her/their place of residence (date mailed, if different _____).

☐ On _____, after attempting service in both manners indicated above, I posted the notice in a conspicuous place at the residence of the resident(s), AND I deposited a true copy in the U.S. Mail, in a sealed envelope with postage fully prepaid, addressed to the resident(s) at his/her/their place of residence (date mailed, if different _____).

☒ On _4/17/XXXX_, in addition to service on the resident(s) as described above, I deposited a true copy of the notice in the U.S. Mail, in a sealed envelope with postage fully prepaid, addressed to the legal and registered owner(s) (if other than resident(s)) as follows: [legal owner] _PACIFIC FINANCE, 32 ORANGE AVE., SUNSET, CA_ ; [registered owner] _____

Executed on _4/17/XXXX_, at _LEMON_, California. Served by _Dan Coffey_

    Copy to:
File Space [number]
Attorney [name of actual attorney
given on final two notices]

The first notice acknowledges that the resident's rent, which is due on the first and delinquent on the seventh of the month at this particular family park, has not been paid. The manager sends the notice on the tenth. Here's the exact wording he uses for this first notice:

Dear [resident], Space [number]:
    Your space rent in the amount
of $xx was due on [date] and be-
came delinquent on [date]. Please
drop this by our office today,
and don't forget to add the late
fee of $xx, too. Your rent is now
late.
    Thank you.

The second notice, sent out five days later if the resident has made no effort to contact the manager with either rent payment or excuses, is more formal than the first one. It reads as follows:

Dear [resident], Space [number]:
    THIS IS A FIVE (5) DAY NOTICE
to pay space rent of $xx due on
[date].
    As stated in your Rental Agree-
ment, "When rent is paid after
the seventh (7th) day of the
month for which rent is due,
Homeowners must pay a late fee of
$xx." The amount due of $xx includes the late fee, as it is now
past the 7th day of the month.
    Preserve your good credit and
pay this amount today.
    Thank you.

The third notice, sent five days following the second notice, assumes that there has been some contact with the resident, that the resident has assured the manager his rent and late fee would be paid by a certain date, and that the resident has failed to perform. It's a little more insistent than the others. Here's what it says:

Dear [resident], Space [number]:
    On [date], you promised to pay
your delinquent space rent of $xx
and a late fee of $xx. This
promise has not been kept. We
shall expect payment within

twenty-four (24) hours!
    Thank you.

The final notice is the most insistent of all and threatens to involve an attorney and court action. It says the following:

Dear [resident], Space [number]:
    We are sorry that you have
failed to pay the delinquent rent
due on Space [number]. Please be
advised that your account will be
turned over to our attorney for
collection processing and eviction action if not paid at our
office by [date given is five
days hence].
    Thank you.

Should the resident fail to respond to this final informal notice from the park, the manager takes the first legal steps required to evict the resident. He completes a 3-Day Notice to Pay Rent or Quit, a 3-Day Notice to Perform Covenant or Quit (necessary to demand payment of the other charges commonly included in mobilehome parks' monthly statements), and a 60-Day Notice to Terminate Tenancy. A single page combining two of the three notices is shown here. The 60-Day Notice must include a bona-fide "good cause," such as "nonpayment of rent" in this case. Use the same 60-Day Notice form shown later in this chapter introduced there for use in cases of noncompliance.

Note that the 3-Day Notice to Pay Rent or Quit includes a warning to the resident about Civil Code §798.56.e.5, which applies to those who are repeatedly late.

Then the manager makes an effort to jolt the resident. He hires any uniformed peace officer (sometimes just a security guard) he can find, someone intimidating and unfamiliar, to serve the notices (within ten days, as required by law, he also sends copies by certified mail, return-receipt requested, to the coach's registered owner and legal owner, if they happen to be someone other than the resident, and to any junior lienholders).

He never serves the notices himself, so he can keep the process on a businesslike level and keep from injecting anything personal into what he now considers a serious matter. Although the resident may have scoffed at the earlier informal notices, he begins to get serious now. He seldom scoffs at these notices, served as they are by a stranger, and somehow he always seems to find the money needed to pay his rent. The manager then drops the matter, having accumulated plenty of paperwork to fatten that resident's file in case it's needed later to substantiate legal action.

Eviction Through Court

If you had to follow up on the notices and pursue your case still further in the courts, here's what you'd do.

You'd wait sixty to sixty-five days before doing anything. (Just like ordinary tenants of houses and apartment houses, mobilehome owners get only three days to pay up. If they don't pay up within that three-day period, they should be looking around for some other place to move their mobilehome. Mind you, they aren't getting the extra time to pay what they owe. They're getting the extra time so they can find a place to move their mobilehome).

Then you'd prepare and file a summons, complaint, a cover sheet, and a Prejudgment Claim of Right to Possession, the same Judicial Council forms covered in chapter 5. You'd wait the appropriate number of days, depending upon the method of service used and whether you'd decided to use the prejudgment claim procedure (recommended because of the long wait following service of notices).

In non-contested cases, you'd file a Request for Entry of Default and a Writ of Possession, and you'd get a lockout date. In contested cases, you'd file a Request to Set Case for Trial, argue your case in court, and if successful, get a judgment, a Writ of Possession, and a lockout date.

With the resident locked out, you'd follow a procedure dictated by whether there's a legal owner different from the registered owner.

If the legal owner and the registered owner were one and the same, you'd get the sheriff or marshal's office to return the Writ of Possession to the court. You'd get a Writ of Execution from the court, and you'd instruct the sheriff or marshal's office to sell the mobilehome to satisfy the judgment. If there were no bidders, you would get the title and could submit the necessary papers to Housing and Community Development (HCD) to clear the title.

If the legal owner were different from the registered owner, you'd give notice of a lien sale and wait ten to fifteen days for the legal owner to pay the lien. If the legal owner were to pay, he would get the mobilehome. If he didn't pay, you'd publish notice of the lien sale and hold the sale. If there were no bidders, you would get title and could clear it with HCD.

Unoccupied Coaches

The ordinary nonpayment problem isn't the only nonpayment problem encountered in mobilehome parks. There's another one which we should consider here, one which is unique to mobilehome parks. It involves unoccupied coaches.

Because fewer than 5% of the mobilehomes placed in parks ever take to the road again, there are always some for sale on their sites when homeowners move on and leave their mobilehomes behind. As far as the park is concerned, if a coach occupies a space, there's rent due on that space, whether anyone is living in it or not. Sometimes absentee homeowners continue paying their space rent while the coach is up for sale and sometimes they don't. When they don't, you as the park owner or manager could initiate an unlawful detainer against the owner of the coach as explained above, but you'll find that it's an exercise in futility. You really needn't bother. You might not want to bother, either, if you're already plagued with vacancies.

Since there's a large asset involved, the coach itself, you're better off being patient about getting paid, but there are a few things you might want to do to safeguard your position. Notify the mobilehome's legal owner about the situation right away (you should have a file of the registered and legal owners of every coach in the park; homeowners are required by law to furnish this information to the park, and you should prod them if they don't respond). The legal owner becomes a kind of bail bondsman trying to preserve the money he put up to finance the coach in the first place. He has an interest in keeping the coach right where it is because a well-situated coach is worth more than a coach which is out on the street, and the lender's depreciated collateral might not be enough to cover the loan balance if he were to foreclose. To protect that interest, he will sometimes promise to pay the space rent while the coach is vacant, although he may not pay it until the coach changes hands.

He may try to sell you his security interest in the mobilehome, but in most cases, you shouldn't buy it because you'd still have to foreclose on the resident to get the space back and the rent owed. Instead, you should refuse the lender's offer and remind him that he may foreclose himself and pay you or he may let you evict the resident and pay yourself out of any proceeds from the lien sale. In other words, you stand to get your money without paying the lender anything for his stake in the coach.

Whatever you do, keep the meter running all this time, and continue calculating the rent and late charges since the rent was last paid. Then, when you approve the new buyer, find out who's handling the escrow on the transaction, and present your claim for the unpaid charges to that escrow holder. If the registered owner's equity is large enough, you'll get the rent from him. If the legal owner has to foreclose on the coach, you'll get the rent from him. Just keep abreast of what's happening, be patient, and you stand a good chance of getting the rent in the end.

Abandonment

Every so often a homeowner will abandon his mobilehome or at least appear to abandon it. Perhaps he'll owe some rent on the space. Perhaps he won't. Perhaps he'll own the mobilehome outright. Perhaps a bank will. The situations vary.

One thing which doesn't vary is this. An abandoned mobilehome has nobody looking after it or its yard. It will soon become a blight on the neighborhood. Because no park can afford to have one abandoned coach or many abandoned coaches dragging it down, you as park management must make a serious effort to contact the registered owners first and the legal owners second to ask permission to take over the maintenance of the space. If you cannot locate anyone with an interest in the coach, you should post a notice about space maintenance on the coach, and then take over.

Keep work records just in case you are able to recover some or all of your costs later, but don't fret if you can't recover anything. The primary reason for your taking over the space maintenance of abandoned coaches is to preserve the park's reputation and value.

With the space maintenance resolved, you can work on sorting out the details of the abandonment in order to restart the income stream which the space should be generating. There are at least three ways to handle abandonments.

The first way is to pursue an ordinary unlawful detainer for nonpayment of rent. Because there's nobody available to accept personal service, you serve the notices by "nailing-and-mailing" and the summons and complaint by posting. Then, when nobody answers your complaint, you get a default judgment and a writ of execution. You go all the way to a lien sale, where the coach is sold, and you either get your money or the title to the coach.

The second way is spelled out in full in CC §798.61. It's a well-defined procedure specifically for handling abandonments. Do note, however, that this second procedure applies only to those mobilehomes (1) which are located in a park on a site for which the rent is at least sixty days in arrears, (2) which are unoccupied, and (3) which reasonably appear to be abandoned.

Should you decide to follow this second procedure, look it up and follow it carefully. It begins with the posting and mailing of a notice and ends with the public sale of the mobilehome and disposition of the proceeds. Because it's not particularly complicated and involves no adversary, you should be able to do it yourself.

The third way, which works only if there is a lienholder, is to conduct a lien sale for the unpaid charges.

Which of the procedures should you use? The answer depends upon whether there's a lienholder. If there is, use the uncomplicated third procedure. If there isn't, the answer depends upon how long you've already waited since the abandonment. If sixty or more days have elapsed since you last received any rent from the resident, you're better off using the second procedure. It assumes that you have been patient, and it gives you a head start as a consequence. If only a few days have elapsed since you last received rent, and you have reason to believe that the coach has been abandoned, use the first procedure.

Noncompliance

Mobilehome parks have their share of uncooperative residents just as other residential rental properties do. These uncooperative residents are the type who let their pets roam about freely, fertilizing the streets. They set up an auto repair business in their front yard. They party late and loudly. They whoop it up and discharge their firearms through the walls. They build unsightly spite fences and paint them gaudy colors, or they find some rule to break just to antagonize their neighbors or the park management.

60-DAY NOTICE TO TERMINATE TENANCY

(Mobilehomes)

TO: Virgil Lutz

Victoria C. Lutz

and all other residents or occupants in possession of the premises described as:

2020 Cherry Hill Rd., Space 19
(Street Address)

Lemon   California   91222
(City)   (State)   (Zip)

PLEASE TAKE NOTICE that you are hereby required within sixty (60) days to remove from and deliver up possession of the above-described premises which you currently hold and occupy.

This notice is intended, pursuant to California Civil Code sections 798-799, commonly known as the "Mobilehome Residency Law," for the purpose of terminating the Rental Agreement by which you now hold possession of the above-described premises.

Should you fail to comply with this notice, legal proceedings will be instituted against you to recover possession, to declare said Lease or Rental Agreement forfeited, and to recover rents and damages for the period of unlawful detention.

This notice is being given for good cause as follows:

Homeowners have been given adequate notice to remove the three
inoperable and unlicensed junk cars and debris on their space. Their
space is unsightly, and they are in violation of park rules, paragraph
22, section 3.

Please be advised that your rent, utility bills, and other charges on said premises are due and payable up to and including the date of termination of your tenancy under this notice.

Dated: 4/15/XXXX   _Dan Coffey_
                                              Owner/Manager

PROOF OF SERVICE (Server should complete this proof of service only AFTER serving tenants.)
I, the undersigned, being at least 18 years of age, declare under penalty of perjury that I served the above notice, of which this is a true copy, on the following resident(s) in possession in the manner(s) indicated below: _VIRGIL LUTZ, VICTORIA LUTZ_

☒ On _4/16/XXXX_ , I handed the notice to the resident(s) personally.

☐ On _____, after attempting personal service, I handed the notice to a person of suitable age and discretion at the residence/business of the resident(s), AND I deposited a true copy in the U.S. Mail, in a sealed envelope with postage fully prepaid, addressed to the resident(s) at his/her/their place of residence (date mailed, if different _____).

☐ On _____, after attempting service in both manners indicated above, I posted the notice in a conspicuous place at the residence of the resident(s), AND I deposited a true copy in the U.S. Mail, in a sealed envelope with postage fully prepaid, addressed to the resident(s) at his/her/their place of residence (date mailed, if different _____).

☒ On _4/16/XXXX_ , in addition to service on the resident(s) as described above, I deposited a true copy of the notice in the U.S. Mail, in a sealed envelope with postage fully prepaid, addressed to the legal and registered owner(s) (if other than resident(s)) as follows:
LEGAL OWNER _BANK OF LEMON, 1 MAIN STREET, LEMON, CALIF._
REGISTERED OWNER _____

Executed on _4/16/XXXX_ , at _LEMON_ , California.
                                    Served by _Dan Coffey_

efc

You will find a blank copy of this form in the FORMS section of this book and in Eviction Forms Creator.

Litigation having become the national pastime that it is, you have to do something about these people or your other residents will haul you into court for failing to act. No matter what you do, you are between Half Dome and a hard place, and your head is hurting so much that even two aspirin won't stop the pain. Only an action plan and some corresponding action will stop the pain.

When you encounter an uncooperative resident, follow the procedure outlined in chapter 2 of this book first, and while you're doing that, consider the role you should be playing. Act more like the park mayor than the park cop. Try to make the resident understand why he should shape up. Take a written agreement with you when you talk with him, and if you can, get him to agree in writing that he will remedy the problem within a given period of time.

When you have exhausted the talking stage without results, you may want to hire an attorney to write the scoundrel a nasty letter outlining the steps you will be forced to take next. Most of the time that works. When it doesn't, consider hiring an attorney to seek an injunction. Unless the court requires the attorney to appear personally to get an Order to Show Cause, in which case an injunction can become rather expensive, an injunction will be cheaper and quicker than an eviction.

To get an injunction, the attorney goes to court and asks for a court order requiring the resident to stop certain behavior, such as threatening his neighbors, discharging his handgun on park property, entertaining a nightly procession of people of the opposite sex, or breaking those particular park rules he's being uncooperative about. After listening to your attorney and examining the declarations of the people affected (they don't have to appear in court), the judge alone makes the decision (juries are never involved).

An injunction is much more effective than your talking with the resident or an attorney's writing to him, for he can be hauled off to jail or fined for failing to observe an injunction. It does have some teeth.

When you're dealing with someone who's truly difficult, though, someone who's hardheaded or downright crazy, you ought to pursue the one solution with plenty of teeth for the situation, an eviction. Whereas the resident might be hauled off to jail or fined as the result of an injunction, he'll be back. You can count on that. After an eviction, he's out for good, although you could get the resident to stipulate to an injunction as a settlement of the eviction case. That can work well, too.

Sometimes, like it or not, the most expeditious and least costly way to "evict" a problem resident in a mobilehome park nowadays is for the park owner to buy that resident's coach and resell it to someone else. Such a solution may not seem fair to the park owner because it ties up his cash, frequently causes him to lose some space rent, and sometimes results in a loss on the sale, but, given the time-consuming and expensive legal alternatives, it should always be considered.

If you've considered every other possibility and you still want to pursue a problem resident's legal eviction, serve him with a Notice to Perform Covenant (7 days), and then, if he persists in his noncompliance after the 7-day period, give him a 60-Day Notice to Terminate Tenancy just like the sample shown here. After that, I'd suggest you hire an attorney to handle the court work because the chances are good that the resident will hire an attorney to defend himself, and you might as well be well prepared for battle.

A Word About Experts

Few attorneys are experts in the laws governing mobilehome parks and recreational vehicle parks. It's a specialty which requires study and experience, and the chances are good that the family attorney who wrote your will, handled your first divorce, or defended your teenage son when he was arrested for drunk driving would not be able to do a good job representing you as a park owner or manager. Most attorneys don't even know that such a thing as the Mobilehome Residency Law exists, so much of what you'd be paying them to represent you would be spent on their schooling to become minimally proficient in this field of law.

To find experts who specialize in mobilehome parks and mobilehome park law, check the attorney listings on the Western Manufactured Housing Communities Association website (wma.org). They're under "Vendors & Services." You'll find more that thirty law offices listed there. Some handle nothing but mobilehome park matters for park owners. Some handle them as a sideline. All of them have attorneys who know much more than the average attorney about the Mobilehome

Residency Law.

As an alternative, you may try calling the Western Manufactured Housing Communities Association at 916.448.7002 or the California Mobilehome Parkowners Alliance at 949.380.3304 and asking them for recommendations.

- Distinguish between recreational vehicles and mobilehomes and treat them appropriately.
- Familiarize yourself with the laws governing mobilehomes and recreational vehicles.
- Adopt a reasonable rent collection routine designed to produce rent monies and keep you out of court.
- Maintain the spaces which have abandoned coaches on them, all the while using every legal means available to you to collect the rent.
- When dealing with park residents, act more like the park mayor than the park cop.
- To get rid of the uncooperative resident without wasting time and money going to court, consider buying his coach and reselling it to someone else.
- Keep an expert attorney in the wings for serious mobilehome and RV evictions.

13
Collecting the Money Judgment

With the actual vacating of your rental dwelling by a nonpaying tenant behind you, you have accomplished only one of the two goals you set for yourself when you began your eviction action for nonpayment of rent. You have forced your tenant out. He's gone, gone, gone. Hooray and hallelujah, he had it comin' to 'im, oo ya! You betcha he did!

Ah, but you still haven't collected any of his back rent, and, in addition, you're now out of pocket more than a few dollars for the various fees and charges you've had to pay to get him out. Your judgment entitles you to all of this money plus interest. That's true. The trouble is that getting what you're entitled to requires still more effort on your part.

Evicted tenants are never going to pay you anything willingly. They tend to think like Abbott, who told Costello in one of their old comedies which you might catch on TV during the wee hours when you're wide awake worrying about some landlording problem or other, "Paying back rent is like betting on a dead horse." Who is stupid enough to bet on a dead horse? Nobody. Nobody is that stupid, not even a pair of dim-witted comedians.

Also, remember that nobody from the courthouse or the local department of law enforcement is going to come forward spontaneously to collect it for you. You are going to have to take some initiative yourself to get what you're entitled to.

Unfortunately, today's laws do not favor creditors as they once did. Gone are the days when you could just walk off with a debtor's belongings and the money that came in his mail, leaving him nothing but a barrel and suspenders. You can't send your deadbeat tenant to debtors' prison any more, and you can't garnish a judgment debtor's checks from sources other than wages (as you shall learn, even wage garnishments have

their limitations nowadays). You can't pull up in front of where he lives with a big sign on top of your car saying "WE COLLECT DEBTS FROM DEADBEATS" to shame him in front of his neighbors. You can't badger him about the debt in front of his boss and his co-workers when he leaves his workplace. You can't hound him wherever he goes and make real or implied threats on his life. You can't keep calling him at all hours and hanging up or calling him repeatedly to tell him he'd better pay up if he values his kneecaps.

Underworld debt collectors who consider themselves outside the law might resort to these very effective methods and worse. You can't. You want to stay within the law. You have to stay within the law. Lawmakers have outlawed these methods. They're called "harassment." You can't use them, not even one of them. Bah, humbug!

So what can you do to collect? Go hat in hand to your tenant asking for spare change to apply to the judgment? Ha, ha! You could do that if you wanted to. I wouldn't. There's no force behind such a plea to pay. He'd laugh in your face. After all, you had to force the tenant to leave. You'll have to force him to pay.

Don't despair. There are still some very legal and very effective things you can do to get your money, and there are also a few little tricks you can use to exact some sweet revenge for all the misery your tenant has put you though.

Before you try any of them, however, you ought to determine whether there's somebody other than the tenant whom you might tap for the money and if not, then whether the tenant himself has the ability to pay you anything at all.

Tapping the Co-signer

When you originally rented to the tenant you evicted, did you happen to secure a co-signer to guarantee the tenant's financial compliance with the rental agreement? You did? Well, aren't you the smart one!

Your foresight may actually pay off now, for you probably have somebody of substance to tap for the judgment, somebody who cares about his credit rating and will do something to protect it. A co-signer is just as liable for paying what's owed to you as is the tenant. A co-signer on a rental agreement is like the co-signer on a bank loan. He's on the hook for the full amount.

Although you could have included him in your unlawful detainer from the very beginning if you'd wanted to, doing so tends to complicate service of the necessary papers. Most landlords, therefore, after being ignored by the co-signer when they've contacted him about the trouble with the tenant, concentrate on getting the tenant evicted first. Then they go after the co-signer in small claims court. Armed with the unlawful detainer judgment against the tenants and the co-signer agreement, the landlord has an open-and-shut case in small claims, and the co-signer has no choice but to pay up or else see his credit rating plummet.

If the co-signer proves to be equally as reluctant to pay as the tenant, you may proceed against him using any of the ways mentioned here just as if he were the deadbeat tenant.

Determining Whether the Tenants Have the Wherewithal to Pay

In many cases there's not a chance in Hades that you'll ever collect one clad dime on your judgment because tenants who have to be evicted tend to lack attachable assets and steady employment. They're what attorneys call "judgment proof." Their pockets are shallow. Their purses are empty. Just as turnips lack blood, they lack money, and whatever they lack to begin with, you'll certainly never be able to squeeze out of them, no matter how hard you try.

The question, then, is this: How do you know whether they really do lack money and attachable assets? They might be fooling you.

You look for clues. That's what you do. Did they pay you the rent with cash or money orders in times past? Then they probably don't use banks and don't have their savings where it can be attached. You can't attach money stored inside a mattress. Did they stay around the house a lot? Did they party all night and sleep all day? Then they probably don't work, at least not steadily, and you won't be able to attach their wages. Do

they drive an old car? Impounding and auctioning the heap would cost you more than what you'd derive from its sale. Are they welfare, disability, Social Security, child care, unemployment insurance, or workers' compensation recipients? Their checks from these sources can't be touched. Are they underground-economy types who handle their money transactions with wads of cash? Maybe the IRS can get to their cash. You can't. Such assets are virtually unattachable.

If you strongly suspect that your evicted tenant has nothing you can get at now and has little hope of ever acquiring anything which you might be able to get at in the future, then you might as well drop the matter before you spend any more of your precious time or good money trying to collect what is quite likely uncollectible. Put this loss behind you and get on with your landlording business. Get busy and find a prompt-paying tenant to replace the deadbeat you have just evicted. Check every applicant's credit thoroughly. You never want to have to go through another eviction for nonpayment of rent, not if you can help it, and you can help it.

Exacting Your Revenge—Part 1

Before you drop the matter entirely, you can, and you should, at the very least smirch the bum's credit rating so that other people proposing to do business with this scoundrel will know what to expect of him and be able to protect themselves if they merely take the precaution of checking him out through a credit bureau or an unlawful detainer registry.

Smirching his credit is easy. In fact, it's automatic when you've already gone to the trouble of securing a money judgment against an evicted tenant and had it recorded. Recorded judgments are public records, and credit bureaus search out such information as a matter of course. They thrive on it. You needn't worry about whether it will get into the tenant's file. It will. Once there, it remains for years, and anyone who bothers to check the file will discover that there was a judgment against the tenant and that it remains unpaid. If it ever is paid, the file will reflect that as well.

When you don't secure a money judgment, however, because the tenant skipped out after receiving your 3-Day Notice to Pay Rent or Quit and you dropped your pursuit even though the tenant left owing you a few hundred dollars, the tenant's credit file will not automatically reflect what he owes you. After all, how could a credit bureau know something like that?

Whereas almost everything pertinent which is a matter of public record will appear in the tenant's file, things which aren't in the public records will appear only if they're reported. That's how a department store's late-payment information, for example, gets there. The department store reports the information to the same credit bureau it uses to secure credit information on applicants for credit. Other businesses which extend credit to their customers do the same.

Although credit reporting agencies won't take nonpayment-of-rent information from every Tom, Dick, and Harriet landlord, they will take such information from their "members." That's right! As a member of a credit reporting agency, you may report negative credit information on your tenants so that it will appear on their credit report (if your apartment and property owners association does credit reports for you, ask whether you may report negative credit information through them).

As a member, you are considered to be a small business owner, and you have the same rights and responsibilities that any small business owner has in using the credit system. You may report a tenant who moves out and owes you money even when you haven't had to evict him through the courts, and there's no public record of what he owes. You may also report a tenant who habitually pays late.

If you haven't been using a credit reporting agency, use the internet to find one. A Google-search on "landlord credit services" will give you a good list of them. Look for one which will provide you with reports for a reasonable fee and enable you to report tenants who skip out owing you money.

By the way, unlawful detainer registries report both filings and judgments, so merely filing against your tenant will alert other landlords that the tenant might be suspect when they order an eviction records search as part of their applicant qualification procedure.

If you want any chance of recouping monies owed to you by a tenant who moved out before you filed court papers against him and you want to smirch his credit rating through public records, go to small claims court and get a judgment against him. That will get the information into the public records and might get you the money, too.

If he moved out after you filed the court papers against him in court but before you had a chance to get his default, go ahead with the case anyway and get the judgment so that it will be duly recorded. You've already paid the bulk of the fees. Getting the judgment and having it recorded won't cost you much more. Following the unlawful detainer through to its conclusion and getting the judgment will ensure that it will appear on the tenant's credit report as a judgment.

Judgments are very black marks on credit reports, blacker than any other derogatory credit information except a bankruptcy.

Exacting Your Revenge—Part 2

There's yet another method you might use to exact your revenge against a former tenant who owes you money which you know you'll never collect. Give him an IRS Form 1099-MISC. The form notifies the IRS that the tenant has received income from you. This "income" is equal to the amount of money the tenant owes you. The tenant will then be liable for paying income tax on this amount.

The tenant may have been able to dodge your every effort to collect, but he won't be able to dodge the IRS. Underworld characters can't even dodge the IRS. Your deadbeat tenant doesn't stand a chance against this formidable adversary.

Please note that if you do elect to file a 1099-MISC, you will be relinquishing all claims to the money the tenant owes you. You are essentially forgiving the debt, and you must file an Acknowledgment of Satisfaction of Judgment form with the court (explained later in this chapter) as well.

Also note that the amount shown on the 1099-MISC should be $600 or more, and that it should be the exact amount owed. You will get yourself into a heap of trouble if you exaggerate the amount. Don't.

In order to complete a 1099-MISC, you will need to include the tenant's name, address, and Social Security number on the form (don't worry too much if you haven't a clue as to the tenant's whereabouts; the IRS will locate him in its files according to his Social Security number). You did get the tenant's Social Security number when he moved in, didn't you? If you didn't, don't despair. For a small fee, you can get it from either a credit reporting agency or a web-based detective agency.

For explicit instructions on preparing and filing a 1099-MISC, go to the IRS website (irs.gov) and download the instruction booklet on the subject or contact the IRS directly and ask for a copy.

Filing an Abstract of Judgment— A Small Gamble

If you've already gone to the trouble of securing a money judgment and you don't want to give up on ever getting the money from the tenant, you might want to take a small gamble. The gamble necessitates your filing a Judicial Council form called an Abstract of Judgment with the county. It's easy, it costs only a few dollars, and it entitles you to payment with interest if the evicted tenant ever attempts to buy or sell any real property in that county during the next ten years (the odds of your getting a payoff on an abstract are a whole lot better than the odds of winning the California lottery). You may file in other counties as well, and you may renew the judgment for a second decade if you wish.

Collecting It Yourself

Depending upon your past relationship with the evicted tenant, your time available, your intestinal fortitude, and your estimate of the ease of collection, you might wish to try collecting the judgment yourself. After all, you evicted the so-and-so yourself, didn't you? Well, there's no reason why you can't try collecting the judgment yourself, too. By that I don't mean you should camp out on his doorstep, follow him around demanding payment, walk off with his coveted black velvet paintings, hotwire his Corvette, take his large-screen Zenith, or petnap his pedigreed Doberman. What I mean by "collecting the judgment yourself" is that you should use the legal recourses available to you through the sheriff or marshal in the county where the tenant's job or assets are located. The sheriff or marshal is duly authorized to collect the judgment on your behalf. You don't have to make personal contact with the tenant and risk bodily injury. All you have to do is point the sheriff or marshal in the right direction and pay some upfront costs.

To collect your judgment, you have to know where the tenant works, where he lives, and/or where he keeps his money. Then you can file the papers necessary to get the sheriff or marshal busy.

Involving the Co-Tenants

Keep in mind that you have the legal right to pursue everyone mentioned in the judgment when you're trying to collect. Each person mentioned is liable for the entire amount, not just a prorated share. You may go after any one of them for the entire amount, but once that entire amount has been paid, you may not try to collect any more money from any of them.

Suppose Richard and Rose Renter, the couple you evicted, have now decided to split up, and you are able to locate Rose working in a neighboring town. You can attach her wages for the entire amount of the judgment if you want to, and she will have to find Richard to collect his share from him. You don't have to collect half from her and then try to find him to get the other half. Once she realizes that she's going to have to pay the entire judgment herself, she may take pains to help you find something of Richard's to attach for at least part of the judgment so she doesn't have to pay it all herself.

Whether you go after one tenant or all of them doesn't really matter so far as you are concerned. What matters is finding somebody, anybody, who has the wherewithal to pay.

Finding Your Former Tenant

Uh, oh, there is one problem you may not have encountered before this. You used to know where to contact the tenant. He was living in your rental dwelling, wasn't he? Now that he doesn't live there anymore, you may not have a clue where to find him, and you have to be able to tell the process server where he is, or you won't be able to get your papers served.

Take heart. Remember that you can have the tenant served anywhere he happens to be. You don't have to know exactly where he's living right now if you know where he's working or what bar he frequents after work or where he bowls every Tuesday or which motorcycle gang he hangs out with on Saturday nights.

Don't be shy about asking your remaining tenants or the neighbors where this former tenant may be found. Sometimes they'll know and won't think twice about divulging the information to you. Sometimes they'll know and won't tell you, but they will tell somebody else. If you don't mind resorting to a little deviousness, have somebody you know, preferably a woman with a smile in her voice, call and say something like this, "Hello, I'm Sally Smith from Smith's Dry Cleaners (or Smith's Photo Shop). Your neighbor, Richard Renter, left some clothes (film) here to be cleaned (developed) quite some time ago, and he hasn't stopped by to pick them (it) up. We think he may have forgotten, and we haven't been able to reach him at the telephone number he gave us. Do you know how we might find him?" It usually works.

If every avenue you take turns into a blind alley, remember that the post office might be of some help. Your tenant wants his mail forwarded; that's pretty sure. He's still expecting his Aunt Nelly to die and leave him a large inheritance, and he certainly wants to get all of his Reader's Digest Sweepstakes mail. He knows that some day he'll be a winner and surprise everyone by paying back his many debts.

To locate him using the post office, ask the postal carrier who delivers mail to the tenant's old address whether there's a change of address on file for him and if so, what it is. If that doesn't work, try dispatching an envelope to the tenant at his old address. Stuff it with a copy of the judgment and your reckoning of his security and cleaning deposits. Include your return address, and write the words "PLEASE FORWARD AND MAIL ADDRESS CORRECTION TO SENDER" below the tenant's address. The post office will send you whatever forwarding address it has on file.

Don't give up. He hasn't vanished off the face of the earth. He's probably even closer than you think. Few people move any great distance from where they've been living unless they're in the armed forces or work for a nationwide company which rotates its employees periodically. They tend to stay within a certain geographical radius because that's where their friends and relatives are, that's where they're accustomed to living and playing, and that's where everything is familiar to them. Your former tenant is around somewhere, and he has left his tracks. Find his tracks, and chase him down.

To locate him using the phone system, dial 411 (directory assistance) and ask for the tenant's current phone number. He may already have a telephone installed at his new place. Once you know it, you may find his current address using a reverse directory on the internet.

To locate him using the internet, consult the nationwide directories now available there. Go to "yahoo.com" and do a "people search"; go to "excite.com" and use the "white pages"; or go to "switchboard.com" and tap into its vast nationwide people database. I've been pleasantly surprised by how many people I've been able to find through these sites. The cost is right, too. It's absolutely free.

Free searches sometimes fail to find elusive people. Fee-based searches seldom fail. They search much larger databases, such as marketing lists, catalog purchasers, magazine subscribers, change of address records, real property records, court records, and business records. Three such fee-based search websites are "intelius.com," "locateamerica.com," and "peopledata.com." They're simple-to-use, quick, effective, and inexpensive.

For specific, helpful hints in tracking down your tenant, consult a book like *How to Find Missing Persons* or *The Complete Idiot's Guide to Private Investigating*.

People who earn their living looking for bail jumpers, child support shirkers, swindlers on the lam, teenage runaways, elusive heirs, and wayward waifs have their own ways of finding those who seem to have vanished as if from a magician's trunk. You may want to use those ways yourself to find your former tenant.

Looking Around for Something to Collect

You may know already where the tenant works or has attachable assets. Good for you! You're smart to have kept track of such things. Now don't wait. Get going. Take this information to the sheriff or marshal and fill out the proper forms so collection can begin right away, before the tenant knows what's happening.

If you suspect that your evicted tenant may have attachable assets, but you don't know what they are or where they are, you may do one or both of two things—run a credit check or order an examination at the courthouse.

Running a credit check has enough advantages so that you ought to think about trying it before resorting to an examination. First, it preserves the element of surprise. You may catch the tenant unawares before he has had an opportunity to hide his attachable assets. Second, it saves you time because you don't have to arrange, prepare

AT-138, EJ-125

ATTORNEY OR PARTY WITHOUT ATTORNEY *(Name, state bar number, and address)*:	FOR COURT USE ONLY
Lester Landlord 123 Neat Street Littletown, California 91111 TELEPHONE NO.: 415-123-4567 FAX NO.: ATTORNEY FOR *(Name)*: Plaintiff in Propria Persona	

NAME OF COURT: Saddleback Superior Court
STREET ADDRESS: 100 State Street
MAILING ADDRESS:
CITY AND ZIP CODE: Littletown, California 91111
BRANCH NAME:

PLAINTIFF: Lester Landlord
            Leslie Landlord
DEFENDANT: Richard Renter, Rose Renter

APPLICATION AND ORDER FOR APPEARANCE AND EXAMINATION	CASE NUMBER:
[✔] **ENFORCEMENT OF JUDGMENT** [ ] **ATTACHMENT (Third Person)** [✔] **Judgment Debtor** [ ] **Third Person**	35791113

ORDER TO APPEAR FOR EXAMINATION

1. TO *(name)*:
2. YOU ARE ORDERED TO APPEAR personally before this court, or before a referee appointed by the court, to
   a. [✔] furnish information to aid in enforcement of a money judgment against you.
   b. [ ] answer concerning property of the judgment debtor in your possession or control or concerning a debt you owe the judgment debtor.
   c. [ ] answer concerning property of the defendant in your possession or control or concerning a debt you owe the defendant that is subject to attachment.

Date: June 29, XXXX   Time: 10:15 A.M.   Dept. or Div.: M-5   Rm.: 212
Address of court [✔] shown above [ ] is:

3. This order may be served by a sheriff, marshal, registered process server, or the following specially appointed person *(name)*:

Date: _____

                                             JUDGE OR REFEREE

This order must be served not less than 10 days before the date set for the examination.
IMPORTANT NOTICES ON REVERSE

APPLICATION FOR ORDER TO APPEAR FOR EXAMINATION

4. [✔] Judgment creditor   [ ] Assignee of record   [ ] Plaintiff who has a right to attach order
   applies for an order requiring *(name)*:   to appear and furnish information
   to aid in enforcement of the money judgment or to answer concerning property or debt.
5. The person to be examined is
   a. [✔] the judgment debtor.
   b. [ ] a third person (1) who has possession or control of property belonging to the judgment debtor or the defendant or (2) who owes the judgment debtor or the defendant more than $250. An affidavit supporting this application under Code of Civil Procedure section 491.110 or 708.120 is attached.
6. The person to be examined resides or has a place of business in this county or within 150 miles of the place of examination.
7. [ ] This court is **not** the court in which the money judgment is entered or *(attachment only)* the court that issued the writ of attachment. An affidavit supporting an application under Code of Civil Procedure section 491.150 or 708.160 is attached.
8. [ ] The judgment debtor has been examined within the past 120 days. An affidavit showing good cause for another examination is attached.

I declare under penalty of perjury under the laws of the State of California that the foregoing is true and correct.
Date: June 12, XXXX

Lester Landlord   ▶ *Lester Landlord*
(TYPE OR PRINT NAME)   (SIGNATURE OF DECLARANT)

(Continued on reverse)

Form Adopted for Mandatory Use Judicial Council of California AT-138, EJ-125 [Rev. July 1, 2000]	**APPLICATION AND ORDER** **FOR APPEARANCE AND EXAMINATION** (Attachment—Enforcement of Judgment)	Code of Civil Procedure, §§ 491.110, 708.110, 708.120

Get a blank copy of this form from the court clerk or at courtinfo.ca.gov/forms/documents/ej125.pdf.

for, and conduct a face-to-face examination. Third, it takes no mental toll on you because you don't have to put yourself in the presence of the lousy scoundrel who's caused you all this trouble in the first place. That's no fun.

Of course, running a credit check does require the tenant's authorization, doesn't it? It does most definitely. But you got that when the tenant first filled out his rental application, didn't you? The rental application I use states specifically: "I authorize verification of my references and credit as they relate to my tenancy and to future rent collections."

The credit report may tell you enough about the tenant's assets to point you in the right direction to get at them, and then again it may not. The information in his credit report may be so dated that you may be able to tell the credit agency things about the tenant which they didn't know before. If so, you will have to go further and order an actual face-to-face examination.

Ordering an Examination

An examination involves personal testimony before a court or before a court-appointed referee. The tenant has no choice but to come. He absolutely has to appear at an examination just as he has to appear in court when subpoenaed or he will be held in contempt of court and will face the humiliation of being arrested and hauled off to jail. He must tell the truth about his assets, too, or he will be guilty of perjury, which carries both a jail sentence and a fine.

To arrange this examination, you must use the Application and Order for Appearance and Examination (Attachment—Enforcement of Judgment) form. You're already familiar with the format of other similar Judicial Council of California forms. This one is simpler than most. Fill it out as shown here and take it to the court clerk's office to get an appointment for the examination. There may be a cost for this hearing, or there may be no cost at all. Ask the court clerk.

Once you have set up the appointment, you may take the order to a sheriff, marshal, registered process server, or a specially appointed third-party, whichever one you believe will serve the papers most cheaply, most correctly, and most promptly. Time is of the essence. The form must be served in person at least ten days prior to the examination.

Generally the examination is held in imper-sonal surroundings at the courthouse in the presence of a clerk. You are the examiner.

The examination, you hope, will be revealing, but you must know what questions to ask, for your former tenant isn't going to volunteer any information. You can be quite sure of that.

To increase the odds that the tenant will answer the questions honestly, bring a recorder and plenty of blank tape and extra batteries to the examination. Announce that you will be recording everything everybody says, and keep the microphone in plain view to remind the tenant that he is being recorded.

Here are some questions you may want to ask:
1) What's your current address? What's your current phone number?
2) Who are your dependents, and how are they related to you?
3) How do you propose to pay me the money you owe me?
4) What's your occupation? Who's your employer? How long have you worked there?
5) What's your salary? How is it paid? When is it paid?
6) What's your spouse's occupation? Who's your spouse's employer? How long has your spouse worked there?
7) What's your spouse's salary? How is it paid? When is it paid?
8) Do you have an interest in any business? How much of an interest do you have? What kind of business is it? How does the business get its money? Where does the business keep its money?
9) What other income do you have?
10) Do you own your own home now? What is the home's value? What mortgages are there on it? Who holds the mortgages? What are the payments? When was your home homesteaded?
11) Are you renting now? How much is the rent? When and how is it paid? What's your landlord's name and address?
12) Do you own any real estate either by yourself or with someone else? Where is it located? How do you hold title to it? Is it mortgaged? Who holds the mortgages? What are the payments?
13) Where do you have your checking account? What's its number? In whose name is it? What's the current balance in

the account? Do you have any checks with you?

14) Where do you have your savings account? What's its number? In whose name is the account?

15) Do you have any more bank accounts? If so, what are the particulars?

16) Do you have any money in an individual retirement account (IRA)? Where is it? Do you have any money in some other retirement account? Where is that?

17) Do you have a safe deposit box? If so, where is it?

18) Do you have anything in your pockets or purse? If so, put it all on the table.

19) Do you have any cash on you other than what is in your pockets or purse, such as in a moneybelt or in a shoe? If so, put it all on the table. Where else do you keep your cash?

20) Do you have any stocks, bonds, or other securities? What are the particulars about them?

21) How much life insurance do you have and with what company is it? Who's your insurance agent?

22) Where is your jewelry kept? What would you estimate its value to be?

23) Do you have a share in someone's will or estate? What are the particulars?

24) Who is the registered owner of the car you drive? Who and where is the legal owner you make payments to? What is the value of your car? How much are your car payments? What is the unpaid balance? You say you don't have a car? Then how did you get here?

25) Do you own or have a share in any other vehicles? What are the particulars?

26) Have you ever filed for bankruptcy before? When? Where?

27) Do you have any property, such as furniture, tools, office equipment, or appliances, which you have pledged to pay a debt? What are the particulars?

28) Who are your parents? Where do they live? What's their telephone number?

29) Give the names of two other relatives or friends who live in the vicinity.

30) Is there anything else relative to your financial situation which I may have overlooked?

Deciding What to Go After

Well, how do things look? You should have a lot of information by now. What are you going to do with it all? Look for things to seize and attach, that's what. Are there forthcoming wages? Is there something of value which your former tenant possesses that you might be able to get your hands on? Did he say during the examination that he had his wallet? Did he say that he had some checks with him?

First things first—if the tenant has a wallet or a purse and puts it on the table, you have the right to go through it looking for cash or anything else of value. You may take all of the cash except for $20, and you may take anything else of value to help satisfy the judgment. Ask him to take out two of those checks he said he has with him and write them to you, one for a third of what he owes you, the other for two-thirds (you want two checks just in case the bank won't cash a check for the entire amount because of insufficient funds; it will cash one for a smaller amount if he has enough in his account). Then run directly to his bank to cash them. If he won't cooperate, get a court order immediately to force his cooperation. Whoever's acting as the impartial third party during the examination will know exactly what to do.

The next best sources of payment after his most readily available assets are wages, a till tap, bank accounts, and vehicles.

Wages are the best of the lot. They're paid on a regular basis, and there's little he can do to stop you from garnishing them, up to a limit of 25% of his take-home pay above the minimum wage. Once you know where he works and how much he earns, you have all the information you need to garnish his wages. The sheriff does the actual garnishing. You will need to provide him with the issued writ and an Application for Earnings Withholding Order, another Judicial Council form, and pay the garnishing fee.

If he's self-employed and he doesn't receive wages, but he does receive monies in his business, you may order a till-tap, a seizure of monies in the "till" conducted by the levying officer in your area.

Bank accounts are too easily transferable. They're good only if you can surprise him and get to them before he has an opportunity to withdraw the funds.

His car would be a good source of funds if he

didn't already owe more on it that it's worth or if he didn't own such a clunker, both of which are likely. The other problem with trying to squeeze money out of a car to satisfy a judgment is the complicated nature of the conversion. Have you ever tried to raise some quick cash by selling a vehicle you own? It can be an involved process, one which never yields as much as you thought it would. Selling a car which someone else owns involves more work and requires more upfront money paid to the sheriff or marshal than the previous two assets. It should be a last resort.

Consider the other assets revealed during the examination for what they're worth. If they look attachable, go after them.

Setting Up the Collection

At this point, do not have a change of heart about the tenant's intentions. Do not set up a payment schedule and have the tenant make payments directly to you. He may implore you not to put his livelihood in danger by garnishing his wages. Don't listen to him. You aren't putting his livelihood in danger unless his wages are already being garnished for some other debts. His employer cannot fire him for one garnishment order. Forego garnishing his wages right away only if he promises to pay the entire judgment to you within three days and if he gives you a plausible source for the funds. Otherwise, get thee to the sheriff or marshal's office, fill out the proper forms there, pay the upfront money required, and let them handle the collection. The tenant has to pay the fees for their service anyway.

The fee for garnishing wages is $25; for attaching a bank account, it's $30; for a till-tap, it's $85; and for selling a vehicle, it's an upfront deposit of $1,000 (these numbers may or may not be exactly what your county charges currently; they are good approximations).

Remember that tenants may try to hide their assets after the examination. Move quickly before they put their assets out of your reach.

Enlisting the Services of a Collection Agency

Sometimes collecting a judgment yourself is easy, and sometimes it's not. After learning what's involved, you may not want to spend your time playing sleuth and trying to collect the judgment yourself. If so, you may get a collection agency to do it for you. Yes, there are people who make

their living collecting other people's debts. They are in business to handle collections impersonally and professionally.

To find a collection agency, use the Yellow Pages or do an internet search. For sums less than $5,000, use an ordinary agency. For sums greater than $5,000, consider using a law firm such as "collectionlawyers.com," which uses lawyers to speed up the collection process.

For their services, collection agencies charge forty to fifty percent of all they collect, but just remember that half of nothing is nothing. If they don't get any money for you, they get none for themselves. Even for a fat forty or fifty percent of a few hundred dollars, they're not going to turn over every rock looking for your debtor and his assets. You should provide them with some solid information so they will know to look only under iron-pyrite rocks weighing about fifty pounds located within the city limits of Bakersfield. That kind of information is helpful.

To enlist the services of a collection agency, give them the judgment form from your court case, sign an "Assignment of Judgment" (they'll have one handy) authorizing them to collect your debt for you, and wait. You may be pleasantly surprised one day long after you've forgotten the matter when checks start coming in the mail. Don't, of course, be the least bit surprised if they don't, because they probably won't. Be content with the tenant's departure, for with that you have accomplished your primary goal anyway—to minimize your losses and regain the possession of a rental dwelling which you can rent to a paying customer.

Selling the Judgment

Don't sell the judgment without first making an effort to collect it yourself. Collecting it might prove to be easier than you thought, and you might be giving it away for pennies on the dollar when you could be collecting every dollar of it yourself without all that much trouble.

Sell it only if you have tried collecting it yourself and failed or if you have decided that collecting it yourself is too much work or if you have no "stomach" for collecting it.

Some savvy people make a good living out of buying money judgments cheaply and then collecting the full amount owed. You may not even have to contact these people. They may contact you. They scour courthouse records looking for the names of judgment creditors.

If nobody contacts you and you're interested in selling your judgment, ask the court clerk for the name of somebody who buys them. She'll know somebody who does.

Depending upon their assessment of your eagerness to sell and the likelihood of their collecting, they will pay you anywhere from 5 to 40% of the judgment. Consider what they first offer you and bargain with them if you'd rather apply your time to things other than collecting judgments. At least they pay you something, and they pay it to you right away. That's better than nothing.

Filing an Acknowledgment of Satisfaction of Judgment

If the tenant ever does pay the entire amount of the judgment, you must file with the court something called an Acknowledgment of Satisfaction of Judgment (EJ-100). It's a form which becomes part of the county's public records, alerting one and all, especially the credit bureaus, that the tenant has paid you everything he owed you as a result of your court case. It's essentially the tenant's "reward" for having paid off the debt. While it doesn't eliminate altogether the appearance of the involuntary judgment indebtedness from the tenant's credit report (that remains for seven years), it does serve as a kind of counterbalance and proves that the tenant does pay up, however reluctantly and however late.

File the form only when the tenant has paid you in full, not before. Ask the court clerk for a blank copy of the form, or download one from the Judicial Council's website (courtinfo.ca.gov). It's a standard Judicial Council form just like the others used in eviction proceedings, and since you have filled out several such forms already, this one won't be any mystery to you.

Because this particular form is used in many kinds of court cases which result in money judgments, not just evictions, you will see some things on the form which don't apply to you. Don't let them confuse you.

Count yourself lucky if you ever have to file one and be sure you file it promptly. You have no right to delay making public the fact that the tenant has paid up.

- Tap the cosigner to pay the evicted tenant's bill.
- One way to exact revenge is to smirch your evicted tenant's credit rating.
- Another is to give him an IRS 1099-MISC.
- File an abstract of judgment in case the tenant ever buys or sells any real property.
- Go after the tenant most likely to have the bucks; he's responsible for the whole judgment.
- Don't assume that a disappearing tenant is gone forever; he's around somewhere.
- Use any of numerous legal ways to discover where the tenant's assets are.
- Make use of the sheriff or marshal to ensure payment.
- Use a collection agency or sell the judgment if you'd rather not collect it yourself.
- File an Acknowledgment of Satisfaction of Judgment when you finally do get paid.

14
Coping with Other Related Matters

Besides regaining possession of your rental dwelling and collecting the money which is owed to you, the primary concerns of previous chapters, you may have occasion to be concerned about a variety of other related matters.

You may need to know what you ought to do with the belongings your tenant left behind when you evicted him, how to handle an apparent abandonment, how to get rid of a renter who stopped paying you his garage rent, how to evict a lodger from your home, how to oust a discharged manager, what to do about squatters, when to pursue a Writ of Immediate Possession, why the baggage lien law is virtually useless to you, what's different about military tenants, how to respond to a landlord who is asking you for a recommendation on the tenant you're evicting, how to evict deadbeats from a commercial property you own, how to handle deposit refunds when the tenant hasn't provided adequate notice that he's vacating, or what to do when you have to evict a Section 8 tenant.

My advice on matters such as these appear in this final chapter, which I hope will help you avoid some unnecessary legal entanglements.

Disposing of the Remains

There is always the slim possibility that an evicted tenant will leave you with a crock full of silver dollars, three Nikons, a signed Picasso print, and an original Tiffany Studios trumpet vine leaded glass lampshade. Unlikely? Yes, unlikely, highly unlikely! More likely, he'll leave you with greasy pots, black kettles, thrift-shop furniture, piles of tattered clothing, dust balls, and dozens of poopy Pampers. You should know how to dispose of these remains legally, exposing yourself to as little liability as possible.

As landlord again in possession of your real property after a tenant's fly-by-night departure or his by-the-book eviction through the courts,

you must take charge of his personal property which remains. You have no choice in the matter, for the sheriff or marshal nowadays can assist you only in removing the humanity left on the premises and not in removing anything else. The sheriff or marshal won't even help you take inventory of the stuff that's left behind. You have to inventory the belongings, decide what to do with them, and then act.

If you can possibly locate your former tenant, try to make arrangements with him to remove his remaining belongings on or before the date set for the eviction.

If you cannot find him anywhere, determine the approximate value of the belongings yourself before doing anything else. As soon as you complete the inventory and appraisal, complete a Notice of Right to Reclaim Abandoned Personal Property, and send it to the tenant at his last known address.

If you believe his belongings have a resale value of less than $300, you may dispose of them after fifteen days in any way you choose. Because you want to prepare the dwelling for new tenants as soon as possible, you will want to remove the belongings from the premises at the first opportunity and store them in a safe place for the fifteen days. After the fifteen days, you may keep all the pennies you find, you may wear the old clothes, toss the Pampers, haul the grease-stained settee to the dump, scrub the pots and kettles, and see what they will fetch on eBay.

If you have any doubts about your own ability to act as an appraiser of secondhand goods, you may want to call a thrift shop and ask them for an estimate, giving them the whole lot as a donation in exchange for an itemized receipt stating that the belongings are worth less than $300.

If you are the least bit suspicious that your former tenant may be trying to lure you into disposing of his worthless belongings, only to claim

NOTICE OF RIGHT TO RECLAIM ABANDONED PERSONAL PROPERTY

TO: Huddle Rund

Address:

458 Sweet Street
(Street Address)

Littletown   California   91111
(City)   (State)   (Zip)

When vacated, the premises described above contained the following personal property:

One green upholstered chair, one black-and-white television, assorted men's clothes, and various kitchen gadgets.

Unless you pay the reasonable cost of storage for all the above-described personal property and take possession of the property which you claim not later than eighteen (18) days after this notice is deposited in the United States Mail, this personal property may be disposed of pursuant to Civil Code Section 1988.

Check the ONE box below which applies:

[X] Because this property is believed to be worth less than $300, it may be kept, sold, or destroyed without further notice if you fail to reclaim it within the time limit indicated below.

[ ] Because this property is believed to be worth more than $300, it will be sold if you fail to reclaim it. It will be sold at a public sale after notice has been given by publication. You have the right to bid on the property at this sale. After the property is sold and the costs of storage, advertising, and sale are deducted, the remaining money will be turned over to the county. You may claim the remaining money at any time within one year after the county receives the money.

Date of mailing this notice: February 7, XXXX

Date of expiration of this notice: February 25, XXXX

You may claim this property at: 444 Neat Street, Littletown, CA 91111

Lester Landlord
_____
Owner/Manager
(signature)

Lester Landlord
123 Neat Street
Littletown, CA 91111
Name & Address of Owner/Manager
(typed or printed)

efc

You will find a blank copy of this form in the FORMS section of this book and in Eviction Forms Creator.

later that they consisted of priceless family heirlooms and an irreplaceable baseball trading card collection, photograph every room and its contents before you ever touch a thing. Then call the thrift-shop appraiser.

If the belongings are worth $300 or more, you may not dispose of them so easily. You should photograph and inventory everything first and then decide whether to leave things where they are or move them. If you leave them in place, you may tally storage charges from the date of the eviction to the date of removal at a daily rate equal to the per-diem rent, but because you cannot rely upon the tenant to resurface anytime soon to redeem his belongings, you should move them into "a place of safekeeping" as soon as possible so you can re-rent the dwelling.

You must return his belongings upon demand, charging only a reasonable sum for the storage itself. Whatever you do, don't hold the tenant's goods until he pays all that he owes you. Be reasonable and you'll stay out of trouble.

According to Civil Code §1983 and §1988, you must keep the goods in storage for at least fifteen days before putting them up for sale, and you must advertise the sale in a local newspaper at least five days before the sale is held. The proceeds must first be applied to the storage costs and to the costs incurred in holding the sale; then they may be applied to your judgment; and after that, whatever is left over must be returned to the tenant. If he is nowhere to be found, the balance must be turned over to the county within thirty days.

Don't be too worried that conducting these sales will interfere with your other leisure-time activities. Tenants simply don't trust their landlords enough to leave valuable belongings behind when they're being evicted. I've never yet had to play auctioneer in such a situation, but I'm glad that I know what's involved anyway, in case I do have to do it someday, just as I'm glad that I can milk a cow, program a computer, fly an airplane, sail a boat, ride a Harley, hit a golfball, and change a flat tire.

Abandonment

Occasionally a tenant, along with all of his belongings, will skip out entirely without your knowledge, or he may simply disappear and leave all of his personal property behind. Maybe he'll owe you some rent, and maybe he won't. Whereas

California law (Civil Code §1951.2 ff.) does have specific procedures to follow in these cases, the procedures do take a minimum of 29 days.

Now, 29 days is a long time to wait if you feel 98% certain that the tenant has already abandoned the place and removed his worldly possessions. You're going to be anxious to get into that empty dwelling to fix it up and get it rented again. But if you are only 71% certain that he has abandoned the place and you want to avoid all the rigmarole of conducting a full-scale unlawful detainer action to regain possession, 29 days might not seem like such a long time.

After all, when you consider that an unlawful detainer filed against a tenant who can't be found and served with any of the required papers in person is going to take a minimum of 28 days, and that's only if all goes extremely well, hey, what's 29 days? Not only that, unlike an unlawful detainer, abandonment procedures bypass the court system altogether, so there's little paperwork to prepare and there's no filing fee to pay.

Think of an abandonment proceeding's 29 days as entirely relative, and don't overlook it as a very useful way to regain possession under certain circumstances.

Whatever the circumstances, you would be wise to try tracking down the missing tenant yourself to learn of his intentions before using this legal procedure. Begin your tracking by looking at the tenant's rental application and telephoning every personal and business reference given there, starting with the "person to contact in an emergency" if there is one on the application. No luck? Try contacting the neighbors for possible clues to his whereabouts. Still no luck? See whether you can find him through one of the many missing-person websites available such as intelius.com. Finally, if all else fails, contact the police. That might yield some leads. If nothing works, use the following legal procedure.

As it does in regular unlawful detainer actions, the law requires that you first notify the tenant in writing of your intentions whenever you suspect abandonment. The notice you must use is called a Notice of Belief of Abandonment, but you may not use it at all until fourteen unpaid rent days have elapsed. Then you may deliver the notice to the tenant in person (yes, that's what the law says), or you may send it by first-class mail (get a "Certificate of Mailing" at the post office as proof that you sent it).

NOTICE OF BELIEF OF ABANDONMENT

(Real Property)

TO: Delwyn Lewno

Muretta Lewno

Address:

999 Sweet Street
(Street Address)

Littletown   California   91111
(City)   (State)   (Zip)

This notice is given pursuant to Section 1951.3 of the California Civil Code concerning the above-described real property rented by you. The rent on this property has been due and unpaid for fourteen (14) or more consecutive days, and the owner/manager believes that you have abandoned the property.

This real property will be deemed abandoned within the meaning of Section 1951.2 of the Civil Code, and your tenancy shall terminate on ___February 25, XXXX___ , which is not less than eighteen (18) days after this notice is deposited in the United States Mail unless before such date the undersigned receives at the address indicated below a written notice from you stating BOTH of the following: (1) Your intent not to abandon the real property, and (2) An address at which you may be served by certified mail in any action for unlawful detainer of the real property.

You are required to pay the rent due and unpaid on this real property as required by your rental agreement. Failure to do so can lead to a court proceeding against you.

Date of mailing this notice: February 7, XXXX

Lester Landlord
Owner/Manager
(signature)

Lester Landlord
123 Neat Street
Littletown, CA 91111
Name & Address of Owner/Manager
(typed or printed)

efc

You will find a blank copy of this form in the FORMS section of this book and in Eviction Forms Creator.

You must wait fifteen days after personal service or eighteen days after service by mail before you can legally claim abandonment. If the tenant does answer your notice, he must do so in writing. He must indicate that he does not intend to abandon the premises, and he must provide you with an address where he may be served by certified mail with a complaint for unlawful detainer.

If the tenant fails to answer your abandonment notice within the prescribed fifteen- or eighteen-day waiting period, you may take possession without ever having to set foot inside the courthouse. Just go right into your rental dwelling, change the locks, and start your usual preparations for new tenants.

Although you do receive possession of your property through this procedure, you do not receive a money judgment. You have to go to court for that. You'll have to decide for yourself how good your chances are of ever collecting. What good's a money judgment if there's nobody available to pay it?

If there is any personal property remaining on the premises when you take possession, you handle it in much the same way you handle the remains left after an eviction. Civil Code §1988 spells out the procedure. You should inventory the property first, store it, and then send the tenant a Notice of Right to Reclaim Abandoned Property, stating that he has eighteen days to reclaim his things. After waiting the full eighteen days, you may keep, sell, or destroy it if you believe it is worth less than $300. If you believe it is worth more than $300, you must advertise that you are auctioning off the property, and then you may go ahead and auction it off. The proceeds of this sale go first to storage costs and sale expenses, then to delinquent rent and costs. Whatever surplus is left over after that must be turned over to the county.

Note that you may proceed with a nonpayment-of-rent unlawful detainer action at the same time you are pursuing an abandonment if you wish, for a Notice of Belief of Abandonment has no effect on the use of a 3-Day Notice to Pay Rent or Quit. They may be used independently of one another and concurrently as well.

Nosy landlords never have abandonment problems. They know what their tenants are up to all the time. You needn't become nosy to avoid abandonment problems. You can avoid them through good communications and circumspection.

Self-Storage Units and Garages

California has a Self-Service Storage Facility Act (Business & Professional Code §21700 ff.) which governs self-storage units and garages used strictly for storing personal property (items used for commercial purposes, such as tools, equipment, and materials, still qualify as "personal property"). Specifically excluded from this act are storage areas or garages rented with a residence, storage areas or garages used as a residence, and warehouses. If you are renting out a garage to somebody and have a separate rental agreement for it, then chances are good that this relationship comes under the SSSFA. Should the renter stop paying you his rent, you'll find that evicting him is relatively easy. The procedure is much like the one used for an abandonment because it calls for similar notice periods and involves no court action in most cases.

Here's what you do when the renter fails to pay his rent.

Wait fourteen days following the rent due date. Then send the renter a Preliminary Lien Notice by certified mail or by first-class mail, verified by a Certificate of Mailing, to his last known address and to whatever alternative address appears on the rental agreement (the agreement must provide a space for an alternative address, whether the renter gives one or not). Here's the notice format:

```
PRELIMINARY LIEN NOTICE
TO [leave a blank for the
renter's name and full address].
   You owe, and have not paid,
rent and/or other charges for the
use of storage [identify the
storage area by space number or
other identifier] at [give the
name and address of the storage
facility].
   These charges total $[amount]
and have been due for more than
14 days. They are itemized as
follows: [give due date, descrip-
tion, and amount].
   If this sum is not paid in full
before [give a date at least 14
days from mailing], your right to
use the storage space will termi-
```

nate, you will be denied access, and an owner's lien on any stored property will be imposed.

You may pay this sum and may contact the owner at [give your name, full address, and your telephone number].

[Date it and sign it.]

Fourteen days later, having received anything less than the full amount of the rent due, you may lock the renter out and enter the space. If you sent the Preliminary Lien Notice by certified mail, you may remove the renter's property to a place of safekeeping. If you sent the notice by first-class mail, you may not remove the renter's property until the termination date of the Notice of Lien Sale, that is, for at least another fourteen days.

In any case, you must then send the renter a Notice of Lien Sale by certified mail. You may not use first-class mail for this notice. Here's the format:

NOTICE OF LIEN SALE

TO [leave a blank for the renter's name and full address].

Your right to use the storage space [identify the storage area by space number or other identifier] at [give the name and address of the storage facility] has terminated. You no longer have access to the stored property.

The stored property is subject to a lien in the amount of [give the same amount shown in the PRELIMINARY LIEN NOTICE].

The stored property will be sold to satisfy this lien after [specify a date not less than fourteen days following the date of mailing] unless the amount of the lien is paid in full or you complete under penalty of perjury and return by certified mail the enclosed DECLARATION IN OPPOSITION TO LIEN SALE form. If you pay the full lien amount prior to the date specified in this paragraph, you may regain full use of the storage space. [This last

sentence is required only if you sent the Preliminary Lien Notice by first-class mail.]

You may claim any excess sale proceeds above the lien amount and the costs of sale at any time within one year following the sale, but after one year, the excess proceeds will be turned over to the county.

[Date it and sign it.]

Along with the Notice of Lien Sale, you must send a relatively simple Declaration in Opposition to Lien Sale form for the renter to fill out. Here's its format:

DECLARATION IN OPPOSITION
TO LIEN SALE

I, [leave a blank for the renter's name], have received the notice of lien sale of the property stored at [leave a blank for the location and space number, if any].

I oppose the lien sale of the property. My address is: [leave a blank for the renter's street address, city, state, and zip].

I understand that the lienholder may file an action in court against me, and if a judgment is given in his or her favor, I may be liable for the court costs. I declare under penalty of perjury that the foregoing is true and correct, and that this declaration was signed by me on [leave a blank for the date] at [leave a blank for the place].

[Leave a blank for the renter's signature.]

If you must take the renter to court because he opposes the lien sale and has returned the declaration, follow the procedure in B&P §21710. If you must hold a sale, follow the procedure in B&P §21707 for advertising it, conducting it, and disposing of the proceeds.

Evicting a Lodger

Should you be renting out a room in your own home to a lodger or a "roomer," as they're sometimes called, and should you want to evict that person because he has stopped paying you the rent money or because you're not getting along well enough to live under one roof anymore, you're probably pretty miserable about the situation. It's much like being stuck in a bad marriage.

Well, consider yourself lucky in this one respect at least, that you do not have to go to all the trouble of filing an unlawful detainer as outlined in chapter 5 in order to evict your lodger. The eviction procedure for lodgers is much simpler than the standard eviction procedure because the law recognizes that you and a lodger with whom you are having a disagreement are living in close proximity under strained circumstances and that you have to resolve the matter between yourselves reasonably quickly, or there could be some "fire" started by the friction.

Take note, however, that you may use this abbreviated procedure only if you have one lodger, no more, and only where you as the owner have retained the "right of access" to your entire dwelling, including the area occupied by the lodger. If you are renting out a self-sufficient in-law apartment located within your dwelling and you have not retained the right of access to the apartment (having keys to the place does not give you the right of access; apartment owners retain keys to their units, but they do not have the right of access), then you cannot use this procedure. You must follow the standard eviction procedure instead.

So what is this abbreviated procedure for evicting lodgers?

Civil Code §1946.5 explains it in legal terms, and you should take a look at the code before you attempt to evict your lodger (see Appendix B).

In layman's terms, it's the simplest procedure possible, one which puts real teeth into notices and real meaning into the time limits given on those notices.

You simply serve the lodger a notice appropriate to the situation, for example, a 3-Day Notice to Pay Rent or Quit in a nonpayment-of-rent situation, the same as you would serve any other tenant (you would be wise to have somebody else serve the notice for you so you'll have someone other than yourself available to testify on your behalf should the lodger later claim in court that nobody served him). If he fails to satisfy the demands of the notice within the time

limits allowed, and he remains on the premises, he has violated California Penal Code §602.3 (see Appendix B), and you may make a "citizen's arrest" under Penal Code §837. If he won't leave, you may call the local law enforcement agency and have him formally arrested. An officer removes him from the premises, and he's gone. He's evicted. That's all there is to it. You do not have to go to all the trouble and expense of getting a court judgment and a Writ of Possession.

This truly is a summary eviction. Would that every landlord could use the same procedure for any tenant who's being evicted!

Unfortunately, there's a horsefly in this salubrious ointment. If the tenant won't cooperate by leaving voluntarily and you have to resort to calling in the troops, you might find yourself at an impasse.

Unless your local law enforcement agency already has experience with this procedure or unless you know the people there and they know you, they're going to be reluctant to help. They're going to want a higher authority. Your word is not enough authority for them. They're so accustomed to acting only when they have some court-generated paperwork that they tend to be lost without it. Consequently, you may have to press your case pretty hard to get any action out of them.

Rather than expecting law enforcement people to jump when you call them to have a lodger evicted bodily, prepare yourself for some resistance. Approach them correctly, however, and you might get the action you want.

Begin by gathering up your paperwork—copies of the rental agreement, the notice you served most recently, and any other relevant papers you may have. Become conversant with the applicable laws. Read them carefully and make copies. Then make an appointment to see somebody at your local law enforcement agency who has the authority to decide whether to take action or not. Argue your case before that person, show him the paperwork, and see what happens.

In spite of what you see in films and on television, law enforcers in real life tend to ask questions first and shoot afterwards. They want to make sure that they are well within the law before they take any action at all. They don't want to do something which will make them look like fools or cause them grief later, especially now that they're fair game for every loaded video camera pointed in their direction. Don't blame them if they're none too eager to drag your lodger out of your house by the scruff of his neck. They know only too well what the consequences might be for them should they make the wrong move.

Because yours may be the one and only lodger eviction case your local law enforcement agency has ever encountered or ever will encounter, you will probably know more about evicting lodgers than they do. Try convincing them that you know what you're doing, that you have complied with the law, and that you would like them merely to carry out the enforcement. Maybe they will help you, and maybe they won't.

If you can't get any action out of your local law enforcement agency, don't despair. You still have any number of choices for getting rid of that lodger. Here are some—intimidate the lodger into leaving by "moving" somebody else into the same room; show him the law about lodger evictions and give him an ultimatum to be out in one hour, at which time you say that you will cause enough of a disturbance so that your neighbors will call the cops and you will have the lodger arrested for trespassing; deny the lodger access to his lodgings, that is, change the locks when he's gone and lock him out; or follow the same formal eviction procedure which everybody else follows at this stage, just as if the lodger were a tenant in your apartment house.

None of these choices is particularly palatable, but then, you're stuck in a disagreeable situation anyway, and you'll likely have to do something disagreeable to force the lodger out and restore your life to normalcy.

Every choice except the last one would seem to be an illegal or quasi-legal "self-help" eviction method. It's not. Remember, your situation is not like that of other landlords. Your "tenant" is living with you, so he's more like a house guest than a tenant, and when you and he are not getting along, he's like a house guest who has overstayed his welcome. The law restores possession to you upon expiration of the notice you gave the lodger.

Just because you can't convince a law enforcement agency to remove the lodger bodily doesn't mean that you have any less of a right to possession. You have every right to possession. You have every right to put him out on the street yourself. Having him arrested is merely a formality, something which puts the law enforcement

establishment's official stamp of approval on the eviction and ensures that nobody gets hurt.

You don't need this stamp of approval, but you do need to ensure that nobody gets hurt, and the best thing you can do to keep the peace is to surround yourself with people. Confront your lodger in the company of others—friends, relatives, or neighbors. You want witnesses. You want moral support. And you want physical support if necessary. If you're too angry with the lodger to talk calmly and you doubt your ability to maintain control over yourself and the situation, you might even want somebody else to do the talking for you.

Whatever you do, be careful. Make absolutely certain that you are in full compliance with the law. Reread the law on the whole lodger eviction procedure. Document and date every step you've taken so far in trying to settle your grievance with the lodger, in giving him proper notice, and in trying to get a law enforcer to remove him. Then take action.

Do nothing to anger the lodger other than put him out. Do not touch him unless he touches you first. Don't even act physically threatening. Return his belongings when he asks for them, return his deposit if you owe him anything, but don't let him back inside the dwelling.

Should he sue you later, you will have what you need to defend yourself in court.

Discharged Manager

Every so often you may be faced with one of the following situations involving a resident manager: You have learned quite by accident that your manager is embezzling funds; you have bought a building which has a manager whom you want to replace; your tenants have begun grumbling to you that the manager is always trying to convert them to his latest religion; you have found your manager drunk on the job; your manager no longer seems interested in exterior maintenance, and the building is beginning to look rundown; over the past three weeks, your manager has given two tenants black eyes; although told repeatedly that the toilet was leaking and the hot water heater wasn't working in Apartment 6, your manager neglected to do anything about these problems, so the tenant withheld his rent, and you failed to evict him when you tried because he rightly used the warranty-of-habitability defense; or you can't seem to get along with your manager, no matter what.

These are distressing situations, to say the least, and you may want to avoid doing anything about them because you know there will only be unpleasantries involved when you do, but you have a business to run. You simply cannot afford to ignore these situations, nor can you afford to get drawn into the personal dramas certain to occur when you discharge a resident manager. You must think of your business first.

So what do you do? What can you do?

If the matter is urgent enough, such as your having caught a manager embezzling funds, you will have to find someone to manage the place immediately on a temporary basis. Once discovered, the embezzler must not be allowed access to your funds. After you have provided for temporary management, you can deal with the villain himself. Threaten to turn him over to the police if he hasn't moved out completely within twenty-four hours. If he doesn't move out, call the police and at the same time serve him with a summons and complaint. The written employment termination notice you give him is the only notice you need to serve to initiate unlawful detainer proceedings against him.

If the matter is not particularly urgent, such as your incompatibility with the manager or the manager's negligence of responsibilities, you should handle the situation differently. Determine, first of all, whether you want to let him continue living where he is. If so, give him a written notice stating when his employment is terminated, when his rent is to begin, and how much that rent will be. Then he won't be able to claim in court that his rent was some other amount. Give him the advance notice you have agreed upon in the management agreement, twenty-four hours, seven days, or at most thirty days. Lacking a management agreement, give him thirty days' notice unless his pay period is every week or twice a month. In that case, the notice period should correspond with his pay period.

If you elect to require him to leave upon termination of his employment (wise in most cases; necessary if there are special resident manager's quarters), state in his notice of termination that you want him to move out. Then, if he doesn't move in the time given for him to move, you may initiate an unlawful detainer against him as soon as his termination becomes effective.

Follow the failure-to-vacate procedure in chap-

ter 8 (you don't need to give him further notice), but you should explain in an attachment to the complaint that the defendant is a licensee, not a tenant, that you and the defendant have had an employer-employee relationship, that you have discharged the defendant from employment, and that you wish to reclaim possession of the dwelling which was first occupied by the defendant as a condition of employment.

Waste no time. A discharged manager who continues living on the premises and bears a grudge against the owner can undermine your control of the property.

Squatters

"Squatters? I've never had any trouble with squatters before. Why would they ever choose my place to squat?"

There are any number of reasons. They might have thought that you didn't care about the property and would be grateful to have someone living there, that you were off on a vacation and wouldn't notice, that you had inherited the property and were waiting for it to clear probate, that you were waiting for a wrecker to tear the place down, that you were a skinflint and should be skinned, that you lived far away and weren't keeping tabs on the place, that you owned so much property you had forgotten about this one, that you were involved in a partnership breakup and couldn't agree what to do with the property, or that you were a government agency with surplus property managed by bureaucrats. Sound crazy? Sure, but there are people in this world who think that you and I owe them a roof over their heads, and given the opportunity, they'll seize that roof. They don't care who owns it.

European landlords know a lot more about squatters than we do. They have been so overwhelmed with squatters that some of them have had to guard their vacant rental properties like fortresses, using 24-hour guards, electronic alarms, Doberman patrols, and all but impregnable locks, just to keep these pesky people out. Some are so persistent and so brazen that they will even try to move in by creating a diversion in order to sneak past the guards.

Fortunately the situation has yet to reach those lows here in California because the housing shortage isn't quite so chronic, and our laws aren't quite so archaic. Still, you may occasionally encounter someone who, unbeknownst to you, has set up housekeeping in one of your vacant rentals, and you may wonder what can be done about it.

Consider, first of all, what has happened, that your real property has actually been stolen out from under your nose just as certainly as someone might break in and steal your laptop, your Colt .45, your Palm PDA, your wedding rings, or your sterling silver. The only difference here is that the squatters can't spirit your property away into hiding. It remains attached to the earth, a particular place with a street address and, of course, a tax assessor's parcel number. You know where the thieves are and you know they aren't going to leave voluntarily, for if they do, they will be relinquishing what they have stolen.

Squatters are committing a criminal act, to be sure, and you have every right to feel wronged. You have been wronged. Consequently, you may tend to cast yourself in the role of a self-appointed vigilante with right on your side. You may want to burst into the place with weapons drawn and boot them out bodily. If you enjoy confrontations and danger and you wouldn't mind risking a few years cooling your heels with society's losers or you have great confidence in your attorney's abilities, strap your six-shooters onto your belt, burst into the place, and go after the squatters with all your firepower. Try to resist this approach if you can. It's unreasonable, it's dangerous, it's illegal, and you're likely to widow your wife and orphan your children.

Instead, call the police and talk the situation over with them. Tell them that someone has "stolen your property," that you know where the thieves are, and that you'd like help from the police in reclaiming it. These are terms understood by police anywhere. Telling the police that there are squatters living in a rental dwelling you own will not elicit the same response.

Incidentally, you or someone representing you should take an active role in this attempt to reclaim your property. Do not leave it entirely up to the police. Accompany them when they first visit the squatters. Help direct the efforts to clarify the situation for everyone and get the squatters out.

So long as the squatters acknowledge that they have no legal claim to possession, the police visit should suffice to get them out. If they claim that they have a legal right, say an oral agreement with the owner, then the police won't be of much help,

and you will have to resort to other means.

If you encounter indifference from the police about your problem, you might find someone else to accompany you on a visit to the premises, in broad daylight if possible. This person who accompanies you ought to have a football player's neck, a basketball player's height, an iron pumper's chest, and a Sicilian surname, but if such a person is unavailable, any adult will do. Together with this person, pull up in front of the property with a U-Haul truck or trailer and get the attention of the squatters. Tell them that you have rented the premises to your friend here and he has a valid rental agreement entitling him to move in that very day. They must leave right now, or you will have to call the police to make them leave. After you've said all that, stay there until they start packing.

As an alternative, you might resort to the primary stratagem used by European landlords who discover squatters on their property, a stratagem similar to what the Feds used when they evicted the Indian squatters from Alcatraz back in June of 1971. Keep watch on the place patiently until all or nearly all of the squatters (at least the ringleaders) have left the premises. Then arrive with a large enough entourage and move the squatters' belongings out into the street. If you have waited until the squatters least expect to be evicted, you should encounter little or no resistance. Should there be any resistance at all, stay right there yourself, and send a cohort to call the police immediately. In a ticklish confrontation like the one you've forced, the police must respond, and now it'll be your word against the squatters', and you should prevail, especially if you have some paperwork to prove your case. Be resolute. Don't leave the place without getting your property back. Then, once you are successful in evicting the squatters, secure the place well and have a neighbor look after it for you.

Should these efforts fail, don't do anything drastic, like burying mines in the yard or setting demolition charges around the periphery of the building and then threatening the squatters' lives if they don't leave. Follow the legal procedure to get them out.

Of course, there is one. It requires serving them with a Notice to Quit first, giving them five days to get out. That's right, I did say five days! Don't ask me why California laws give a squatter more notice time than a deadbeat tenant; they just do.

Use the straightforward Notice to Quit form for starters. Mention that the occupants are in violation of California law regarding "forceable entry" and put a "5" in the line next to "days."

Try various subterfuges to get the squatters' names if possible (question the neighbors or literally sift through the squatters' garbage looking for names if you have to). On the notice you may list the names as numbered "Does," but you'll need to know their real names by the time you get the judgment because the sheriff or marshal will not be able to carry out the Writ of Possession unless the actual names of the occupants are listed.

After that, you should proceed not with an unlawful detainer, but rather with a forcible detainer according to CCP §1159-60. Consult the latest edition of the *Landlord-Tenant California Practice Guide* in your court's law library for more information and the proper forms.

Writ of Immediate Possession

You may still file for a Writ of Immediate Possession just as you may still file a lien against your tenant's personal property using the baggage lien law, but neither one is used that much anymore. In 1970, the writ was emasculated just enough to make it virtually useless except for a narrow range of applications.

Today, according to CCP §1166a, a writ will be issued only if you can prove any one of the following: 1) the defendant resides out of state; 2) he has departed from the state; 3) he cannot, after due diligence, be found in the state; or 4) he has concealed himself to avoid service of summons.

Prior to 1970, one could get a Writ of Immediate Possession in California by proving either that the tenant was bankrupt or that he lacked resources sufficient to repay the damages sought by the landlord. As you might imagine, those two grounds, when added to the four above, made this writ quite a bit more useful then as compared to its restricted version now.

Still, if you feel you can prove that your tenant falls into any of the four categories above, you might want to secure a Writ of Immediate Possession because it will do exactly what its name says it will do, give you immediate possession, after you make a court appearance.

The procedure starts out like any other un-

lawful detainer and changes only when the process server who is trying to serve the tenants informs you that they are avoiding service or could be out of state. That's when you file a motion for writ of possession per CCP §1166a (see Appendix B).

This motion must state that the writ of possession you are requesting applies to all tenants, subtenants, if any, named claimants, if any, and any other occupants of the premises, and it must ask for an order shortening the time of notice of the hearing on the motion because the underlying unlawful detainer action is entitled to a summary proceeding.

After you learn from the court when the hearing on your motion will be held, you must serve the tenants with a notice informing them of the date and time of the hearing (served according to CCP §1011). The notice must state that they have the right to file affidavits with the court and to appear and testify at the hearing. It must also state that if the tenants do not appear, the plaintiff/landlord will apply to the court for a writ of possession.

Then comes something different. The judge will require you to "file an undertaking," that is, post a bond, which would be used to compensate the tenants for damages if you later fail to get a judgment for possession or if your unlawful detainer action is later dismissed.

Be aware that some judges are very reluctant to grant an order for immediate possession because they believe that tenants should have their "day in court."

Be aware that local eviction control ordinances may prohibit the use of CCP §1166a entirely.

Be aware that you should submit a written declaration of facts before the hearing and that your declaration should be specific about where the tenants are and how you discovered their whereabouts. It should give whatever information you have about how the premises are being damaged, if they are being damaged, and about how the premises are being used for illegal acts, if they are. You should get a declaration from the process server, too, listing all of his previously unsuccessful attempts to serve the tenants.

Be aware that an order for immediate possession is different from a judgment for possession even though they both result in an eviction of the tenants. Once you receive an order for immediate possession, you may still have to seek an official termination of the tenancy from the court, but at least you'd be rid of the tenants in short order.

In spite of these drawbacks, which you should be aware of before using CCP §1166a, you might find certain occasions when this procedure will serve you well.

The Baggage Lien Law

You've heard of the baggage lien law, haven't you? Yes, there truly is such a thing, but, no, it's not of much use to you. You can't just walk right into the dwelling of a tenant who's behind in the

rent and seize his belongings any more.

The correct lawful procedure is so involved, and the exemptions are so numerous as to render this law virtually useless to landlords. You must first file a suit and obtain a court order before you may legally remove any of the tenant's nonexempted possessions, and, to be sure, you will find little of what most tenants own is not exempt from seizure. Even if you do get a court order to remove those household and personal items which are not considered basic under the law, you may remove them only during daylight hours. Then you must obtain a court judgment against the tenant and give the tenant another month to redeem his goods. Finally, at long last, you do get to dispose of the seized possessions at a public sale after first giving adequate notice of the sale.

Even though the law as it now reads is virtually useless to you, don't become so disgusted that you try summarily confiscating the tenant's belongings anyway to compensate yourself for rent owed. Tenants become ruffled when that happens, and you can get into more trouble than you can handle.

Some time ago, a landlady in Germany seized an American serviceman's stereo set for nonpayment of rent, so he stole a cannon from the armory, wheeled it up in front of his apartment house, and threatened to blow the place up.

There's enough tension in this business without your raising the level higher.

Forget about the baggage lien law. Instead, follow the appropriate eviction proceedings, get the tenant out, and get a money judgment as well. Money is better than baggage any day.

The Military Tenant

You may have noticed that the Request for Entry of Default introduced in chapter 5 includes a Declaration of Non-Military Status that you have to fill out if you want your long-sought default entered as a matter of record. You cannot obtain a default judgment and get the tenant evicted without first signing this request declaring that your tenant is a civilian.

Well, then, what happens if you have been blithely pursuing an unlawful detainer action against a military tenant, only to discover at this juncture that you can't get a default judgment unless you swear to a falsehood? Is all your work thus far for naught?

Maybe it is and maybe it isn't.

Here's one possibility. If you also named the military person's spouse in your suit, proceed against him or her alone just as you would against any other civilian. When the spouse is evicted, the military tenant will generally accompany him or her.

Here's another possibility. Hope that the military tenant will go ahead and make a response to your complaint so that you won't have to complete a Declaration of Non-Military Status. The only place one appears, remember, is on the Request for Entry of Default, and you won't have to file a request if your military tenant responds to the complaint.

Here's still another possibility. Skip the normal court procedure altogether when you're dealing with a military tenant. Because military people are subject to military procedures (you know how Beetle Bailey's sergeant treats him in the famous comic strip), you could proceed against your military tenant by calling the commanding officer and asking for help in resolving the payment or tenancy problem, whatever it is. The armed services have the power to order a pay allotment proportional to salary to pay for rent of any premises occupied by a military person or the military person's spouse, child, or other dependents. You'll likely be pleasantly surprised by the speedy response.

By the way, whenever there is any major military activity, watch the media for possible temporary restrictions on rent collections and on evictions as they affect military personnel. To find this information using the internet, do a "google-search" (google.com) on "Soldiers' and Sailors' Civil Relief Act." You'll see something relevant among the list of items Google finds for you. Pay great heed to whatever restrictions happen to be current, keep alert for changes in the restrictions, and be patient. You'll get all the rent owed to you eventually, and you'll get the military miscreant evicted eventually, too.

Tenant Recommendations

The tenants you evict are going to find someone else to rent from when they move out of your rental property. They're not going to disappear off the face of the earth, idle a while in purgatory, be jailed for a few years, live in their monstrous SUV very long, or wander the streets with other homeless nomads just because you have evicted them. No, they're not. They're going to be out there looking for another place to live just as soon as you kick them out, and they'll find one, too.

So what do you say when another landlord calls you to ask for a recommendation on someone you're in the process of evicting? Do you tell the whole truth and risk not being able to get rid of the tenants promptly because you gave them a bad recommendation? Do you tell none or only part of the truth, just to slough your lousy tenants off on some other unsuspecting landlord?

You'll be especially tempted to give the tenants an undeserved good recommendation when you're in the early stages of an eviction and you're trying hard to get them to leave voluntarily without your having to go to court and lose lots of money and time. Later in the process, when you know you have won the court battle and their eviction is assured, you won't be so tempted.

The truth is that you don't have to lie about the tenants you're evicting, nor do you want to lie about them and compromise your reputation as a trustworthy landlord. Not only is lying bad for your reputation, it will fill you with regrets later.

You do not have to tell the whole truth about the tenants, either. That'll also fill you with regrets. Instead, don't say anything either positive or negative about them. Say something like this, "I have been advised not to give recommendations on any of my tenants because you might sue me if I give them a good recommendation and they turn out to be bad tenants for you, and they might sue me if I give them a bad recommendation and my judgment is proven wrong." Almost every landlord can understand that explanation, concerned as all of us are about potential lawsuits.

Let the other landlord figure out whether to rent to your old tenants from other information available to him. At least you will have a clear conscience that you haven't wronged either him, your departing tenants, or yourself.

NOTICE TO PAY RENT OR QUIT

(Commercial Property)

TO: _ROBERT JONES_

and all other tenants in possession of the premises described as:

2222 MAIN STREET

(Street Address)

LITTLETOWN   _CALIFORNIA_   _91111_

(City)   (State)   (Zip)

PLEASE TAKE NOTICE that the rent is now due and payable on the above-described premises which you currently hold and occupy.

Your rental account is delinquent for the period from _SEPTEMBER 1, XXXX_ through _SEPTEMBER 30, XXXX_.

Item 1) _BASE RENT_   Amount due $ _695.00_
Item 2) _COMMON AREA MAINTENANCE_   Amount due $ _38.00_
Item 3) _PROPERTY TAX_   Amount due $ _72.00_

[OWNER: Include common area maintenance, taxes,   TOTAL DUE $ _805.00_
insurance, and other such items above ONLY if the   less partial payment $ _∅_
rental agreement contains an "additional rent" clause.]   equals TOTAL BALANCE DUE $ _805.00_

Total balance due is [X] exact amount of rent owed [ ] reasonable ESTIMATE of rent owed.

You are hereby required to pay said rent in full within _THREE (3)_ days or to remove from and deliver up possession of the above-described premises, or legal proceedings will be instituted against you to recover possession of said premises, to declare the forfeiture of the Lease or Rental Agreement under which you occupy said premises and to recover rents and damages, together with court costs and attorney fees, according to the terms of your Lease or Rental Agreement.

Rent must be paid in full and in person to the following person or entity:
Name: _PETER SMYTHE_   Phone _555-101-2345_
Address where rent is to be paid _2225 MAIN ST, LITTLETOWN, CA_
Usual days and times for payment of rent _M-F, 9A-5P; SAT 10A-4P_
Please phone in advance to make sure that someone will be available to accept payment.

Owner's acceptance of a partial rent payment after service of this notice upon you or after commencement of an unlawful detainer based upon this notice shall not constitute a waiver of any rights, including any rights Owner may have to recover possession of the premises (CCP §1161.1).

Dated: _9/18/XXXX_   _Peter Smythe_
                                              Owner/Manager

PROOF OF SERVICE   (Server should complete this proof of service only AFTER serving tenants.)

I, the undersigned, being at least 18 years of age, declare under penalty of perjury that I served the above notice, of which this is a true copy, on the above-mentioned tenant(s) in possession in the manner(s) indicated below:

[X] On _9/18/XXXX_, I handed the notice to the tenant(s) personally.

[ ] On _____, after attempting personal service, I handed the notice to a person of suitable age and discretion at the residence/business of the tenant(s).

[ ] On _____, after attempting service in both manners indicated above, I posted the notice in a conspicuous place at the residence of the tenant(s).

[ ] On _____, I sent by [cross out the one(s) not used] (first-class) (registered) (certified) mail a true copy of the notice addressed to the tenant(s) at his/her/their place of residence.

Executed on _9/18/XXXX_, at _LITTLETOWN_, California.
                              Served by _Peter Smythe_

You will find a blank copy of this form in the FORMS section of this book.

Commercial Property

When your bagel shop tenant goes out of business and disappears, and the rent payments stop; when your beauty shop tenant sells her shop to a scatterbrained beautician and leaves town, and the rent payments stop; when your restaurant tenant padlocks his doors and tells you he's broke, and the rent payments stop, you will have to become familiar with how to evict tenants from the commercial property you thought would be so much easier to manage than an apartment house.

Except for the section on evicting renters from storage units, this book deals entirely with residential property. Covering fully the subject of evicting tenants from commercial property would require a book at least the size of this one. Nah, it would be bigger, much bigger. There are all kinds of wrinkles in commercial property evictions because attorneys have devoted more thought to them than to residential property evictions. There's usually more money involved.

Nonetheless, I do not want to ignore the subject entirely. I want to give the hapless landlord faced with a commercial property eviction a head start on the procedure. Here are the basics for handling a simple eviction when a commercial property tenant has stopped paying rent.

Although a commercial property eviction is different from a residential property eviction, it's not so completely different that you must always call for help, that is, unless the tenancy is complicated or unless there are big bucks at stake.

A commercial property tenancy becomes "complicated" when the original tenant has assigned or sublet the premises, when the commercial property includes a residence, when there's a dispute about the principals' obligations under the lease, when the tenant has declared bankruptcy, when the tenant has made substantial improvements, or when the tenancy itself has positive or negative value to the owner. Those tenancies and others like them tend to complicate a commercial property eviction, and you should consult experienced legal counsel for guidance when faced with such complications.

A simple commercial property tenancy is one where the tenant pays a certain rent every month and perhaps something extra according to the business income or the utilities used. That's a tenancy much like a residential property tenancy, and in that case, you may want to pursue the eviction yourself when the tenant stops paying rent and hasn't declared bankruptcy and isn't disputing the landlord's obligations.

Before you take the legal steps necessary to evict the tenant, read chapter 2 of this book again and try some of its ideas. Perhaps you can get the tenants to vacate without taking them to court. If so, celebrate! If not, get out their rental agreement and read it. Read it twice. Study it. What it says about your remedy for dealing with them as nonpaying tenants is what you must do now.

See what it says about the person or entity who is responsible for paying the rent. Is that party still responsible? Has the individual who originally rented from you become a partnership or a corporation? If you believe so, you may want to list both the individual and the ownership entity on the notice and serve both. Has the agreement been assigned or is there a sublessee? If it's been assigned, serve the assignee because that person or entity is the only one with the right to possession. If there is a sublessee, serve both the sublessor and the sublessee. You want to identify in the notice and serve the notice to whoever has possession, and that's almost always the party or entity who's been paying the rent lately.

See what the agreement says about the number of days the tenant has to pay the rent after service of notice. The tenant may have three, five, ten, fifteen, or even thirty days to pay. Whatever it is, your notice must conform to the rental agreement. If the agreement says the tenant is allowed ten days to pay, then you must use a ten-day notice. If the agreement says nothing about the notice duration, you may use a three-day notice. Your notice, by the way, must conform exactly to the rental agreement. If you mistakenly serve a three-day notice and learn later that it should have been a five-day notice, you must serve another notice, a five-day notice. You may not just wait an extra two days.

See what the agreement says about the tenant's monetary obligations. There may be a base rent plus other obligations like a percentage of the business revenues at that location, a pro-rata share of the common-area maintenance costs, a pro-rata share of the property taxes, and a pro-rata share of the liability insurance. What does the agreement say that the tenant is supposed to pay? Does it say that these other obligations, if any, are considered "additional rent"? The verbiage would be something like this, "All monetary obligations shall be deemed additional rent." If the agreement does contain an "additional rent" clause, you may include the base rent and the other obligations in the Notice to Pay Rent or Quit. If it doesn't and there are other obligations, you must list them in a Notice to Perform Covenant, which you may serve together with the notice to pay.

Use a Notice to Pay Rent or Quit designed for commercial property tenancies so you may take advantage of certain rights you have that residential property owners do not.

CCP §1161.1, quoted in Appendix B, gives commercial property owners the right to estimate the rent rather than state it precisely, so long as the estimate is labeled an "estimate" in the notice, the complaint, and the evidence produced at trial, and so long as it is "reasonable."

This code section also gives commercial property owners the right to accept partial rent after serving the notice and even after filing the complaint, all without waiving any rights whatsoever. Residential property owners would have to start from scratch if they were to accept partial rent after serving the notice or filing the complaint.

If you know the precise amount of rent owed, use that figure rather than an estimated amount because there are a few disadvantages to using the estimated amount (see *Landlord-Tenant California Practice Guide*, 7:104.6). If you don't know the precise amount, by all means, use an estimated amount.

Whether you use a precise or an estimated amount, make sure it includes whatever the agreement identified as additional rent. For the sake of clarity, you may want to itemize the various rent and additional rent items on the notice, starting with the base rent.

Having settled upon the person or entity to identify and serve, the length of time they have to pay following service, and the amount of the demand, we need to consider one more detail, forfeiture of the agreement. There are pro's and con's about electing forfeiture in the notice.

Most landlords elect forfeiture because they know that they aren't going to collect anything by holding a deadbeat tenant to lease terms following an eviction. Electing forfeiture gives the tenant only the days allowed in the notice to pay the rent and no more. It also enables the landlord to get relief from stay in bankruptcy court more easily. Not electing forfeiture gives the tenant the right to pay the rent at any time during the unlawful detainer, even after the judgment, and still retain possession. You don't want that.

The notice here assumes you want to elect forfeiture. Change it if you wish.

Serve the notice as specified in the rental agreement. If the agreement says nothing about how notices are to be served, serve it just as you would if you were serving a nonpaying residential tenant, that is, according to CCP §1162.

Remember now. You're handling a commercial property eviction. You may accept partial rent without having to start all over again. Take whatever monies your tenant offers you after he gets the notice. You have nothing to lose by taking it. The eviction clock keeps right on ticking. If he doesn't come up with all the rent money he owes you within three days, you continue with the eviction. You file the summons and complaint.

You may use the Judicial Council complaint form, or you may draft one yourself. If you elect to draft one, follow the model in the *Landlord-Tenant California Practice Guide*. If you elect to use the Judicial Council form, you'll need to adapt it slightly for your purposes. It's designed more for residential evictions, but because it does refer specifically to commercial property evictions in section 8a(5), you need have no qualms about using it for your commercial property eviction.

Here's what you should do when using the Judicial Council complaint. Enter what's called for throughout the complaint, paying special heed to the following: In section 6a(2), where you're supposed to enter the rent as a dollar figure, enter the precise amount of rent originally agreed upon. If there is no precise amount, enter "See Attach. 6a(2)" in the space, and include an attachment identified as Attachment 6a(2) to explain the original rent calculation, including whatever the agreement calls "additional rent." Check box 6e, and attach a copy of the written agreement as Exhibit 1. It explains the original rent arrangement better than anything else. Check box 7e, and attach a copy of the notice as Exhibit 2.

Wherever you are supposed to enter precise figures for rent and damages on page 2 of the complaint, enter precise figures if you have them. If you are using estimated figures, enter them along with an asterisk, and explain at the bottom of the page, below item 18, that the asterisk means the figure is a reasonable estimate.

Everything else follows the same steps as a residential property eviction.

Deposit Refunds

Now and again, tenants will give you an indefinite notice that they plan to move and then give you a definite moving date four days before they actually do move. Naturally, they believe that if they leave the place reasonably clean and undamaged, and if they are current in their rent, you owe them their entire deposit plus whatever rent they have paid for those days following the day they are planning to vacate.

The truth is that if they have a month-to-month tenancy and pay their rent every month, they owe you rent for thirty days following the day when they give you a 30-day notice in writing that they intend to move, unless you have agreed with them in advance to a shorter notice period.

For example, if they have paid you their rent for all of May and they tell you on May 12th that they're leaving May 16th, they owe you rent through June 11th, rather than through May 16th, and you may take the balance out of their security deposit if you choose.

As a practical matter, however, you would be wise to compromise on the rent you charge vacating tenants, especially if you can reasonably expect to find another tenant quickly. The law does not allow you to collect double rent, so if you argue with the vacating tenants over how much rent they owe and you succeed in collecting the rent from them for twenty days following their move-out date, you're going to have to refund any rent they paid for the period beginning with the first day you receive rent from a new tenant anyway. Why should you provoke them and distress yourself by pressing them for the maximum amount of rent they owe? You shouldn't. Compromise with them. Tell them what you could do by law, and then tell them what you will do to make them happy.

There's another practical matter you should keep in mind. You want to make certain that there is enough of a deposit refund available as an incentive for the vacating tenants to leave the place in good condition. The more of a refund they expect to receive, the better they'll leave the place.

When a tenant gives me one week's notice and asks me how much of his deposit he'll get back if he leaves the place clean, I tell him he'll get back all of it except for a hundred or two hundred dollars (generally it's a hundred when the rent is less than $750 and two hundred when it's more),

which I tell him is to compensate for his giving such short notice. I could hold back more of the deposit because of the short notice, maybe all of it, and still be within the law, but that's not going to get me a clean, perhaps even a ready-to-rent, dwelling.

Evicting the Section 8 Tenant

Section 8 tenants know that the rental assistance they get through HUD's Section 8 housing program is a good deal. They get to live in rental housing which isn't located in a "housing project" where there are hundreds of other po' folks, and they pay only a fraction of the market rent for their dwelling. The government pays the balance.

They know that they had to do a lot to qualify for Section 8 assistance, and they know that Section 8 funds are limited.

Many people who have qualified for assistance aren't receiving any because there's almost always a shortage of funds. They just have to wait until more funds become available or until somebody currently receiving funds is disqualified or drops dead.

So, if some Section 8 tenants lose their entitlement by increasing their income or doing something foolish like failing to make their rent payments, they lose out on the assistance for a long time to come, perhaps forever. If they can succeed somehow in getting requalified, they must go to the end of the line and wait for funds to become available.

While they're receiving assistance, Section 8 tenants tend to behave. They pay their rent on time, and they abide by whatever rules apply to them as tenants. They don't want to lose out on a good deal.

Of course, there are always some Section 8 tenants who have to be evicted because they stop paying their share of the rent money or they break the rules.

Evicting them does involve a little extra work, I'll grant you, but considering all that you have to do for an ordinary eviction anyway, this extra work doesn't amount to much.

Let's see what's involved should you ever have to evict Section 8 tenants yourself.

First, we'll assume that you have already exhausted every amicable method you know of to resolve whatever it is that is causing you to think about evicting your Section 8 tenants. Having done that, you must serve the tenants with an appropriate notice, and the notice must include a "good cause."

Notices for some good causes, such as failure to pay, serious or repeated lease violations, and breaking the law, may be served at any time and call for the same notice compliance period you'd give any tenant.

Notices for other good causes, such as the landlord's wanting to occupy or remodel the premises or end Section 8 involvement, would apply only upon or after the expiration of the initial fixed-term agreement and require a 90-day notice rather than a 30- or 60-day notice.

At the same time that you serve the tenants with a notice, you must notify the agency administering your local Section 8 program that you intend to evict the tenants. Sending them a copy of the notice along with a note advising them of your intention to evict the tenants is sufficient. The agency does not get involved in the eviction. The matter is between you and the tenants.

The agency even continues making payments to you during the eviction. As you know, if the tenants were paying all of the rent themselves and you served them with a notice to pay rent or quit or a notice to terminate tenancy, you must not accept any rent from them to cover the period following the expiration date of the notice. Were you to accept any rent for that period, the tenant could argue that you had nullified the notice or that you had entered into a new agreement.

In the case of Section 8 tenants, however, they are the ones paying "rent." The agency is not. The agency is merely making housing assistance payments to the landlord to make up the shortfall between the market rent and the rent paid by the tenant. Housing assistance payments are not rent. They're an independent subsidy made on behalf of the tenant and on the basis of an agreement between HUD and the landlord. You may continue accepting HUD's payments even during an eviction [*Savett v. Davis* (1994) 29 CA4th Supp. 13, 19-20, 34 CR2d 550, 554].

As for what you should include on a notice to pay rent or quit issued to a Section 8 tenant, you should include just what the tenant is obligated to pay and nothing more. That's the "rent." Don't even mention what HUD is paying you. That's not rent.

These few considerations aside, evicting a Section 8 tenant is no different from evicting any

other tenant, but you might want to contact your local housing agency to ask them for help and suggestions before you serve the tenant with the notice and certainly before you file your paperwork with the court. You want to make sure that your timing is correct, and the agency will know whether it is.

- Unload abandoned personal goods legally.
- If you suspect abandonment, try to locate the tenant yourself while you follow the legal procedure to reclaim the premises.
- Use the Self-Service Storage Facility Act procedure for evicting renters from storage areas.
- To evict a lodger from your home, use the uncomplicated and speedy eviction procedure especially designed for such situations.
- Settle rental dwelling questions concurrently with discharging a manager.
- Play a squatter's game to get squatters out.
- Forget about using the baggage lien law.
- Consider using a writ of immediate possession when tenants can't be found or when you know they're avoiding service.
- You can't evict military tenants through superior court, so use other methods.
- When asked, give neither a positive nor a negative recommendation about a tenant you're evicting.
- Commercial property evictions are different from residential property evictions in some respects. Learn what the differences are, and decide whether your circumstances warrant handling such an eviction yourself or hiring it done.
- Be fair in calculating deposit refunds, but don't cheat yourself.
- Go ahead and evict your Section 8 tenants when you must, but remember that you must have a good cause and you must inform the agency responsible for administering the program.

Forms

Page Numbers

To assist you in finding the blank forms you're looking for, we put small page numbers in the forms' corners. When you go to copy the forms, either white-out the page numbers, cut them off, or fold the corners of the pages over so the numbers will not show up on your copies.

Number of Copies to Make

The numbers in parentheses following the form names above are the number of copies, in-cluding the original, which you should make if you are dealing with a single defendant. Add one copy of each form for each additional defendant.

Whatever notice you use, make an original plus a copy first. Serve the copy and keep the original. (NOTE: You may serve notices to tenants collectively or individually. If you serve them collectively, you won't need an extra copy for each additional defendant. If you serve them individually, you will need an extra copy for each additional defendant.) Then, if you have to pursue the eviction as an unlawful detainer later, you will be able to make more copies.

If you decide to attach a copy of the notice to the complaint as an exhibit, you will need an additional copy for each copy of the complaint you prepare. If you do not attach a copy to the complaint, you won't need to make any more copies of the notice, no matter how many co-tenants you're trying to evict.

You will need to serve separate notices to subtenants (anyone who is subletting) and to cosigners, if there are any.

When using the prejudgment claim procedure, you will need to make three copies of the Prejudgment Claim of Right to Possession form and three additional copies of the summons and complaint. Do not fill out the prejudgment form. It's for the tenant to fill out. You may not even have to supply copies of the form. Some process servers will supply them for you as a matter of course.

For each defendant who must be served by substituted service or posting, add one copy of the summons, complaint, exhibits, and attachments.

Remember, the numbers given here are minimums. Follow this rule of thumb whenever you're in doubt: *Always make enough copies of every form so that you have one for yourself, preferably the original.* Then, if need be, you can make more copies of that form instead of having to make up another "original" or pay the clerk a dollar apiece for every copy she makes on the court's copy machine. The dollar-per-copy charge is supposed to discourage you from using the court as a copy service. Take the hint!

Except for the double-sided Judicial Council forms, copy all forms on one side only. Your copies should have one blank side.

Judicial Council Forms

The forms with the capitalized names have been approved or adopted by the Judicial Council of California and are available directly from the courts. They are also available for downloading from the Judicial Council's website (courtinfo.ca.gov/).

Some Judicial Council forms are double-sided. Their front sides are printed right side up, and their back sides are printed upside down. Copy them that way if you can. If you can't, copy them on separate sheets of paper, and organize them so they are all right side up when you present them to the clerk.

Local Forms

Courts have certain forms of their own for routine tasks, such as the Application for Writ of Possession. Likewise, sheriffs' and marshals' offices have their own forms for routine tasks, such as the Instructions to Levying Officer Serving Writ form.

Sometimes you absolutely must use the forms which they provide, and sometimes you may use a similar generic form designed for the same purpose, such as those provided here.

Before you go to all the trouble of completing any form which might be available in a local version, check your court's website to see whether there is a local version, and ask the court clerk whether you must use it or whether you may use a generic form for the same purpose.

Unlawful Detainer Case Summary

Not mentioned anywhere in the text, the optional Unlawful Detainer Case Summary form shown on page 227 merely summarizes your case. It's a cover sheet of sorts to accompany your paperwork.

Clerks like the form because they prefer to see everything in one place so they don't have to waste time shuffling through a bunch of papers looking for the pertinent facts of each case. By using the form, you may actually expedite your case somewhat because the clerk knows she can process your paperwork quickly. She can look at one form and find everything she needs.

Although you may use this form at any time, the most appropriate time to use it is when you are applying for your judgment.

Latest Forms

Be aware that both Judicial Council and local forms change periodically. As a rule, the Judicial Council introduces new forms and changes to old forms twice a year, in January and July. There is no rule for the introduction of new local forms or changes to old ones. They may change at any time. As a consequence, the forms in this book may have changed since the book was published.

To check the currency of the forms you plan to use, visit the websites of the Judicial Council, the superior court, and the bankruptcy court. One or all of them may have updated forms for you to download and use.

Most courts will accept the old forms for a while, but the time will come when they no longer will. Whenever possible, use the latest forms.

PAYMENT PLEDGE

Dear Landlord/Landlady:

On or before _____, I promise to pay you
$_____ for rent and other charges now owing on the dwelling
which I rent from you located at the following address:

_____
(Street Address)

_____
(City)   (State)   (Zip)

I expect to be receiving sufficient funds to pay you from the
following sources:

Name   Address   Phone   Amount Expected

_____

_____

_____

Should you wish to, you have my authorization to verify
these sources.

If I fail to honor this pledge, I understand that I will be
evicted and that this pledge will be used against me as evidence
of my bad faith in paying what I owe.

____ I acknowledge receipt of a 3-Day Notice to Pay Rent or
Quit as required by law to begin eviction proceedings. I
understand that the 3-Day Notice may show a balance owed which is
different from that given above because a 3-Day Notice by law can
demand only delinquent rent. I also understand that the
three-day period mentioned in this Notice is being extended to
the date given above, at which time I promise to pay you what I
owe. If I fail to pay on or before that date, you have the right
to continue the legal eviction (unlawful detainer) procedure
against me without having to serve me another 3-Day Notice to Pay
Rent or Quit. I have already been served. I am being given the
extra time to pay only as a courtesy and only this once.

Signed _____

Dated _____

194

192

3-DAY NOTICE TO PAY RENT OR QUIT

TO: _____

_____

and all other occupants, tenants, and subtenants in possession of the premises described as:

_____
(Street Address)

_____
(City)   (State)   (Zip)

PLEASE TAKE NOTICE that the rent is now due and payable on the above-described premises which you currently hold and occupy.

Your rental account is delinquent in the amount itemized as follows:

Rental period _____ through _____ RENT DUE $_____

less partial payment of $_____

equals TOTAL RENT DUE of $_____

YOU ARE HEREBY REQUIRED to pay said rent in full within three (3) days or to remove from and deliver up possession of the above-described premises, or legal proceedings will be instituted against you to recover possession of said premises, to declare the forfeiture of the Lease or Rental Agreement under which you occupy said premises and to recover rents and damages, together with court costs and attorney's fees, according to the terms of your Lease or Rental Agreement.

RENT MUST BE PAID IN FULL AND IN PERSON TO THE FOLLOWING PERSON OR ENTITY:
Name _____ Phone _____
Address where rent is to be paid _____
Usual days and times for payment of rent _____
Please phone in advance to make sure that someone will be available to accept payment.

Dated: _____   _____
                              Owner/Manager

PROOF OF SERVICE (Server should complete this proof of service only AFTER serving tenants.)

I, the undersigned, being at least 18 years of age, declare under penalty of perjury that I served the above notice, of which this is a true copy, on the following tenant(s) in possession in the manner(s) indicated below: _____

☐ On _____, I handed the notice to the tenant(s) personally.

☐ On _____, after attempting personal service, I handed the notice to a person of suitable age and discretion at the residence/business of the tenant(s), AND I deposited a true copy in the U.S. Mail, in a sealed envelope with postage fully prepaid, addressed to the tenant(s) at his/her/their place of residence (date mailed, if different _____).

☐ On _____, after attempting service in both manners indicated above, I posted the notice in a conspicuous place at the residence of the tenant(s), AND I deposited a true copy in the U.S. Mail, in a sealed envelope with postage fully prepaid, addressed to the tenant(s) at his/her/their place of residence (date mailed, if different _____).

Executed on _____, at _____, California.

Served by _____

efc

3-DAY NOTICE TO PAY RENT OR QUIT

This notice supersedes any previously served 3-day notice to pay rent or quit.

TO: _____

_____
and all other occupants, tenants, and subtenants in possession of the premises described as:

_____
(Street Address)

_____
(City)   (State)   (Zip)

Penal Code Section 594 states, "Every person who maliciously injures or destroys any real or personal property not his own... is guilty of a misdemeanor."

(LANDLORD: Include the names of all known adult occupants. Include only rent which is due and delinquent. Do not include rent due and delinquent for longer than twelve months. Do not include items such as unpaid late fees, damages, utilities, deposits, etc. Put them in a separate 3-day notice to perform covenant. Serve a 30- or 60-day notice to terminate tenancy concurrently with this notice to those month-to-month tenants you wish to evict even if they comply with this notice.)

PLEASE TAKE NOTICE that the rent is now due and payable on the above-described premises which you currently hold and occupy.

Your rental account is delinquent in the amount itemized as follows:

Rental period _____ through _____ RENT DUE $_____

less partial payment of $_____

equals TOTAL RENT DUE of $_____

YOU ARE HEREBY REQUIRED to pay said rent in full within three (3) days or to remove from and deliver up possession of the above-described premises, or legal proceedings will be instituted against you to recover possession of said premises, to declare the forfeiture of the Lease or Rental Agreement under which you occupy said premises and to recover rents and damages, together with court costs and attorney's fees, according to the terms of your Lease or Rental Agreement.

RENT MUST BE PAID IN FULL AND IN PERSON TO THE FOLLOWING PERSON OR ENTITY:
Name _____ Phone _____
Address where rent is to be paid _____
Usual days and times for payment of rent _____
Please phone in advance to make sure that someone will be available to accept payment.

Dated: _____   _____
                                   Owner/Manager

(OCCUPANTS: If you receive other notices along with this notice, you must comply with all of them. Compliance with this notice alone does not entitle you to remain in possession. Be advised that your landlord has the right to make a negative credit report to a credit reporting agency if you fail to meet your payment obligations.)

PROOF OF SERVICE

(SERVER: Complete this proof of service only AFTER serving tenants. Serve every adult occupant, whether named in the rental agreement or not. Try the first method, personal delivery, first; if unsuccessful, try the second, substituted service. Only if both methods are unsuccessful should you try the third, posting and mailing.)

I, the undersigned, being at least 18 years of age, declare under penalty of perjury that I served the above notice, of which this is a true copy, on the following tenant(s) in possession in the manner(s) indicated below: _____

☐ On _____, I handed the notice to the tenant(s) personally.
☐ On _____, after attempting personal service, I handed the notice to a person of suitable age and discretion at the residence/business of the tenant(s), AND I deposited a true copy in the U.S. Mail, in a sealed envelope with postage fully prepaid, addressed to the tenant(s) at his/her/their place of residence (date mailed, if different _____).
☐ On _____, after attempting service in both manners indicated above, I posted the notice in a conspicuous place at the residence of the tenant(s), AND I deposited a true copy in the U.S. Mail, in a sealed envelope with postage fully prepaid, addressed to the tenant(s) at his/her/their place of residence (date mailed, if different _____).

Executed on _____, at _____, California.

Served by _____

efc

NOTICE TO PAY RENT OR QUIT

(Commercial Property)

TO: _____
and all other tenants in possession of the premises described as:

_____
(Street Address)

_____
(City)   (State)   (Zip)

PLEASE TAKE NOTICE that the rent is now due and payable on the above-described premises which you currently hold and occupy.

Your rental account is delinquent for the period from _____ through _____ .

Item 1) _____ Amount due $_____
Item 2) _____ Amount due $_____
Item 3) _____ Amount due $_____
[OWNER: Include common area maintenance, taxes,   TOTAL DUE $_____
insurance, and other such items above ONLY if the   less partial payment $_____
rental agreement contains an "additional rent" clause.]   equals TOTAL BALANCE DUE $_____
Total balance due is [ ] exact amount of rent owed [ ] reasonable ESTIMATE of rent owed.

You are hereby required to pay said rent in full within _____ days or to remove from and deliver up possession of the above-described premises, or legal proceedings will be instituted against you to recover possession of said premises, to declare the forfeiture of the Lease or Rental Agreement under which you occupy said premises and to recover rents and damages, together with court costs and attorney fees, according to the terms of your Lease or Rental Agreement.

Rent must be paid in full and in person to the following person or entity:
Name:_____ Phone _____
Address where rent is to be paid _____
Usual days and times for payment of rent _____
Please phone in advance to make sure that someone will be available to accept payment.

Owner's acceptance of a partial rent payment after service of this notice upon you or after commencement of an unlawful detainer based upon this notice shall not constitute a waiver of any rights, including any rights Owner may have to recover possession of the premises (CCP §1161.1).
Dated: _____

_____
Owner/Manager

PROOF OF SERVICE   (Server should complete this proof of service only AFTER serving tenants.)
I, the undersigned, being at least 18 years of age, declare under penalty of perjury that I served the above notice, of which this is a true copy, on the above-mentioned tenant(s) in possession in the manner(s) indicated below:
[ ] On _____, I handed the notice to the tenant(s) personally.
[ ] On _____, after attempting personal service, I handed the notice to a person of suitable age and discretion at the residence/business of the tenant(s).
[ ] On _____, after attempting service in both manners indicated above, I posted the notice in a conspicuous place at the residence of the tenant(s).
[ ] On _____, I sent by [cross out the one(s) not used] (first-class) (registered) (certified) mail a true copy of the notice addressed to the tenant(s) at his/her/their place of residence.
Executed on _____, at_____, California.
Served by_____

NOTICE TO PERFORM COVENANT

TO: _____
_____
_____
_____

and all other tenants in possession of the premises described as:

_____
(Street Address)

_____
(City)   (State)   (Zip)

PLEASE TAKE NOTICE that you have violated the following covenant(s) in your Lease or Rental Agreement:

You are hereby required within _____ days to perform the aforesaid covenant(s) or to deliver up possession of the above-described premises which you currently hold and occupy.

If you fail to do so, legal proceedings will be instituted against you to recover said premises and such damages as the law allows.

This notice is intended to be a _____-day notice to perform the aforesaid covenant(s). It is not intended to terminate or forfeit the Lease or Rental Agreement under which you occupy said premises. If, after legal proceedings, said premises are recovered from you, the owners will try to rent the premises for the best possible rent, giving you credit for sums received and holding you liable for any deficiencies arising during the term of your Lease or Rental Agreement.

Dated: _____   _____
                                                      Owner/Manager

PROOF OF SERVICE (Server should complete this proof of service only AFTER serving tenants.)

I, the undersigned, being at least 18 years of age, declare under penalty of perjury that I served the above notice, of which this is a true copy, on the following tenant(s) in possession in the manner(s) indicated below: _____

☐ On _____, I handed the notice to the tenant(s) personally.

☐ On _____, after attempting personal service, I handed the notice to a person of suitable age and discretion at the residence/business of the tenant(s), AND I deposited a true copy in the U.S. Mail, in a sealed envelope with postage fully prepaid, addressed to the tenant(s) at his/her/their place of residence (date mailed, if different _____).

☐ On _____, after attempting service in both manners indicated above, I posted the notice in a conspicuous place at the residence of the tenant(s), AND I deposited a true copy in the U.S. Mail, in a sealed envelope with postage fully prepaid, addressed to the tenant(s) at his/her/their place of residence (date mailed, if different _____).

Executed on _____, at _____, California.

Served by _____

efc

NOTICE TO TERMINATE TENANCY

TO: _____

_____

_____

_____

and all other tenants in possession of the premises described as:

_____
(Street Address)

_____
(City)   (State)   (Zip)

PLEASE TAKE NOTICE that you are hereby required within _____ days to remove from and deliver up possession of the above-described premises, which you currently hold and occupy.

This notice is intended for the purpose of terminating the Lease or Rental Agreement by which you now hold possession of the above-described premises, and should you fail to comply, legal proceedings will be instituted against you to recover possession, to declare said Lease or Rental Agreement forfeited, and to recover rents and damages for the period of the unlawful detention.

Dated: _____   _____
                                                    Owner/Manager

PROOF OF SERVICE (Server should complete this proof of service only AFTER serving tenants.)
   I, the undersigned, being at least 18 years of age, declare under penalty of perjury that I served the above notice, of which this is a true copy, on the following tenant(s) in possession in the manner(s) indicated below: _____

☐ On _____, I handed the notice to the tenant(s) personally.

☐ On _____, after attempting personal service, I handed the notice to a person of suitable age and discretion at the residence/business of the tenant(s), AND I deposited a true copy in the U.S. Mail, in a sealed envelope with postage fully prepaid, addressed to the tenant(s) at his/her/their place of residence (date mailed, if different _____).

☐ On _____, after attempting service in both manners indicated above, I posted the notice in a conspicuous place at the residence of the tenant(s), AND I deposited a true copy in the U.S. Mail, in a sealed envelope with postage fully prepaid, addressed to the tenant(s) at his/her/their place of residence (date mailed, if different _____).

☐ On _____, I sent by certified mail a true copy of the notice addressed to the tenant(s) at his/her/their place of residence.

Executed on _____, at _____, California.

Served by _____

efc

3-DAY NOTICE TO QUIT
FOR WASTE, NUISANCE, OR UNLAWFUL ACTS

TO: _____

_____

_____

_____

and all other tenants in possession of the premises described as:

_____
(Street Address)

_____
(City)   (State)   (Zip)

PLEASE TAKE NOTICE that you are hereby required within three (3) days to deliver up possession of the above-described premises which you currently hold and occupy because you have committed the following waste, nuisance, or unlawful act(s):

As a consequence of your having committed the foregoing acts, your Lease or Rental Agreement is hereby declared canceled under California law (CCP §1161.4).

Should you fail to comply with this notice, legal proceedings will be instituted against you to recover said premises and such damages as the law allows.

Dated: _____   _____

Owner/Manager

PROOF OF SERVICE (Server should complete this proof of service only AFTER serving tenants.)

I, the undersigned, being at least 18 years of age, declare under penalty of perjury that I served the above notice, of which this is a true copy, on the following tenant(s) in possession in the manner(s) indicated below: _____

☐ On _____, I handed the notice to the tenant(s) personally.

☐ On _____, after attempting personal service, I handed the notice to a person of suitable age and discretion at the residence/business of the tenant(s), AND I deposited a true copy in the U.S. Mail, in a sealed envelope with postage fully prepaid, addressed to the tenant(s) at his/her/their place of residence (date mailed, if different _____).

☐ On _____, after attempting service in both manners indicated above, I posted the notice in a conspicuous place at the residence of the tenant(s), AND I deposited a true copy in the U.S. Mail, in a sealed envelope with postage fully prepaid, addressed to the tenant(s) at his/her/their place of residence (date mailed, if different _____).

Executed on _____, at _____, California.

Served by _____

efc

NOTICE TO QUIT

TO: _____

_____

_____

_____

and all other persons in possession of the premises described as:

_____
(Street Address)

_____
(City)   (State)   (Zip)

PLEASE TAKE NOTICE that your possession of the above-described premises is without the consent of the owner and is in violation of California law regarding

You are hereby required to remove from and deliver up possession of said premises within _____ days, or legal proceedings will be instituted against you to recover said premises and such damages as the law allows.

Dated: _____   _____
                                                      Owner/Manager

---

PROOF OF SERVICE (Server should complete this proof of service only AFTER serving tenants.)
   I, the undersigned, being at least 18 years of age, declare under penalty of perjury that I served the above notice, of which this is a true copy, on the following person(s) in possession in the manner(s) indicated below: _____

☐ On _____, I handed the notice to the person(s) in possession personally.

☐ On _____, after attempting personal service, I handed the notice to a person of suitable age and discretion at the residence/business of the person(s) in possession, AND I deposited a true copy in the U.S. Mail, in a sealed envelope with postage fully prepaid, addressed to the person(s) in possession at his/her/their place of residence (date mailed, if different _____).

☐ On _____, after attempting service in both manners indicated above, I posted the notice in a conspicuous place at the residence of the person(s) in possession, AND I deposited a true copy in the U.S. Mail, in a sealed envelope with postage fully prepaid, addressed to him/her/them at his/her/their place of residence (date mailed, if different _____).

Executed on _____, at _____, California.

Served by _____

efc

72-HOUR NOTICE TO VACATE

(Recreational Vehicles)

TO: _____
_____
_____
_____

and all other occupants in possession of the premises described as:

_____
(Street Address)

_____
(City)   (State)   (Zip)

PLEASE TAKE NOTICE that you have failed to pay for your occupancy or failed to comply with the reasonable written rules and regulations of the park provided to you upon registration. You are hereby required within seventy-two (72) hours to remove from and deliver up possession of the above-described premises which you currently hold and occupy.

Should you fail to comply with this notice, your recreational vehicle will be removed from the park pursuant to the procedure described in that part of the California Civil Code (CCC §799.20 et seq.) commonly known as the Recreational Vehicle Park Occupancy Law.

Dated: _____   _____
                                            Owner/Manager

PROOF OF SERVICE (Server should complete this proof of service only AFTER serving tenants.)

I, the undersigned, being at least 18 years of age, declare under penalty of perjury that I served the above notice, of which this is a true copy, on the person(s) indicated below and in the manner(s) indicated below: _____

☐ On _____, I handed the notice to the occupant(s) personally.

☐ On _____, after attempting personal service, I handed the notice to a person of suitable age and discretion at the address above or at the place of business of the occupant(s), AND I posted a true copy in a conspicuous place at the address above, AND I deposited a true copy in the U.S. Mail, in a sealed envelope with postage fully prepaid, addressed to the occupant(s) at the address above. I also deposited a true copy in the U.S. Mail, in a sealed envelope with postage fully prepaid, addressed to the occupant(s) at the following address given on their registration agreement:

_____

☐ On _____, I [cross out one] (sent by certified mail) (hand-delivered) a true copy of the notice to the police or sheriff's department serving the area where the premises are located.

Executed on _____, at _____, California.
                          Served by _____

efc

200

30-DAY NOTICE TO VACATE

(Recreational Vehicles)

TO: _____
_____
_____
_____

and all other tenants in possession of the premises described as:

_____
(Street Address)

_____
(City)   (State)   (Zip)

PLEASE TAKE NOTICE that you are hereby required within thirty (30) days to remove your recreational vehicle from and deliver up possession of the above-described premises which you currently hold and occupy.

This notice is intended, pursuant to California Civil Code §799.66, for the purpose of terminating the right of occupancy by which you now hold possession of the above-described premises.

Should you fail to comply with this notice, legal proceedings will be instituted against you to remove your recreational vehicle from the above-described premises, to recover possession of the above-described premises, to declare forfeited whatever rental agreement you may have, and to recover rents and damages for the period of unlawful detention.

Dated: _____   _____
                                                    Owner/Manager

PROOF OF SERVICE (Server should complete this proof of service only AFTER serving tenants.)

I, the undersigned, being at least 18 years of age, declare under penalty of perjury that I served the above notice, of which this is a true copy, on the following tenant(s) in possession in the manner(s) indicated below: _____

☐ On _____, I handed the notice to the tenant(s) personally.

☐ On _____, after attempting personal service, I handed the notice to a person of suitable age and discretion at the address above or at the place of business of the tenant(s), AND I deposited a true copy in the U.S. Mail, in a sealed envelope with postage fully prepaid, addressed to the tenant(s) at the address above (date mailed, if different _____).

☐ On _____, after attempting service in both manners indicated above, I posted the notice in a conspicuous place at the address above, AND I deposited a true copy in the U.S. Mail, in a sealed envelope with postage fully prepaid, addressed to the tenant(s) at the address above (date mailed, if different _____).

☐ On _____, I sent by certified mail one true copy of the notice addressed to the tenant(s) at the address above and another addressed to the tenant(s) at the following address given on their registration agreement _____.

Executed on _____, at _____, California.

Served by _____

efc

WARNING: This notice is the _____ three-day notice for nonpayment of rent, utility charges, or other reasonable incidental services that has been served upon you in the last 12 months. Pursuant to Civil Code Section 798.56(e)(5), if you have been given a three-day notice to either pay rent, utility charges, or other reasonable incidental services or to vacate your tenancy on three or more occasions within a 12-month period, management is not required to give you a further three-day period to pay rent or vacate the tenancy before your tenancy can be terminated.

3-DAY NOTICE TO PAY RENT OR QUIT

TO: _____
_____ and all other residents or occupants in possession of the premises described as: _____
_____

PLEASE TAKE NOTICE that the rent is now due and payable on the above-described premises which you currently hold and occupy. Your rental account is delinquent in the amount itemized as follows:

Rental period _____ through _____   RENT DUE $_____
less partial payment of $_____
equals TOTAL RENT DUE of $_____

YOU ARE HEREBY REQUIRED to pay said rent in full within three (3) days or to deliver up possession of the above-described premises to the park manager, who is authorized to receive same, or legal proceedings will be instituted against you to recover possession of said premises, to declare the forfeiture of the Lease or Rental Agreement under which you occupy said premises and to recover rents and damages, together with court costs and attorney's fees, according to the terms of your Lease or Rental Agreement.

RENT MUST BE PAID IN FULL AND IN PERSON TO THE FOLLOWING PERSON OR ENTITY:
Name _____ Phone _____
Address where rent is to be paid _____
Usual days and times for payment of rent _____
Please phone in advance to make sure that someone will be available to accept payment.

3-DAY NOTICE TO PERFORM COVENANT OR QUIT

PLEASE TAKE NOTICE that you have also failed to perform that covenant in your Lease or Rental Agreement requiring that certain other charges be paid along with your rent. These charges are itemized as follows:
Other charges _____ TOTAL other charges due $ _____
You are hereby required to perform this covenant within three (3) days or to deliver up possession of the above-described premises to the park manager. If you fail to do so, legal proceedings will be instituted against you to recover said charges and to recover said premises and such damages as the law allows.

PLEASE NOTE: If you fail to pay the total amount of rent and other charges due and owing within three days, your tenancy is terminated. The additional time period allowed in the "60-Day Notice" which accompanies this three-day notice is strictly to give you time to locate a place to move your mobilehome or to find a qualified buyer. It does not extend the time you have to pay what you owe.

Should you sell or transfer the mobilehome, you must pay what you owe upon the sale or transfer.

Whoever resides in the mobilehome after service of this notice shall continue to be subject to the Mobilehome Residency Law and park rules and regulations, including rules regarding space maintenance.

Dated: _____   _____
Owner/Manager

PROOF OF SERVICE   (Server should complete this proof of service only AFTER serving residents.)
I, the undersigned, being at least 18 years of age, declare under penalty of perjury that I served the above notice, of which this is a true copy, on the above-mentioned resident(s) in possession in the manner(s) indicated below:

☐ On _____, I handed the notice to the resident(s) personally.
☐ On _____, after attempting personal service, I handed the notice to a person of suitable age and discretion at the residence/business of the resident(s), AND I deposited a true copy in the U.S. Mail, in a sealed envelope with postage fully prepaid, addressed to the resident(s) at his/her/their place of residence (date mailed, if different _____).
☐ On _____, after attempting service in both manners indicated above, I posted the notice in a conspicuous place at the residence of the resident(s), AND I deposited a true copy in the U.S. Mail, in a sealed envelope with postage fully prepaid, addressed to the resident(s) at his/her/their place of residence (date mailed, if different _____).
☐ On _____, in addition to service on the resident(s) as described above, I deposited a true copy of the notice in the U.S. Mail, in a sealed envelope with postage fully prepaid, addressed to the legal and registered owner(s) (if other than resident(s)) as follows: [legal owner] _____; [registered owner] _____.

Executed on _____, at _____, California.   Served by _____

60-DAY NOTICE TO TERMINATE TENANCY

(Mobilehomes)

TO: _____

_____

_____

_____

and all other residents or occupants in possession of the premises described as:

_____
(Street Address)

_____
(City)   (State)   (Zip)

PLEASE TAKE NOTICE that you are hereby required within sixty (60) days to remove from and deliver up possession of the above-described premises which you currently hold and occupy.

This notice is intended, pursuant to California Civil Code sections 798-799, commonly known as the "Mobilehome Residency Law," for the purpose of terminating the Rental Agreement by which you now hold possession of the above-described premises.

Should you fail to comply with this notice, legal proceedings will be instituted against you to recover possession, to declare said Lease or Rental Agreement forfeited, and to recover rents and damages for the period of unlawful detention.

This notice is being given for good cause as follows:

Please be advised that your rent, utility bills, and other charges on said premises are due and payable up to and including the date of termination of your tenancy under this notice.

Dated: _____   _____
                                                        Owner/Manager

---

PROOF OF SERVICE (Server should complete this proof of service only AFTER serving tenants.)

I, the undersigned, being at least 18 years of age, declare under penalty of perjury that I served the above notice, of which this is a true copy, on the following resident(s) in possession in the manner(s) indicated below: _____

☐ On _____, I handed the notice to the resident(s) personally.

☐ On _____, after attempting personal service, I handed the notice to a person of suitable age and discretion at the residence/business of the resident(s), AND I deposited a true copy in the U.S. Mail, in a sealed envelope with postage fully prepaid, addressed to the resident(s) at his/her/their place of residence (date mailed, if different _____).

☐ On _____, after attempting service in both manners indicated above, I posted the notice in a conspicuous place at the residence of the resident(s), AND I deposited a true copy in the U.S. Mail, in a sealed envelope with postage fully prepaid, addressed to the resident(s) at his/her/their place of residence (date mailed, if different _____).

☐ On _____, in addition to service on the resident(s) as described above, I deposited a true copy of the notice in the U.S. Mail, in a sealed envelope with postage fully prepaid, addressed to the legal and registered owner(s) (if other than resident(s)) as follows:

LEGAL OWNER _____

REGISTERED OWNER _____

Executed on _____, at _____.

Served by _____

efc

NOTICE OF BELIEF OF ABANDONMENT

(Real Property)

TO: _____

_____

_____

_____

Address:

_____
(Street Address)

_____
(City)   (State)   (Zip)

This notice is given pursuant to Section 1951.3 of the California Civil Code concerning the above-described real property rented by you. The rent on this property has been due and unpaid for fourteen (14) or more consecutive days, and the owner/manager believes that you have abandoned the property.

This real property will be deemed abandoned within the meaning of Section 1951.2 of the Civil Code, and your tenancy shall terminate on _____, which is not less than eighteen (18) days after this notice is deposited in the United States Mail unless before such date the undersigned receives at the address indicated below a written notice from you stating BOTH of the following: (1) Your intent not to abandon the real property, and (2) An address at which you may be served by certified mail in any action for unlawful detainer of the real property.

You are required to pay the rent due and unpaid on this real property as required by your rental agreement. Failure to do so can lead to a court proceeding against you.

Date of mailing this notice: _____

_____
Owner/Manager
(signature)

_____
_____
Name & Address of Owner/Manager
(typed or printed)

204

NOTICE OF RIGHT TO RECLAIM
ABANDONED PERSONAL PROPERTY

TO: _____
_____
_____
_____

Address:
_____
(Street Address)

_____
(City)   (State)   (Zip)

When vacated, the premises described above contained the following personal property:

Unless you pay the reasonable cost of storage for all the above-described personal property and take possession of the property which you claim not later than eighteen (18) days after this notice is deposited in the United States Mail, this personal property may be disposed of pursuant to Civil Code Section 1988.

Check the ONE box below which applies:

☐ Because this property is believed to be worth less than $300, it may be kept, sold, or destroyed without further notice if you fail to reclaim it within the time limit indicated below.

☐ Because this property is believed to be worth more than $300, it will be sold if you fail to reclaim it. It will be sold at a public sale after notice has been given by publication. You have the right to bid on the property at this sale. After the property is sold and the costs of storage, advertising, and sale are deducted, the remaining money will be turned over to the county. You may claim the remaining money at any time within one year after the county receives the money.

Date of mailing this notice: _____

Date of expiration of this notice: _____

You may claim this property at:

_____
Owner/Manager
(signature)

_____
_____
Name & Address of Owner/Manager
(typed or printed)

efc

CM-010

ATTORNEY OR PARTY WITHOUT ATTORNEY (Name, State Bar number, and address):	FOR COURT USE ONLY
TELEPHONE NO.: FAX NO.:	
ATTORNEY FOR (Name):	

SUPERIOR COURT OF CALIFORNIA, COUNTY OF
STREET ADDRESS:
MAILING ADDRESS:
CITY AND ZIP CODE:
BRANCH NAME:

CASE NAME:

CIVIL CASE COVER SHEET	**Complex Case Designation**	CASE NUMBER:
☐ **Unlimited** (Amount demanded exceeds $25,000) ☐ **Limited** (Amount demanded is $25,000 or less)	☐ **Counter** ☐ **Joinder** Filed with first appearance by defendant (Cal. Rules of Court, rule 1811)	JUDGE: DEPT:

Items 1–5 below must be completed (see instructions on page 2).

1. Check **one** box below for the case type that best describes this case:

Auto Tort
☐ Auto (22)
☐ Uninsured motorist (46)

Other PI/PD/WD (Personal Injury/Property Damage/Wrongful Death) Tort
☐ Asbestos (04)
☐ Product liability (24)
☐ Medical malpractice (45)
☐ Other PI/PD/WD (23)

Non-PI/PD/WD (Other) Tort
☐ Business tort/unfair business practice (07)
☐ Civil rights (08)
☐ Defamation (13)
☐ Fraud (16)
☐ Intellectual property (19)
☐ Professional negligence (25)
☐ Other non-PI/PD/WD tort (35)

Employment
☐ Wrongful termination (36)
☐ Other employment (15)

Contract
☐ Breach of contract/warranty (06)
☐ Collections (09)
☐ Insurance coverage (18)
☐ Other contract (37)

Real Property
☐ Eminent domain/Inverse condemnation (14)
☐ Wrongful eviction (33)
☐ Other real property (26)

Unlawful Detainer
☐ Commercial (31)
☐ Residential (32)
☐ Drugs (38)

Judicial Review
☐ Asset forfeiture (05)
☐ Petition re: arbitration award (11)
☐ Writ of mandate (02)
☐ Other judicial review (39)

Provisionally Complex Civil Litigation (Cal. Rules of Court, rules 1800–1812)
☐ Antitrust/Trade regulation (03)
☐ Construction defect (10)
☐ Mass tort (40)
☐ Securities litigation (28)
☐ Environmental/Toxic tort (30)
☐ Insurance coverage claims arising from the above listed provisionally complex case types (41)

Enforcement of Judgment
☐ Enforcement of judgment (20)

Miscellaneous Civil Complaint
☐ RICO (27)
☐ Other complaint (not specified above) (42)

Miscellaneous Civil Petition
☐ Partnership and corporate governance (21)
☐ Other petition (not specified above) (43)

2. This case ☐ is ☐ is not complex under rule 1800 of the California Rules of Court. If the case is complex, mark the factors requiring exceptional judicial management:
   a. ☐ Large number of separately represented parties
   b. ☐ Extensive motion practice raising difficult or novel issues that will be time-consuming to resolve
   c. ☐ Substantial amount of documentary evidence
   d. ☐ Large number of witnesses
   e. ☐ Coordination with related actions pending in one or more courts in other counties, states, or countries, or in a federal court
   f. ☐ Substantial postjudgment judicial supervision

3. Type of remedies sought (check all that apply):
   a. ☐ monetary   b. ☐ nonmonetary; declaratory or injunctive relief   c. ☐ punitive

4. Number of causes of action (specify):

5. This case ☐ is ☐ is not a class action suit.

6. If there are any known related cases, file and serve a notice of related case. (You may use form CM-015.)

Date:

▶

_____   _____
(TYPE OR PRINT NAME)   (SIGNATURE OF PARTY OR ATTORNEY FOR PARTY)

NOTICE
- Plaintiff must file this cover sheet with the first paper filed in the action or proceeding (except small claims cases or cases filed under the Probate Code, Family Code, or Welfare and Institutions Code). (Cal. Rules of Court, rule 201.8.) Failure to file may result in sanctions.
- File this cover sheet in addition to any cover sheet required by local court rule.
- If this case is complex under rule 1800 et seq. of the California Rules of Court, you must serve a copy of this cover sheet on **all** other parties to the action or proceeding.
- Unless this is a complex case, this cover sheet will be used for statistical purposes only.

Page 1 of 2

Form Adopted for Mandatory Use
Judicial Council of California
CM-010 [Rev. January 1, 2006]

CIVIL CASE COVER SHEET

Cal. Rules of Court, rules 201.8, 1800–1812;
Standards of Judicial Administration, § 19
www.courtinfo.ca.gov

American LegalNet, Inc.
www.USCourtForms.com

INSTRUCTIONS ON HOW TO COMPLETE THE COVER SHEET

To Plaintiffs and Others Filing First Papers

If you are filing a first paper (for example, a complaint) in a civil case, you **must** complete and file, along with your first paper, the *Civil Case Cover Sheet* contained on page 1. This information will be used to compile statistics about the types and numbers of cases filed. You must complete items 1 through 5 on the sheet. In item 1, you must check **one** box for the case type that best describes the case. If the case fits both a general and a more specific type of case listed in item 1, check the more specific one. If the case has multiple causes of action, check the box that best indicates the **primary** cause of action. To assist you in completing the sheet, examples of the cases that belong under each case type in item 1 are provided below. A cover sheet must be filed only with your initial paper. You do not need to submit a cover sheet with amended papers. Failure to file a cover sheet with the first paper filed in a civil case may subject a party, its counsel, or both to sanctions under rules 201.8(c) and 227 of the California Rules of Court.

To Parties in Complex Cases

In complex cases only, parties must also use the *Civil Case Cover Sheet* to designate whether the case is complex. If a plaintiff believes the case is complex under rule 1800 of the California Rules of Court, this must be indicated by completing the appropriate boxes in items 1 and 2. If a plaintiff designates a case as complex, the cover sheet must be served with the complaint on all parties to the action. A defendant may file and serve no later than the time of its first appearance a joinder in the plaintiff's designation, a counter-designation that the case is not complex, or, if the plaintiff has made no designation, a designation that the case is complex.

CASE TYPES AND EXAMPLES

Auto Tort
Auto (22)–Personal Injury/Property
Damage/Wrongful Death
Uninsured Motorist (46) *(if the
case involves an uninsured
motorist claim subject to
arbitration, check this item
instead of Auto)*

**Other PI/PD/WD (Personal Injury/
Property Damage/Wrongful Death)
Tort**
Asbestos (04)
Asbestos Property Damage
Asbestos Personal Injury/
Wrongful Death
Product Liability *(not asbestos or
toxic/environmental)* (24)
Medical Malpractice (45)
Medical Malpractice–
Physicians & Surgeons
Other Professional Health Care
Malpractice
Other PI/PD/WD (23)
Premises Liability (e.g., slip
and fall)
Intentional Bodily Injury/PD/WD
(e.g., assault, vandalism)
Intentional Infliction of
Emotional Distress
Negligent Infliction of
Emotional Distress
Other PI/PD/WD

Non-PI/PD/WD (Other) Tort
Business Tort/Unfair Business
Practice (07)
Civil Rights (e.g., discrimination,
false arrest) *(not civil
harassment)* (08)
Defamation (e.g., slander, libel)
(13)
Fraud (16)
Intellectual Property (19)
Professional Negligence (25)
Legal Malpractice
Other Professional Malpractice
(not medical or legal)
Other Non-PI/PD/WD Tort (35)

Employment
Wrongful Termination (36)
Other Employment (15)

Contract
Breach of Contract/Warranty (06)
Breach of Rental/Lease
Contract *(not unlawful detainer
or wrongful eviction)*
Contract/Warranty Breach–Seller
Plaintiff *(not fraud or negligence)*
Negligent Breach of Contract/
Warranty
Other Breach of Contract/Warranty
Collections (e.g., money owed, open
book accounts) (09)
Collection Case–Seller Plaintiff
Other Promissory Note/Collections
Case
Insurance Coverage *(not provisionally
complex)* (18)
Auto Subrogation
Other Coverage
Other Contract (37)
Contractual Fraud
Other Contract Dispute

Real Property
Eminent Domain/Inverse
Condemnation (14)
Wrongful Eviction (33)
Other Real Property (e.g., quiet title) (26)
Writ of Possession of Real Property
Mortgage Foreclosure
Quiet Title
Other Real Property *(not eminent
domain, landlord/tenant, or
foreclosure)*

Unlawful Detainer
Commercial (31)
Residential (32)
Drugs (38) *(if the case involves illegal
drugs, check this item; otherwise,
report as Commercial or
Residential)*

Judicial Review
Asset Forfeiture (05)
Petition Re: Arbitration Award (11)
Writ of Mandate (02)
Writ–Administrative Mandamus
Writ–Mandamus on Limited Court
Case Matter
Writ–Other Limited Court Case
Review
Other Judicial Review (39)
Review of Health Officer Order
Notice of Appeal–Labor
Commissioner Appeals

**Provisionally Complex Civil Litigation
(Cal. Rules of Court Rules 1800–1812)**
Antitrust/Trade Regulation (03)
Construction Defect (10)
Claims Involving Mass Tort (40)
Securities Litigation (28)
Environmental/Toxic Tort (30)
Insurance Coverage Claims
*(arising from provisionally
complex case type listed above)*
(41)

Enforcement of Judgment
Enforcement of Judgment (20)
Abstract of Judgment (Out of
County)
Confession of Judgment *(non-
domestic relations)*
Sister State Judgment
Administrative Agency Award
(not unpaid taxes)
Petition/Certification of Entry of
Judgment on Unpaid Taxes
Other Enforcement of Judgment
Case

Miscellaneous Civil Complaint
RICO (27)
Other Complaint *(not specified
above)* (42)
Declaratory Relief Only
Injunctive Relief Only *(non-
harassment)*
Mechanics Lien
Other Commercial Complaint
Case *(non-tort/non-complex)*
Other Civil Complaint
(non-tort/non-complex)

Miscellaneous Civil Petition
Partnership and Corporate
Governance (21)
Other Petition *(not specified above)*
(43)
Civil Harassment
Workplace Violence
Elder/Dependent Adult
Abuse
Election Contest
Petition for Name Change
Petition for Relief from Late
Claim
Other Civil Petition

SUM-130

SUMMONS
(CITACION JUDICIAL)
UNLAWFUL DETAINER—EVICTION
(RETENCIÓN ILÍCITA DE UN INMUEBLE—DESALOJO)

NOTICE TO DEFENDANT:
(AVISO AL DEMANDADO):

YOU ARE BEING SUED BY PLAINTIFF:
(LO ESTÁ DEMANDANDO EL DEMANDANTE):

FOR COURT USE ONLY
(SOLO PARA USO DE LA CORTE)

You have **5 CALENDAR DAYS** after this summons and legal papers are served on you to file a written response at this court and have a copy served on the plaintiff. (To calculate the five days, count Saturday and Sunday, but do not count other court holidays. If the last day falls on a Saturday, Sunday, or a court holiday then you have the next court day to file a written response.) A letter or phone call will not protect you. Your written response must be in proper legal form if you want the court to hear your case. There may be a court form that you can use for your response. You can find these court forms and more information at the California Courts Online Self-Help Center (www.courtinfo.ca.gov/selfhelp), your county law library, or the courthouse nearest you. If you cannot pay the filing fee, ask the court clerk for a fee waiver form. If you do not file your response on time, you may lose the case by default, and your wages, money, and property may be taken without further warning from the court.

There are other legal requirements. You may want to call an attorney right away. If you do not know an attorney, you may want to call an attorney referral service. If you cannot afford an attorney, you may be eligible for free legal services from a nonprofit legal services program. You can locate these nonprofit groups at the California Legal Services Web site (www.lawhelpcalifornia.org), the California Courts Online Self-Help Center (www.courtinfo.ca.gov/selfhelp), or by contacting your local court or county bar association.

Tiene 5 DÍAS DE CALENDARIO después de que le entreguen esta citación y papeles legales para presentar una respuesta por escrito en esta corte y hacer que se entregue una copia al demandante. (Para calcular los cinco días, cuente los sábados y los domingos pero no los otros días feriados de la corte. Si el último día cae en sábado o domingo, o en un día en que la corte esté cerrada, tiene hasta el próximo día de corte para presentar una respuesta por escrito). Una carta o una llamada telefónica no lo protegen. Su respuesta por escrito tiene que estar en formato legal correcto si desea que procesen su caso en la corte. Es posible que haya un formulario que usted pueda usar para su respuesta. Puede encontrar estos formularios de la corte y más información en el Centro de Ayuda de las Cortes de California (www.courtinfo.ca.gov/selfhelp/espanol/), en la biblioteca de leyes de su condado o en la corte que le quede más cerca. Si no puede pagar la cuota de presentación, pida al secretario de la corte que le dé un formulario de exención de pago de cuotas. Si no presenta su respuesta a tiempo, puede perder el caso por incumplimiento y la corte le podrá quitar su sueldo, dinero y bienes sin más advertencia.

Hay otros requisitos legales. Es recomendable que llame a un abogado inmediatamente. Si no conoce a un abogado, puede llamar a un servicio de remisión a abogados. Si no puede pagar a un abogado, es posible que cumpla con los requisitos para obtener servicios legales gratuitos de un programa de servicios legales sin fines de lucro. Puede encontrar estos grupos sin fines de lucro en el sitio web de California Legal Services, (www.lawhelpcalifornia.org), en el Centro de Ayuda de las Cortes de California, (www.courtinfo.ca.gov/selfhelp/espanol/) o poniéndose en contacto con la corte o el colegio de abogados locales.

---

1. The name and address of the court is:
   (El nombre y dirección de la corte es):

CASE NUMBER:
(Número del caso):

2. The name, address, and telephone number of plaintiff's attorney, or plaintiff without an attorney, is:
   (El nombre, la dirección y el número de teléfono del abogado del demandante, o del demandante que no tiene abogado, es):

3. *(Must be answered in all cases)* An **unlawful detainer assistant (Bus. & Prof. Code, §§ 6400–6415)** ☐ did **not** ☐ did for compensation give advice or assistance with this form. *(If plaintiff has received any help or advice for pay from an unlawful detainer assistant, complete item 6 on the next page.)*

Date: Clerk, by _____ , Deputy
(Fecha)   *(Secretario)*   *(Adjunto)*

(For proof of service of this summons, use Proof of Service of Summons (form POS-010).)
(Para prueba de entrega de esta citación use el formulario Proof of Service of Summons, (POS-010)).

[SEAL]

4. **NOTICE TO THE PERSON SERVED:** You are served
   a. ☐ as an individual defendant.
   b. ☐ as the person sued under the fictitious name of *(specify):*
   c. ☐ as an occupant
   d. ☐ on behalf of *(specify):*
      under: ☐ CCP 416.10 (corporation)   ☐ CCP 416.60 (minor)
             ☐ CCP 416.20 (defunct corporation) ☐ CCP 416.70 (conservatee)
             ☐ CCP 416.40 (association or partnership) ☐ CCP 416.90 (authorized person)
             ☐ CCP 415.46 (occupant)   ☐ other *(specify):*
5. ☐ by personal delivery on *(date):*

Page 1 of 2

PLAINTIFF *(Name):*	CASE NUMBER:
DEFENDANT *(Name):*	

6. **Unlawful detainer assistant** *(complete if plaintiff has received any help or advice for pay from an unlawful detainer assistant):*

   a. Assistant's name:

   b. Telephone no.:

   c. Street address, city, and ZIP:

   d. County of registration:

   e. Registration no.:

   f. Registration expires on *(date):*

POS-010

ATTORNEY OR PARTY WITHOUT ATTORNEY *(Name, State Bar number, and address):*	FOR COURT USE ONLY
TELEPHONE NO.: FAX NO. *(Optional):* E–MAIL ADDRESS *(Optional):* ATTORNEY FOR *(Name):*	

| SUPERIOR COURT OF CALIFORNIA, COUNTY OF
    STREET ADDRESS:
    MAILING ADDRESS:
    CITY AND ZIP CODE:
    BRANCH NAME: | |

PLAINTIFF/PETITIONER: DEFENDANT/RESPONDENT:	CASE NUMBER:
PROOF OF SERVICE OF SUMMONS	Ref. No. or File No.:

(Separate proof of service is required for each party served.)

1. At the time of service I was at least 18 years of age and not a party to this action.

2. I served copies of:

   a. ☐   summons

   b. ☐   complaint

   c. ☐   Alternative Dispute Resolution (ADR) package

   d. ☐   Civil Case Cover Sheet *(served in complex cases only)*

   e. ☐   cross-complaint

   f. ☐   other *(specify documents):*

3. a. Party served *(specify name of party as shown on documents served):*

   b. Person served: ☐ party in item 3a   ☐ other *(specify name and relationship to the party named in item 3a):*

4. Address where the party was served:

5. I served the party *(check proper box)*

   a. ☐   **by personal service.** I personally delivered the documents listed in item 2 to the party or person authorized to receive service of process for the party   (1) on *(date):*   (2) at *(time):*

   b. ☐   **by substituted service.** On *(date):*   at *(time):*   I left the documents listed in item 2 with or in the presence of *(name and title or relationship to person indicated in item 3b):*

        (1) ☐   **(business)** a person at least 18 years of age apparently in charge at the office or usual place of business of the person to be served. I informed him or her of the general nature of the papers.

        (2) ☐   **(home)** a competent member of the household (at least 18 years of age) at the dwelling house or usual place of abode of the party. I informed him or her of the general nature of the papers.

        (3) ☐   **(physical address unknown)** a person at least 18 years of age apparently in charge at the usual mailing address of the person to be served, other than a United States Postal Service post office box. I informed him or her of the general nature of the papers.

        (4) ☐   I thereafter mailed (by first-class, postage prepaid) copies of the documents to the person to be served at the place where the copies were left (Code Civ. Proc., § 415.20). I mailed the documents on *(date):*   from *(city):*   **or** ☐ a declaration of mailing is attached.

        (5) ☐   I attach a **declaration of diligence** stating actions taken first to attempt personal service.

Page 1 of 2

c. ☐ **by mail and acknowledgment of receipt of service.** I mailed the documents listed in item 2 to the party, to the address shown in item 4, by first-class mail, postage prepaid,

    (1) on *(date):*   (2) from *(city):*

    (3) ☐ with two copies of the *Notice and Acknowledgment of Receipt* and a postage-paid return envelope addressed to me. *(Attach completed* Notice and Acknowledgement of Receipt.*)* (Code Civ. Proc., § 415.30.)

    (4) ☐ to an address outside California with return receipt requested. (Code Civ. Proc., § 415.40.)

d. ☐ **by other means** *(specify means of service and authorizing code section):*

    ☐ Additional page describing service is attached.

6. The "Notice to the Person Served" (on the summons) was completed as follows:
   a. ☐ as an individual defendant.
   b. ☐ as the person sued under the fictitious name of *(specify):*
   c. ☐ as occupant.
   d. ☐ On behalf of *(specify):*
     under the following Code of Civil Procedure section:

        ☐ 416.10 (corporation)   ☐ 415.95 (business organization, form unknown)
        ☐ 416.20 (defunct corporation)   ☐ 416.60 (minor)
        ☐ 416.30 (joint stock company/association) ☐ 416.70 (ward or conservatee)
        ☐ 416.40 (association or partnership)   ☐ 416.90 (authorized person)
        ☐ 416.50 (public entity)   ☐ 415.46 (occupant)
                                ☐ other:

7. **Person who served papers**
   a. Name:
   b. Address:
   c. Telephone number:
   d. **The fee** for service was: $
   e. I am:

     (1) ☐ not a registered California process server.
     (2) ☐ exempt from registration under Business and Professions Code section 22350(b).
     (3) ☐ registered California process server:
       (i) ☐ owner ☐ employee ☐ independent contractor.
       (ii) Registration No.:
       (iii) County:

8. ☐ **I declare** under penalty of perjury under the laws of the State of California that the foregoing is true and correct.

   or

9. ☐ **I am a California sheriff or marshal and** I certify that the foregoing is true and correct.

Date:

_____   ▶   _____
(NAME OF PERSON WHO SERVED PAPERS/SHERIFF OR MARSHAL)   (SIGNATURE)

UD-100

ATTORNEY OR PARTY WITHOUT ATTORNEY *(Name, State Bar number, and address)*:	*FOR COURT USE ONLY*
TELEPHONE NO.: FAX NO. *(Optional)*:	
E-MAIL ADDRESS *(Optional)*:	
ATTORNEY FOR *(Name)*:	

SUPERIOR COURT OF CALIFORNIA, COUNTY OF
STREET ADDRESS:
MAILING ADDRESS:
CITY AND ZIP CODE:
BRANCH NAME:

PLAINTIFF:

DEFENDANT:

☐ DOES 1 TO _____

COMPLAINT — UNLAWFUL DETAINER* ☐ **COMPLAINT** ☐ **AMENDED COMPLAINT** *(Amendment Number)*: _____	CASE NUMBER:

Jurisdiction *(check all that apply)*:
☐ **ACTION IS A LIMITED CIVIL CASE**
    Amount demanded ☐ **does not exceed $10,000**
                             ☐ **exceeds $10,000 but does not exceed $25,000**
☐ **ACTION IS AN UNLIMITED CIVIL CASE** (amount demanded exceeds $25,000)
☐ **ACTION IS RECLASSIFIED** by this amended complaint or cross-complaint *(check all that apply)*:
    ☐ from unlawful detainer to general unlimited civil (possession not in issue)   ☐ from limited to unlimited
    ☐ from unlawful detainer to general limited civil (possession not in issue)   ☐ from unlimited to limited

1. PLAINTIFF *(name each)*:

   alleges causes of action against DEFENDANT *(name each)*:

2. a. Plaintiff is   (1) ☐ an individual over the age of 18 years.   (4) ☐ a partnership.
                (2) ☐ a public agency.   (5) ☐ a corporation.
                (3) ☐ other *(specify)*:

    b. ☐ Plaintiff has complied with the fictitious business name laws and is doing business under the fictitious name of *(specify)*:

3. Defendant named above is in possession of the premises located at *(street address, apt. no., city, zip code, and county)*:

4. Plaintiff's interest in the premises is ☐ as owner ☐ other *(specify)*:

5. The true names and capacities of defendants sued as Does are unknown to plaintiff.

6. a. On or about *(date)*:   defendant *(name each)*:

     (1) agreed to rent the premises as a ☐ month-to-month tenancy ☐ other tenancy *(specify)*:
     (2) agreed to pay rent of $ payable ☐ monthly ☐ other *(specify frequency)*:
     (3) agreed to pay rent on the ☐ first of the month ☐ other day *(specify)*:
   b. This ☐ written ☐ oral agreement was made with
     (1) ☐ plaintiff.   (3) ☐ plaintiff's predecessor in interest.
     (2) ☐ plaintiff's agent.   (4) ☐ other *(specify)*:

* NOTE: Do not use this form for evictions after sale (Code Civ. Proc., § 1161a).

                                              Page 1 of 3

Form Approved for Optional Use   **COMPLAINT—UNLAWFUL DETAINER**   Civil Code, § 1940 et seq.
Judicial Council of California   Code of Civil Procedure §§ 425.12, 1166
UD-100 [Rev. July 1, 2005]   www.courtinfo.ca.gov

American LegalNet, Inc.
www.USCourtForms.com

6. c. ☐ The defendants not named in item 6a are

    (1) ☐ subtenants.

    (2) ☐ assignees.

    (3) ☐ other (specify):

  d. ☐ The agreement was later changed as follows (specify):

  e. ☐ A copy of the written agreement, including any addenda or attachments that form the basis of this complaint, is attached and labeled Exhibit 1. (Required for residential property, unless item 6f is checked. See Code Civ. Proc., § 1166.)

  f. ☐ (For residential property) A copy of the written agreement is **not** attached because (specify reason):

    (1) ☐ the written agreement is not in the possession of the landlord or the landlord's employees or agents.

    (2) ☐ this action is solely for nonpayment of rent (Code Civ. Proc., § 1161(2)).

7. ☐ a. Defendant (name each):

    was served the following notice on the same date and in the same manner:

    (1) ☐ 3-day notice to pay rent or quit   (4) ☐ 3-day notice to perform covenants or quit

    (2) ☐ 30-day notice to quit   (5) ☐ 3-day notice to quit

    (3) ☐ 60-day notice to quit   (6) ☐ Other (specify):

  b. (1) On (date):   the period stated in the notice expired at the end of the day.

    (2) Defendants failed to comply with the requirements of the notice by that date.

  c. All facts stated in the notice are true.

  d. ☐ The notice included an election of forfeiture.

  e. ☐ A copy of the notice is attached and labeled Exhibit 2. (Required for residential property. See Code Civ. Proc., § 1166.)

  f. ☐ One or more defendants were served (1) with a different notice, (2) on a different date, or (3) in a different manner, as stated in Attachment 8c. (Check item 8c and attach a statement providing the information required by items 7a–e and 8 for each defendant.)

8. a. ☐ The notice in item 7a was served on the defendant named in item 7a as follows:

    (1) ☐ by personally handing a copy to defendant on (date):

    (2) ☐ by leaving a copy with (name or description):

    a person of suitable age and discretion, on (date):   at defendant's

    ☐ residence ☐ business AND mailing a copy to defendant at defendant's place of residence on (date):   because defendant cannot be found at defendant's residence or usual place of business.

    (3) ☐ by posting a copy on the premises on (date): ☐ AND giving a copy to a person found residing at the premises AND mailing a copy to defendant at the premises on (date):

      (a) ☐ because defendant's residence and usual place of business cannot be ascertained OR

      (b) ☐ because no person of suitable age or discretion can be found there.

    (4) ☐ (Not for 3-day notice; see Civil Code, § 1946 before using) by sending a copy by certified or registered mail addressed to defendant on (date):

    (5) ☐ (Not for residential tenancies; see Civil Code, § 1953 before using) in the manner specified in a written commercial lease between the parties.

  b. ☐ (Name):

    was served on behalf of all defendants who signed a joint written rental agreement.

  c. ☐ Information about service of notice on the defendants alleged in item 7f is stated in Attachment 8c.

  d. ☐ Proof of service of the notice in item 7a is attached and labeled Exhibit 3.

PLAINTIFF (Name):	CASE NUMBER:
DEFENDANT (Name):	

9. ☐ Plaintiff demands possession from each defendant because of expiration of a fixed-term lease.

10. ☐ At the time the 3-day notice to pay rent or quit was served, the amount of **rent due** was $

11. ☐ The fair rental value of the premises is $ per day.

12. ☐ Defendant's continued possession is malicious, and plaintiff is entitled to statutory damages under Code of Civil Procedure section 1174(b). *(State specific facts supporting a claim up to $600 in Attachment 12.)*

13. ☐ A written agreement between the parties provides for attorney fees.

14. ☐ Defendant's tenancy is subject to the local rent control or eviction control ordinance of *(city or county, title of ordinance, and date of passage):*

Plaintiff has met all applicable requirements of the ordinances.

15. ☐ Other allegations are stated in Attachment 15.

16. Plaintiff accepts the jurisdictional limit, if any, of the court.

17. **PLAINTIFF REQUESTS**
    a. possession of the premises.
    b. costs incurred in this proceeding:
    c. ☐ past-due rent of $
    d. ☐ reasonable attorney fees.
    e. ☐ forfeiture of the agreement.
    f. ☐ damages at the rate stated in item 11 from *(date):*   for each day that defendants remain in possession through entry of judgment.
    g. ☐ statutory damages up to $600 for the conduct alleged in item 12.
    h. ☐ other *(specify):*

18. ☐ Number of pages attached *(specify):* _____

UNLAWFUL DETAINER ASSISTANT (Bus. & Prof. Code, §§ 6400–6415)

19. *(Complete in all cases.)* An unlawful detainer assistant ☐ did **not** ☐ did for compensation give advice or assistance with this form. *(If plaintiff has received **any** help or advice for pay from an unlawful detainer assistant, state:)*

    a. Assistant's name:
    b. Street address, city, and zip code:

    c. Telephone No.:
    d. County of registration:
    e. Registration No.:
    f. Expires on *(date):*

Date:

▶

_____
(TYPE OR PRINT NAME)

_____
(SIGNATURE OF PLAINTIFF OR ATTORNEY)

VERIFICATION

(Use a different verification form if the verification is by an attorney or for a corporation or partnership.)

I am the plaintiff in this proceeding and have read this complaint. I declare under penalty of perjury under the laws of the State of California that the foregoing is true and correct.

Date:

▶

_____
(TYPE OR PRINT NAME)

_____
(SIGNATURE OF PLAINTIFF)

214

Name, Address, and Telephone No. of Attorney(s)

Space Below for Use of Court Clerk Only

Attorney(s) for

| AMENDMENT TO COMPLAINT | SUPERIOR COURT OF CALIFORNIA
COUNTY OF _____
_____ JUDICIAL DISTRICT | CASE NUMBER: |

vs.

Plaintiff(s)   Defendant(s)

FICTITIOUS NAME (NO ORDER REQUIRED)

Upon filing the complaint herein, plaintiff(s) being ignorant of the true name of a defendant, and having designated said defendant in the complaint by the fictitious name of

and having discovered the true name of said defendant to be

hereby amends the complaint by inserting such true name in place and stead of such fictitious name wherever it appears in said complaint.

Plaintiff(s)/Attorney(s) for Plaintiff(s)

INCORRECT NAME/ADDRESS (ORDER REQUIRED)

Plaintiff(s) having designated a defendant in the complaint by the incorrect name/address of

and having discovered the true name/address of said defendant to be

hereby amends the complaint by inserting such true name/address in place and stead of such incorrect name/address wherever it appears in said complaint.

Plaintiff(s)/Attorney(s) for Plaintiff(s)

ORDER

Proper cause appearing, the above amendment to the complaint is allowed.

Dated: _____   _____
                                                        Presiding Judge

AMENDMENT TO COMPLAINT
CCP §§473-474

efc

NOTICE: EVERYONE WHO LIVES IN THIS RENTAL UNIT MAY BE EVICTED BY COURT ORDER. READ THIS FORM IF YOU LIVE HERE AND IF YOUR NAME IS NOT ON THE ATTACHED SUMMONS AND COMPLAINT.

1. If you live here and you do not complete and submit this form within 10 days of the date of service shown on this form, you will be evicted without further hearing by the court along with the persons named in the Summons and Complaint.
2. If you file this form, your claim will be determined in the eviction action against the persons named in the Complaint.
3. If you do not file this form, you will be evicted without further hearing.

CLAIMANT OR CLAIMANT'S ATTORNEY *(Name and Address)*	TELEPHONE NO.:	FOR COURT USE ONLY

NAME OF COURT:
STREET ADDRESS:
MAILING ADDRESS:
CITY AND ZIP CODE:
BRANCH NAME:

PLAINTIFF:

DEFENDANT:

PREJUDGMENT CLAIM OF RIGHT TO POSSESSION

CASE NUMBER:

Complete this form only if ALL of these statements are true:
1. **You are NOT named in the accompanying Summons and Complaint.**
2. **You occupied the premises on or before the date the unlawful detainer (eviction) Complaint was filed.**
3. **You still occupy the premises.**

(To be completed by the process server)
DATE OF SERVICE:

(Date that this form is served or delivered, and posted, and mailed by the officer or process server)

I DECLARE THE FOLLOWING UNDER PENALTY OF PERJURY:

1. My name is *(specify)*:

2. I reside at *(street address, unit No., city and ZIP code)*:

3. The address of "the premises" subject to this claim is *(address)*:

4. On *(insert date)* : _____, the landlord or the landlord's authorized agent filed a complaint to recover possession of the premises. *(This date is the court filing date on the accompanying Summons and Complaint.)*

5. I occupied the premises on the date the complaint was filed *(the date in item 4)*. I have continued to occupy the premises ever since.

6. I was at least 18 years of age on the date the complaint was filed *(the date in item 4)*.

7. I claim a right to possession of the premises because I occupied the premises on the date the complaint was filed *(the date in item 4)*.

8. I was not named in the Summons and Complaint.

9. I understand that if I make this claim of right to possession, I will be added as a defendant to the unlawful detainer (eviction) action.

10. *(Filing fee)* I understand that I must go to the court and pay a filing fee of $ _____ or file with the court the form "Application for Waiver of Court Fees and Costs." I understand that if I don't pay the filing fee or file with the court the form for waiver of court fees within 10 days from the date of service on this form (excluding court holidays), I will not be entitled to make a claim of right to possession.

(Continued on reverse)

CP10.5 (New January 1, 1991)   **PREJUDGMENT CLAIM OF RIGHT TO POSSESSION**   Code of Civil Procedure, §§ 415.46, 715.010, 715.020, 1174.25

PLAINTIFF (Name):	CASE NUMBER:
DEFENDANT (Name):	

> **NOTICE: If you fail to file this claim, you will be evicted without further hearing.**

11. *(Response required within five days after you file this form)* I understand that I will have *five days* (excluding court holidays) to file a response to the Summons and Complaint after I file this Prejudgment Claim of Right to Possession form.

12. **Rental agreement.** I have *(check all that apply to you)*:
   a. ☐ an oral rental agreement with the landlord.
   b. ☐ a written rental agreement with the landlord.
   c. ☐ an oral rental agreement with a person other than the landlord.
   d. ☐ a written rental agreement with a person other than the landlord.
   e. ☐ other *(explain)*:

I declare under penalty of perjury under the laws of the State of California that the foregoing is true and correct.

> **WARNING: Perjury is a felony punishable by imprisonment in the state prison.**

Date:

▶

. . . .
(TYPE OR PRINT NAME)   (SIGNATURE OF CLAIMANT)

> **NOTICE:** If you file this claim of right to possession, the unlawful detainer (eviction) action against you will be determined at trial. At trial, you may be found liable for rent, costs, and, in some cases, treble damages.

—NOTICE TO OCCUPANTS—

YOU MUST ACT AT ONCE if all the following are true:
   1. **You are NOT named in the accompanying Summons and Complaint.**
   2. **You occupied the premises on or before the date the unlawful detainer (eviction) complaint was filed.** *(The date is the court filing date on the accompanying Summons and Complaint.)*
   3. **You still occupy the premises.**

(Where to file this form) You can complete and SUBMIT THIS CLAIM FORM WITHIN 10 DAYS from the date of service (on the reverse of this form) at the court where the unlawful detainer (eviction) complaint was filed.

(What will happen if you do not file this form) If you do not complete and submit this form (and pay a filing fee or file the form for proceeding in forma pauperis if you cannot pay the fee), YOU WILL BE EVICTED.

After this form is properly filed, you will be added as a defendant in the unlawful detainer (eviction) action and your right to occupy the premises will be decided by the court. *If you do not file this claim, you will be evicted without a hearing.*

CP 10.5 [New January 1, 1991]   **PREJUDGMENT CLAIM OF RIGHT TO POSSESSION**   Page two

UD-116

ATTORNEY OR PARTY WITHOUT ATTORNEY *(Name, state bar number, and address):*	*FOR COURT USE ONLY*
TELEPHONE NO.: FAX NO. *(Optional):*	
E-MAIL ADDRESS *(Optional):*	
ATTORNEY FOR *(Name):*	

SUPERIOR COURT OF CALIFORNIA, COUNTY OF

    STREET ADDRESS:

    MAILING ADDRESS:

    CITY AND ZIP CODE:

    BRANCH NAME:

    PLAINTIFF:

    DEFENDANT:

DECLARATION FOR DEFAULT JUDGMENT BY COURT **(Unlawful Detainer—Code Civil Proc., § 585(d))**	CASE NUMBER:

1. My name is *(specify):*
   a. ☐ I am the plaintiff in this action.
   b. I am
      (1) ☐ an owner of the property   (3) ☐ an agent of the owner
      (2) ☐ a manager of the property   (4) ☐ other *(specify):*

2. The property concerning this action is located at *(street address, apartment number, city, and county):*

3. Personal knowledge. I personally know the facts stated in this declaration and, if sworn as a witness, could testify competently thereto. I am personally familiar with the rental or lease agreement, defendant's payment record, the condition of the property, and defendant's conduct.

4. Agreement was ☐ written ☐ oral as follows:
   a. On or about *(date):*   defendant *(name each):*

   (1) agreed to rent the property for a ☐ month-to-month tenancy ☐ other tenancy *(specify):*
   (2) agreed to pay rent of $ payable ☐ monthly ☐ other *(specify frequency):*
       with rent due on the ☐ first of the month ☐ other day *(specify):*

   b. ☐ Original agreement is attached *(specify):* ☐ to the original complaint.
        ☐ to the *Application for Immediate Writ of Possession.* ☐ to this declaration, labeled Exhibit 4b.
   c. ☐ Copy of agreement with a declaration and order to admit the copy is attached *(specify):*
        ☐ to the *Application for Immediate Writ of Possession.* ☐ to this declaration, labeled Exhibit 4c.

5. ☐ Agreement changed.
   a. ☐ More than one change in rent amount *(specify history of all rent changes and effective dates up to the last rent change)* on *Attachment 5a (form MC-025).*
   b. ☐ Change in rent amount *(specify the last rent change).* The rent was changed from $ to $, which became effective on *(date):*   and was made
      (1) ☐ by agreement of the parties and subsequent payment of such rent.
      (2) ☐ by service on defendant of a notice of change in terms pursuant to Civil Code section 827 *(check item 5d).*
      (3) ☐ pursuant to a written agreement of the parties for change in terms *(check item 5e or 5f).*
   c. ☐ Change in rent due date. Rent was changed, payable in advance, due on *(specify day):*
   d.
   e. ☐ Original agreement for change in terms is attached *(specify):* ☐ to the original complaint.
        ☐ to the *Application for Immediate Writ of Possession.* ☐ to this declaration, labeled Exhibit 5e.
   f. ☐ Copy of agreement for change in terms with a a declaration and order to admit the copy is attached *(specify):*
        ☐ to the *Application for Immediate Writ of Possession.* ☐ to this declaration, labeled Exhibit 5f.

Page 1 of 3

PLAINTIFF:	CASE NUMBER:
DEFENDANT:	

6. Notice to quit.
   a. ☐ Defendant was served with a
      (1) ☐ 3-day notice to pay rent or quit   (4) ☐ 3-day notice to quit
      (2) ☐ 3-day notice to perform covenants or quit   (5) ☐ 30-day notice to quit
      (3) ☐ other *(specify):*

   b. ☐ The 3-day notice to pay rent or quit demanded rent due in the amount of *(specify):* $ for the rental period beginning on *(date)*   and ending on *(date)*

   c. ☐ The total rent demanded in the 3-day notice under item 6b is different from the agreed rent in item 4a(2) *(specify history of dates covered by the 3-day notice and any partial payments received to arrive at the balance)* on Attachment 6c (form MC-025).

   d. ☐ The original or copy of the notice specified in item 6a is attached to *(specify):* ☐ the original complaint.
           ☐ this declaration, labeled Exhibit 6d. *(The original or a copy of the notice MUST be attached to this declaration if not attached to the original complaint.)*

7. Service of notice.
   a. The notice was served on defendant *(name each):*
      (1) ☐ personally on *(date):*
      (2) ☐ by substituted service, including a copy mailed to the defendant, on *(date):*
      (3) ☐ by posting and mailing on *(date mailed):*
   b. ☐ A prejudgment claim of right to possession was served on the occupants pursuant to Code of Civil Procedure section 415.46.

8. Proof of service of notice. The original or copy of the proof of service of the notice in item 6a is attached to *(specify):*
   a. ☐ the original complaint.
   b. ☐ this declaration, labeled Exhibit 8b. *(The original or copy of the proof of service MUST be attached to this declaration if not attached to the original complaint.)*

9. Notice expired. On *(date):*   the notice in item 6 expired at the end of the day and defendant failed to comply with the requirements of the notice by that date. No money has been received and accepted after the notice expired.

10. The fair rental value of the property is $ per day, calculated as follows:
    a. ☐ (rent per month) x (0.03288) *(12 months divided by 365 days)*
    b. ☐ rent per month divided by 30
    c. ☐ other valuation *(specify):*

11. Possession. The defendant
    a. ☐ vacated the premises on *(date):*
    b. ☐ continues to occupy the property on *(date of this declaration):*

12. ☐ Holdover damages. Declarant has calculated the holdover damages as follows:
    a. Damages demanded in the complaint began on *(date):*
    b. Damages accrued through *(date specified in item 11):*
    c. Number of days that damages accrued *(count days using the dates in items 12a and 12b):*
    d. Total holdover damages *((daily rental value in item 10) x (number of days in item 12c)):* $

13. ☐ Reasonable attorney fees are authorized in the lease or rental agreement pursuant to paragraph *(specify):* and reasonable attorney fees for plaintiff's attorney *(name):*   are $

14. ☐ Court costs in this case, including the filing fee, are $

UD-116 [New January 1, 2003]   **DECLARATION FOR DEFAULT JUDGMENT BY COURT**   Page 2 of 3
(Unlawful Detainer—Code Civil Proc., § 585(d))

218

PLAINTIFF:	CASE NUMBER:
DEFENDANT:	

15. ☒ Declarant requests a judgment on behalf of plaintiff for:
  a. ☐ A money judgment as follows:

(1) ☐ Past-due rent *(item 6b)*	$	
(2) ☐ Holdover damages *(item 12d)*	$	
(3) ☐ Attorney fees *(item 13)**	$	⋆ ☐ Attorney fees are to be paid by *(name)* only.
(4) ☐ Costs *(item 14)*	$	
(5) ☐ Other *(specify):* Interest Special Damages	$	
(6) **TOTAL JUDGMENT**	$	

  b. ☐ Possession of the premises in item 2 *(check only if a clerk's judgment for possession was **not** entered)*.
  c. ☐ Cancellation of the rental agreement.   ☐ Forfeiture of the lease.

I declare under penalty of perjury under the laws of the State of California that the foregoing is true and correct.

Date:

_____ _____
(TYPE OR PRINT NAME) (SIGNATURE OF DECLARANT)

Summary of Exhibits

16. ☐ Exhibit 4b: Original rental agreement.
17. ☐ Exhibit 4c: Copy of rental agreement with declaration and order to admit the copy.
18. ☐ Exhibit 5d: Copy of notice of change in terms.
19. ☐ Exhibit 5e: Original agreement for change of terms.
20. ☐ Exhibit 5f: Copy of agreement for change in terms with declaration and order to admit copy.
21. ☐ Exhibit 6d: Original or copy of the notice to quit under item 6a *(MUST be attached to this declaration if it is not attached to original complaint)*.
22. ☐ Exhibit 8b: Original or copy of proof of service of notice in item 6a *(MUST be attached to this declaration if it is not attached to original complaint)*.
23. ☐ Other exhibits *(specify number and describe):*

DECLARATION FOR DEFAULT JUDGMENT BY COURT (Unlawful Detainer—Code Civil Proc., § 585(d))

1

2

3

4

5

6

7

8

9

10

11

12

13

14

15

16

17

18

19

20

21

22

23

24

25

26

27

28

29

IN THE SUPERIOR COURT OF _____ JUDICIAL DISTRICT,

COUNTY OF _____, STATE OF CALIFORNIA

_____,)
                  Plaintiff,)   NO.
     vs.   )
)   DECLARATION FOR
_____,)   DEFAULT JUDGMENT
               Defendant.)   IN LIEU OF PERSONAL
_____)   TESTIMONY (CCP 585.4)

I, _____, declare

that if sworn as a witness, I would testify competently within my

personal knowledge to the following facts:

1. That I am the plaintiff herein and the owner of the premises

located at _____, in the City of

_____, County of _____,

State of California.

2. That on _____, prior to filing this

action, the defendant rented said premises from me by _____

agreement and agreed to pay the sum of $_____ per month rental,

payable in advance on the _____ day of each and every calendar month

thereafter, current per month rental value being the sum of $_____

or $_____ per day.

3. That by virtue of said agreement, defendant went into

possession of said premises and still continues to hold and occupy same.

4. That on _____, I caused the
defendant to be served with a written notice stating the amount of
rent due and requiring payment thereof or possession of the premises
within three days after service of the notice.

5. That when at least three days had elapsed after service of
said notice on defendant and no part of said rent had been paid, I
caused the defendant to be served with a Summons and Complaint on

_____.

6. Said defendant has failed to answer the Summons and Complaint
within five days following service.

WHEREFORE, I pray that this Court render a judgment by default
against the defendant for restitution of said premises, for costs of
$_____, for past due rent of $_____, for damages at the rate
of $_____ per day, and for forfeiture of the agreement.

I declare under penalty of perjury that the foregoing is true and
correct.

Executed on _____, at City of _____,
County of _____, State of California.

_____
                                    Plaintiff

ATTORNEY OR PARTY WITHOUT ATTORNEY *(Name, State Bar number, and address):*	FOR COURT USE ONLY

TELEPHONE NO.: FAX NO. *(Optional):*
E-MAIL ADDRESS *(Optional):*
ATTORNEY FOR *(Name):*

SUPERIOR COURT OF CALIFORNIA, COUNTY OF

STREET ADDRESS:
MAILING ADDRESS:
CITY AND ZIP CODE:
BRANCH NAME:

PLAINTIFF/PETITIONER:

DEFENDANT/RESPONDENT:

REQUEST FOR (Application)	☐ **Entry of Default** ☐ **Clerk's Judgment** ☐ **Court Judgment**	CASE NUMBER:

1. TO THE CLERK: On the complaint or cross-complaint filed
   a. on *(date):*
   b. by *(name):*
   c. ☐ Enter default of defendant *(names):*

   d. ☐ I request a court judgment under Code of Civil Procedure sections 585(b), 585(c), 989, etc., against defendant *(names):*

   (Testimony required. Apply to the clerk for a hearing date, unless the court will enter a judgment on an affidavit under Code Civ. Proc., § 585(d).)
   e. ☐ Enter clerk's judgment
      (1) ☐ for restitution of the premises only and issue a writ of execution on the judgment. Code of Civil Procedure section 1174(c) does not apply. (Code Civ. Proc., § 1169.)
       ☐ Include in the judgment all tenants, subtenants, named claimants, and other occupants of the premises. The *Prejudgment Claim of Right to Possession* was served in compliance with Code of Civil Procedure section 415.46.
      (2) ☐ under Code of Civil Procedure section 585(a). *(Complete the declaration under Code Civ. Proc., § 585.5 on the reverse (item 5).)*
      (3) ☐ for default previously entered on *(date):*

2. **Judgment to be entered.**

	Amount	Credits acknowledged	Balance
a. Demand of complaint	$	$	$
b. Statement of damages *			
(1) Special	$	$	$
(2) General	$	$	$
c. Interest	$	$	$
d. Costs *(see reverse)*	$	$	$
e. Attorney fees	$	$	$
f. TOTALS	$	$	$

   g. **Daily damages** were demanded in complaint at the rate of: $ per day beginning *(date):*
   (* Personal injury or wrongful death actions; Code Civ. Proc., § 425.11.)

3. ☐ *(Check if filed in an unlawful detainer case)* **Legal document assistant or unlawful detainer assistant** information is on the reverse *(complete item 4).*

Date:

▶

_____ (TYPE OR PRINT NAME)   _____ (SIGNATURE OF PLAINTIFF OR ATTORNEY FOR PLAINTIFF)

FOR COURT USE ONLY	(1) ☐ Default entered as requested on *(date):* (2) ☐ Default NOT entered as requested *(state reason):*

Clerk, by _____, Deputy

Page 1 of 2

Form Adopted for Mandatory Use
Judicial Council of California
982(a)(6) [Rev. February 18, 2005]

REQUEST FOR ENTRY OF DEFAULT
(Application to Enter Default)

Code of Civil Procedure,
§§ 585–587, 1169
www.courtinfo.ca.gov

4. **Legal document assistant or unlawful detainer assistant (Bus. & Prof. Code, § 6400 et seq.).** A legal document assistant or unlawful detainer assistant ☐ did ☐ did **not** for compensation give advice or assistance with this form. *(If declarant has received **any** help or advice for pay from a legal document assistant or unlawful detainer assistant, state):*

  a. Assistant's name:
  b. Street address, city, and zip code:

  c. Telephone no.:
  d. County of registration:
  e. Registration no.:
  f. Expires on *(date):*

5. ☐ **Declaration under Code of Civil Procedure Section 585.5** *(required for entry of default under Code Civ. Proc., § 585(a)).* This action

  a. ☐ is ☐ is not on a contract or installment sale for goods or services subject to Civ. Code, § 1801 et seq. (Unruh Act).
  b. ☐ is ☐ is not on a conditional sales contract subject to Civ. Code, § 2981 et seq. (Rees-Levering Motor Vehicle Sales and Finance Act).
  c. ☐ is ☐ is not on an obligation for goods, services, loans, or extensions of credit subject to Code Civ. Proc., § 395(b).

6. **Declaration of mailing (Code Civ. Proc., § 587).** A copy of this *Request for Entry of Default* was

  a. ☐ **not mailed** to the following defendants, whose addresses are **unknown** to plaintiff or plaintiff's attorney *(names):*

  b. ☐ **mailed** first-class, postage prepaid, in a sealed envelope addressed to each defendant's attorney of record or, if none, to each defendant's last known address as follows:

    (1) Mailed on *(date):*
    (2) To *(specify names and addresses shown on the envelopes):*

I declare under penalty of perjury under the laws of the State of California that the foregoing items 4, 5, and 6 are true and correct.
Date:

▶

(TYPE OR PRINT NAME)	(SIGNATURE OF DECLARANT)

7. **Memorandum of costs** *(required if money judgment requested).* Costs and disbursements are as follows (Code Civ. Proc., § 1033.5):

  a. Clerk's filing fees . . . . $
  b. Process server's fees . . . . $
  c. Other *(specify):* . . . . $
  d. . . . . $
  e. **TOTAL** . . . . $ _____

  f. ☐ Costs and disbursements are waived.

  g. I am the attorney, agent, or party who claims these costs. To the best of my knowledge and belief this memorandum of costs is correct and these costs were necessarily incurred in this case.

I declare under penalty of perjury under the laws of the State of California that the foregoing is true and correct.
Date:

▶

(TYPE OR PRINT NAME)	(SIGNATURE OF DECLARANT)

8. ☐ **Declaration of nonmilitary status** *(required for a judgment).* No defendant named in item 1c of the application is in the military service so as to be entitled to the benefits of the Servicemembers Civil Relief Act (50 U.S.C. App. § 501 et seq.).

I declare under penalty of perjury under the laws of the State of California that the foregoing is true and correct.
Date:

▶

(TYPE OR PRINT NAME)	(SIGNATURE OF DECLARANT)

UD-110

ATTORNEY OR PARTY WITHOUT ATTORNEY *(Name, state bar number, and address):*	FOR COURT USE ONLY
TELEPHONE NO.: FAX NO. *(Optional)*: E-MAIL ADDRESS *(Optional)*: ATTORNEY FOR *(Name)*: ☐ ATTORNEY FOR ☐ JUDGMENT CREDITOR ☐ ASSIGNEE OF RECORD	

SUPERIOR COURT OF CALIFORNIA, COUNTY OF

STREET ADDRESS:

MAILING ADDRESS:

CITY AND ZIP CODE:

BRANCH NAME:

PLAINTIFF:

DEFENDANT:

JUDGMENT—UNLAWFUL DETAINER	CASE NUMBER:
☐ **By Clerk** ☐ **By Default** ☐ **After Court Trial** ☐ **By Court** ☐ **Possession Only** ☐ **Defendant Did Not Appear at Trial**	

JUDGMENT

1. ☐ **BY DEFAULT**

    a. Defendant was properly served with a copy of the summons and complaint.

    b. Defendant failed to answer the complaint or appear and defend the action within the time allowed by law.

    c. Defendant's default was entered by the clerk upon plaintiff's application.

    d. ☐ **Clerk's Judgment** (Code Civ. Proc., § 1169). For possession only of the premises described on page 2 (item 4).

    e. ☐ **Court Judgment** (Code Civ. Proc., § 585(b)). The court considered

    (1) ☐ plaintiff's testimony and other evidence.

    (2) ☐ plaintiff's or others' written declaration and evidence (Code Civ. Proc., § 585(d)).

2. ☐ **AFTER COURT TRIAL.** The jury was waived. The court considered the evidence.

    a. The case was tried on *(date and time)*:

    before *(name of judicial officer)*:

    b. Appearances by:

    ☐ Plaintiff *(name each)*:   ☐ Plaintiff's attorney *(name each)*:

                                                                          (1)

                                                                          (2)

    ☐ Continued on *Attachment 2b* (form MC-025).

    ☐ Defendant *(name each)*:   ☐ Defendant's attorney *(name each)*:

                                                                          (1)

                                                                          (2)

    ☐ Continued on *Attachment 2b* (form MC-025).

    c. ☐ Defendant did not appear at trial. Defendant was properly served with notice of trial.

    d. ☐ A statement of decision (Code Civ. Proc., § 632) ☐ was not ☐ was requested.

Form Approved for Optional Use
Judicial Council of California
UD-110 [New January 1, 2003]

JUDGMENT—UNLAWFUL DETAINER

Code of Civil Procedure, §§ 415.46,
585(d), 664.6, 1169

JUDGMENT IS ENTERED AS FOLLOWS BY: ☐ **THE COURT**   ☐ **THE CLERK**

3. **Parties.** Judgment is

    a. ☐ for plaintiff *(name each):*

      and against defendant *(name each):*

      ☐ Continued on *Attachment* 3a (form MC-025).

    b. ☐ for defendant *(name each):*

4. ☐ Plaintiff ☐ Defendant is entitled to possession of the premises located at *(street address, apartment, city, and county):*

5. ☐ Judgment applies to all occupants of the premises including tenants, subtenants if any, and named claimants if any (Code Civ. Proc., §§ 715.010, 1169, and 1174.3).

6. **Amount and terms of judgment**

    a. ☐ Defendant named in item 3a above must pay plaintiff on the complaint:

    b. ☐ Plaintiff is to receive nothing from defendant named in item 3b.

      ☐ Defendant named in item 3b is to recover costs: $

       ☐ and attorney fees: $

(1) ☐ Past-due rent	$	
(2) ☐ Holdover damages	$	
(3) ☐ Attorney fees	$	
(4) ☐ Costs	$	
(5) ☐ Other *(specify):* Int. Special Damages	$	
(6) **TOTAL JUDGMENT**	$	

    c. ☐ The rental agreement is canceled.   ☐ The lease is forfeited.

7. ☐ **Conditional judgment.** Plaintiff has breached the agreement to provide habitable premises to defendant as stated in *Judgment—Unlawful Detainer Attachment* (form UD-110S), which is attached.

8. ☐ **Other** *(specify):*

    ☐ Continued on *Attachment* 8 (form MC-025).

Date: ☐ _____

                             JUDICIAL OFFICER

Date: ☐ Clerk, by _____ , Deputy

[SEAL]

CLERK'S CERTIFICATE *(Optional)*

I certify that this is a true copy of the original judgment on file in the court.

Date:

Clerk, by _____ , Deputy

UD-110 [New January 1, 2003]   **JUDGMENT—UNLAWFUL DETAINER**   Page 2 of 2

Court Date: Time: Dept: Judge:

UNLAWFUL DETAINER CASE SUMMARY

CASE
Title:
Number:
Defendant(s):

Property Address:

TENANCY
Date Tenancy Began:
Initial Rent:
Current Rent:
Security Deposit:

NOTICE
Notice Served:
Date of Notice:
Date Notice Expired:

SUMMONS/COMPLAINT
Date Summons/Complaint Filed:
Date Summons/Complaint Served:

REQUEST
1) Forfeiture of the Agreement
2) Past Due Rent . . . .
3) HOLDOVER DAMAGES
       Date Damages Begin:
       Date Damages End:
       Damages Per Day:
       TOTAL DAMAGES:
4) Costs . . . .
5) Restitution of the Premises

JUDGMENT
Immediate Possession   OR   Stay of _____ Days (circle one)

Past Due Rent $_____

Damages $_____

Costs $_____

Judge (name) _____ Dept./Time_____

228

<table>
<tr><td>ATTORNEY OR PARTY WITHOUT ATTORNEY (Name and Address):

ATTORNEY FOR (Name):</td><td>TELEPHONE NO.:</td><td rowspan="2">FOR COURT USE ONLY</td></tr>
<tr><td colspan="2">NAME OF COURT AND ADDRESS:</td></tr>
<tr><td colspan="2">PLAINTIFF:</td><td></td></tr>
<tr><td colspan="2">DEFENDANT:</td><td>CASE NUMBER:</td></tr>
</table>

**AMENDED
UNLAWFUL DETAINER
DEFAULT JUDGMENT**

The Defendant(s) hereinafter named, having been regularly served with summons and copy of complaint, having failed to appear and answer plaintiff's complaint within the time allowed by law, and the default of said defendant(s) having been duly entered, and after having heard the testimony and considered the evidence, or pursuant to affidavit on file herein, the Court ordered the following JUDGMENT:

IT IS ORDERED AND ADJUDGED that Plaintiff(s)

have and recover from Defendant(s)

the restitution and possession of those certain premises situated, lying and being in the County of _____, State of California, and more particularly described as follows, to-wit:

_____

possession of premises restored to plaintiff on _____ through judgment pursuant to CCP §1169 dated _____
It is further Ordered, Adjudged, and Decreed that said plaintiff(s) have and recover from said defendant(s)

Rents and Damages	
Interest	
Costs	
Attorney Fees	
TOTAL	

And that the lease or agreement under which said defendant(s) hold(s) said premises be, and the same is hereby declared, forfeited, void, and of no effect.

Dated: _____   _____
                                          Judge of the Superior Court
I hereby certify this to be a true copy of the Judgment in the above action.

Judgment entered on _____ _____, Clerk

Judgment Book _____ Page _____ By _____, Deputy Clerk

CCP 585, 664, 668, 1033 1/2, 1169, 1174
AMENDED UNLAWFUL DETAINER DEFAULT JUDGMENT

efc

UD-115

ATTORNEY OR PARTY WITHOUT ATTORNEY *(Name, state bar number, and address)*:	FOR COURT USE ONLY
TELEPHONE NO.: FAX NO. *(Optional)*: E-MAIL ADDRESS *(Optional)*: ATTORNEY FOR *(Name)*:	

SUPERIOR COURT OF CALIFORNIA, COUNTY OF

STREET ADDRESS:

MAILING ADDRESS:

CITY AND ZIP CODE:

BRANCH NAME:

PLAINTIFF:

DEFENDANT:

STIPULATION FOR ENTRY OF JUDGMENT (Unlawful Detainer)	CASE NUMBER:

1. IT IS STIPULATED by plaintiff *(name each)*:   and

    defendant *(name each)*:

2. ☐ Plaintiff ☐ Defendant *(specify name)*:   is awarded

    a. ☐ possession of the premises located at *(street address, apartment number, city, and county)*:

    b. ☐ cancellation of the rental agreement.   ☐ forfeiture of the lease.

    c. ☐ past due rent $

    d. ☐ total holdover damages $

    e. ☐ attorney fees $

    f. ☐ costs $

    g. ☐ deposit of $ ☐ See item 3.

    h. ☐ other *(specify)*:   Interest   Special Damages

    i. Total $ to be paid by ☐ *(date)*:   ☐ installment payments (see item 5)

3. ☐ Deposit. If not awarded under item 2g, then plaintiff must _____

    a. ☐ return deposit of $ to defendant by *(date)*:

    b. ☐ give an itemized deposit statement to defendant within three weeks after defendant vacates the premises
        (Civ. Code. § 1950.5).

    c. ☐ mail the ☐ deposit ☐ itemized statement   to the defendant at *(mailing address)*:

                                     _____

4. ☐ A writ of possession will issue immediately, but there will be no lockout before *(date)*:

5. ☐ AGREEMENT FOR INSTALLMENT PAYMENTS

    a. Defendant agrees to pay $ on the *(specify day)*   day of each month beginning
        on *(specify date)*   until paid in full.

    b. If any payment is more than *(specify)*   days late, the entire amount in item 2i will become immediately due and
        payable plus interest at the legal rate.

6. a. ☐ Judgment will be entered now.

    b. ☐ Judgment will be entered only upon default of payment of the amount in item 2i or the payment arrangement in item 5a.
        The case is calendared for dismissal on *(date and time)*   in
        department *(specify)*   unless plaintiff or defendant otherwise notifies the court.

    c. ☐ Judgment will be entered as stated in Judgment—Unlawful Detainer Attachment (form UD-110S), which is attached.

    d. ☐ Judgment will be entered as stated in item 7.

Page 1 of 2

7. ☐ Plaintiff and defendant further stipulate as follows *(specify):*

8. a. **The parties named in item 1 understand that they have the right to (1) have an attorney present and (2) receive notice of and have a court hearing about any default in the terms of this stipulation.**

   b. Date:

        (TYPE OR PRINT NAME)

▶ _____
      (SIGNATURE OF PLAINTIFF OR ATTORNEY)

        (TYPE OR PRINT NAME)

▶ _____
      (SIGNATURE OF PLAINTIFF OR ATTORNEY)

    ☐ Continued on *Attachment* 8b (form MC-025).

   c. Date:

        (TYPE OR PRINT NAME)

▶ _____
      (SIGNATURE OF DEFENDANT OR ATTORNEY)

        (TYPE OR PRINT NAME)

▶ _____
      (SIGNATURE OF DEFENDANT OR ATTORNEY)

        (TYPE OR PRINT NAME)

▶ _____
      (SIGNATURE OF DEFENDANT OR ATTORNEY)

    ☐ Continued on *Attachment* 8c (form MC-025).

9. IT IS SO ORDERED.

Date:

_____
             JUDICIAL OFFICER

230

UD-150

ATTORNEY OR PARTY WITHOUT ATTORNEY *(Name, State Bar number, and address)*:	*FOR COURT USE ONLY*
TELEPHONE NO.: FAX No. *(Optional)*: E-MAIL ADDRESS *(Optional)*: ATTORNEY FOR *(Name)*:	

SUPERIOR COURT OF CALIFORNIA, COUNTY OF

STREET ADDRESS:

MAILING ADDRESS:

CITY AND ZIP CODE:

BRANCH NAME:

PLAINTIFF:

DEFENDANT:

☐ REQUEST ☐ COUNTER-REQUEST TO SET CASE FOR TRIAL—UNLAWFUL DETAINER ☐ Plaintiff ☐ Defendant	CASE NUMBER:

1. ☐ **Plaintiff's request.** I represent to the court that all parties have been served with process and have appeared or have had a default or dismissal entered against them. I request that this case be set for trial.

2. **Trial preference.** The premises concerning this case are located at *(street address, apartment number, city, zip code, and county)*:

   a. ☐ To the best of my knowledge, the right to possession of the premises is still in issue. This case is entitled to legal preference under Code of Civil Procedure section 1179a.

   b. ☐ To the best of my knowledge, the right to possession of the premises is no longer in issue. No defendant or other person is in possession of the premises.

3. **Jury or nonjury trial.** I request ☐ a jury trial ☐ a nonjury trial.

4. **Estimated length of trial.** I estimate that the trial will take *(check one)*:

   a. ☐ days *(specify number)*:   b. ☐ hours *(specify if estimated trial is less than one day)*:

5. **Trial date.** I am not available on the following dates *(specify dates and reasons for unavailability)*:

UNLAWFUL DETAINER ASSISTANT (Bus. & Prof. Code, §§ 6400–6415)

6. *(Complete in all cases.)* An unlawful detainer assistant ☐ did **not** ☐ did for compensation give advice or assistance with this form. *(If declarant has received **any** help or advice for pay from an unlawful detainer assistant, complete a–f.)*

   a. Assistant's name: c. Telephone no.:

   b. Street address, city, and zip code: d. County of registration:

                                                    e. Registration no.:

                                                    f. Expires on *(date)*:

I declare under penalty of perjury under the laws of the State of California that the foregoing is true and correct.

Date:

▶

_____   _____
(TYPE OR PRINT NAME)   (SIGNATURE OF PARTY OR ATTORNEY FOR PARTY)

NOTICE

- An unlawful detainer case must be set for trial on a date not later than **20 days after the first request** to set the case for trial is made (Code Civ. Proc., § 1170.5(a)).
- If a jury is requested, $150 must be deposited with the court 5 days before trial (Code Civ. Proc., § 631).
- Court reporter and interpreter services vary. Check with the court for availability of services and fees charged.
- If you cannot pay the court fees and costs, you may apply for a fee waiver. Ask the court clerk for a fee waiver form.

Form Adopted for Mandatory Use
Judicial Council of California
UD-150 [New January 1, 2005]

**REQUEST/COUNTER-REQUEST TO SET CASE
FOR TRIAL—UNLAWFUL DETAINER**

Code of Civil Procedure, §§ 631,
1170.5(a), 1179a
www.courtinfo.ca.gov

PLAINTIFF:	CASE NUMBER:
DEFENDANT:	

PROOF OF SERVICE BY MAIL

Instructions: *After having the parties served by mail with the* Request/Counter-Request to Set Case for Trial—Unlawful Detainer, *(form UD-150), have the person who mailed the form UD-150 complete this* Proof of Service by Mail. *An **unsigned** copy of the* Proof of Service by Mail *should be completed and served with form UD-150. Give the* Request/Counter-Request to Set Case for Trial —Unlawful Detainer *(form UD-150) and the completed* Proof of Service by Mail *to the clerk for filing. If you are representing yourself, someone else must mail these papers and sign the* Proof of Service by Mail.

1. I am over the age of 18 and **not a party to this case.** I am a resident of or employed in the county where the mailing took place.
2. My residence or business address is *(specify):*

3. I served the *Request/Counter-Request to Set Case for Trial—Unlawful Detainer* (form UD-150) by enclosing a copy in an envelope addressed to each person whose name and address are shown below AND

    a. ☐ **depositing** the sealed envelope in the United States mail on the date and at the place shown in item 3c with the postage fully prepaid.

    b. ☐ **placing** the envelope for collection and mailing on the date and at the place shown in item 3c following ordinary business practices. I am readily familiar with this business's practice for collecting and processing correspondence for mailing. On the same day that correspondence is placed for collection and mailing, it is deposited in the ordinary course of business with the United States Postal Service in a sealed envelope with postage fully prepaid.

    c. (1) Date mailed:

       (2) Place mailed *(city and state):*

I declare under penalty of perjury under the laws of the State of California that the foregoing is true and correct:

Date:

_____   ▶   _____
(TYPE OR PRINT NAME)   (SIGNATURE OF PERSON WHO MAILED *FORM UD-150*)

NAME AND ADDRESS OF EACH PERSON TO WHOM NOTICE WAS MAILED

	Name	Address *(number, street, city, and zip code)*
4.		
5.		
6.		
7.		
8.		
9.		

☐ List of names and addresses continued on a separate attachment or form MC-025, titled Attachment to Proof of Service by Mail.

    REQUEST/COUNTER-REQUEST TO SET CASE FOR TRIAL—UNLAWFUL DETAINER

MC-025

SHORT TITLE:

CASE NUMBER:

ATTACHMENT *(Number):* _____
(This Attachment may be used with any Judicial Council form.)

Page _____ **of** _____
(Add pages as required)

1
2
3
4
5
6
7
8
9
10
11
12
13
14
15
16
17
18
19
20
21
22
23
24
25
26
27

(If the item that this Attachment concerns is made under penalty of perjury, all statements in this Attachment are made under penalty of perjury.)

Form Approved for Optional Use
Judicial Council of California
MC-025 [New July 1, 2002]

ATTACHMENT
to Judicial Council Form

Cal. Rules of Court, rule 982

234

	COURT USE ONLY
COURT ADDRESS:	
PLAINTIFF:	
DEFENDANT:	

APPLICATION FOR ISSUANCE OF WRIT OF : ☐ POSSESSION ☐ SALE ☐ OTHER	**CASE NUMBER**

I, the undersigned, say : I am the ☐ Judgment Creditor

☐ attorney for the Judgment Creditor

☐ assignee of record of the Judgment Creditor

in the above-entitled action and that the following judgment was: (check if applicable)

☐ entered on _____ .

☐ entered on _____ .

In favor of the Judgment Creditor as follows (name and address) :

against the Judgment Debtor(s) as follows (name and address) :

for the amount of :

$ _____ Principal

$ _____ Accrued Costs

$ _____ Attorney Fees

$ _____ Interest

$ _____ TOTAL

and the possession of the premises located at :

The daily rental value of the property as of the date the complaint was filed is :

$ _____

It is prayed that a writ as checked above be issued to the _____

The writ will be directed to _____

(Law Enforcement Agency and Location)

I declare under the penalty of perjury under the Laws of the State of California that the foregoing is true and correct.

Executed on _____ at _____ , California

_____
Signature

APPLICATION FOR WRIT OF POSSESSION / SALE

efc

EJ-130

ATTORNEY OR PARTY WITHOUT ATTORNEY *(Name, State Bar number and address)*:	*FOR COURT USE ONLY*
TELEPHONE NO.: FAX NO. *(Optional)*:	
E-MAIL ADDRESS *(Optional)*:	
ATTORNEY FOR *(Name)*:	
☐ ATTORNEY FOR ☐ JUDGMENT CREDITOR ☐ ASSIGNEE OF RECORD	

SUPERIOR COURT OF CALIFORNIA, COUNTY OF
STREET ADDRESS:
MAILING ADDRESS:
CITY AND ZIP CODE:
BRANCH NAME:

PLAINTIFF:

DEFENDANT:

WRIT OF	☐ **EXECUTION (Money Judgment)** ☐ **POSSESSION OF** ☐ **Personal Property** ☐ **Real Property** ☐ **SALE**	CASE NUMBER:

1. **To the Sheriff or Marshal of the County of:**

   You are directed to enforce the judgment described below with daily interest and your costs as provided by law.

2. **To any registered process server:** You are authorized to serve this writ only in accord with CCP 699.080 or CCP 715.040.

3. *(Name):*
   is the ☐ judgment creditor ☐ assignee of record   whose address is shown on this form above the court's name.

4. **Judgment debtor** *(name and last known address):*

   ☐ Additional judgment debtors on next page

5. **Judgment entered** on *(date):*

6. ☐ **Judgment renewed** on *(dates):*

7. **Notice of sale** under this writ
   a. ☐ has not been requested.
   b. ☐ has been requested *(see next page).*
8. ☐ Joint debtor information on next page.

   [SEAL]

9. ☐ See next page for information on real or personal property to be delivered under a writ of possession or sold under a writ of sale.
10. ☐ This writ is issued on a sister-state judgment.
11. Total judgment . . . . $
12. Costs after judgment (per filed order or memo CCP 685.090) . . . . $
13. Subtotal *(add 11 and 12)* . . . . $ _____
14. Credits . . . . $
15. Subtotal *(subtract 14 from 13)* . . . . . . $ _____
16. Interest after judgment (per filed affidavit CCP 685.050) (not on GC 6103.5 fees). . . $
17. Fee for issuance of writ . . . . $
18. **Total** *(add 15, 16, and 17)* . . . . $ _____
19. Levying officer:
    (a) Add daily interest from date of writ *(at the legal rate on 15)* (not on GC 6103.5 fees) of . . . . . . $
    (b) Pay directly to court costs included in 11 and 17 (GC 6103.5, 68511.3; CCP 699.520(i)) . . . . $
20. ☐ The amounts called for in items 11–19 are different for each debtor. These amounts are stated for each debtor on Attachment 20.

Issued on *(date):*   Clerk, by _____ , Deputy

NOTICE TO PERSON SERVED: SEE NEXT PAGE FOR IMPORTANT INFORMATION.

Page 1 of 2

Form Approved for Optional Use
Judicial Council of California
EJ-130 [Rev. January 1, 2006]

WRIT OF EXECUTION

Code of Civil Procedure, §§ 699.520, 712.010,
Government Code, § 6103.5
www.courtinfo.ca.gov
American LegalNet, Inc.
www.USCourtForms.com

PLAINTIFF:	CASE NUMBER:
DEFENDANT:	

— Items continued from page 1—

21. ☐ **Additional judgment debtor** (name and last known address):

22. ☐ **Notice of sale** has been requested by (name and address):

23. ☐ **Joint debtor** was declared bound by the judgment (CCP 989–994)
   a. on (date):
   b. name and address of joint debtor:
   a. on (date):
   b. name and address of joint debtor:

   c. ☐ additional costs against certain joint debtors (itemize):

24. ☐ (Writ of Possession or Writ of Sale) **Judgment** was entered for the following:
   a. ☐ Possession of real property: The complaint was filed on (date):
      (Check (1) or (2)):
      (1) ☐ The Prejudgment Claim of Right to Possession was served in compliance with CCP 415.46.
         The judgment includes all tenants, subtenants, named claimants, and other occupants of the premises.
      (2) ☐ The Prejudgment Claim of Right to Possession was NOT served in compliance with CCP 415.46.
         (a) $ was the daily rental value on the date the complaint was filed.
         (b) The court will hear objections to enforcement of the judgment under CCP 1174.3 on the following
            dates (specify):
   b. ☐ Possession of personal property.
      ☐ If delivery cannot be had, then for the value (itemize in 9e) specified in the judgment or supplemental order.
   c. ☐ Sale of personal property.
   d. ☐ Sale of real property.
   e. Description of property:

NOTICE TO PERSON SERVED

WRIT OF EXECUTION OR SALE. Your rights and duties are indicated on the accompanying *Notice of Levy* (Form EJ-150).
WRIT OF POSSESSION OF PERSONAL PROPERTY. If the levying officer is not able to take custody of the property, the levying officer will make a demand upon you for the property. If custody is not obtained following demand, the judgment may be enforced as a money judgment for the value of the property specified in the judgment or in a supplemental order.
WRIT OF POSSESSION OF REAL PROPERTY. If the premises are not vacated within five days after the date of service on the occupant or, if service is by posting, within five days after service on you, the levying officer will remove the occupants from the real property and place the judgment creditor in possession of the property. Except for a mobile home, personal property remaining on the premises will be sold or otherwise disposed of in accordance with CCP 1174 unless you or the owner of the property pays the judgment creditor the reasonable cost of storage and takes possession of the personal property not later than 15 days after the time the judgment creditor takes possession of the premises.
► A Claim of Right to Possession form accompanies this writ (unless the Summons was served in compliance with CCP 415.46).

WRIT OF EXECUTION

INSTRUCTIONS TO LEVYING OFFICER SERVING WRIT
(POSSESSION OF REAL PROPERTY)

Plaintiff

-vs-

Date

Defendant

Court (Case) Number

To:

By virtue of the accompanying Writ in the above entitled action, you are hereby instructed to RETURN POSSESSION OF THE PROPERTY DESCRIBED BELOW TO THE CREDITOR:

Street Address (include apt. no.)

City/Zip Code

WHEN YOU ARE READY TO DELIVER POSSESSION OF THE PROPERTY, CONTACT:

Name

Address

City/Zip Code

Phone (8 AM - 11 AM)

Signature (Creditor or Creditor's Attorney)

Print/Type Name

Address

City/State/Zip Code

Phone (8 AM - 5 PM)

efc

238

ATTORNEY OR PARTY WITHOUT ATTORNEY (Name and Address)

TELEPHONE NO.:

FOR COURT USE ONLY

ATTORNEY FOR (Name)

Insert name of court and name of judicial district and branch court, if any:

PLAINTIFF/PETITIONER:

DEFENDANT/RESPONDENT:

REQUEST FOR DISMISSAL

[ ] **Personal Injury, Property Damage, or Wrongful Death**
    [ ] **Motor Vehicle**   [ ] **Other**
[ ] **Family Law**
[ ] **Eminent Domain**
[X] **Other** *(specify)*: Unlawful Detainer

CASE NUMBER:

— A conformed copy will not be returned by the clerk unless a method of return is provided with the document. —

1. **TO THE CLERK:** Please **dismiss** this action as follows:

  a. (1) [ ] With prejudice   (2) [ ] Without prejudice

  b. (1) [X] Complaint   (2) [ ] Petition
     (3) [ ] Cross-complaint filed by (name):   on (date):
     (4) [ ] Cross-complaint filed by (name):   on (date):
     (5) [ ] Entire action of all parties and all causes of action
     (6) [ ] Other (specify) :*

Date:

▶

. . . .
(TYPE OR PRINT NAME OF [ ] ATTORNEY [ ] PARTY WITHOUT ATTORNEY)

(SIGNATURE)
Attorney or party without attorney for:

* If dismissal requested is of specified parties only, of specified causes of action only, or of specified cross-complaints only, so state and identify the parties, causes of action, or cross-complaints to be dismissed.

[X] Plaintiff/Petitioner   [ ] Defendant/Respondent
[ ] Cross-complainant

---

2. **TO THE CLERK:** Consent to the above dismissal is hereby given.**
Date:

▶

. . . .
(TYPE OR PRINT NAME OF [ ] ATTORNEY [ ] PARTY WITHOUT ATTORNEY)

(SIGNATURE)
Attorney or party without attorney for:

**If a cross-complaint--or Response (Family Law) seeking affirmative relief--is on file, the attorney for cross-complainant (respondent) must sign this consent if required by Code of Civil Procedure section 581(i) or (j).

[X] Plaintiff/Petitioner   [ ] Defendant/Respondent
[ ] Cross-complainant

(To be completed by clerk)

3. [ ] Dismissal entered as requested on (date):
4. [ ] Dismissal entered on (date):   as to only (name):
5. [ ] Dismissal **not entered** as requested for the following reasons (specify):

6. [ ] a. Attorney or party without attorney notified on (date):
      b. Attorney or party without attorney not notified. Filing party failed to provide
         [ ] a copy to conform   [ ] means to return conformed copy

Date: _____   Clerk, by _____, Deputy

Form Adopted by the
Judicial Council of California
982 (a)(5) [Rev. January 1, 1997]

REQUEST FOR DISMISSAL

Code of Civil Procedure, § 581 et seq.
Cal. Rules of Court, rules 383, 1233

IN THE SUPERIOR COURT OF _____ JUDICIAL DISTRICT,

COUNTY OF _____, STATE OF CALIFORNIA

_____,)
               Plaintiff,)   No.
       vs.   )
)   APPLICATION AND
_____,)   DECLARATION FOR
              Defendant.)   ORDER OF POSTING
_____)   OF SUMMONS

Application is hereby made for an order directing service of summons in the above-entitled matter on above-named Defendant by posting of said summons on the premises located at

The complaint in this action, which is for unlawful detainer, was filed on _____, and the summons was duly issued on

Said Defendant is a necessary party to this action. Said Defendant cannot, with reasonable diligence, be served in any other manner specified by Section 415.47 of the Code of Civil Procedure. Defendant's place of employment is unknown to the Plaintiff, and a reasonable search of public records does not disclose any address for said Defendant; hence, said Defendant's whereabouts are unknown.

Reasonable diligence in attempting service is set forth in the

1 Declaration of   on file herein and attached hereto.

2   WHEREFORE, Plaintiff prays that the Court issue its order

3 directing service of the summons against the Defendant by posting of

4 the summons at

5 pursuant to provisions of Section 415.45 of the Code of Civil

6 Procedure.

7   I declare under penalty of perjury that the foregoing is true and

8 correct.

9   Executed on   , at City of   ,

10 County of   , State of California.

11

12

13   _____

14   Plaintiff

15

16

17

18

19

20

21

22

23

24

25

26

27

28

29

1

2

3

4

5

6

7

8   IN THE SUPERIOR COURT OF _____ JUDICIAL DISTRICT,

9   COUNTY OF _____, STATE OF CALIFORNIA

10

11   _____,)
                        Plaintiff,)
12   vs.   )   NO.
)
13   _____,)   ORDER FOR
                        Defendant.)   POSTING OF SUMMONS
14   _____)   (CCP 415.45)

15   Upon reading and filing the Plaintiff's Application and

16   Declaration for Order of Posting of Summons, the Court appears

17   satisfied therefrom that a cause of action for unlawful detainer exists

18   against Defendant in the above-mentioned action and that summons on the

19   complaint has been duly issued out of the above-entitled court in this

20   action and that said Defendant cannot with reasonable diligence be

21   served in any manner specified by Section 415.10 and 415.50 of the Code

22   of Civil Procedure for the reasons that the whereabouts of said

23   Defendant are unknown, and that reasonable diligence has been expended

24   in attempting to serve the summons as set forth in the declaration on

25   file herein.

26

27   IT IS HEREBY ORDERED that the service of said summons in this action be

28   made on Defendant by posting of the summons for a period of not less

29

1 than ten (10) days on the premises located at

2

3

4 THE COURT ALSO ORDERS that a copy of the summons and complaint

5 shall be mailed forthwith by certified mail to Defendant at his

6 last known address, to wit:

7

8 Dated:

9 _____

   JUDGE OF THE SUPERIOR COURT

10

11

12

13

14

15

16

17

18

19

20

21

22

23

24

25

26

27

28

29

1

2

3

4

5

6

7

8   IN THE SUPERIOR COURT OF _____ JUDICIAL DISTRICT,

9   COUNTY OF _____, STATE OF CALIFORNIA

10

11   _____,)
                          Plaintiff,)
12   vs.   )   NO.
)
13   _____,)   COMPLAINT FOR
                          Defendant.)   UNLAWFUL DETAINER
14   _____)   (CCP §1161a)

15   Plaintiff alleges as follows:

16   1. At all times mentioned herein, plaintiff was and now is a

17   competent adult residing in the City of _____, County of

18   _____, State of California.

19   2. Plaintiff is the owner of the premises located at

20   _____ in the City

21   of _____, County of _____, State of

22   California.

23   3. Plaintiff believes that defendants are competent adults

24   residing in the City of _____, County of

25   _____, State of California.

26   4. The true names and capacities of defendants sued as Does are

27   unknown to plaintiff. Plaintiff will seek leave of court to amend this

28   complaint when said true names and capacities have been determined.

29   5. At all times mentioned herein, each of the defendants,

including the defendants served as Does herein, was the agent and/or employee of each of the remaining defendants and in doing what is mentioned herein was acting within the scope of such agency and/or employment. Plaintiff is further informed and believes and thereupon alleges that each of the defendants, including the defendants served as Does herein, claims some type of possessory interest in the premises.

6. Defendants entered into possession of the Premises as owners of record. Defendants are no longer owners of record, nor are they tenants of the current owner of record.

7. Plaintiff has acquired ownership interest in the premises and consequent right to possession. Plaintiff is now the owner of record, holding legal entitlement to the premises as [select one]:

[ ] purchaser from the defendants through a voluntary sale.

[ ] purchaser upon foreclosure against the defaulting defendants.

[ ] purchaser under writ of execution against the defendants.

[ ] purchaser under a power of sale provision contained in a deed of trust executed by the defendants.

[ ] purchaser under the default provisions of a conditional sale contract or security agreement.

8. Plaintiff has complied with all legal requirements for perfecting the title as evidenced by Exhibit A.

9. Plaintiff caused the defendants to be served with a written notice to quit. Said notice required defendants to deliver possession of the premises within three days following service of the notice. A copy of this notice is attached hereto as Exhibit B and incorporated herein by this reference.

10. The notice to quit was served on the defendants pursuant to CCP Section 1162 in the manner shown on the Proof of Service, which is a part of Exhibit B.

11. The period stated in the notice to quit expired on

_____, and defendants failed to comply with the notice by that date, that is, they failed to quit the premises and deliver up possession to plaintiff.

12. Defendants continue in possession of the premises without plaintiff's permission or consent.

14. Plaintiff is entitled to immediate possession of the premises.

13. Plaintiff is informed and believes and thereupon alleges that the reasonable rental value of the premises is the sum of $_____ per day, and damages to plaintiff caused by defendants' unlawful detention thereof have accrued at said rate since _____ [date after notice to quit expired] and will continue to accrue at said rate so long as defendants remain in possession of the premises.

WHEREFORE, plaintiff prays judgment against defendants, and each of them, as follows:

1. For immediate possession of the premises;

2. For damages at the rate of $_____, according to proof at trial, for each day defendants continue in possession of the premises, commencing _____.

3. For costs of suit incurred herein; and

4. For such other and further relief as the court may deem just and proper.

DATED: _____   SIGNED: _____

[Verification attached]

246

VERIFICATION

I, the undersigned, certify and declare that I have read the foregoing complaint and know its contents. The statement following the box checked is applicable.

[ ] I am a party to this action. The matters stated in the document described above are true of my own knowledge and belief except as to those matters stated on information and belief, and as to those matters I believe them to be true.

[ ] I am [ ] an officer [ ] a partner [ ] a _____ of _____, a party to this action, and am authorized to make this verification on its behalf. I am informed and believe and on that ground allege that the matters stated in the document described above are true.

[ ] I am the attorney, or one of the attorneys for _____, a party to this action. Such party is absent from the county where I or such attorneys have their offices and is unable to verify the document described above. For that reason, I am making this verification for and on behalf of that party. I am informed and believe and on that ground allege that the matters stated in said document are true.

Executed on _____, at _____.

I declare under penalty of perjury under the laws of the State of California that the foregoing is true and correct.

SIGNED: _____

Appendix A

Posting

Posting, one of the options available to you for serving especially elusive tenants a Summons and Complaint, involves several steps [see CCP §415.45(b); see also *Green v. Lindsey* (U.S. Sup.Ct. 1982) 102 S.Ct. 1874, 72 L.Ed.2d 249]:

1. Instruct the process server to make three attempts to serve the papers and then return them to you with enough information so you can proceed to get an order for posting.

2. Check the information regarding the process server's three attempts and make sure that they were made on three different days, each at a different time of the day. Two might be made in the morning and one in the evening, for example.

3. Prepare an Application and Declaration for Order of Posting of Summons and an Order for Posting of Summons as shown in this appendix.

4. Take to the court clerk the process server's signed statement that the defendant could not be found, as well as the two forms just mentioned for securing the order of posting. Ask her to submit them to a judge for a signature. Depending on how busy everybody is, you may be able to wait for them then or you may have to return and pick them up later.

5. Take your papers back to the sheriff or marshal and have him post the Summons and Complaint on the tenant's main entry and also send a copy of each by certified mail to the defendant at his last known address. The posting must take place before the mailing.

6. Wait fifteen days for a response [CCP §415.45(c)].

Does

Whenever you discover that the fictitious "DOES 1 to 10," whom you referred to in your Summons and Complaint, are real people with real names, you'll have to amend the Complaint or you won't be able to evict them.

Once you find out who they are, which is sometimes the most difficult part of all and may involve your having to "sift through the garbage" (attorneys' expression not necessarily meant to be literal) looking for their real names, you may file an Amendment to Complaint form and then have them served with a copy of the Summons, Complaint, and the Amendment.

In the absence of a Judicial Council form for this purpose, the form provided here should suffice to substitute a real person's name for a Doe. This is a dual-purpose form which works both for changing fictitious names to real names and for changing incorrect names to real names. "Does" are fictitious names and changing them does not require that you secure a judge's signature. You need use only the top two-thirds of the form for changing fictitious names. If you want to, you may use the same form for changing more than one fictitious name at a time.

These are the steps you should take to change "Does" to real names:

1. Make sure that your original Summons and Complaint always include "DOES 1 to 10" (10 is usually enough to include everybody who wasn't specifically named, but there's nothing to prevent you from using a larger number) as defendants.

2. Find out the real names of any adults living on the premises whom you didn't know before.

3. Complete the upper two-thirds of the Amendment to Complaint form.

4. File the Amendment to Complaint form with the court clerk.

5. Serve each of your newly discovered Does individually with a copy of the Summons, Complaint, and the Amendment to Complaint.

6. Wait five days following service for these defendants to respond.

7. Continue the eviction as usual.

Attorney Verification (Complaint)

Attorneys may verify a complaint using these words: "I am an attorney at law admitted to practice before all courts of the State of California and have my office in XXX County, California. I am the attorney for the plaintiff in this proceeding. I declare that plaintiff is unable to make the verification because plaintiff is absent from XXX County and for that reason affiant makes this verification on plaintiff's behalf. I declare that I have read the foregoing complaint and am informed and believe the matters therein to be true and on that ground allege that the matters stated therein are true." [Dated] [Signed]

```
 1   Lester Landlord & Leslie Landlord
     123 Neat Street
 2   Littletown, California 91111
     415-123-4567
 3   Plaintiff in Propria Persona

 4

 5

 6

 7

 8       IN THE SUPERIOR COURT OF  LITTLETOWN        JUDICIAL DISTRICT,

 9       COUNTY OF ____SADDLEBACK_____, STATE OF CALIFORNIA

10
     LESTER LANDLORD
11   LESLIE LANDLORD                  ,)
                          Plaintiff,)      No. 1234567890
12            vs.                    )
     RICHARD ROTTER                  )      APPLICATION AND
13   HAZEL ROTTER                  ,)       DECLARATION FOR
                        Defendant.)         ORDER OF POSTING
14   _____)          OF SUMMONS

15       Application is hereby made for an order directing service of

16   summons in the above-entitled matter on above-named Defendant by

17   posting of said summons on the premises located at

18                       456 Sweet Street

19                  Littletown, California 91111

20       The complaint in this action, which is for unlawful detainer, was

21   filed on  July 2, XXXX        , and the summons was duly issued on

22   July 2, XXXX.

23       Said Defendant is a necessary party to this action.  Said

24   Defendant cannot, with reasonable diligence, be served in any other

25   manner specified by Section 415.47 of the Code of Civil Procedure.

26   Defendant's place of employment is unknown to the Plaintiff, and a

27   reasonable search of public records does not disclose any address for

28   said Defendant; hence, said Defendant's whereabouts are unknown.

29       Reasonable diligence in attempting service is set forth in the
```

You will find a blank copy of this form in the FORMS section of this book and in Eviction Forms Creator.

1 Declaration of   Sheriff   on file herein and attached hereto.

2   WHEREFORE, Plaintiff prays that the Court issue its order

3 directing service of the summons against the Defendant by posting of

4 the summons at 456 Sweet Street, Littletown, California

5 pursuant to provisions of Section 415.45 of the Code of Civil

6 Procedure.

7   I declare under penalty of perjury that the foregoing is true and

8 correct.

9   Executed on July 7, XXXX   , at City of Littletown   ,

10 County of Saddleback   , State of California.

11

12

13 _____

                       Plaintiff

14

15

16

17

18

19

20

21

22

23

24

25

26

27

28

29

```
 1 │ Lester Landlord & Leslie Landlord
   │ 123 Neat Street
 2 │ Littletown, California 91111
   │ 415-123-4567
 3 │ Plaintiff in Propria Persona
 4
 5
 6
 7
 8 │      IN THE SUPERIOR COURT OF _____LITTLETOWN_____ JUDICIAL DISTRICT,
 9 │      COUNTY OF _____SADDLEBACK_____, STATE OF CALIFORNIA
10 │ LESTER LANDLORD
   │ LESLIE LANDLORD
11 │ _____, )
   │              Plaintiff, )
12 │        vs.               )        NO. 1234567890
   │ RICHARD ROTTER           )
13 │ HAZEL ROTTER             )
   │ _____, )                ORDER FOR
   │              Defendant. )         POSTING OF SUMMONS
14 │ _____ )         (CCP 415.45)
15 │      Upon reading and filing the Plaintiff's Application and
16 │ Declaration for Order of Posting of Summons, the Court appears
17 │ satisfied therefrom that a cause of action for unlawful detainer exists
18 │ against Defendant in the above-mentioned action and that summons on the
19 │ complaint has been duly issued out of the above-entitled court in this
20 │ action and that said Defendant cannot with reasonable diligence be
21 │ served in any manner specified by Section 415.10 and 415.50 of the Code
22 │ of Civil Procedure for the reasons that the whereabouts of said
23 │ Defendant are unknown, and that reasonable diligence has been expended
24 │ in attempting to serve the summons as set forth in the declaration on
25 │ file herein.
26
27 │ IT IS HEREBY ORDERED that the service of said summons in this action be
28 │ made on Defendant by posting of the summons for a period of not less
29
```

You will find a blank copy of this form in the FORMS section of this book and in Eviction Forms Creator.

than ten (10) days on the premises located at

456 Sweet Street, Littletown, California 91111

THE COURT ALSO ORDERS that a copy of the summons and complaint shall be mailed forthwith by certified mail to Defendant at his last known address, to wit:

456 Sweet Street, Littletown, California 91111

Dated: July 7, XXXX

Denise Berger
———————————————————
JUDGE OF THE SUPERIOR COURT

You will find a blank copy of this form in the FORMS section of this book and in Eviction Forms Creator.

Name, Address, and Telephone No. of Attorney(s)

Lester Landlord & Leslie Landlord
123 Neat Street
Littletown, California 91111

415-123-4567

Attorney(s) for Plaintiff in Propria Persona

Space Below for Use of Court Clerk Only

AMENDMENT TO COMPLAINT	SUPERIOR COURT OF CALIFORNIA COUNTY OF SADDLEBACK LITTLETOWN JUDICIAL DISTRICT	CASE NUMBER: 1234567890

Lester Landlord
Leslie Landlord

Otto Rowe

vs.

Plaintiff(s)   Defendant(s)

FICTITIOUS NAME (NO ORDER REQUIRED)
Upon filing the complaint herein, plaintiff(s) being ignorant of the true name of a defendant, and having designated said defendant in the complaint by the fictitious name of

Doe 1 and Doe 2

and having discovered the true name of said defendant to be

Jennifer Rowe and Max Rowe

hereby amends the complaint by inserting such true name in place and stead of such fictitious name wherever it appears in said complaint.

Lester Landlord

Plaintiff(s)/Attorney(s) for Plaintiff(s)

INCORRECT NAME/ADDRESS (ORDER REQUIRED)
Plaintiff(s) having designated a defendant in the complaint by the incorrect name/address of

and having discovered the true name/address of said defendant to be

hereby amends the complaint by inserting such true name/address in place and stead of such incorrect name/address wherever it appears in said complaint.

Plaintiff(s)/Attorney(s) for Plaintiff(s)

ORDER
Proper cause appearing, the above amendment to the complaint is allowed.

Dated: _____

_____
Presiding Judge

AMENDMENT TO COMPLAINT
CCP §§473-474

efc

You will find a blank copy of this form in the FORMS section of this book and in Eviction Forms Creator.

Appendix B
Codes Relevant to Unlawful Detainers

Code of Civil Procedure §1161.1.

With respect to application of Section 1161 in cases of possession of commercial real property after default in the payment of rent:

(a) If the amount stated in the notice provided to the tenant pursuant to subdivision (2) of Section 1161 is clearly identified by the notice as an estimate and the amount claimed is not in fact correct, but it is determined upon the trial or other judicial determination that rent was owing, and the amount claimed in the notice was reasonably estimated, the tenant shall be subject to judgment for possession and the actual amount of rent and other sums found to be due. However, if (1) upon receipt of such a notice claiming an amount identified by the notice as an estimate, the tenant tenders to the landlord within the time for payment required by the notice, the amount which the tenant has reasonably estimated to be due and (2) if at trial it is determined that the amount of rent then due was the amount tendered by the tenant or a lesser amount, the tenant shall be deemed the prevailing party for all purposes. If the court determines that the amount so tendered by the tenant was less than the amount due, but was reasonably estimated, the tenant shall retain the right to possession if the tenant pays to the landlord within five days of the effective date of the judgment (1) the amount previously tendered if it had not been previously accepted, (2) the difference between the amount tendered and the amount determined by the court to be due, and (3) any other sums as ordered by the court.

(b) If the landlord accepts a partial payment of rent, including any payment pursuant to subdivision (a), after serving notice pursuant to Section 1161, the landlord, without any further notice to the tenant, may commence and pursue an action under this chapter to recover the difference between the amount demanded in that notice and the payment actually received, and this shall be specified in the complaint.

(c) If the landlord accepts a partial payment of rent after filing the complaint pursuant to Section 1166, the landlord's acceptance of the partial payment is evidence only of that payment, without waiver of any rights or defenses of any of the parties. The landlord shall be entitled to amend the complaint to reflect the partial payment without creating a necessity for the filing of an additional answer or other responsive pleading by the tenant, and without prior leave of court, and such an amendment shall not delay the matter from proceeding. However, this subdivision shall apply only if the landlord provides actual notice to the tenant that acceptance of the partial rent payment does not constitute a waiver of any rights, including any right the landlord may have to recover possession of the property.

(d) "Commercial real property" as used in this section, means all real property in this state except dwelling units made subject to Chapter 2 (commencing with Section 1940) of Title 5 of Part 4 of Division 3 of the Civil Code, mobilehomes as defined in Section 798.3 of the Civil Code, or recreational vehicles as defined in Section 799.24 of the Civil Code.

(e) For the purposes of this section, there is a presumption affecting the burden of proof that the amount of rent claimed or tendered is reasonably estimated if, in relation to the amount determined to be due upon the trial or other judicial determination of that issue, the amount claimed or tendered was no more than 20 percent more or less than the amount determined to be due. However, if the rent due is contingent upon information primarily within the knowledge of the one party to the lease and that information has been furnished to, or has not accurately been furnished to, the other party, the court shall consider that fact in determining the reasonableness of the amount of rent claimed or tendered pursuant to subdivision (a).

Code of Civil Procedure §1166a

(a) Upon filing the complaint, the plaintiff may, upon motion, have immediate possession of the premises by a writ of possession of a manufactured home, mobilehome, or real property issued by the court and directed to the sheriff of the county, or constable or marshal, for execution, where it appears to the satisfaction of the court, after a hearing on the motion, from the verified complaint and from any affidavits filed or oral testimony given by or on behalf of the parties, that the defendant resides out of state, has departed from the state, cannot, after due diligence, be found within the state, or has concealed himself or herself to avoid the service of summons. The motion shall indicate that the writ applies to all tenants, subtenants, if any, named claimants, if any, and any other occupants of the premises.

(b) Written notice of the hearing on the motion shall be served on the defendant by the plaintiff in accordance with the provisions of Section 1011, and shall inform the defendant as follows: "You may file affidavits on your own behalf with the court and may appear and present testimony on your own behalf. However, if you fail to appear, the plaintiff will apply to the court for a writ of possession of a manufactured home, mobilehome, or real property."

(c) The plaintiff shall file an undertaking in such sum as shall be fixed and determined by the judge, to the effect that, if the plaintiff fails to recover judgment against the defendant for the possession of the premises or if the suit is dismissed, the plaintiff will pay to the defendant such damages, not to exceed the amount fixed in the undertaking, as may be sustained by the defendant by reason of such dispossession under the writ of possession of a manufactured home, mobilehome, or real property.

(d) If, at the hearing on the motion, the findings of the court are in favor of the plaintiff and against the defendant, an order shall be entered for the immediate possession of the premises.

(e) The order for the immediate possession of the premises may be enforced as provided in Division 3 (commencing with Section 712.010) of Title 9 of Part 2.

(f) For the purposes of this section, references in Division

3 (commencing with Section 712.010) of Title 9 of Part 2 and in subdivisions (e) to (m), inclusive, of Section 1174, to the "judgment debtor" shall be deemed references to the defendant, to the "judgment creditor" shall be deemed references to the plaintiff, and to the "judgment of possession or sale of property" shall be deemed references to an order for the immediate possession of the premises.

Code of Civil Procedure §1169

If at the time appointed any defendant served with a summons does not appear and defend, the clerk, or the judge if there is no clerk, upon written application of the plaintiff and proof of the service of summons and complaint, shall enter the default of any defendant so served, and, if requested by the plaintiff, immediately shall enter judgment for restitution of the premises and shall issue a writ of execution thereon. Thereafter, the plaintiff may apply to the court for any other relief demanded in the complaint, including the costs, against the defendant, or defendants, or against one or more of the defendants.
[NOTE: Attorneys generally advise landlords to wait until the tenant has been evicted before going back into court for a money judgment. They fear that the two judgments, the earlier of which might be superseded by the latter, could result in confusion and delay.]

Code of Civil Procedure §715.050

Except with respect to enforcement of a judgment for money, a writ of possession issued pursuant to a judgment for possession in an unlawful detainer action shall be enforced pursuant to this chapter without delay, notwithstanding receipt of notice of the filing by the defendant of a bankruptcy proceeding.

This section does not apply to a writ of possession issued for possession of a mobilehome or manufactured home, as those terms are defined in subdivision (a) of Section 1161a, and does not apply to a writ of possession issued for possession of real property in a mobilehome park subject to the Mobilehome Residency Law (Chapter 2.5 (commencing with Section 798) of Title 2 of Part 2 of Division 2 of the Civil Code), or to a manufactured housing community, as defined in Section 18801 of the Health and Safety Code.

Civil Code §1946.5

(a) The hiring of a room by a lodger on a periodic basis within a dwelling unit occupied by the owner may be terminated by either party giving written notice to the other of his or her intention to terminate the hiring, at least as long before the expiration of the term of the hiring as specified in Section 1946. The notice shall be given in a manner prescribed in Section 1162 of the Code of Civil Procedure or by certified or registered mail, restricted delivery, to the other party, with a return receipt requested.

(b) Upon expiration of the notice period provided in the notice of termination given pursuant to subdivision (a), any right of the lodger to remain in the dwelling unit or any part thereof is terminated by operation of law. The lodger's removal from the premises may thereafter be effected pursuant to the provisions of Section 602.3 of the Penal Code or other applicable provisions of law.

(c) As used in this section, "lodger" means a person contracting with the owner of a dwelling unit for a room or room and board within the dwelling unit personally occupied by the owner, where the owner retains a right of access to all areas of the dwelling unit occupied by the lodger and has overall control of the dwelling unit.

(d) This section applies only to owner-occupied dwellings where a single lodger resides. Nothing in this section shall be construed to determine or affect in any way the rights of persons residing as lodgers in an owner-occupied dwelling where more than one lodger resides.

Penal Code §602.3

(a) A lodger who is subject to Section 1946.5 of the Civil Code and who remains on the premises of an owner-occupied dwelling unit after receipt of a notice terminating the hiring, and expiration of the notice period, provided in Section 1946.5 of the Civil Code is guilty of an infraction and may, pursuant to Section 837, be arrested by the owner for the offense. Notwithstanding Section 853.5, the requirement of that section for release upon a written promise to appear shall not preclude an assisting peace officer from removing the person from the owner-occupied dwelling unit.

(b) The removal of a lodger from a dwelling unit by the owner pursuant to subdivision (a) is not a forcible entry under the provisions of Section 1159 of the Code of Civil Procedure and shall not be a basis for civil liability under that section.

(c) Chapter 5 (commencing with Section 1980) of Title 5 of Part 4 of Division 3 of the Civil Code applies to any personal property of the lodger which remains on the premises following the lodger's removal from the premises pursuant to this section.

(d) Nothing in this section shall be construed to limit the owner's right to have a lodger removed under other provisions of law.

(e) Except as provided in subdivision (b), nothing in this section shall be construed to limit or affect in any way any cause of action an owner or lodger may have for damages for any breach of the contract of the parties respecting the lodging.

(f) This section applies only to owner-occupied dwellings where a single lodger resides. Nothing in this section shall be construed to determine or affect in any way the rights of persons residing as lodgers in an owner-occupied dwelling where more than one lodger resides.

References

Books & Booklets

(Your county has a law library which is usually located in or near the courthouse and is open to everyone, not just to attorneys. You'll find most of these books and booklets available there; those which aren't, you'll likely find at your public library. Because some of them are expensive (as much as $270) and tend to become dated rather quickly, take a close look at them before you decide to add them to your own library.)

Brown, David; Ralph Warner and Janet Portman. *The California Landlord's Law Book: Rights and Responsibilities*. Nolo Press, 950 Parker St., Berkeley, CA 94710. (nolo.com) 800.728.3555.

Two attorneys wrote this book specifically to demystify the law for California landlords and landladies. By and large, they succeed.

Brown, David. *The California Landlord's Law Book: Evictions*. Nolo Press, 950 Parker St., Berkeley, CA 94710. (nolo.com) 800.728.3555.

Should you want a second opinion on eviction matters, take a look at this book. It covers pretty much the same ground as *The Eviction Book for California*, and it's pretty expensive, but it bears the distinction of having been written by an attorney, for whatever that's worth to you.

California Apartment Association. *Managing Rental Housing*. California Apartment Association, 980 Ninth St., Suite 2150, Sacramento, CA 95814. (caanet.org) 800.967.4222.

This one-volume "encyclopedia" (yes, it's a formidable book) contains the laws, case citings, and forms which are relevant to the landlording business in California today. Having your own copy handy will save you the time required to look up this law or that case over the internet or to make numerous trips down to the library. It has over a hundred forms which have been reviewed by the CAA and its attorneys and also by the State Attorney General's office, so you can expect them to incorporate whatever's pertinent in the latest laws and legal interpretations. It even includes a rental application and a rental agreement in Spanish.

California Department of Consumer Affairs Legal Office. *California Tenants, A Guide to Residential Tenants' and Landlords' Rights and Responsibilities*. Department of Consumer Affairs, P.O. Box 989004, Sacramento, CA 95798-0004. (dca.ca.gov) 800.952.5210.

Although this booklet covers landlord-tenant matters from a tenant's point of view, landlords find it helpful, too. Not only does it provide a succinct overview of the eviction procedure, it examines the rental process from the git-go, when tenants first start looking for a place to live, and it serves as a good introduction to the many laws which apply to residential tenancies. You may download the booklet from the Department of Consumer Affair's website or send for a free printed copy. For a printed copy, write to the address above with your request. Enclose a stamped (postage sufficient for four ounces), self-addressed envelope (at least 7" x 10") for delivery, and while you're at it, ask for a list of other Consumer Affairs' publications.

California Department of Consumer Affairs Legal *Office. The Dos and Don'ts of Using the Small Claims Court*. Department of Consumer Affairs, P.O. Box 989004, Sacramento, CA 95798-0004. (dca.ca.gov)

If you wish to pursue your case in small claims court or if your tenant is suing you there, you should read this booklet to learn how to prepare and present your side of the case most effectively. Like the booklet above, this one is free, and it's available in both electronic and printed forms.

Eriksen, Ronald. *How to Find Missing Persons*. Loompanics Unlimited, P.O. Box 1197, Port Townsend, WA 98368. (loompanics.com) 360.385.2230.

Before the internet, there was this book, helping people find people who didn't want to be found. You might not need it now unless you cannot find someone using all the internet resources available. Then you will need it. Though most of what is in this book is scrupulous stuff, some of it is not, but then you just may have to check your scruples at the door before you go out hunting for an unscrupulous tenant who's disappeared owing you a bunch of money.

Fisher, Roger; William Ury and Bruce M. Patton. *Getting to Yes: Negotiating Agreement Without Giving In*. Penguin Books, 375 Hudson St., New York, NY 10014. (us.penguingroup.com)

Written by three professors who have spent years studying how people can best resolve their conflicts without giving in to the opposition and without resorting to physical force or the legal system, this very practical manual offers scores of ideas which you might try when you're having tenant problems. Because some of the book's examples are drawn from landlord-tenant situations, you can see how the ideas apply directly to you as a landlord.

Friedman, Terry; David Garcia; and Mark Hagarty. *California Practice Guide: Landlord-Tenant.* The Rutter Group, 15760 Ventura Blvd., Suite 630, Encino, CA 91436. (ruttergroup.com) 800.747.3161.

Three attorneys with vastly different perspectives on landlord-tenant matters collaborated to write this guide. One usually represents landlords; one usually represents tenants; and the third is a judge who has heard more than his share of landlord-tenant litigation. They have examined the subject backwards, forwards, rightside-up, upside-down, and inside-out. Though written for attorneys, it has a practical side as well and can prove useful to the landlord who handles his own evictions. Unfortunately, it's the most expensive of all the books listed here.

HALT. *Using the Law Library, A Nonlawyer's Guide.* HALT, 1612 K St., NW, Suite 510, Washington, DC 20006. (halt.org) 888.367.4258.

Part of HALT's Citizens Legal Manuals series, this particular volume prepares the nonlawyer to use the resources of a law library as knowledgeably as any bona fide member of the bar, maybe even as knowledgeably as any jailhouse lawyer. HALT, by the way, is an acronym for "Help Abolish Legal Tyranny," a national public interest organization "dedicated to the principle that all people in the United States should be able to dispose of their legal affairs in a simple, affordable and equitable manner." That's just what you're trying to do in handling an eviction yourself, isn't it? HALT is worthy of your support. With membership, it makes a copy of its most popular Citizens Legal Manuals series book, *Using a Lawyer...And What to Do if Things Go Wrong,* available as a premium.

Moskovitz, Myron; Ralph Warner. *California Tenants' Rights.* Nolo Press, 950 Parker St., Berkeley, CA 94710. (nolo.com) 800.728.3555.

Tenants who are having trouble with their land-lord seek out this book and scour it for remedies. Some landlords and landladies think of it as the enemy's battle plan and consider it offensive. Some of it is. But it's primarily defensive, and it gives you a chance to consider the tenant's point of view for a change.

National Housing Law Project. *HUD Housing Programs: Tenants' Rights.* National Housing Law Project, 614 Grand Avenue, Suite 320, Oakland, CA 94610. (nhlp.org) 510.251.9400.

You think you got problems! Take a look at this enormous book sometime. It'll remove the blinders from your eyeballs. It cites case after case which legal-aid attorneys have brought against public housing projects; that's right, public housing projects! You might conclude from a cursory examination that public housing administrators are bumbling fools, that poor people are more litigious than a lawyer's daughter, that legal-aid attorneys are relentless, and that whoever is paying the bills must be as blind as justice herself, and you wouldn't be far wrong. As Pogo was wont to say, "I has met the enemy, and he is us."

TRG California Practice Guides. *Legal Professional's Handbook.* The Rutter Group, 15760 Ventura Blvd., Suite 630, Encino, CA 91436. (ruttergroup.com) 800.747.3161.

This informational cornucopia is a two-volume "law library" for the real workhorses in law offices, the staff. It includes only one chapter on unlawful detainers specifically, but it has much information on other related matters, such as motions, appeals, writs, demurrers, pleadings, attachments, general procedures, court filing fees, and the like. In addition, there are samples galore.

Weller, Louis; Drucker, Cecily; Moskovitsz, Myron; et *al. California Eviction Defense Manual.* California Continuing Education of the Bar, 300 Frank H. Ogawa Plaza, Suite 410, Oakland, CA 94612. (ceb.ucop.edu) 800.232.3444.

This book comes in two looseleaf volumes totaling a whopping 1,100 pages! It's a formidable tome written for tenants' attorneys and updated annually. It offers some valuable insights into the defenses concocted by those who consider most landlords unscrupulous. Such people must certainly lie awake nights thinking up new legal stratagems to thwart all of us filthy-rich landlords and landladies.

Computer Software

Eviction Forms Creator™ (California). (Windows and Macintosh) ExPress, P.O. Box 1639, El Cerrito, CA 94530-4639. (landlording.com) 800.307.0789.

Sooner or later, somebody had to write a computer program which could fill out all the forms required to do an eviction in California. Because nobody else did it, I wrote it myself. Whether you're doing one eviction or hundreds, this program will save you both time and frustration. You enter information only once, and that same information is used wherever it's needed to fill out virtually all the eviction forms, including the notices, the Judicial Council forms, and the local forms. I'm adding more and more of the local forms with each revision. The program is simple to understand and easy to use. It works either with or without Pushbutton Landlording as a source of tenant data.

Take a look at its main menu in the back of this book.

Periodicals

Apartment and Property Owners Association Magazine. Your Association, (see association listings for the one nearest you). 6, 10, or 12 issues a year, advertising; included with membership.

Most California apartment and property owners associations publish their own magazines or newsletters which, among other things, help to keep their members up-to-date on legal matters.

The Robert Bruss California Real Estate Law Newsletter. Robert Bruss, 251 Park Rd., Suite 200, Burlingame, CA 94010. (bobbruss.com) 800.736.1736. 12 issues a year, no advertising.

In this fascinating eight-page newsletter, Robert Bruss, the nationally syndicated real estate writer, reviews current California court decisions involving real estate. As you might imagine, a fair number of these decisions affect landlord-tenant disputes in general and evictions specifically. Mr. Bruss uses his skills as an attorney, real estate entrepreneur, and real estate writer to detail each case, analyze the resulting decision, and explain why this particular case is important, all in layman's terms. Anyone with an interest in California real estate can understand and profit from this information.

Services

Tele-Lawyer. Tele-Lawyer, P.O. Box 12927, Las Vegas, NV 89112. (telelaw.com) 800.835.3529. Monday through Friday, 9 a.m. to 5 p.m.

What won't "they" think of next? Now you can dial an 800 number, give the operator your MasterCard or Visa number, ask to speak to a lawyer specializing in landlord-tenant matters, ask your specific legal questions, and get an expert's legal opinion without having to wait for an appointment, without even having to leave your home or office. The expert who will be answering your queries will have years of experience in this field and should know the answers straightaway. If not, he will research the matter and call you back. Tele-Lawyer charges $3 per minute and claims that most calls require ten to fifteen minutes. That works out to $30-45 for the average call.

The Tele-Lawyer law firm neither makes referrals nor accepts cases. It generates revenue strictly by selling "legal expertise by the minute" over the telephone. Consequently, when you call Tele-Lawyer, you won't encounter anybody who is trying to sell you the services of a particular lawyer in order to get a referral fee, nor will you encounter anybody who wants to take your case. A Tele-Lawyer lawyer simply wants to give you the best possible answers to your questions while you're on the telephone.

Don't call Tele-Lawyer if you feel completely overwhelmed by an eviction you're pursuing. In that situation, call a local lawyer who specializes in landlord-tenant law and turn over your case to him.

Call Tele-Lawyer if you feel that the answers to a few unsettling questions will help you pursue your case on your own.

Websites

(Where the internet will take us in the future is anybody's guess, but it has already changed the way we gather information. It can save you a lot of time when you're pursuing an eviction because it enables you to verify court information, check for changes in the law, and even download the most current forms.)

caanet.org/—The California Apartment Association's website offers members of local chapters all kinds of assistance relevant to evictions, including issue insights, legal briefings, state laws that have taken effect over the past four years, and a legal center with an ask-an-attorney section. Non-members visiting the site have limited access but will still find something of value such as the frequently asked questions and the history of California's landlord-tenant laws.

cacb.uscourts.gov, caeb.uscourts.gov, canb.uscourts. gov, casb.uscourts.gov—California's four federal bankruptcy court districts maintain these websites to provide case information, calendars, filing and fee information, office locations and hours, forms, and guidance for debtors and creditors. If your tenant declares bankruptcy while you are pursuing his eviction and you have to file papers with the bankruptcy court to lift the automatic stay, go to the court's website for help.

ci.berkeley.ca.us/rent/—Berkeley's Rent Stabilization Board maintains this site to help tenants and landlords in Berkeley. It's helpful to tenants and landlords elsewhere as well. It has a "reference kit" for landlords with links to all kinds of information applicable anywhere in California.

courtinfo.ca.gov/forms/—Here's where you'll find a complete list of all the Judicial Council forms. If you suspect that a certain form has changed, but you want to verify that it has and also obtain a copy in the Adobe Acrobat format (pdf), go to this site. Always download the fillable versions of the forms so you can use a computer to enter your data directly into the fields provided and then print out the completed form. Otherwise, you'll have to use a typewriter to enter your data on the blank form once you print it on your computer's printer.

courtinfo.ca.gov/otherwebsites.htm—Here's where you'll find a list of the county courts which have their own websites. If your county court is on the list, there will be a link to its site, and you should find information about the locations of the courts in your county, their hours, and their fees.

google.com—Go here to search for reverse directories (get an address from a phone number) and skip tracing websites. Reverse directories are free. Skip tracing is not. Skip tracing prices do vary, as does the effectiveness of the tracing. Check out several sites.

intelius.com—This skip tracing website has always "found my man." Enter what you know about somebody, and it will search billions of records to find that person, records such as marketing lists, catalog purchases, magazine subscriptions, change of address records, real property records, court records, and business records. Upon concluding the search, it will tell you whether it was successful and give you partial information, including the person's approximate age, so you can determine whether the person it found is the person you're looking for. If you want to see more, you will have to pay $8 per inquiry or a flat fee of $20 for unlimited inquiries over a period of 24 hours.

kts-law.com—The law firm of Kimball, Tirey & St. John, with offices in northern and southern California, specializes in both residential and commercial landlord-tenant matters and makes a very useful "resource library" available on their website. Check out their preventive law handbooks.

landlording.com—This is my own website where you will find current information about my books and software. You will also find a page called "What's New?" where I comment on subjects of current interest to landlords.

leginfo.ca.gov/calaw.htm—Maintained by the State of California, this site makes available all of the state's current codes (laws), including those found in the Code of Civil Procedure and the Civil Code, which are the codes most relevant to evictions. Because the state itself maintains this site, you know that the codes are current.

switchboard.com—Go here first to locate a former tenant who seems to have vanished. At no cost to you, you can search phone directories throughout the country for someone's address and phone number. All you need to enter is the person's name.

tenant.net—Maintained by tenant advocates, this site has nothing good to say about landlords and landladies. Indeed, it likens us to vermin, but it has some links which may prove useful if you want to find the particulars about the rent control board in your area.

wma.org—Mobilehome park owners and managers will find the Western Manufactured Housing Communities Association's website useful for legislative information and vendor listings.

Glossary

Abandonment—giving up possession without notifying the landlord.

Abstract of Judgment—a lien recorded in a county where a judgment debtor (someone owing money as a result of a judgment) has assets.

Accrue—accumulating or adding up over a period of time; rent "accrues" every day the tenant remains in possession of the landlord's real property.

Additional Rent Clause—wording in a commercial rental agreement necessary for landlord to include charges other than base rent in a notice to pay or quit; sample wording: "All monetary obligations shall be deemed additional rent."

Affidavit—a sworn, written statement.

Affirmative Defense—a defense based more on new evidence than on a denial of the charges.

Alternative—a choice given to the tenant in a notice such as a 3-Day Notice to Pay Rent or Quit; the tenant may either pay up or vacate.

Answer—legal paper filed soon after summons which states the defendant's defense in response to the plaintiff's complaint; it assures the defendant of a trial.

Arbitration—a truncated "trial" conducted to avoid the costs and time delays of a court trial; an arbitrator acts as judge, listening to arguments and handing down a decision based upon the arguments; resulting decision may be binding or not and may or may not be converted into a legal judgment upon application to the court.

Automatic Stay (Bankruptcy Court)—halt of a case's legal proceedings as a result of a bankruptcy filing by either plaintiff or defendant; legal "monkey wrench" used by tenants who want to delay their evictions.

Baggage Lien Law—lodging facility owners may use this law to attach a guest's belongings for unpaid room charges; rental property owners cannot use it to attach a tenant's belongings for unpaid rent.

Breach of Contract—breaking something agreed upon in a lease or rental agreement.

Case Number—number assigned by the court clerk when the legal papers are filed; thereafter, the case is known by that number.

Civil Code—state laws relating to noncriminal matters; includes laws such as those covering discrimination, tenants' rights, and security deposits; abbreviated as CC.

Code of Civil Procedure—state laws governing how civil matters are to be conducted legally; abbreviated as CCP.

Complaint—a statement of the plaintiff's case.

Constructive Eviction—either an actual disturbance by the landlord of the tenant's possession of the premises or any substantial interference with the tenant's quiet enjoyment of the premises; examples are removing the front door or cutting down the stairway to a second-floor entrance.

Constructive Service—serving a notice without giving it to the defendant personally; leaving it with someone of "suitable age and discretion" and mailing a copy or posting it in a conspicuous place at the residence and mailing a copy.

Court of Jurisdiction—court which has the responsibility for deciding matters concerning property in its general area.

Covenant—an expressed or implied promise appearing in a lease or rental agreement; here's a sample of a covenant: "Tenants agree to keep from making loud noises and disturbances and to play music and broadcast programs at all times so as not to disturb other people's peace and quiet."

Covenant of Quiet Enjoyment—landlord's implied promise that he will allow the tenant to enjoy the premises in peace.

Damages—amount of money awarded by the court to compensate for loss or injury; in nonpayment cases, damages equal unpaid rent following the final rental period mentioned in the 3-day notice.

Declaration for Default Judgment in Lieu of Personal Testimony per CCP 585.4—sworn, written statement by the plaintiff, restating what was included in the complaint and asking the court to enter a judgment in the plaintiff's favor because the defendant failed to answer the summons; it takes the place of a personal appearance at a prove-up trial; availability of this declaratory procedure is up to the discretion of each judicial district.

Declaration of Service—a statement signed by one who served certain papers and attesting to how and when they were served.

Default—failure to respond to a court summons within a given time limit.

Defendant—one against whom a case is brought; one who is being sued; opposite of plaintiff.

Demurrer—legal paper responding to plaintiff's complaint and asserting that there is no cause of action at all; in a demurrer the defendant is saying, in effect, that even if what the plaintiff states in his complaint is true, the plaintiff still doesn't have a case; the defendant's response is essentially, "So what?"

Entry of Default—recording in public records the lack of a defendant's response to the filing of a lawsuit.

Estoppel Defense—legal defense alleging that the plaintiff may not depart from precedents already set in order to win a judgment; in an unlawful detainer for nonpayment, a 3-Day Notice to Pay Rent or Quit would be considered premature if served before the date when the landlord was accustomed to collecting rent and not considering it late.

Eviction—the actual removal of tenants from real property through a legal process; loosely used to refer to the process itself as well as to the removal of tenants even though there has been no legal process.

Execution—carrying out of the judgment; in an unlawful detainer action, an execution no longer results in the hanging or other permanent dispatch of the tenant; execution results only in the tenant's expulsion from the property and in an effort to collect monies owed.

Ex Parte—Latin for "on behalf of a single party"; an "ex parte" action is the legal equivalent of a surprise attack because it gives the other party, the adversary, no notice nor any opportunity to respond; "ex parte" actions are subject to a speedy review upon application by the adversary.

Filing—entering your legal papers into the records of the court; accomplished after you have prepared the summons and complaint.

Forcible Entry—taking possession without a legal right to the property; a landlord using a passkey to dispossess a tenant who has a legal right to live where he is and a squatter who takes over a vacant residence are both guilty of forcible entry.

Forfeiture—loss of the right to possess a property for failure to comply with the rental agreement.

Injunction—a court order restraining someone from a certain activity; it is supposed to prevent future injuries, not compensate for past injuries.

In Forma Pauperis—this Latin expression means literally "in the manner of a pauper"; someone who claims to be too poor to pay normal court costs may file a paper to this effect and not have to pay the costs.

In Re—another Latin expression, it means "in the matter of," as in *In Re Smith*; captions of legal citations regarding nonadversarial judicial proceedings, such as bankruptcies and probates, use the *in re* format; adversarial judicial proceedings are commonly referred to in the *plaintiff v. defendant* format.

Judicial Council of California—state agency charged by the legislature with the responsibility for providing both the layout and the content of various forms used in courts throughout California.

Judgment—outcome of a court hearing or trial.

Judgment by Default—ruling made by a judge in the landlord's favor after the tenant has been given a certain period of time to respond to the summons and complaint and has failed to do so; landlord must apply for the judgment by default; it is not granted automatically.

Lien Sale—procedure necessary for recouping monies owed by self-service storage renters who stop paying their rent or abandon their property.

Mediation—meeting of disputants and a third-party who listens to both sides and suggests possible solutions.

Memorandum to Set Case for Trial—form used to secure a trial in a contested case; same as a Request for Setting.

Motion to Quash Service—legal paper responding to the plaintiff's complaint; may assert that the summons itself or its service is somehow defective or that the cause of action is not really for unlawful detainer and hence fails to qualify for summary proceedings.

Motion to Strike—legal paper responding to the plaintiff's complaint and asserting that there are irrelevancies or redundancies in the complaint or that it contains some other defect, such as the absence of a verification or an improper request for damages.

Movant—a party not named in an action who brings a motion into court.

Nail and Mail—expression used to characterize service which involves posting a copy of the paper to be served and mailing a copy to the defendant at his last known address.

Notice to Pay Rent or Quit—a notice advising the delinquent tenant that he must either pay the rent owing within a certain period, generally three days, or move out; this notice must precede any unlawful detainer for nonpayment of rent.

Notice to Perform Covenant—a notice advising the tenant that he is breaking his lease or rental agreement; this notice must precede any unlawful detainer for breach of contract.

Notice to Terminate Tenancy—a notice used in situations where you want tenants to leave for reasons of your own; this notice must precede any eviction for failure to vacate; in certain California cities, notably those with rent control, this notice may be used only for "just cause," e.g., demolition, occupancy by a close relative, etc.

Notice to Vacate—sheriff or marshal's final five-day warning before actual removal of the tenants.

Nuisance—anything harmful to the health, offensive to the senses, or otherwise adversely affecting the enjoyment of life or property.

Order for Posting—see "posting."

Penal Code—state laws governing criminal matters; includes information about performing a citizen's arrest in the eviction of a lodger; abbreviated as PC; don't confuse this abbreviation with "personal computer" or "politically correct."

Performance of Covenants—fulfilling the obligations agreed upon in a contract.

Personal Service—serving legal documents by handing them directly to the person who must be served, usually the defendant.

Place Plaintiff in Quiet Possession—court instruction to the sheriff or marshal to evict a tenant and give possession to the plaintiff who won an eviction action.

Plaintiff—the one bringing a case to court; the one suing.

Plaintiff in Propria Persona—"in propria persona" is a Latin expression meaning literally that the plaintiff is "in his own person" or is representing himself before the court; usually the expression is shortened to "Plaintiff in Pro Per" or even to "In Pro Per"; in a legal context, it means the same as "Pro Se."

Pleading Paper—paper with line numbers down the left side; used to create any legal document for which there is no state or local form equivalent.

Posting—alternative method of service; requires court order and adds ten days to time allowed for answer but requires no one to be present to receive the papers; papers are taped, stapled, or otherwise attached to a conspicuous place on the property.

Pray—ask or plead.

Prejudgment Claim of Right to Possession—form served along with the summons and complaint; anyone filing this claim becomes a defendant; all others give up their right to claim later that they had a right of possession.

Prima Facie—a Latin phrase which means "at first sight"; "prima facie evidence" is evidence which would seem to support a fact, although it might be refuted.

Process—legal papers bringing a matter before a court of law.

Process Server—someone who serves legal papers; cannot be party to the suit.

Proof of Service—see "declaration of service."

Pro Se—another Latin phrase meaning "for oneself"; anyone acting as his own attorney is acting "Pro Se"; in a legal context, it means the same as "In Pro Per."

Prove-up Trial—plaintiff's personal appearance in court to prove the allegations made in the complaint and ask for a default judgment.

Pursuant to—according to or following.

Quit—take your belongings and leave the property.

Relief from Automatic Stay—permission from a bankruptcy court enabling a landlord to proceed with eviction proceedings against a tenant who has filed for bankruptcy.

Request for Entry of Default—a request for the clerk to record that the defendant has failed to respond to the summons.

Request for Setting—see "Memorandum to Set

Case for Trial."

Restitution—return; ordinarily the plaintiff in an unlawful detainer asks for the "restitution" or return of the premises among other things.

Retaliatory Eviction—unlawful detainer defense used when the landlord is alleged to be getting revenge against his tenants for exercising their legal rights.

Self-Help Eviction—use of any methods, legal or illegal, which do not involve court proceedings and result ultimately in the tenant's vacating the premises; bribery and cutting off utilities are both self-help methods; bribery is legal; cutting off utilities is not.

Service—the serving of legal papers on someone affected by them.

Small Claims Court—a civil court where people argue their own cases without attorneys; unlawful detainers are no longer heard in small claims court.

Stay—a postponement or delay, as in a "stay of execution"; generally, a stay is a win for a tenant and a loss for a landlord because it means that the tenant gets more time to occupy the premises without having to pay rent.

Stipulation—agreement between plaintiff and defendant as to how a judge is to decide an issue.

Substituted Service—serving legal papers on a substitute rather than handing them directly to the defendant; extends the waiting period by ten days.

Summons—a notice requiring that one appear in court or before a court official.

Summary Proceeding—a prompt and simple hearing which is abbreviated by law; unlawful detainers are summary proceedings.

Superior Court—court used for unlawful detainers.

Three-Day Notice—any of several different kinds of 3-day notices, the two most common being for nonpayment of rent and for breach of contract.

Unlawful Detainer—wrongfully keeping real property that belongs to someone else; see "unlawful detainer proceeding."

Unlawful Detainer Proceeding—the legal proceeding necessary for eviction; frequently abbreviated as "unlawful detainer."

Verification—a statement required at the end of every complaint to acknowledge that the facts are as stated.

Warehouseman's Lien—in the case of a mobilehome park eviction, the park owner's right to sell the mobilehome to satisfy the amount owed by the mobilehome's legal owner.

Warranty of Habitability—landlord's implied obligation to provide a dwelling which is fit for human occupancy; this right of the tenant cannot be signed away.

Waste—destruction of property.

Writ—written authority from a court for the sheriff or marshal to carry out a judgment.

Writ of Execution—court authorization for the sheriff or marshal to seize a defendant's property or money in order to satisfy a judgment.

Writ of Immediate Possession—the result of a procedure used when tenants are hiding to avoid service or are known to be out of state.

Writ of Possession—court authorization for the sheriff or marshal to remove a tenant from a property and return possession to the plaintiff who successfully sued for eviction.

California Apartment and Property Owners Associations

ALAMEDA COUNTY
(NORTHERN)
Rental Housing Association of
Northern Alameda County
2201 Broadway, Suite 311
Oakland, CA 94612
510.893.9873
rhanac.org

ALAMEDA COUNTY
(SOUTHERN)
Rental Housing Owners
Association of Southern
Alameda County
1264 "A" St.
Hayward, CA 94541
510.537.0340
rhosource.com

BERKELEY
Berkeley Property Owners
Association
2005 Hopkins
Berkeley, CA 94707
510.525.3666
bpoa.org

CAA CENTRAL COAST
CAA CENTRAL VALLEY
CAA CONTRA COSTA
CAA GREATER FRESNO
CAA LOS ANGELES
CAA MERCED COUNTY
CAA NAPA/SOLANO
("Direct Member" territories
managed by the California
Apartment Association (CAA)
with help from an advisory
committee of active local prop-
erty owners and managers; see
state association listing)

CHICO
(See North Valley)

FOOTHILL
Foothill Apartment Association
424 N. Lake Ave., Suite 104
Pasadena, CA 91101-1202
626.793.5873
foothillapartmentassociation.com

INLAND EMPIRE
Apartment Association of
Greater Inland Empire
10630 Town Center Dr.,
Suite 116
Rancho Cucamonga, CA
91730
909.948.0784
aagie.com

KERN COUNTY
Income Property
Association of Kern
P.O. Box 809
Bakersfield, CA 93302
661.322.3288

LONG BEACH/
SOUTHERN CITIES
Apartment Association
California Southern Cities
333 W. Broadway St.,
Suite 101
Long Beach, CA 90802
562.426.8341
apt-assoc.com

Apartment Owners Association
4611-A East Anaheim St.
Long Beach, CA 90804
562.597.2422
aoausa.com

LOS ANGELES COUNTY
Apartment Association of
Greater Los Angeles
621 S. Westmoreland Ave.
Los Angeles, CA 90005
213.384.4131
aagla.org

Apartment Owners Association
5455 Wilshire Blvd., #1009
Los Angeles, CA 90036
323.937.8811
aolusa.com

MARIN COUNTY
Marin Income Prop. Assn.
P.O. Box 150315
San Rafael, CA 94915
415.491.4461

MONTEREY COUNTY
Apt. Assn of Monterey County
975 Cass St.
Monterey, CA 93940
831.649.4704

NAPA COUNTY
(See CAA Napa/Solano)

NORTH COAST
North Coast Rental Housing
Association
P.O. Box 12172
Santa Rosa, CA 95406
707.526.9526

NORTH VALLEY
North Valley Property Owners
Association
813 East Fifth Ave.
Chico, CA 95926-2702
530.345.1321
nvpoa.com

NORTHERN CALIFORNIA
Apartment Owners Association
1128 Lincoln Ave.
Alameda, CA 94501
510.769.7521
aoausa.com

ORANGE COUNTY
Apartment Association
of Orange County
12822 Garden Grove Blvd.,
Suite D
Garden Grove, CA 92843
714.638.5550
aaoc.com

Apartment Owners Association
11752 Garden Grove Blvd.,
Suite 110
Garden Grove, CA 92843
714.539.6000
aoausa.com

PASADENA
(See Foothill)

POMONA VALLEY
(See Inland Empire)

RIVERSIDE COUNTY
(See Inland Empire)

SACRAMENTO COUNTY
Rental Housing Association
of Sacramento Valley
221 Lathrop Way, Suite C
Sacramento, CA 95815
916.920.1120
rha.org

SAN BERNARDINO
COUNTY
(See Inland Empire)

SAN DIEGO COUNTY
San Diego County
Apartment Association
3702 Ruffin Road
San Diego, CA 92123
858.278.8070
sdcaa.com

Apartment Owners Association
3110 Camino Del Rio South,
Suite A214
San Diego, CA 92108
619.280.7007
aoausa.com

SAN FERNANDO VALLEY
Apartment Owners Association
6445 Sepulveda Blvd.,
Suite 300
Van Nuys, CA 91411
818.988.9200
aoausa.com

SAN FRANCISCO
San Francisco
Apartment Association
265 Ivy Street
San Francisco, CA 94102
415.255.2288
sfaa.org

SAN JOAQUIN COUNTY
San Joaquin
Rental Property Association
1122 N. El Dorado Street
Stockton, CA 95202
209.944.9266
sjcrpa.org

SAN MATEO COUNTY
(See Santa Clara County)

SANTA BARBARA COUNTY
Santa Barbara
Rental Property Association
3887 State St., Suite 7
Santa Barbara, CA 93105
805.687.7007
sbrpa.org

SANTA CLARA COUNTY
Tri-County
Apartment Association
20863 Stevens Creek Blvd.,
Suite 250
Cupertino, CA 95014
408.873.1599
tcaa.org

SANTA CRUZ COUNTY
(See Santa Clara County)

SANTA MONICA
Action Apartment Association
2812 Santa Monica Blvd.,
Suite 203
Santa Monica, CA 90403
310.828.7628
action-wam.com

SOLANO COUNTY
(See CAA Napa/Solano)

SOUTH BAY/
SOUTHERN CITIES
(See Long Beach/Southern
Cities)

SOUTH COAST
South Coast
Apartment Association
2102 Business Center Drive
Irvine, CA 92612
949.253.4123

VENTURA COUNTY
(See San Fernando Valley)

CALIFORNIA
(State Association)
California
Apartment Association (CAA)
980 Ninth St., Suite 200
Sacramento, CA 95814
800.967.4222
caanet.org

Index

Eviction Forms Creator™

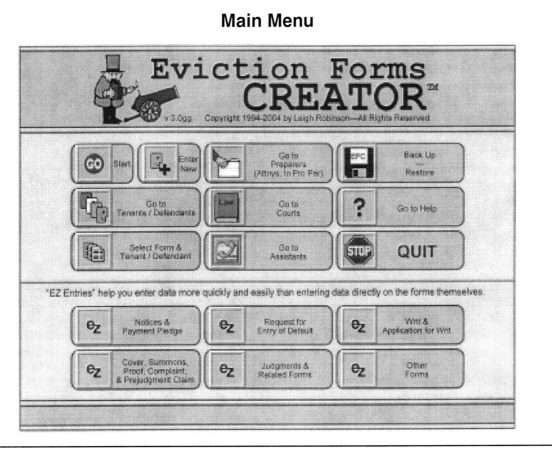

Eviction Forms Creator creates the various forms you need to evict a tenant legally through the California court system. It creates them the modern way, on a computer, rather than the old fashioned way, on a typewriter.

Using Eviction Forms Creator, even the worst of typists, those who have to eyeball the key caps and strike the right keys with conscious effort, can create perfect eviction forms which are sure to please the people who count whenever there's an eviction in the legal works, that is, the court clerk and the judge.

Eviction Forms Creator is designed to be so easy to use that it doesn't require a thick user's manual and hours of study time. In fact, once you understand a little bit about what makes the program "tick," what you need to do to load it onto your computer, what you need to do to navigate through it easily, and what you need to do to get it to print the forms correctly, you'll be ready to crank out great-looking eviction forms from sunup to sundown.

When using Eviction Forms Creator, you save time because you enter information only once, and that same information is used wherever it's needed to fill out all the forms. Once you enter information about yourself as the preparer of the forms, for example, you never have to enter that information again. The same goes for the court(s) you use and for each of the tenants you are evicting.

The forms you can create with Eviction Forms Creator begin with the various legal notices designed to alert tenants to the owner's intent to evict, and they end with the Writ of Execution, which gives the sheriff or marshal the authority to turn the tenants out and return possession of the property to the rightful owner.

These forms include both those which have specific legal wording requirements and those which have specific legal wording and formatting requirements, that is, the Judicial Council forms. (The Judicial Council is charged by the state legislature with the responsibility of providing uniformity in the forms used in state courts.)

The program works just as well for those who

do their own evictions as it does for those who do evictions for others.

Here is a list of all the forms included in Eviction Forms Creator (the names of the sixteen Judicial Council forms are capitalized):

Payment Pledge
Notice to Pay Rent or Quit [three versions]
Notice to Pay, etc. (Mobilehomes)
Notice to Perform Covenant
Notice to Terminate Tenancy
Notice to Quit for Waste, Nuisance, or Unlawful Acts
Notice to Quit
Notice to Terminate Tenancy (Mobilehomes)
72-Hour Notice to Vacate (RVs)
30-Day Notice to Vacate (RVs)
Notice of Belief of Abandonment
Notice of Right to Reclaim Abandoned Personal Property
COVER SHEET CM-010
Cover Sheet Addendum (Los Angeles) CIV 109 03-04
SUMMONS SUM-130
PROOF OF SERVICE POS-010
COMPLAINT UD-100
PREJUDGMENT CLAIM OF RIGHT TO POSSESSION CP 10.5
REQUEST FOR ENTRY OF DEFAULT 982(a)(6)
JUDGMENT UD-110
JUDGMENT ATTACHMENT UD-110S
Multipurpose Judgment
Application for Clerk's Judgment
Clerk's Default Judgment [six versions]
Clerk's Interlocutory Judgment
Plaintiff's Declaration
Court's Default Judgment [three versions]
Judgment After Trial [three versions]
Amended Judgment [three versions]
DECLARATION FOR DEFAULT JUDGMENT BY COURT UD-116

Declaration for Default Judgment in Lieu of Personal Testimony
STIPULATION FOR ENTRY OF JUDGMENT UD-115
Judgment Pursuant to Stipulation
WRIT OF EXECUTION EJ-130
Application for Writ [three versions]
Statement of Classification
Application for Posting of Summons
Order for Posting of Summons
ATTACHMENT MC-025 (two copies of the same form)
Attachment (two copies of the same form)
DECLARATION MC-030
ATTACHED DECLARATION MC-031
Amendment to Complaint
REQUEST/COUNTER REQUEST TO SET CASE FOR TRIAL UD-150
Proof of Service (Memo to Set)
Case Summary
Instructions to Officer [four versions]
REQUEST FOR DISMISSAL 982(a)(5)
NOTICE OF ENTRY OF DISMISSAL 982(a)(5.1)

Version 3.0 of Eviction Forms Creator includes seventy-two forms in all, twenty more than the previous version of the program.

You may use Eviction Forms Creator on a computer running Windows or on an Apple Macintosh running System 7.0 or higher or System 10. The program does run native under MacOS 10.

The Windows computer must be running Windows 98 or later. It must have a hard drive, Microsoft Universal Printer Driver 3.1.4 or later, a pointing device (mouse or trackball), and a dot matrix, laser, or ink-jet printer capable of printing in Arial and New Courier fonts.

The Macintosh must have a hard drive and a dot-matrix, laser, or ink-jet printer, capable of printing in Helvetica and Courier fonts.

Order Forms

ExPRESS, P.O. BOX 1639, EL CERRITO, CA 94530-4639

Dear ExPress:

I'm a scrupulous property owner, and I'd like copies of your materials for my very own. Hurry up with my order. I need all the help I can get right now.

Please send me:

_____ copies of *Landlording*	@ $27.95	$_____
_____ copies of *What's a Landlord to Do?*	@ $21.95	$_____
_____ copies of *The Eviction Book for California*	@ $24.95	$_____
_____ copies of *Landlording® on Disk (The Forms)*	@ $39.95	$_____
_____ copies of *Eviction Forms Creator™*	@ $79.95	$_____
_____ copies of *Pushbutton Landlording®*	@ $149.95	$_____
> > > > SALES TAX FOR CALIFORNIA RESIDENTS > > > >		$_____
Shipping and handling		$ 4.00

My computer disk format is Windows___, Macintosh___   TOTAL $_____

PLEASE SEND TO

_____

_____

_____

ExPRESS, P.O. BOX 1639, EL CERRITO, CA 94530-4639

Dear ExPress:

I'm an unscrupulous property owner who's merciless, lowdown, and greedy, and I'll pay double the usual price for your stuff just to lay my hands on all that great information. It may even reform me. Who knows?

Please send me:

_____ copies of *Landlording*	@ $55.90	$_____
_____ copies of *What's a Landlord to Do?*	@ $43.90	$_____
_____ copies of *The Eviction Book for California*	@ $49.90	$_____
_____ copies of *Landlording® on Disk (The Forms)*	@ $79.90	$_____
_____ copies of *Eviction Forms Creator™*	@ $159.90	$_____
_____ copies of *Pushbutton Landlording®*	@ $299.90	$_____
> > > > SALES TAX FOR CALIFORNIA RESIDENTS > > > >		$_____
Shipping and handling		$ 8.00

My computer disk format is Windows___, Macintosh___   TOTAL $_____

PLEASE SEND TO

_____

_____

_____

ExPRESS, P.O. BOX 1639, EL CERRITO, CA 94530-4639

Dear ExPress:

I'm not a property owner yet, but I think I'd like to be one some day, and I'd certainly like to know what I'm doing. Show me.

Please send me:

_____ copies of *Landlording*	@ $27.95	$_____
_____ copies of *What's a Landlord to Do?*	@ $21.95	$_____
_____ copies of *The Eviction Book for California*	@ $24.95	$_____
_____ copies of *Landlording® on Disk (The Forms)*	@ $39.95	$_____
_____ copies of *Eviction Forms Creator™*	@ $79.95	$_____
_____ copies of *Pushbutton Landlording®*	@ $149.95	$_____
> > > > SALES TAX FOR CALIFORNIA RESIDENTS > > > >		$_____
Shipping and handling		$ 4.00

My computer disk format is Windows___, Macintosh___   TOTAL $_____

PLEASE SEND TO

_____

_____

_____

Use one of these forms and mail it with your check or money order, OR
call ExPRESS at 800.307.0789 and charge to your MasterCard, Visa, or American Express.
Our pricing changes periodically. Visit our website (landlording.com) for current pricing.